# Egypt Unexpected

# Egypt Unexpected

## 1001 Days in Photographs

Silvia Dogliani

in collaboration with
Theresa Everline

The American University in Cairo Press
Cairo New York

*Passages in this book written by Silvia Dogliani are signed* S. D.*;*
*those written by Theresa Everline are signed* T. E.
*The interview with Tahani El-Gebali was conducted with the help of Réhab El-Bakry.*


The American University in Cairo Press
113 Sharia Kasr el Aini, Cairo, Egypt
420 Fifth Avenue, New York, NY 10018
www.aucpress.com



Dar el Kutub No. 17952/03
ISBN 977 424 851 1

Design by **AGENZIA ITALIANA,** Cairo
Printed in Egypt

# Contents

# Preface

When I try to describe Egypt to people, I listen to what I am saying and realize that the exact opposite is often just as true. I moved to this country in the summer of 2002, discovering that it was very similar to what I imagined it would be like. It was also utterly different than what I had expected. Those kinds of contradictions have persisted.

The culture is warmly welcoming. It is also standoffish and suspicious. It is an easy place for a foreigner to live, full of wonderfully helpful people. It is also a terribly difficult place for a foreigner to live, with a society that is in many ways impenetrable to outsiders. And so on. Because of these contradictions, I find that when I talk about Egypt, the discussions are hopelessly inadequate. Either that, or they go on for a very long time.

When Silvia Dogliani approached me to help her write the text of this book, one of the main reasons that I immediately agreed was because of her desire to get at the complexities of Egypt. I was impressed that she wanted to avoid so much of the 'typical' Egypt, the aspects that are remarkably unimportant in day-to-day life. Although I have visited, and been impressed by, many of the tourist sites—the Valley of the Kings, the Pyramids, Karnak Temple, and so forth—these reveal next to nothing about a country that is the most populous in the Middle East, a region that has become so central to current events in the world. I was particularly eager to work on this project because Silvia wanted to include other people's perspectives.

I also wanted to collaborate with Silvia because her photographs are so beautiful and accomplished, something I recognized immediately when we started working together at a magazine in Cairo. Hopefully the book's images and interviews begin to create a sense of Egypt's shifting identity—something I am still trying to grasp.

*Theresa Everline*

# Introduction

My Italian grandmother was born in Alexandria and lived there with her family, who ran a building company before the Revolution. When she met and married my grandfather, she left the country and moved first to Greece and then to Italy. So since I was a child, Egypt has been mentioned often in my family, like a mysterious land in a children's fairy tale. My imagination has always been lively, and many were the thoughts and the dreams that I privately fabricated about my grandmother's native country. When my husband and I planned to move to Egypt, I really did not know what to expect.

I arrived in Egypt at the end of 2000 to become a foreign resident—a *khawaga.* It is strange not being a tourist in a country so well known for its famous sites. My first day here was intense. I remember that my growing feelings for this country mingled with the variety of different sights that my eyes captured and recorded. Cairo looked like a huge construction site. The noise was powerful, and one color—green—was missing.

I have traveled around the world and visited many places, but things look different when you realize that you are not just visiting a country but taking up residence there, that you are deciding whether to go forward and experience, or backward and feel safe. Each detail of the country becomes important in your decision.

Before arriving in Cairo I had been told that Zamalek, on an island in the Nile, was one of pleasantest residential neighborhoods, and I visited this area first. I took a carriage, perhaps searching for the romantic side of such a busy town. Although the result was not too positive, we decided to live there. And at night the city changed completely: the noise turned into music, the lights into colors, and the crowds into life. I was happy to be here.

Perhaps as with any country, Egypt is like a coin, with two faces: on one side the well-known history and the popular scenery, which has become so much part of the Egyptian culture that even locals forget the other side—life as it is lived by the people.

What does everybody see, know, and think of Egypt, both here and abroad? This is a question I asked myself many times when I first arrived. It took me only a few months to settle in with my family in Cairo, but it took almost three years to answer to that question! This book is my personal answer: the unexpected face of the coin.

*Egypt Unexpected* is my personal vision of this country, divided into three main coexistences and six strong subjects: **Noise**—what I first felt here, the explosion of many indiscreet and varying sounds across the surface of life—and **Silence**—what I discovered later—secretly hidden and constantly desired; **Movement**—the daily reality I lived, the action of lively faces and places—and **Spirit**—what attracted me, a fascinating labyrinth of beliefs; **Past**—my dreams and my thoughts through my family's stories, the magnificent memories touched by nostalgia—and **Future**—the unexpected I found, the fervent wish for improvement.

The pictures I took over the course of three years are small but intense moments, which can speak without words. They are complemented here by other people's experiences: informal interviews that Theresa Everline and I conducted with Egyptians and foreign residents from all walks of life—both the famous and the not so famous.

I remember the man I photographed once when I was stuck in the middle of the Cairo traffic, waiting for a minister to pass by with his large escort. He was standing by his car, looking impassively at the horizon, without hope. We spent more than an hour without moving, surrounded by honking horns. Nobody became upset, something that would never happen in Western countries.

A sign on the road to Ain Sukhna on Egypt's eastern coast took me by surprise. It read "ROSSI, Italian Ristorante 400 km." There were no directions, just that extraordinary distance, teasing a hungry traveler with a mysterious restaurant, located somewhere in the desert!

Sharm al-Sheikh and Hurghada are the best known Red Sea holiday destinations, along with others such as Marsa Alam, Taba, Dahab, and El Gouna. The Egyptian North Coast is not so popular (at least with foreigners), although its beauty is unique: the magnificent white sand bathed in the deep turquoise Mediterranean can shock anyone. The Egyptian Mediterranean has nothing to do with the south European one: it is another sea.

The mystical atmosphere that you breathe in Cairo, while walking through the hectic old Islamic core of the city, brings you to a small door, hidden among the crowded, narrow streets. Behind it lies the recently restored *samakhana,* a picturesque, small, round theater that once a year hosts the spiritual performance of the Mawlawi Dervish dancers, an order that dates back to the fifteenth century.

Mysterious and extraordinary too is the life of the residents of the City of the Dead, whose destiny it is to live among the tombs of Cairo. This unusual cemetery, known to locals as *al-Qarafa*, has become a city in its own right, with running water, electricity, a post office, a police station, shops, tea houses, and even factories. This may sound sad, but in my walks there I met only smiling faces. The residents live in small villas, where the rooms for the dead are separated by a green patio from the rooms for the living, far from the polluted metropolis.

Egypt is movement, past, spirit, noise, silence—but it is also future. My daughter Vittoria Valeria Gertrud was born in Cairo. I felt I could trust this country, and I have been impressed by the professionalism of doctors and by the excellent service of the local hospitals. Sabina Pilgram, a foreign resident whom I met and interviewed here, told me about her similar experience.

The great new library of Alexandria—the Bibliotheca Alexandrina—is a piece of history as well as a piece of art, an unexpected example of the future digital age. I visited several times, but once, when the library was closed, I had the privilege of being there alone, without other visitors: while looking at its impressive structure I felt small and powerless in such a space full of knowledge.

The images and the words of this book are an attempt to show the noise, the silence, the spirit, the movement, the past, and the future of Egypt, the unexpected side of the country I found while living here. What does everybody see, know, and think of Egypt, both here and abroad? —Is my answer to this question an accurate one? A critical eye will tell.

*Silvia Dogliani*

*I dedicate this book to my husband Alberico, who shared all these photographs and experiences with me and who encouraged and pushed me in realizing this project.*
*I also dedicate all these images to my daughter Vittoria Valeria Gertrud, so that she will remember forever this fascinating country where she was born two years ago, a land that gave all of us unique emotions and memories.*
*Important thanks go to my family in Italy, who have always trusted me and my work.*

*Silvia Dogliani*

# Noise

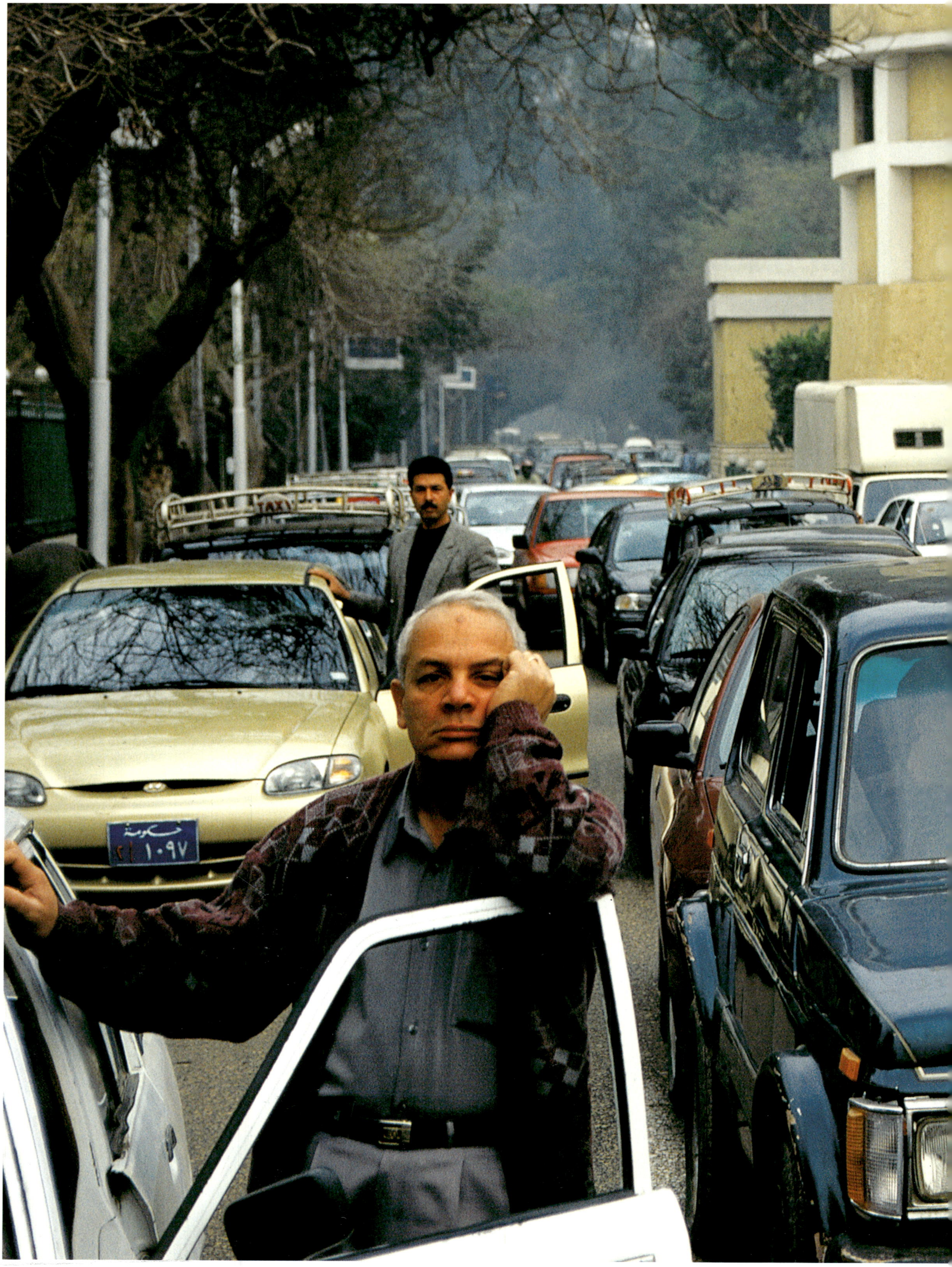
حكومة

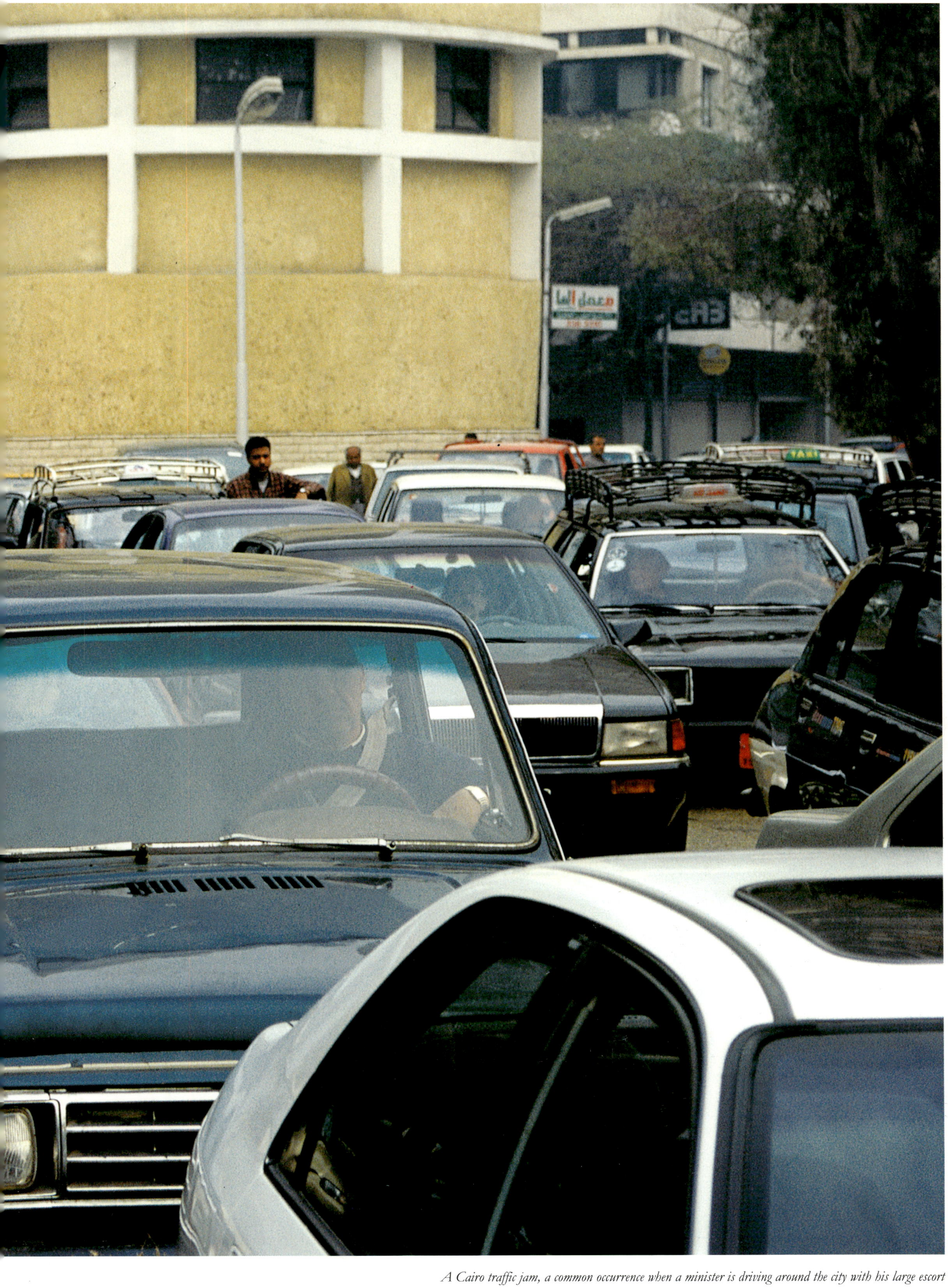

*A Cairo traffic jam, a common occurrence when a minister is driving around the city with his large escort*

Social traditions in Egypt keep everyone literally close to each other: strong family ties cause most people to live with or near their relatives for their entire lives. The landscape of Egypt also pulls everyone together: like a magnet, the River Nile attracts life. Around 95 percent of Egyptians live on just 5 percent of the country's land. Of those people, most are crowded together in Cairo, a city of 16 million people (or more, depending on who is doing the counting). All these souls squeeze into a mere 679 square kilometers of space, making for a population density of more than 30,000 people per square kilometer. In contrast, the population density of London is only 4,500 people per square kilometer. Egyptians seem to be constantly searching for extra space where they can build yet more places to live and work—whether it is between the already tight spaces of Cairo or in desert land reclaimed and made into well-groomed suburbs like Sixth of October City.

As a result of this squeeze, Cairo is vibrant and busy. It is also very noisy. More than anything else, the sound of the city is the sound of a giant tangle of millions of cars honking their horns simultaneously, while harried policemen try unsuccessfully to keep the chaotic traffic under control.

Egyptian drivers have developed an elaborate language of horn honks that can communicate an impressive array of sentiments. And drivers always seem to have a lot to say—most often simply, "Hey, I'm here", a warning to other drivers not to change lanes and to pedestrians not to follow that impulse to step into the street in front of a car heedlessly barreling down the road. Out of necessity, every Cairene learns when to tune out the sound of all those cars and when to pay attention to them.

Of course, the call to prayer also defines the sound of Egypt, as with any Islamic country. Five times a day the muezzins lift their voices to God, and the prayers fall upon the city like a sudden rain. In certain areas of Cairo where several mosques are within a few blocks of each other, the prayers weave and overlap, sounding both mournful and exhilarated. On Fridays at most mosques there is not enough space for people to pray, and thus the devout spill out onto the streets, blocking the road.

In recent years, Egypt has increasingly buzzed to the sound of satellite televisions stations. On the tops of every building the satellite dishes crowd together, like proper Cairenes living close to each other for support. And this phenomenon is not limited to the modern city dwellers. Satellite dishes can be seen perched atop the mud-brick houses of Dakhla Oasis, eight hundred kilometers from Cairo.

The resorts on the Red Sea coast are bustling meeting places for Egyptians as well as foreigners. People splash and yell and laugh, overjoyed by the beauty of the waveless crystal-blue water. Once they put on snorkels and masks, the underwater world becomes another crowded thoroughfare. As people glide past each other to gaze at some of the most stunning coral reefs in the world, the sound of the kicking of their brightly colored flippers creates another sort of cacophony, one far removed from the roar of Cairo traffic.

*T. E.*

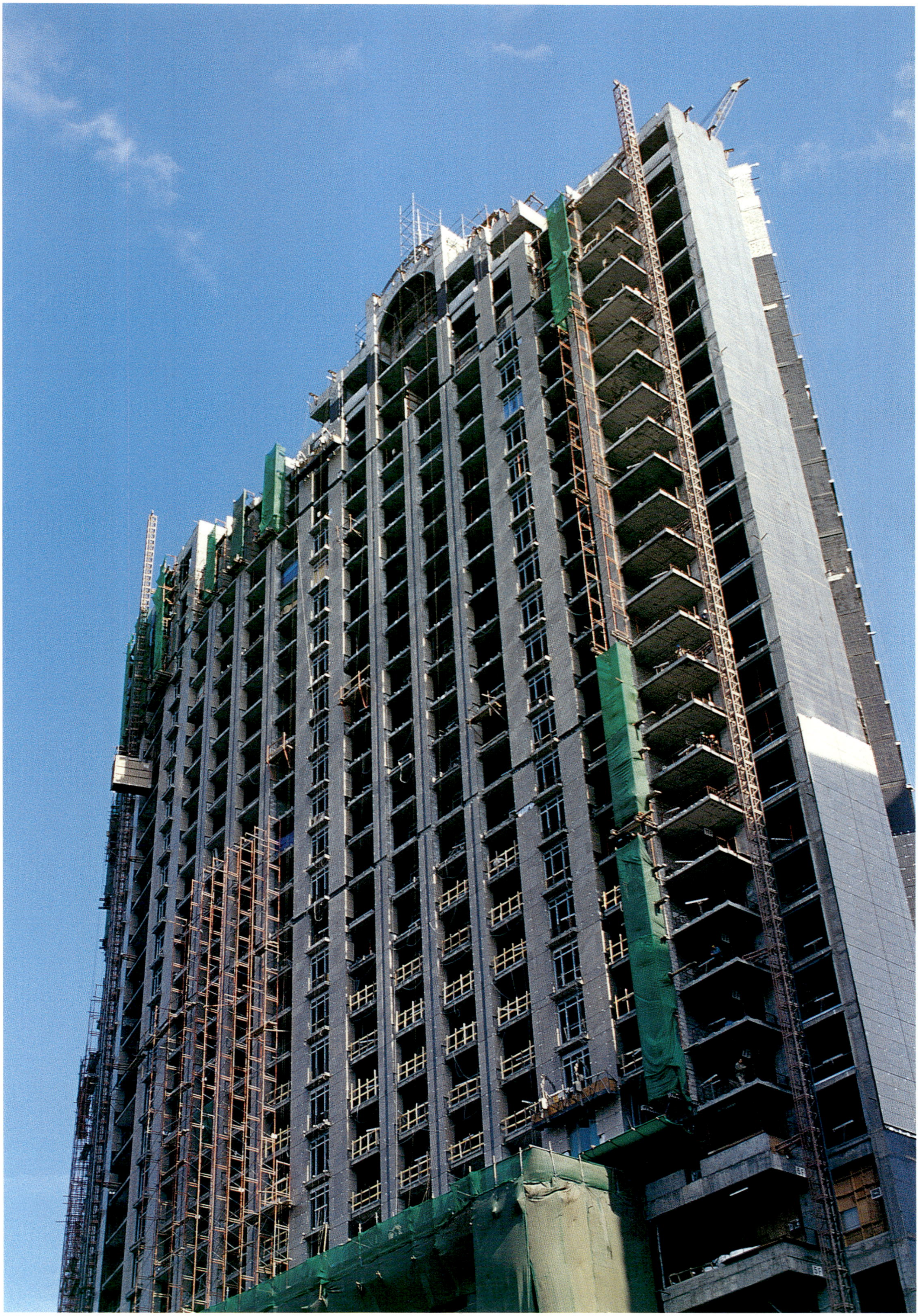

*A hotel under construction, Cairo*

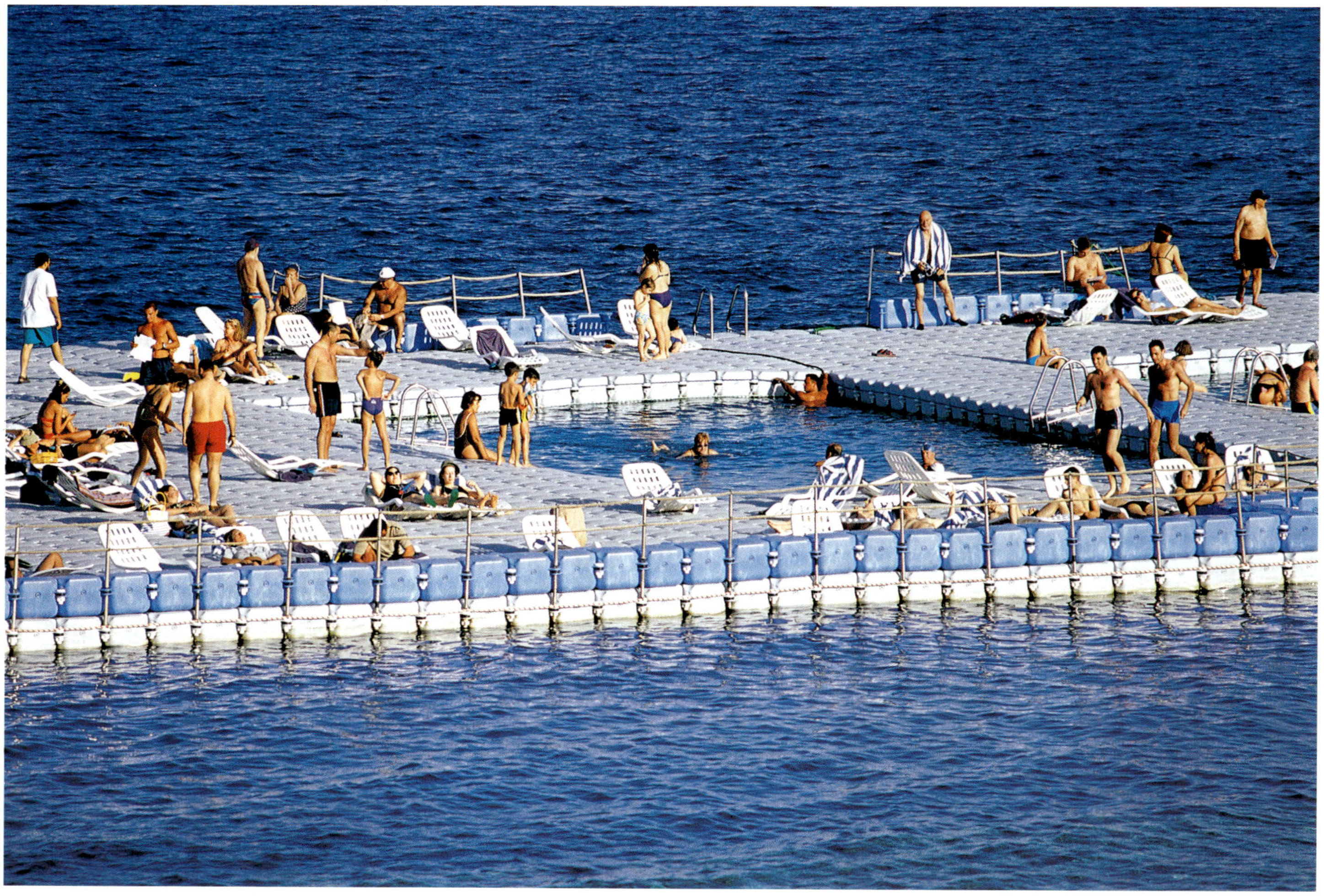

*An unusual swimming pool at Coral Bay Resort, Sharm al-Sheikh*

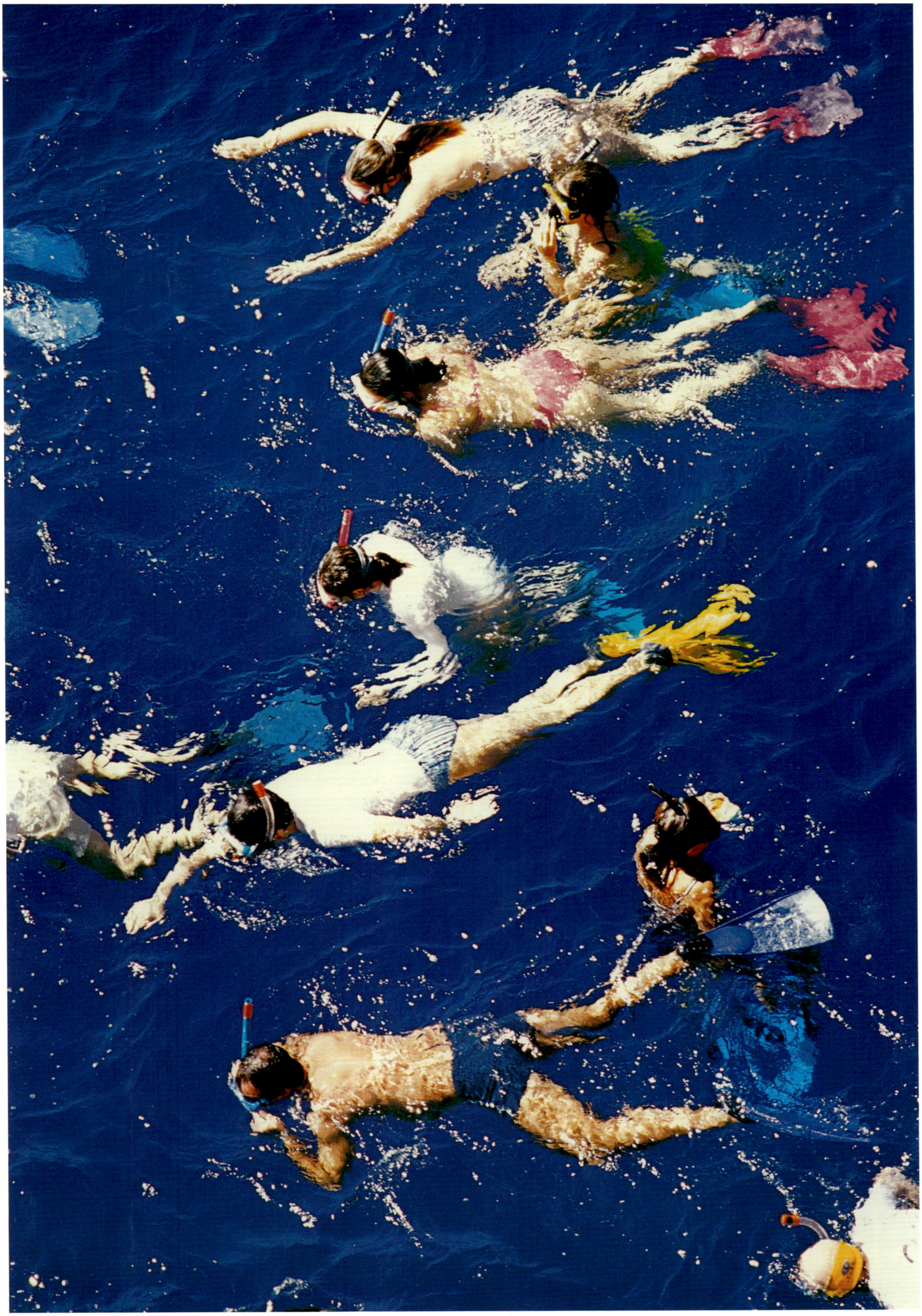

*The underwater world becomes a crowded thoroughfare, Ras Muhammad, Sinai*

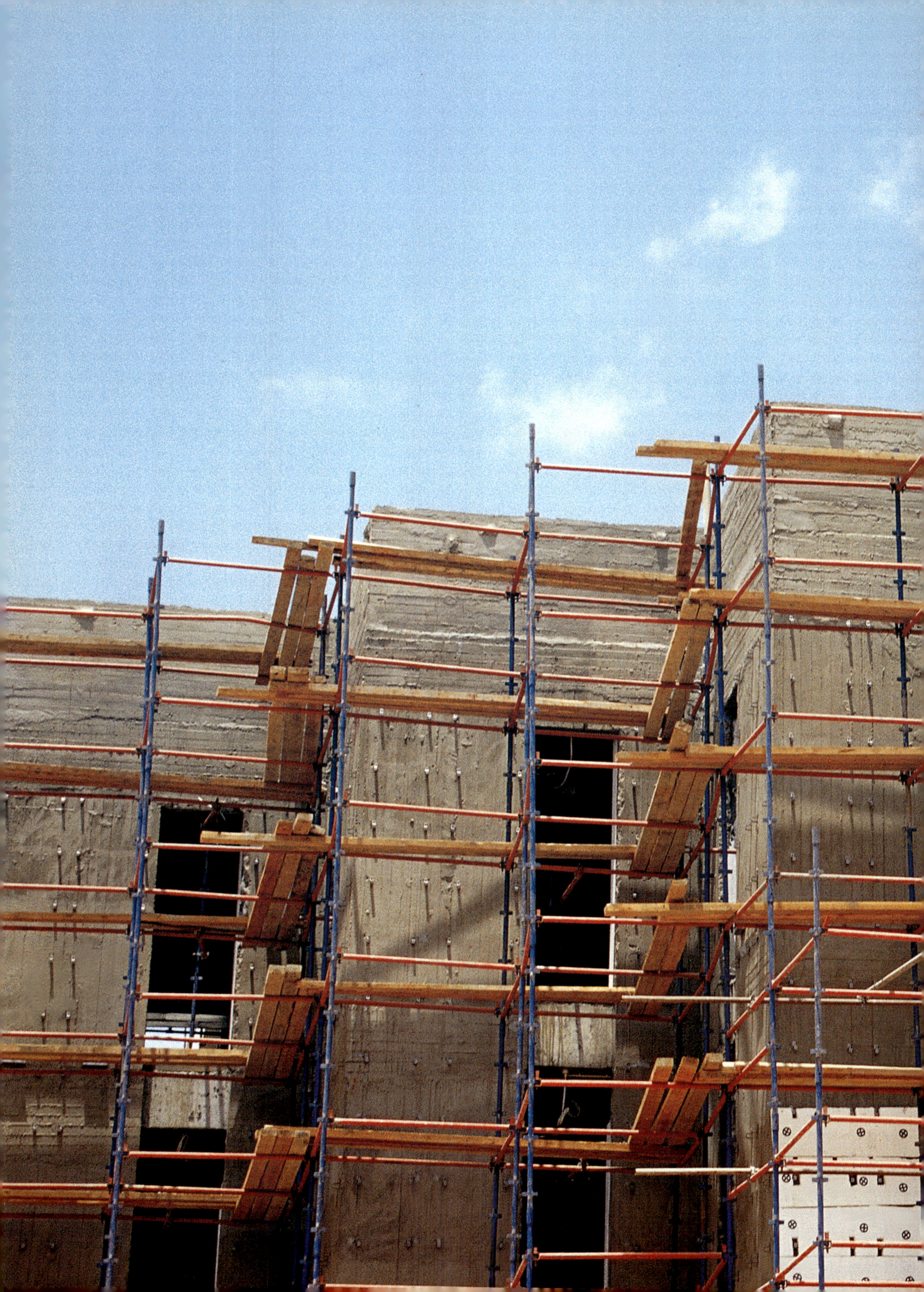

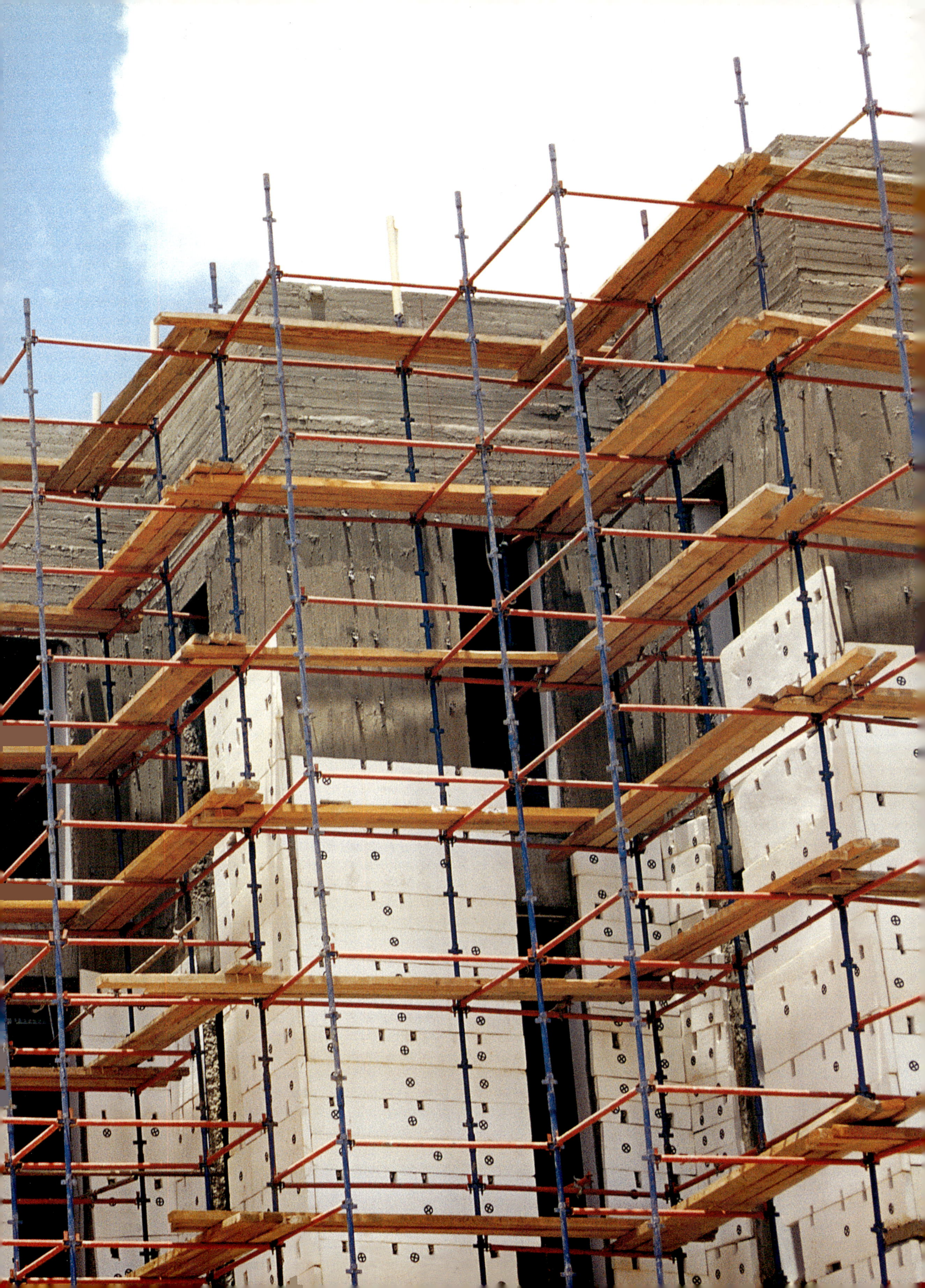

## Mohamed Abdel Salam El Mahgoub

*Governor of Alexandria*

"It is terrible to hear the noise! Myself, as a person, I hate it. As a governor, I am working hard to prevent it," says Mohamed Abdel Salam El Mahgoub, the governor of Alexandria.

El Mahgoub thinks that Egyptians would rather avoid noise. "It is in their genes," he says. "Ninety percent of the population come from the country. They are farmers. It is very quiet there. I am sure they would love to go back to their original style of life, but perhaps they need someone to guide them with an initiative."

When El Mahgoub came to Alexandria in July 1997, the city was very noisy, like Cairo. What is the first thing that comes to mind when he thinks about the noise in Alexandria? "Horns!" he says immediately. The honking, he notes, "is a habit, like smoking. We must insist, and the habit will disappear."

El Mahgoub has indeed insisted: he created a law against excessive horn use. This is just one of the many improvements that El Mahgoub has promoted in his Mediterranean city. "More than 85 percent of Alexandrians now don't use their horn. If they do, they pay a fine." But it is not only a matter of a fine, the governor insists. The reality is that "the citizens are with me. They really want this law," he says.

The governor also relocated the industries to the city's outskirts and moved noisy workshops out of Alexandria. "Fifty years ago the factories were built out of the town. As Alexandria developed, the factories are now inside," he explains. "We are giving the owners almost free land to move out to. It is good for the Alexandrians, but economically it is also good for the factory owners," the governor stresses.

Reducing the traffic in a city like Alexandria is not easy. The town is long and thin, and each summer around three and a half million visitors swarm into the city. El Mahgoub's strategies have included renovating the Corniche, the main coast road, constructing a bridge across Stanley Bay (in a design that echoes Alexandria's historic Montazah Palace), and building two ring roads to access the port without going through the city.

The governor is also thinking about the future of his town. "We are now working on synchronization between traffic lights and car speed: if you drive sixty kilometers per hour on any of the roads of Alexandria, you will find only green traffic lights, and you will never have to stop," explains El Mahgoub. In the summer of 2004 he will introduce a new traffic information system. "I will encourage Alexandrians to use the radio to keep informed on the current traffic situation. We suffered a lot last summer," he admits.

El Mahgoub's previous experience includes thirty years in Egypt's General Intelligence Service and a previous appointment as governor of Ismailia (Egyptian governors are chosen by the president for an unlimited period of time). He is intent on making all the improvements he can before retiring. "My real success is in creating a system. I have done that. Now, with me or anyone else as governor here, the system will continue."

El Mahgoub has worked to privatize services in Alexandria, such as the water company and the garbage collection service, which is now handled by a French contractor. "Now the city looks clean," he says proudly. "If the young generation learn what having clean streets means, they will refuse anything dirty in the future."

The fate of the next generation is important to the governor. Two years ago he started an educational program in cooperation with the Ministry of Education, USAID, and a non-governmental organization. They chose a small number of schools to begin with, trying to improve them in the areas of science, math, computers, and foreign languages. The aim is eventually to extend the program to other governorates, and finally to the whole country.

It is impossible to refrain from asking El Mahgoub why Cairo is not able to follow Alexandria in terms of making serious improvements to the quality of life. "Cairo is a very big city with many problems," he says. Cairo developed without any plan. From El Mahgoub's point of view the only solution is to establish another capital city elsewhere.

"Developing and modernizing a city is the vision for the future," points out the governor, who sees a chance for Alexandria to return to the peaceful beauty it held in the past. "Step by step, the citizens and I will reach this goal: Alexandria will become again the best city on the Mediterranean, a place that everyone wants to see."

*S. D.*

*Previous page: A building under construction, Sixth of October City, near Cairo*

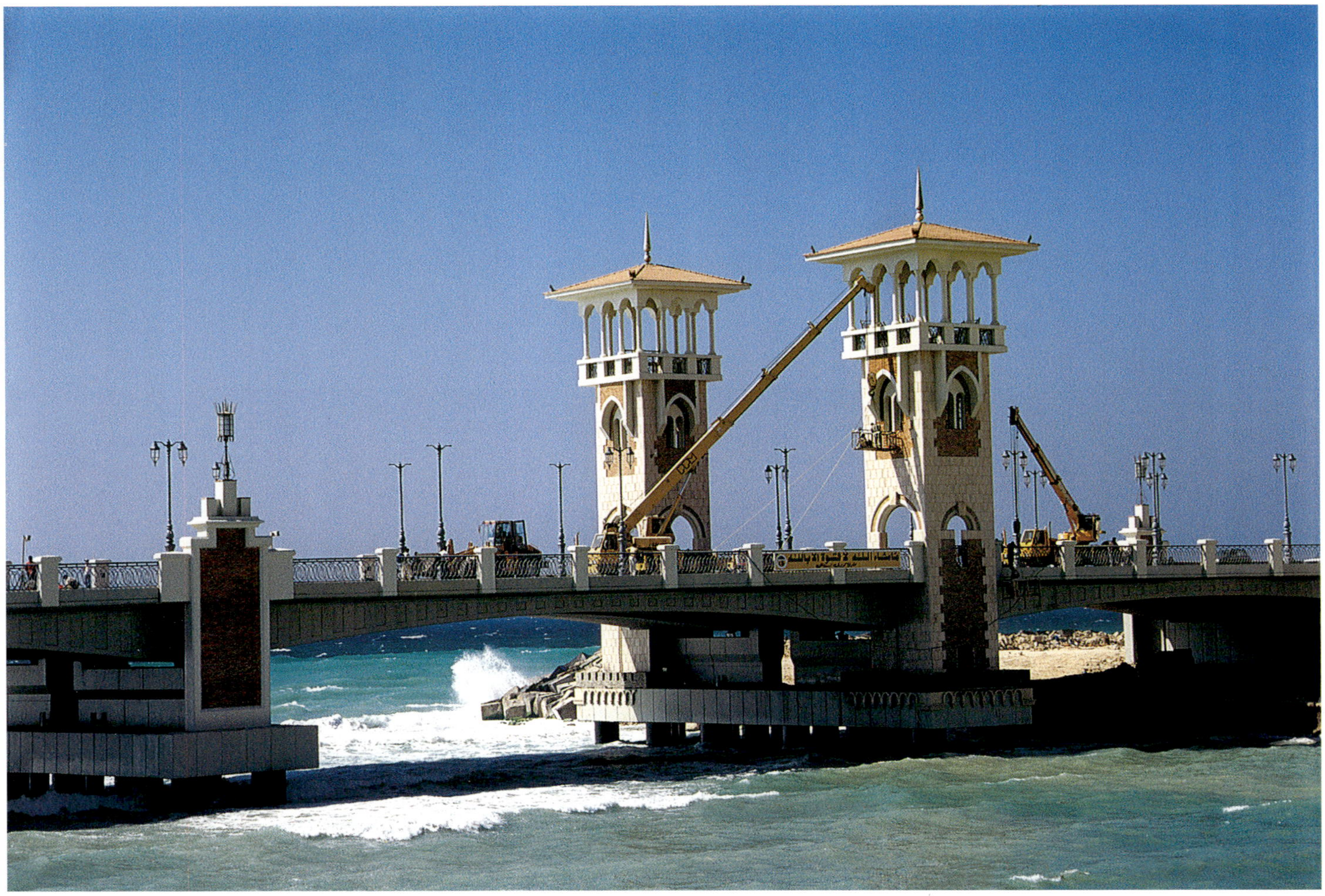

*The Stanley Bridge under construction, Alexandria*

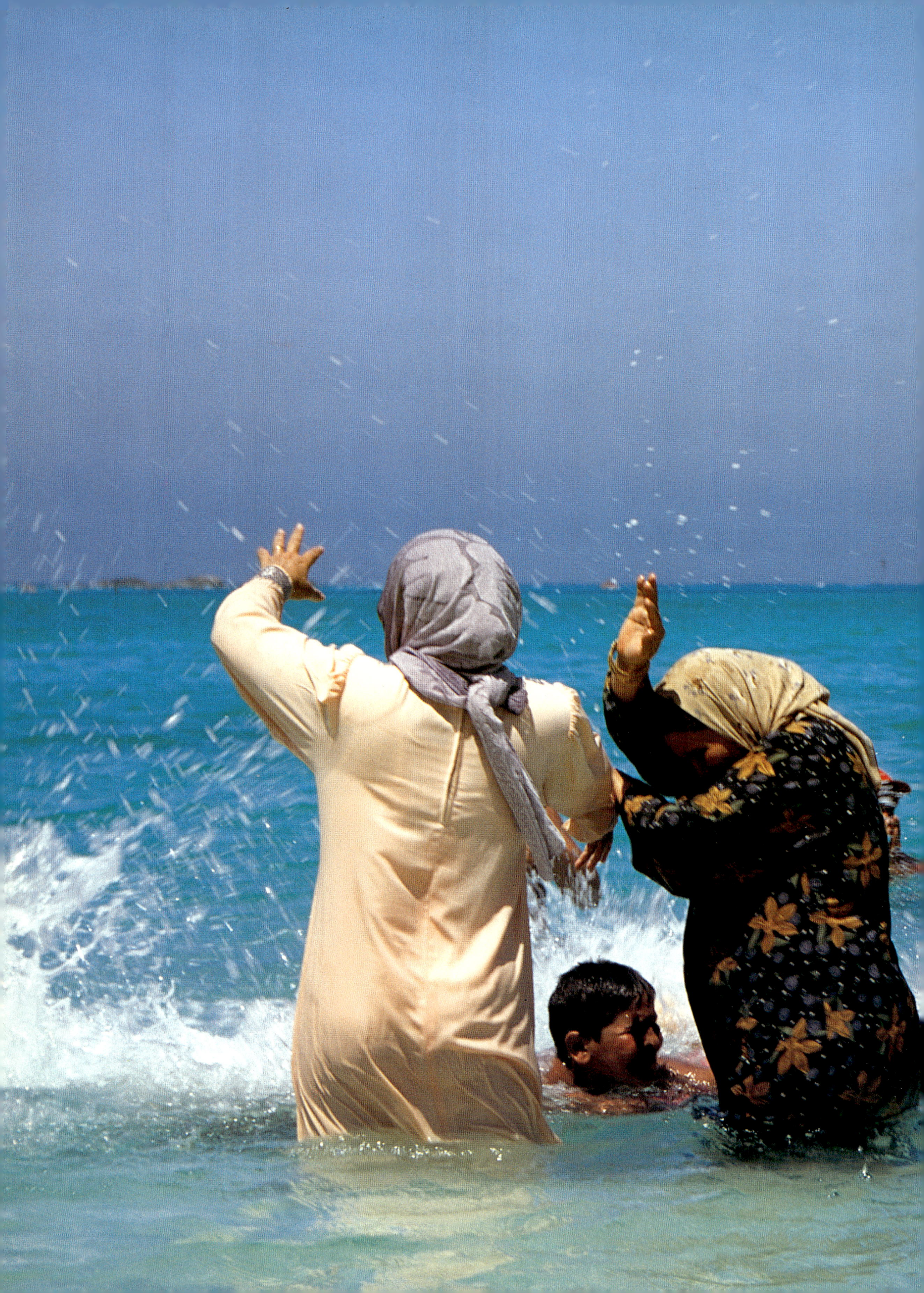

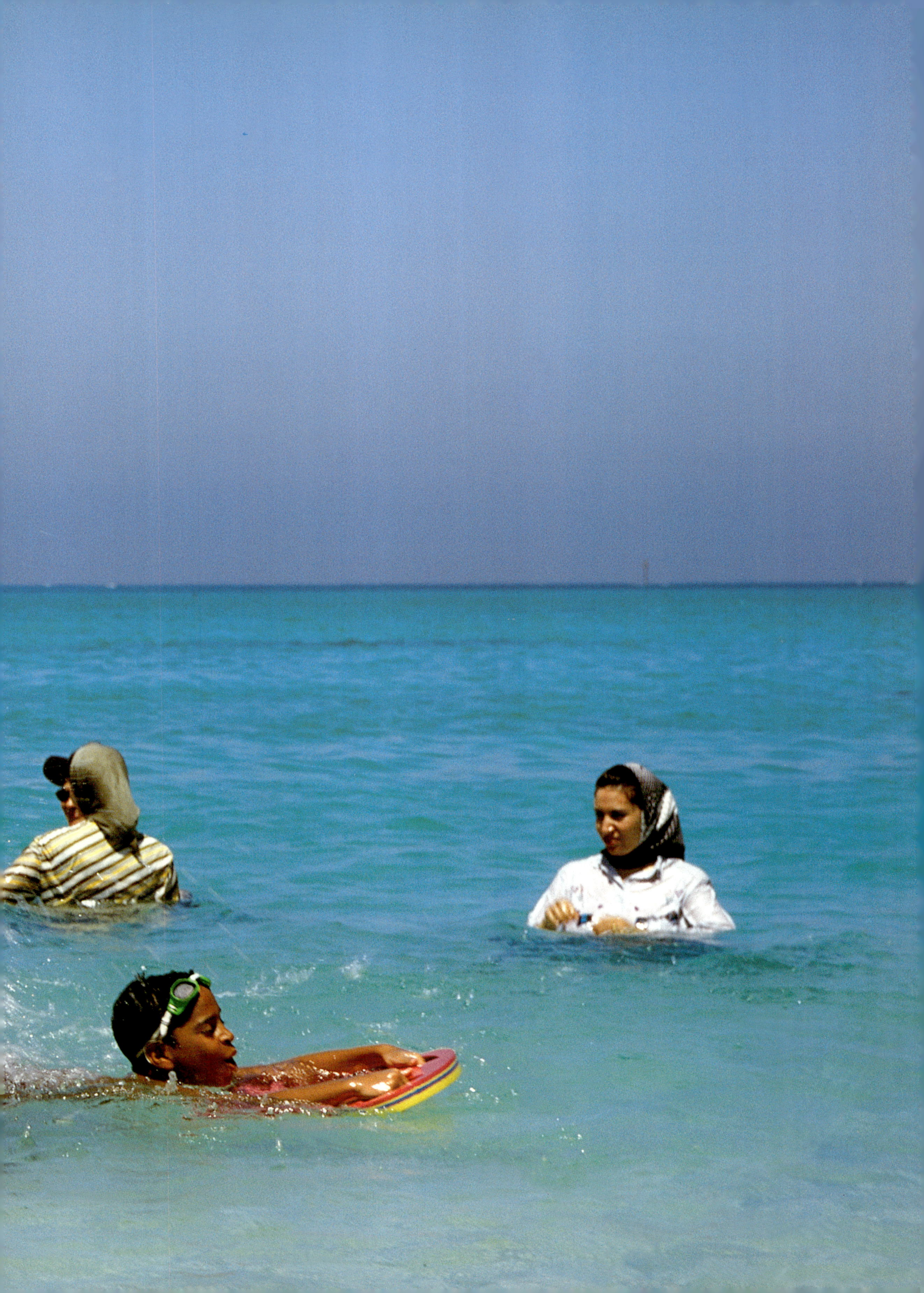

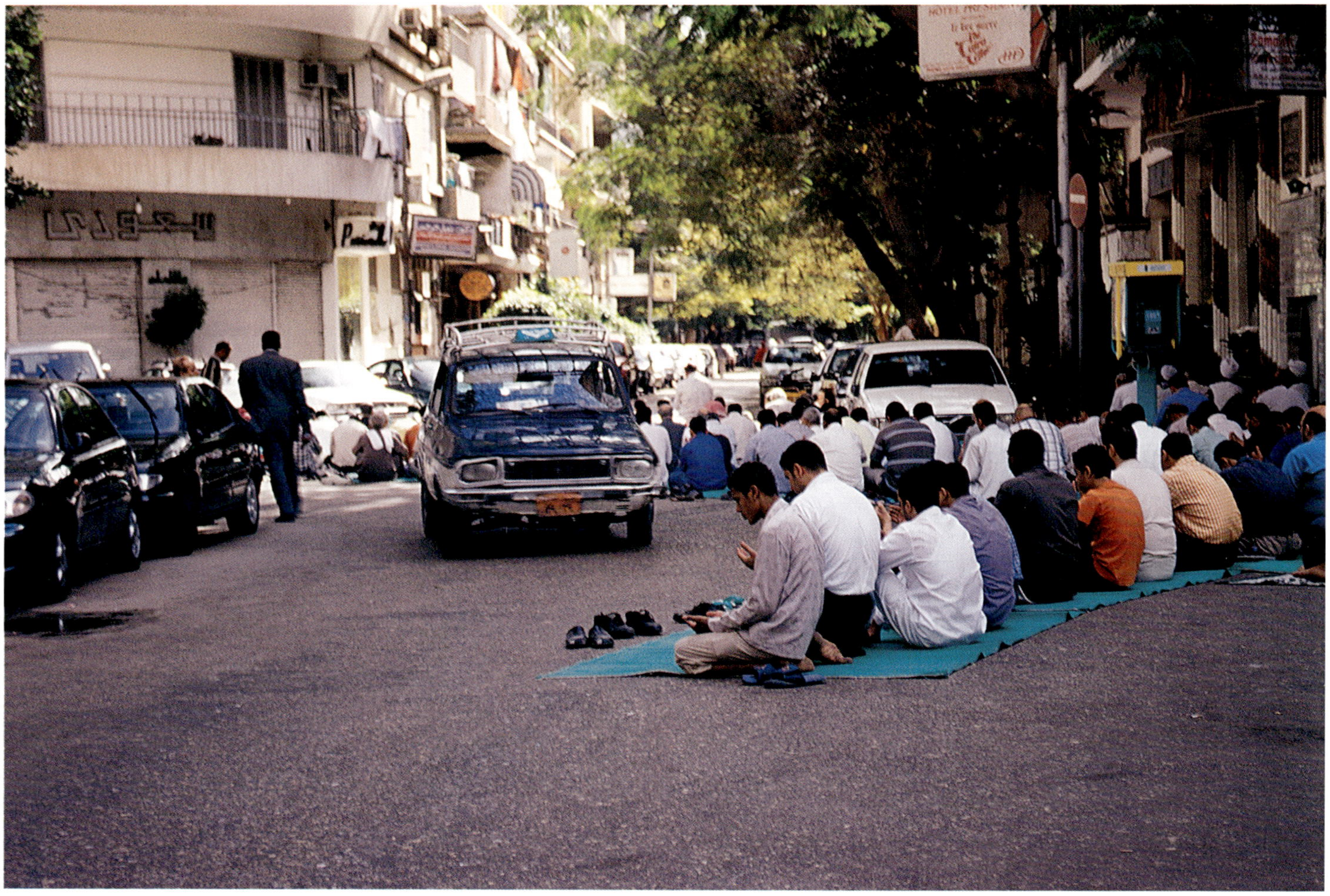

*On Fridays, most mosques do not have enough room for everyone to pray, and the devout spill out onto the streets, blocking the road, Zamalek, Cairo*

*Previous page: Bathing in the Mediterranean, Marsa Matruh*

*Satellite television dishes facing the Nile, Cairo*

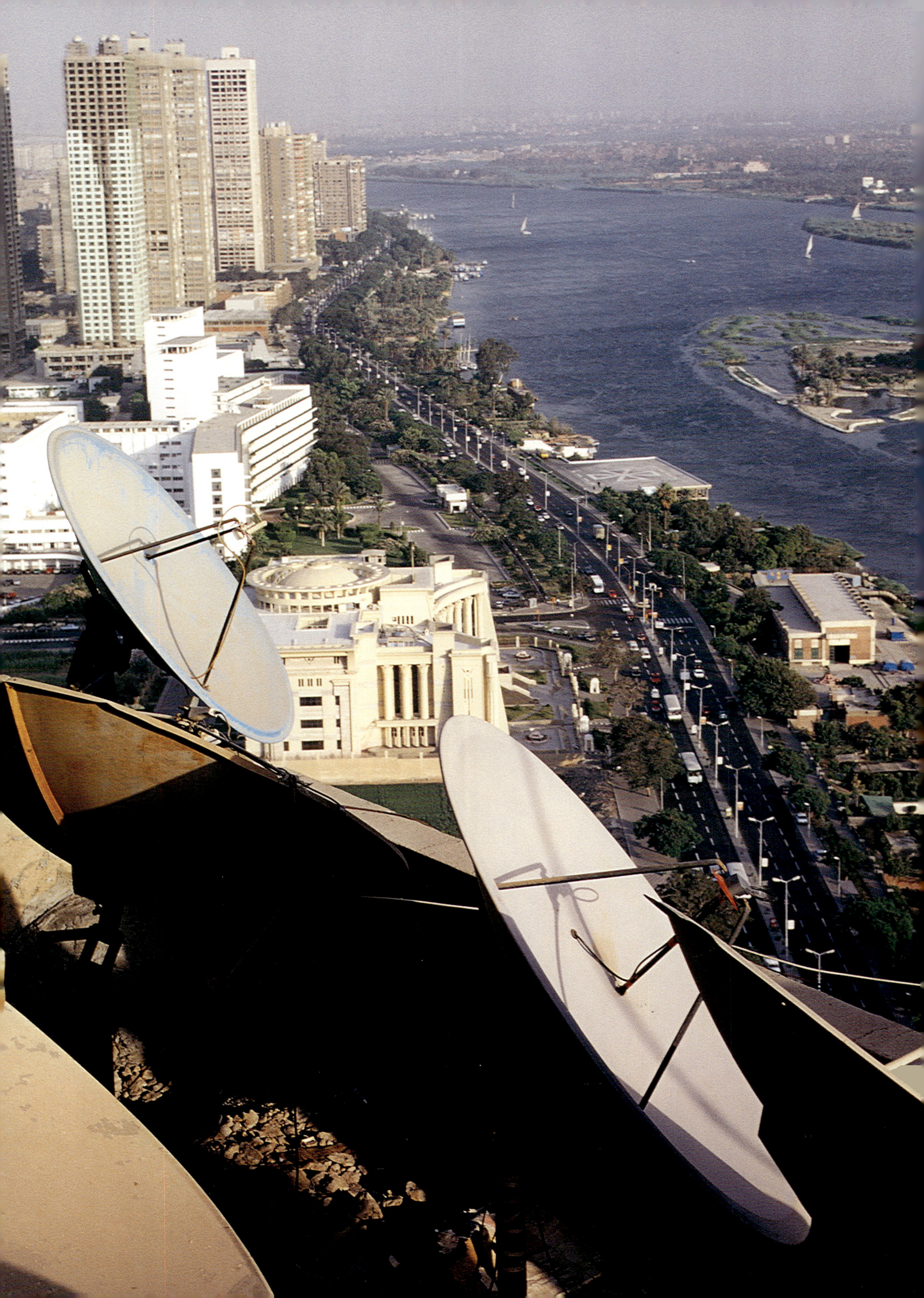

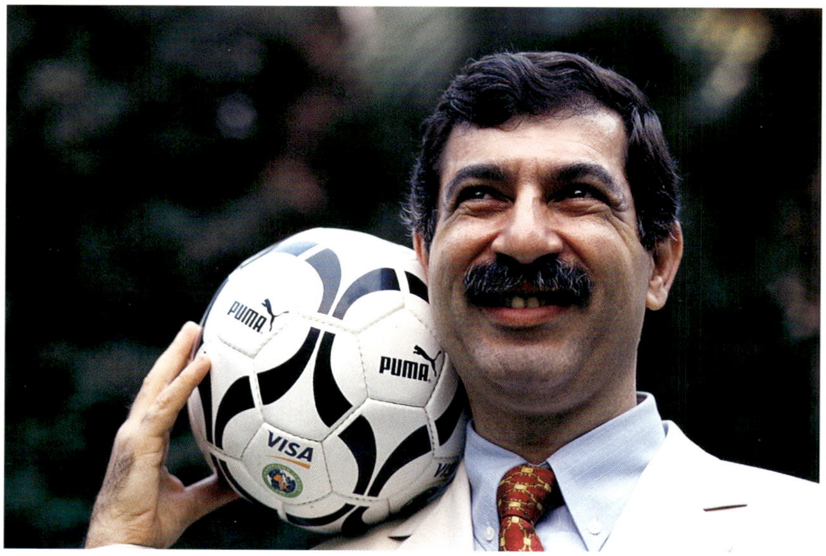


*Alaa Sadek, sports journalist*

## Alaa Sadek

*Sport journalist*

"I like the noise. It's part of my job," says Dr. Alaa Sadek, an Egyptian journalist specializing in sports writing. "I like to hear people talking. It makes life in Egypt different from life in other places in the world. I don't like the silence. In the football stadium you hear three types of noise: from the fans in the stadium, from the players on the pitch, and from the whistle of the referee. That's the noise I like!" The atmosphere on the field is not the only place that provides Sadek with the sound and energy he enjoys. "As a journalist I make other people talk, and as a commentator I talk. The noise of words is part of my life!" he says.

Sadek always had a passion for sport. When he was eight he used to memorize match results. His career path, however, started off in another direction. After he graduated from high school, his family forced him to enroll in the Medical College of Alexandria. After all, medicine and engineering were the most respected faculties in Egypt. But while he was a medical student he also worked as a journalist, which made his decision easier: "As soon as I had the chance to change my career from doctor to journalist, I did." In 1979, two years after he graduated, Sadek closed an important chapter of his life. "Since then I have not practiced medicine, even on the level of advice to family and friends," he concludes.

He has become famous throughout Egypt and the Middle East for his thoughtful journalistic style and his elegant classical Arabic. "I didn't choose a style. It comes naturally," he explains, and credits the influence of his late father. "My father was a very good writer and taught me the classical language, which I use everywhere: in the taxi, at home, in the bus, on television. Everyone here normally speaks colloquial Arabic. I was an exception, as I used classical Arabic instead. This gave me the chance to be unique."

Sadek keeps himself informed about the world of sport by reading about it every day for two to four hours. "It helps me to get closer to people's hearts," he says. "They know I search hard to get the information they want. I am very frank. This is probably why people respect me and appreciate my work," he says with a smile. Such popularity is sometimes difficult to maintain. "The competition here in Egypt is very aggressive, very unfair," Sadek admits. "A dirty campaign from colleagues or a powerful boss is quite common."

Sadek continues to broaden his working life: not only is he a journalist for important newspapers and local and foreign television programs, but also a sports adviser via the telephone and the internet, and a writer. "I normally write two books a year. I've had fifty-three published so far!" he says proudly.

Sadek stresses the long history that sport has in Egypt: "We were the first country in the world to practice sport," he explains, and lists a variety of sports the ancient Egyptians used to play. He also mentions several noteworthy events: "In 1912 Egypt participated in the Olympic Games in Stockholm and in 1934 in the Second World Cup in Italy; in 1949 Egypt was the winner of the European basketball championship in Cairo; and in 1928 in Amsterdam, 1936 in Berlin, and 1948 in London, Egypt won the most gold medals in weightlifting in the Olympic Games."

The current situation is not so good. "In recent times we have deteriorated, because of bad economic conditions and because of administrative problems as a result of three wars against Israel. Unfortunately we are now outsiders in sport," he says sadly. "Our history and our culture are good, but our present is bad!"

Improvement will come when the Egyptian idea of sport changes. "Sport is not entertainment, as many of our ministers and upper-class minds think," says Sadek. "Sport is a very important part of our life. In Egypt they can quickly build a new city with lots of infrastructure, such as schools, hospitals, and factories, but not a single football field, and not a single sports club. We must change our view so that sport in Egypt will play an important role in our society again."

The attitude of players likewise must change. "Egyptians only like victory," Sadek points out. "Sport means to win or to lose. We have to accept both results with pride. We miss sportsmanship because our leaders and our heroes never accepted defeat." The perfect role model for an athlete, according to Sadek, is soccer player Mahmoud al-Khatib, who was the national team's star in the 1980s. "He was the best player ever in Egyptian sports history," says Sadek, praising not only al-Khatib's talent but the man's professionalism and courtesy.

Sadek does not hesitate to admit the connection that has developed between sport and money. "The amateur field has been deteriorating since 1992," he says. "Sport now depends on money and on how much you can spend. The richest counties are now the giants in the world of sport. Yes, money is now sport!"

This is true even on the local level. "The chance foreigners have to play sport in Egypt is much higher than it is for locals," he points out. "Hotels and private clubs are the only places available for playing sports. Money is therefore essential in sport, not only for competition but also for practicing," he concludes. "Whoever can pay can play!"

*S. D.*

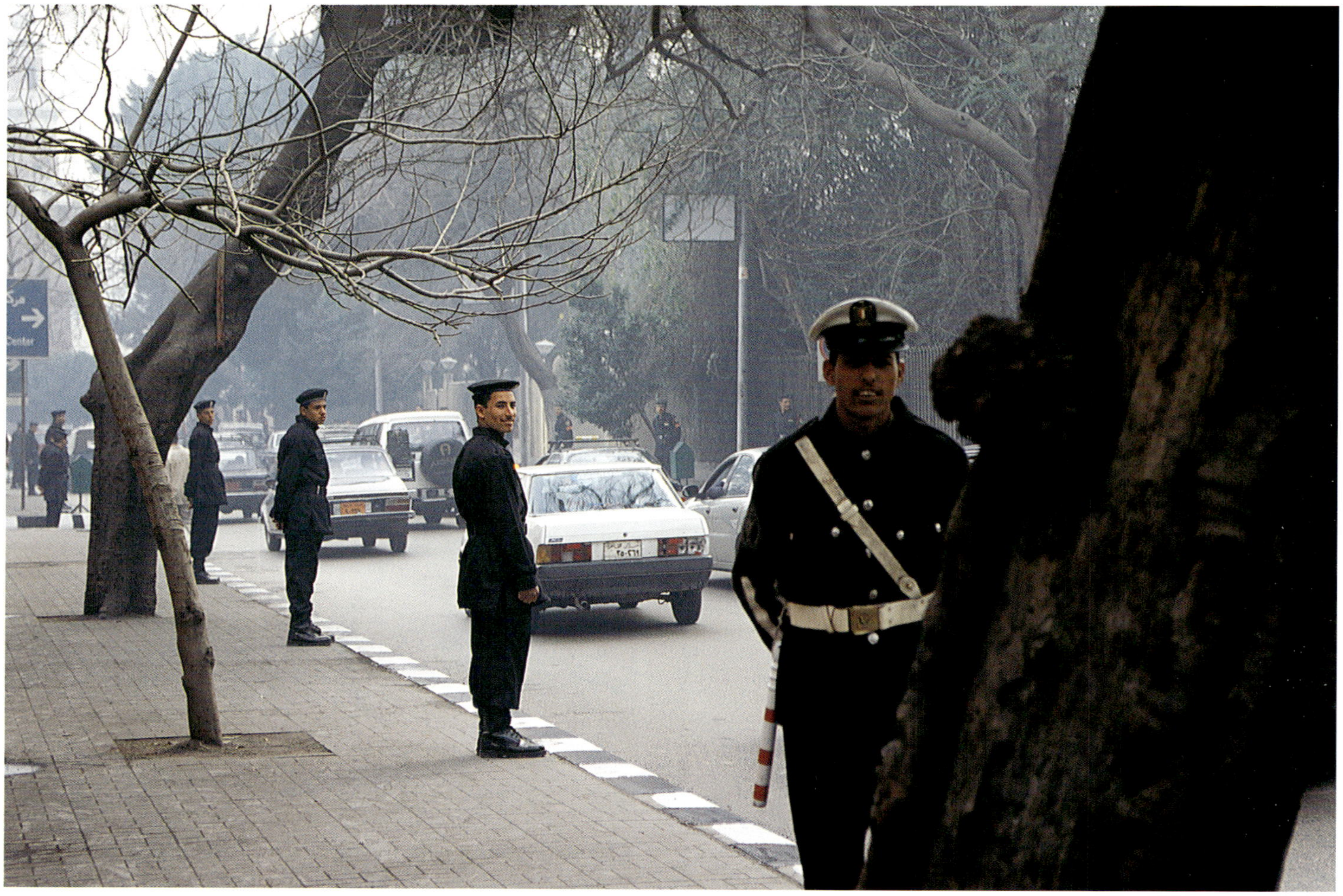


*Policemen line the street before a minister's car and his escort pass by, Zamalek, Cairo*

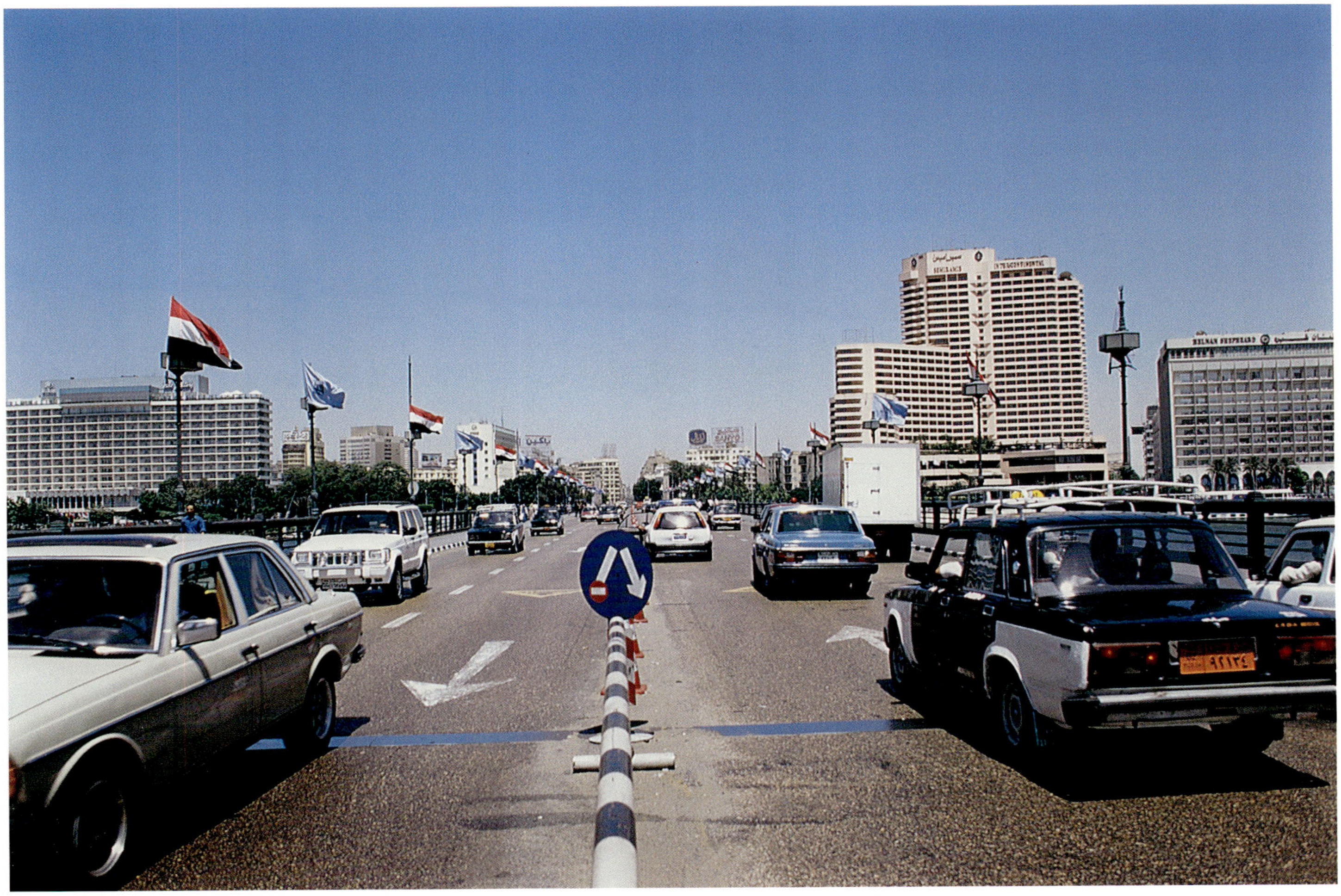

*Qasr al-Nil Bridge, Cairo*

## Mohamed

*Policeman*

"I've never been ill," says Mohamed. Then he starts coughing. Mohamed is a thirty-three-year-old policeman, and he has been working in the streets of Cairo since 1990, breathing the polluted air and being bombarded by the noise of the city.

"Of course I love the quiet, but this is my job. I got used to the noise. It took me almost a year," he confesses.

Originally from the Delta town of Damietta, Mohamed moved to the capital and started work in the poorest areas of Imbaba and Shubra, until he was promoted. Now he works in Zamalek, one of the most affluent residential neighborhoods. He stands for eight hours a day on the chaotic 26 July Street, keeping an eye not only on the traffic but also on crime.

Does he like his job? "Of course!" he immediately says. "I like it when everything runs smoothly, as often happens in the morning. But when someone double parks, blocking the other cars, or doesn't stop at the red light, it drives me crazy," he admits with a smile.

There are good days, on which Mohamed never gives a ticket, and bad ones, on which he spends most of his time writing down plate numbers. "Once I gave seventy tickets in a day," he remembers.

Dressed in a perfectly ironed jacket, Mohamed notes that "Egyptians respect the uniforms more than the rules." Uniforms are certainly a symbol of a hierarchy. Policemen sporting gold stars or white helmets are surely more intimidating than the ones who wear the orange plastic jackets.

There are several levels of policemen in Egypt: at the top is the police officer, who starts his career after graduating from the Police Academy; next is the *amin shurta,* who has a high school education and has graduated from the Police Institute; at the bottom the *'askari,* who enlists in the police and applies for special police training, hoping to reach the rank of *sul.* Mohamed is an *amin shurta*: during the winter he wears a black uniform, in summer a white one.

"If I were the governor of Cairo? I don't know what I would do to make improvements in the city," admits Mohamed. "Perhaps I would apply my attention to the pedestrians and to the overuse of horns."

Although Mohamed will not divulge his salary, it is well known in Egypt that a policemen's monthly earnings are low. An *'askari* might be paid 90 Egyptian pounds—the equivalent of about $15. A *sul* might get 120 pounds, and an *amin shurta*, like Mohamed from 150 to 200. The police officer is the privileged one, starting with a monthly salary of 450 pounds, with the potential to reach almost 2,000.

Mohamed's hopes are very few beyond his job. "I want to work until I retire. When I retire I won't do anything else. But yes, I have a dream: to go to Mecca at least once in my life."

*S. D.*

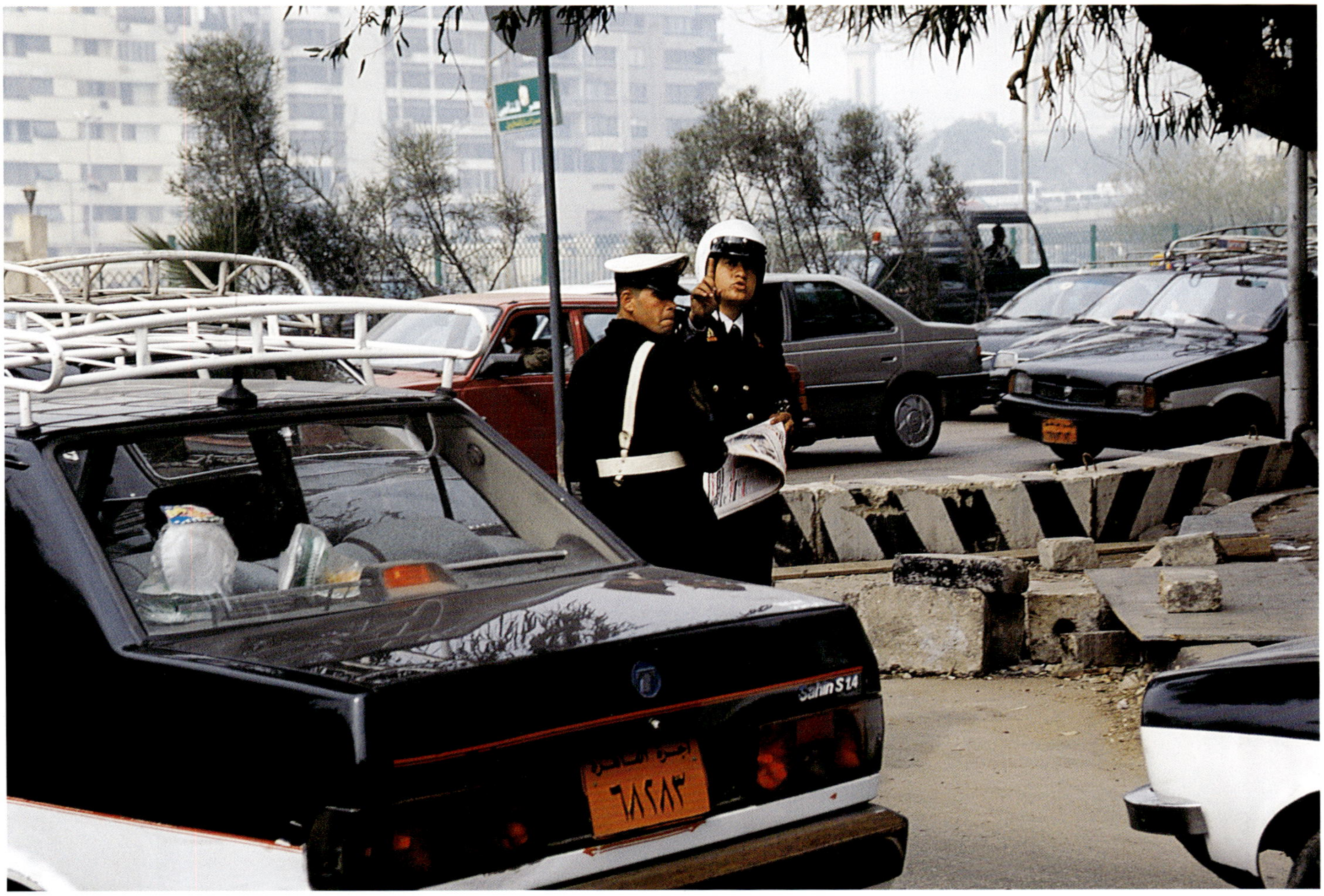


*Policemen in the middle of the daily traffic, Cairo*

# Silence

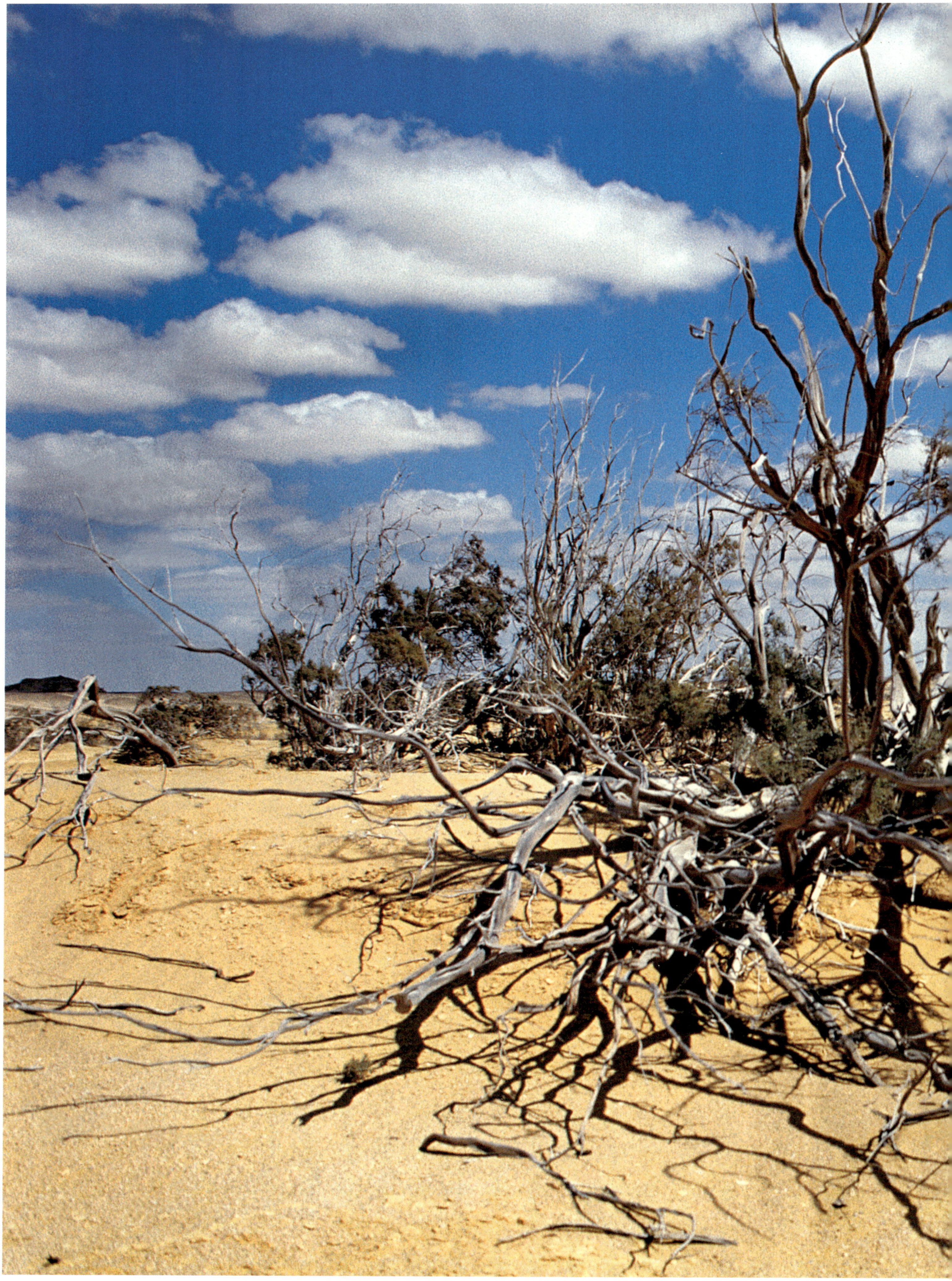

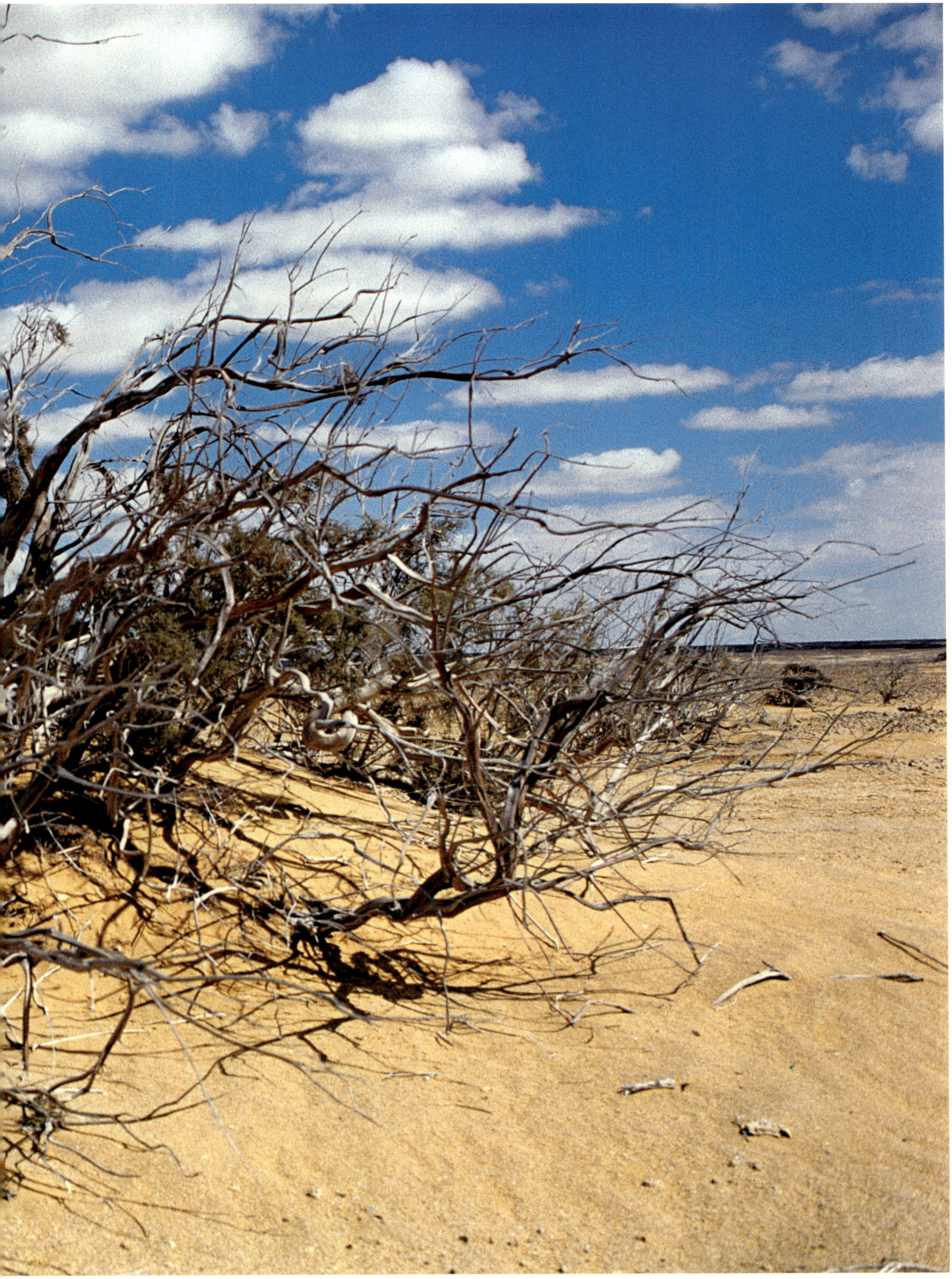

*A plant in the Western Desert*

When prayer time is finished, the inside of a mosque is shrouded in silence. Shoes have been left outside. Barefoot people glide soundlessly along the carpeted floors. A few devout souls may be mumbling prayers under their breath, kneeling, then touching their foreheads to their prayer rugs, their eyes closed. The glorious al-Hakim Mosque in Cairo enhances the quiet. Begun in 990, the mosque features a lovely open central courtyard that encourages contemplation. More typically, mosques are topped with a high domed ceiling stretching toward heaven. Sunlight falls through the windows, and dust swirls through the beams of light. Inside such places, it is so quiet, it is as if time has slowed.

Despite Egypt's dense cities with their gnarled traffic, loud street vendors, and garish billboards, a person can find a remarkable number of sites that hold an ancient kind of silence. Medieval mosques might be sitting in some of the oldest and most crowded parts of town, but step inside and it is as if someone has flipped a switch to turn off all the noise. The same thing happens when you push off onto the Nile in a small sailboat, known as a felucca: the roar of Cairo falls away, and nothing can be heard except the boat's sails softly struggling against the breeze and the light splash of the water against the hull.

A special kind of silence can be experienced during the holy month of Ramadan: the wordlessness of anticipation. During Ramadan, observant Muslims do not eat from sunrise to sunset and then break their fast with a meal called *iftar*. In Cairo during these thirty days, you can see long tables in alleys and on sidewalks set up by philanthropists who provide an *iftar* meal to the neighborhood's poorer residents. Just as the sun is about to set, all take their seats and wait anxiously for the moment when the food can be consumed. The young fidget. The old take a moment to reflect on the lessons of fasting, one of the five requirements of Islam.

Egypt's natural landscapes provide the deepest sort of silence. The waters of the Red Sea and the Mediterranean border the east and the north of the country, with endless quiet vistas. On the Sinai Peninsula, the craggy mountains glow bronze and copper when dawn breaks. Sand dunes as tall as office buildings ripple the desert, looking like golden silk billowing in the breeze. Over time the dunes creep along through the emptiness, inch by inch burying anything in their way. Animals and plants from millions of years ago lie in quiet repose in the form of fossils in the desert's rocks. The landscape's sand, mountains, and caves provide a true experience of solitude: silence stretching from horizon to horizon, and far beyond.

*T. E.*

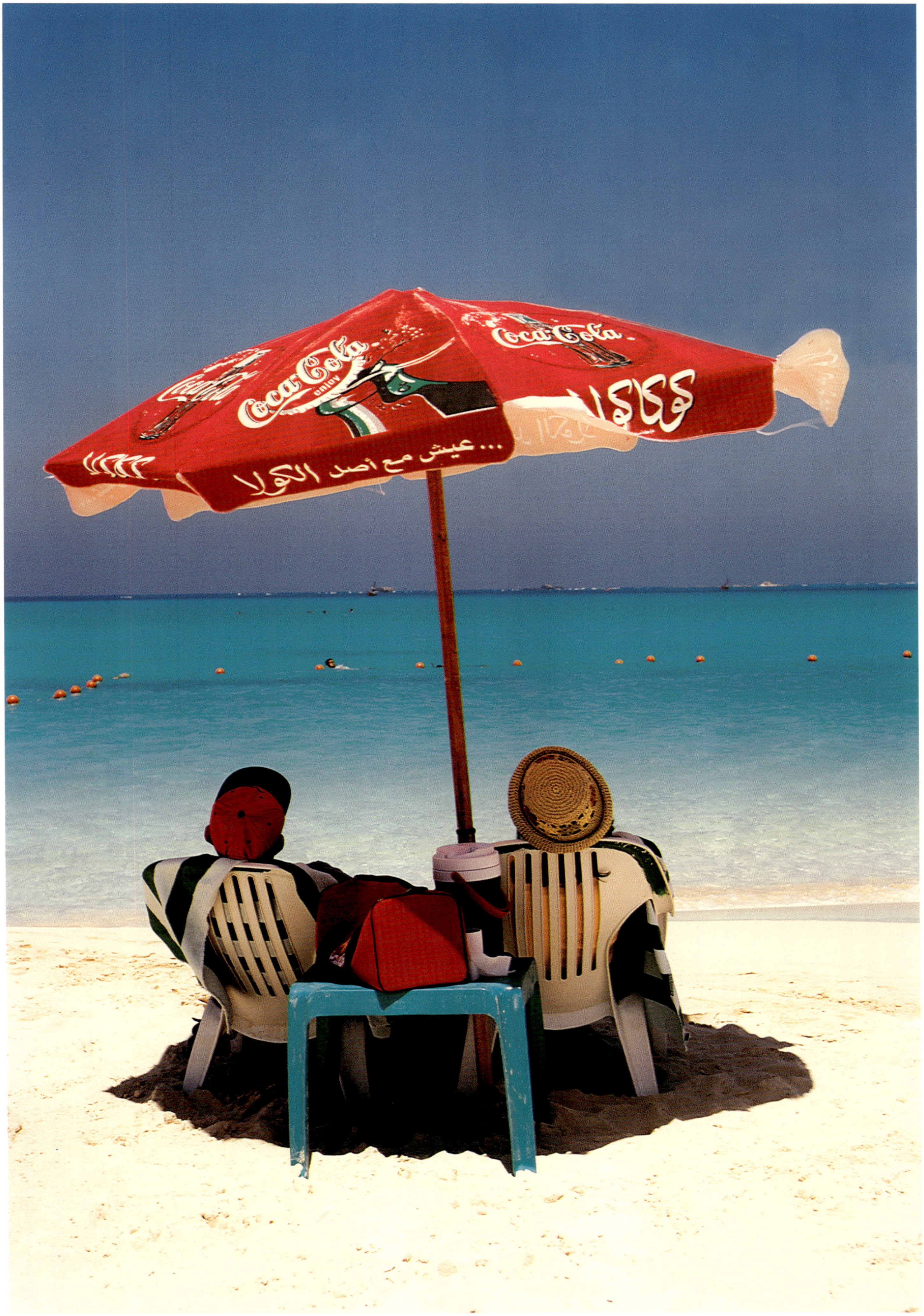


*The turquoise water of the Mediterranean, Marsa Matruh*

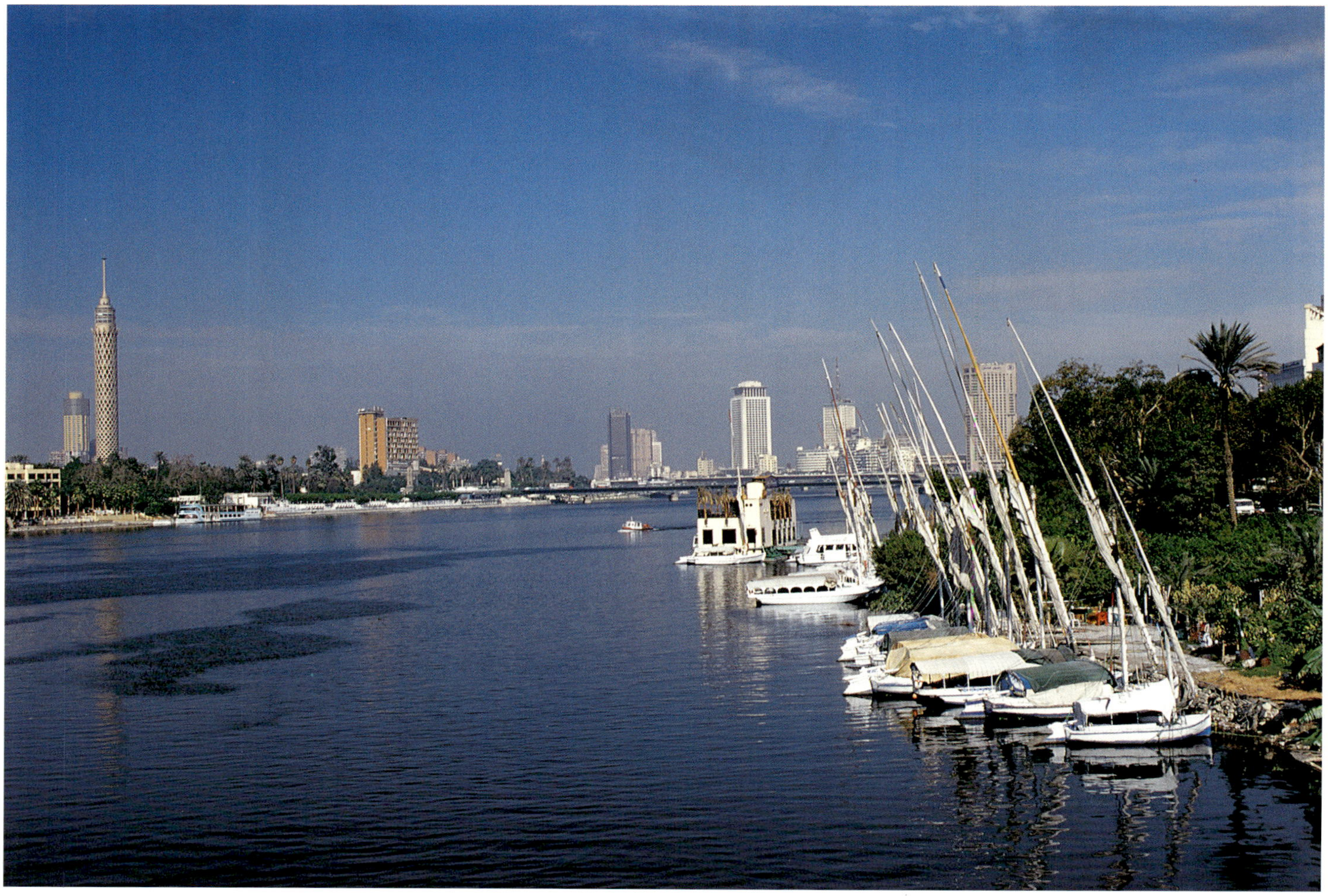

*Feluccas on the Nile, Cairo*

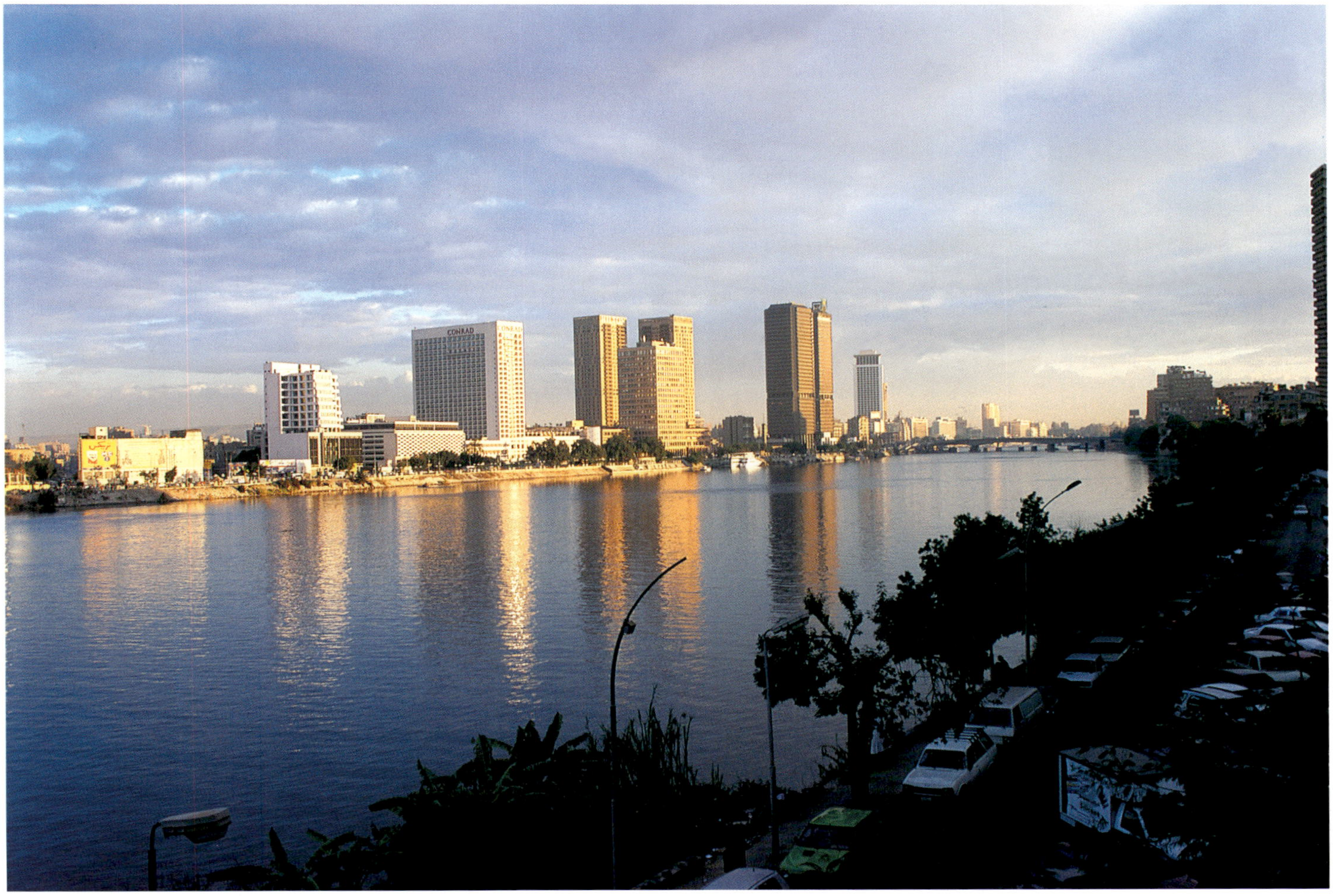


*Sunset from Montaza Street, also known as Lovers' Street, Cairo*

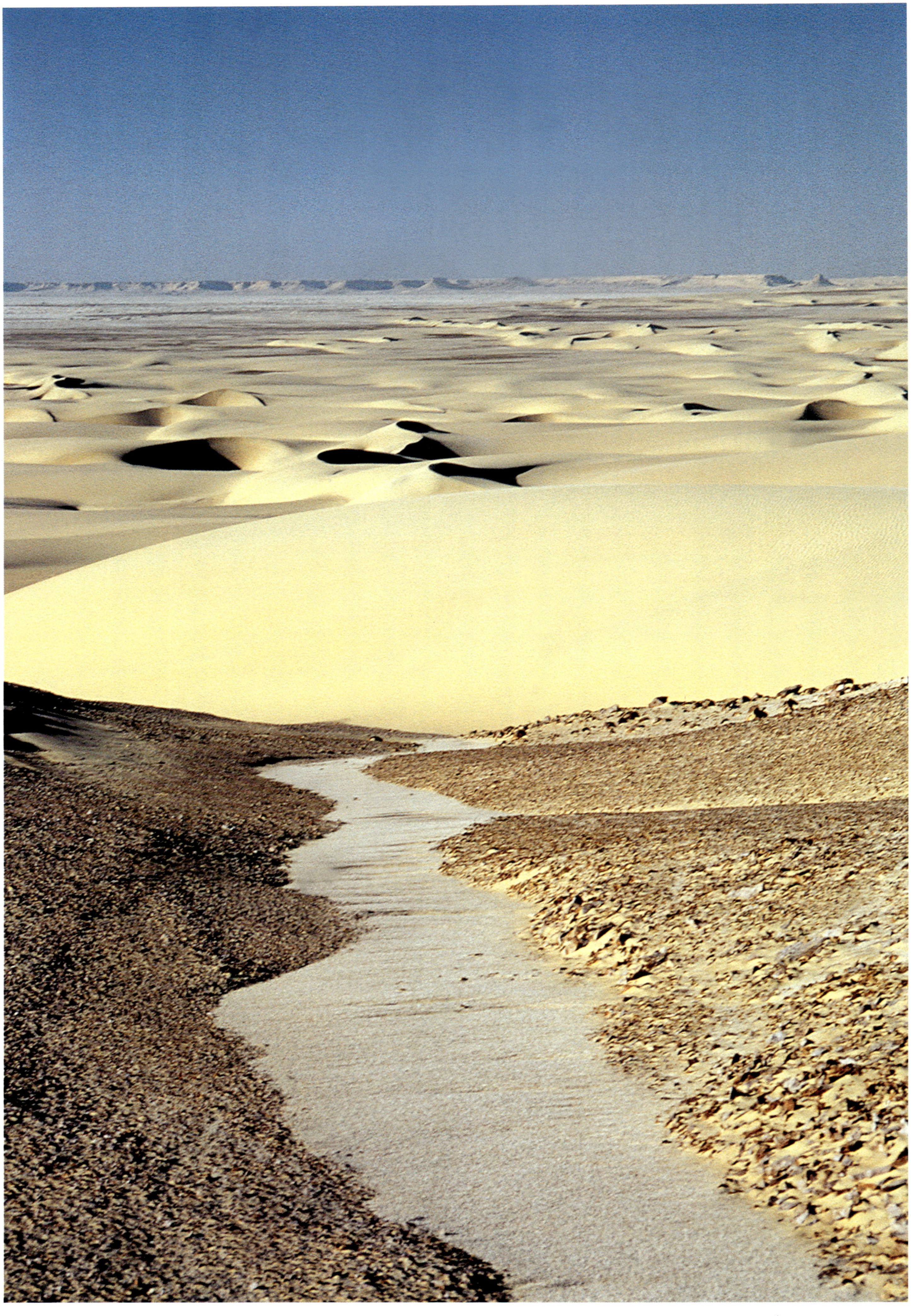

*Sand dunes ripple in the desert, like golden silk billowing in the breeze, Western Desert*

*The White Desert's rock formations, Western Desert*

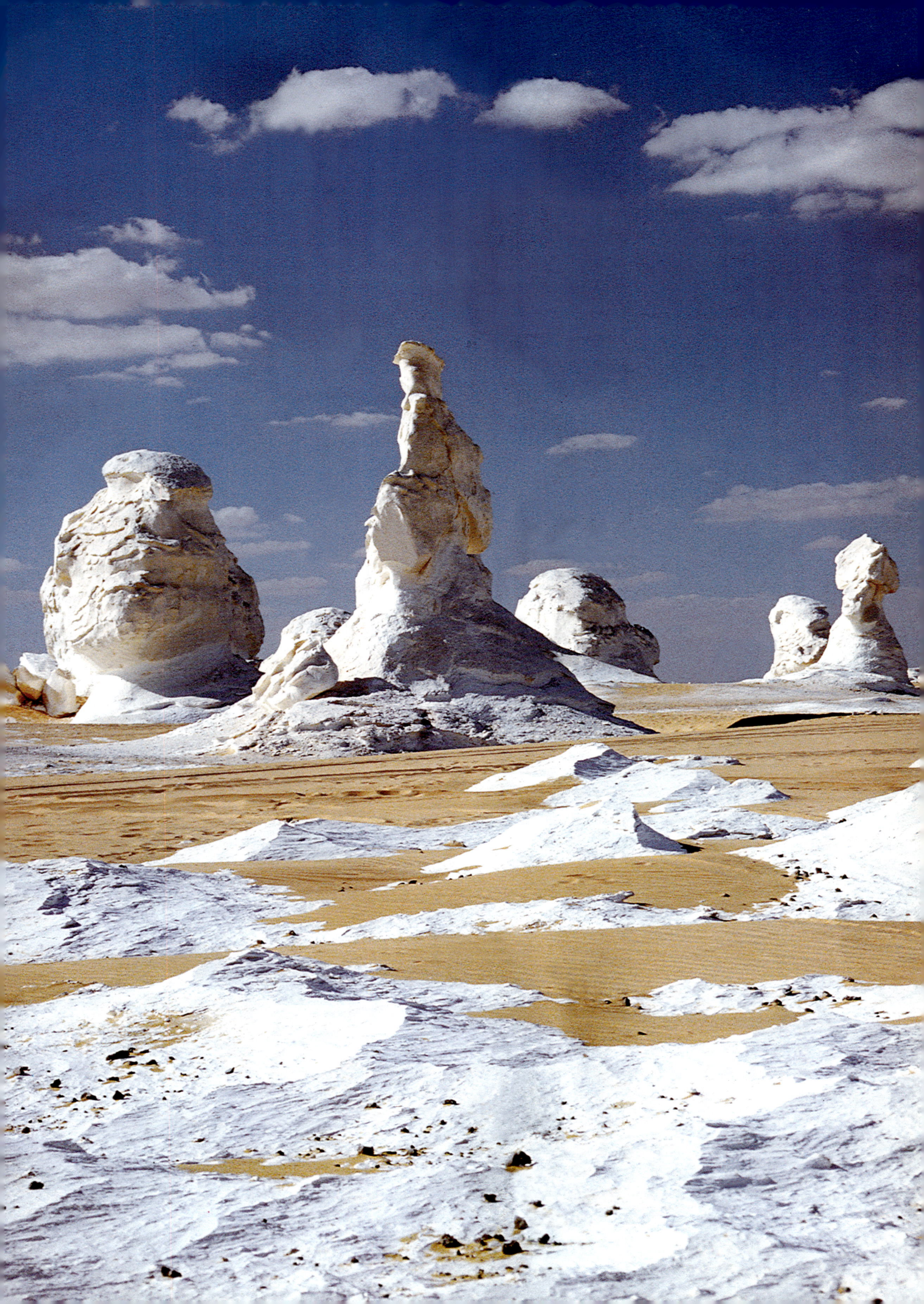

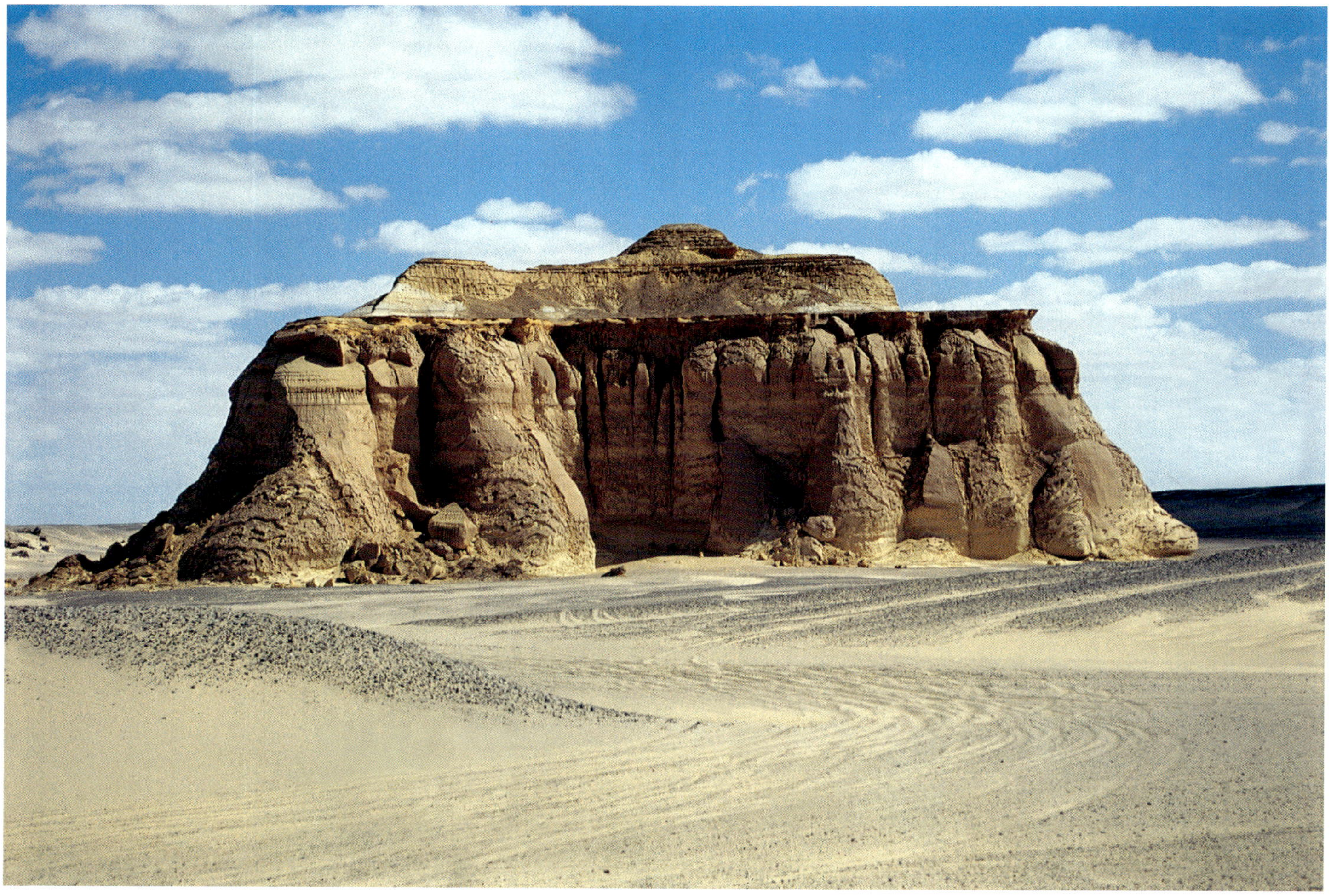

*Surreal rock formations in the Valley of the Whales, Western Desert*

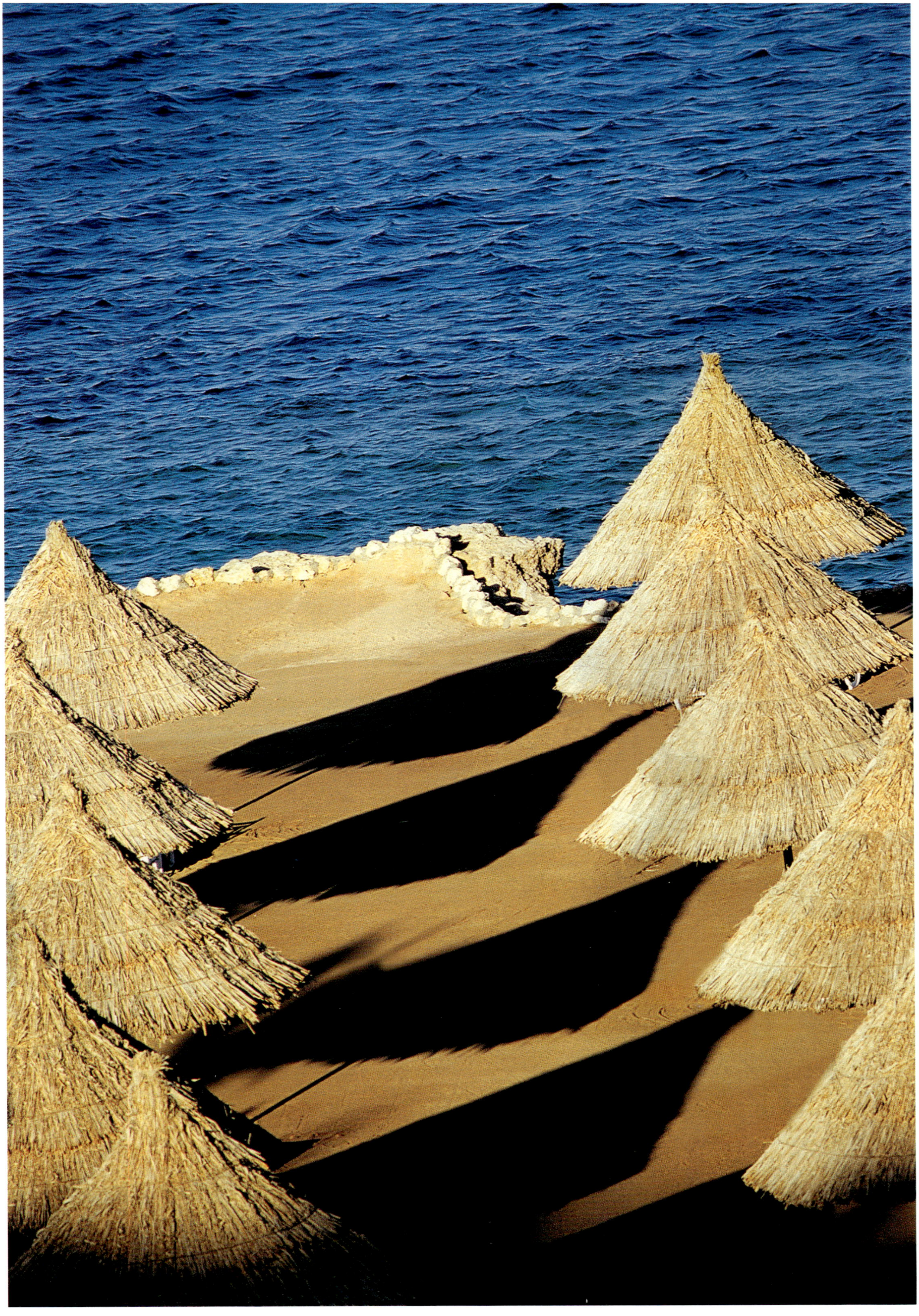

*A quiet beach, Sharm al-Sheikh*

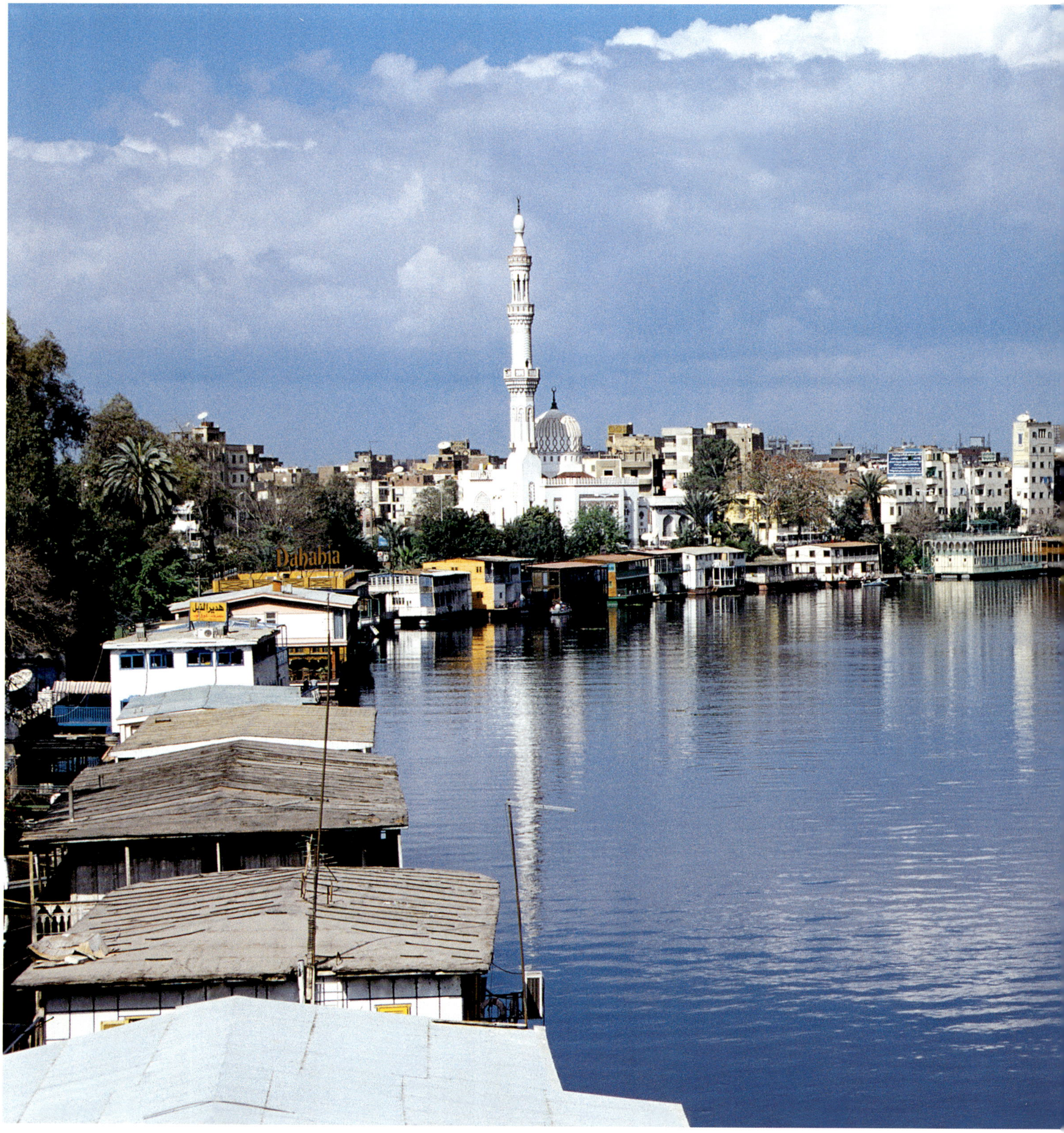


**Gamal Bakry**

*Architect and urban planner*

Architect Gamal Bakry designs exceptionally sleek, modern buildings. And yet surprisingly, one of his inspirations is the silent peacefulness of old Egyptian houses. "You enter them, and then you reach a courtyard, and all the rooms are looking into that inner space."

It is such simplicity that appeals to Bakry. He believes in "architecture without cosmetics." He admits that this motto presents a difficult challenge for an architect, particularly one working in Egypt, but after forty-eight years in the business, he is sure of his ability to carry it out.

"Cosmetics" for Bakry are details that appear without meaning—things that are added randomly, to create an "expected" look. "There must be a reason, there must be logic, there must be something related to the tradition," says Bakry, whose office and living space are a creativity-filled refuge three

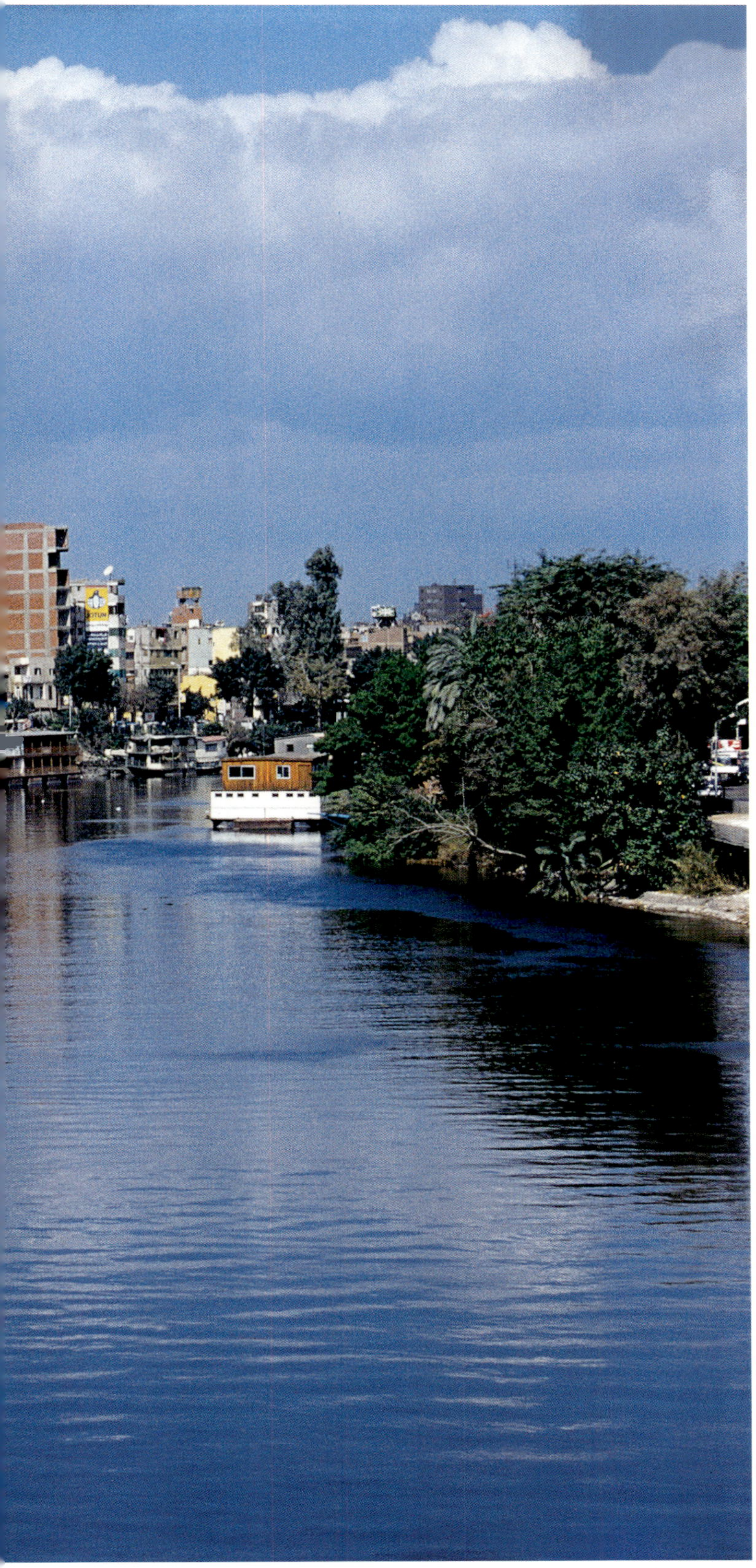

floors above a busy Cairo street. But for Bakry, using Egyptian tradition does not mean designing imposing pharaonic columns or sticking on hieroglyph-like decorations; those additions are precisely the kind of cosmetics that he deplores.

Bakry's designs are not in any way old-style. He respects tradition and yet updates it. The architect, who was born in Egypt's north-coast town of Port Said in 1931, creates buildings that are very fluid and exceptionally modern. He has designed a History Garden in Port Said, touristic villages in Dahab and Alexandria, the Arab Lawyers' Union building in Cairo, the Egyptian Embassy and Egyptian ambassador's residence in Berlin, a theater/convention hall for Cairo University, and numerous hotels, office buildings, and villas. All of them are ultra-sleek. "When I design a modern house, the client will look at it and say, 'Is it a hospital?'" Bakry says with a smile. "But I don't care. You don't choose your life—you are born with it. If you don't make peace with yourself and do what you really can do, you'll be a failure."

When he is not faced with resistance to his ideas from his clients, he is frustrated by contractors who want to alter his designs to make the construction easier or cheaper. "The owner and the contractor speak the same language—the language of money," Bakry sighs. Sadly, the language of art is not something everyone can hear.

Bakry discovered the lines and curves for his elegant modernism by improvising on another traditional element: the Islamic or Arabesque style. "This comes from the motion of the circle, because they saw the sun, the moon, the motion of them," explains Bakry. He then demonstrates what he's saying by showing how the interlocking circles on a piece of paper create Islamic-style patterns.

Bakry also devotes a portion of his time to creating abstract paintings. True to form, his paintings are full of fluid energy. He explains his process by saying that he first follows his intuition, quickly covering the paper with an elaborate, criss-crossing line. Then he contemplates what sections need color. "I take time to consider where should I leave the void and where should I paint," he says. Once again there's a connection to the old Egyptian houses: open, silent spaces surrounded by the activity of life.

*T. E.*

*Houseboats on the Nile, Cairo*

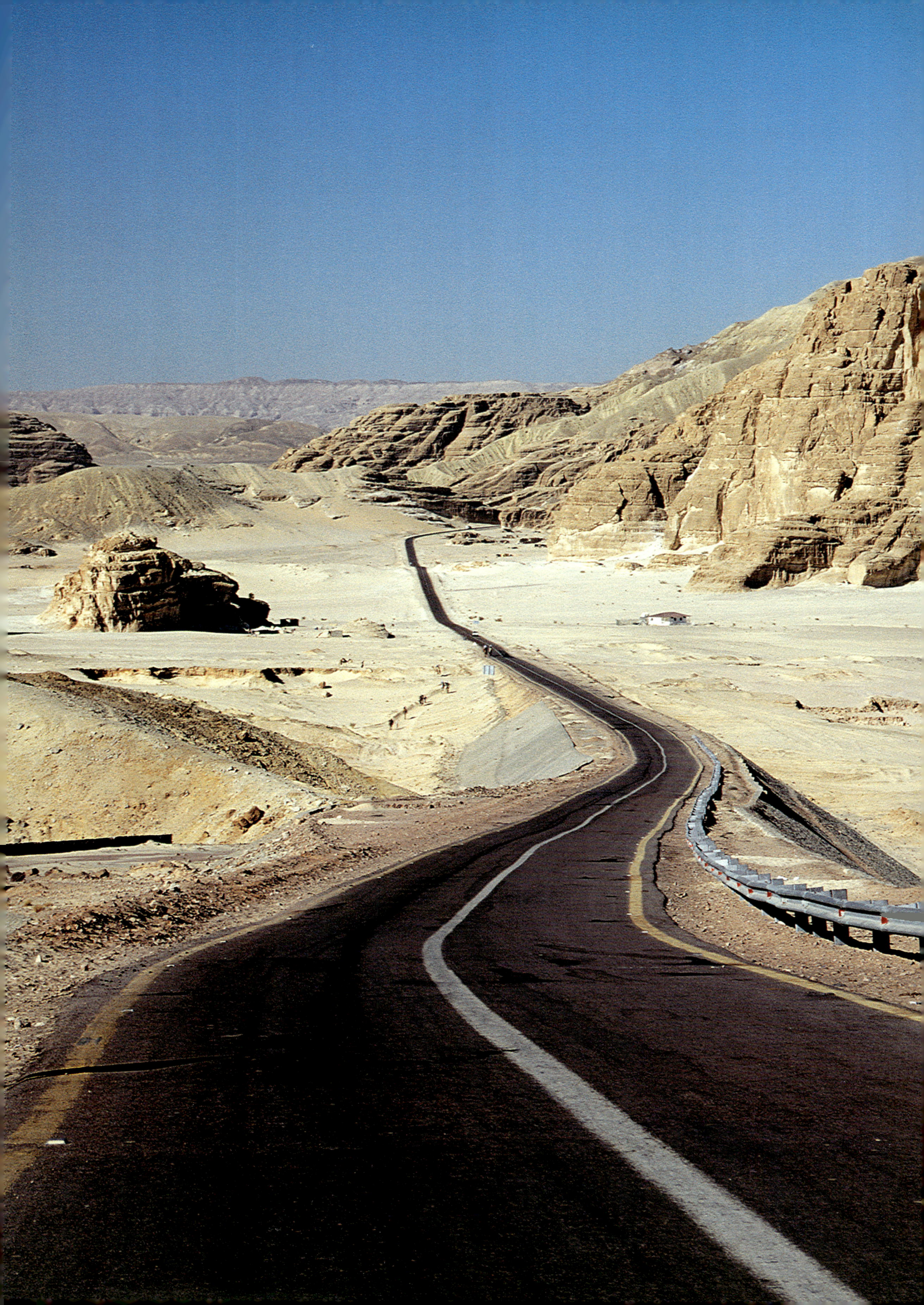

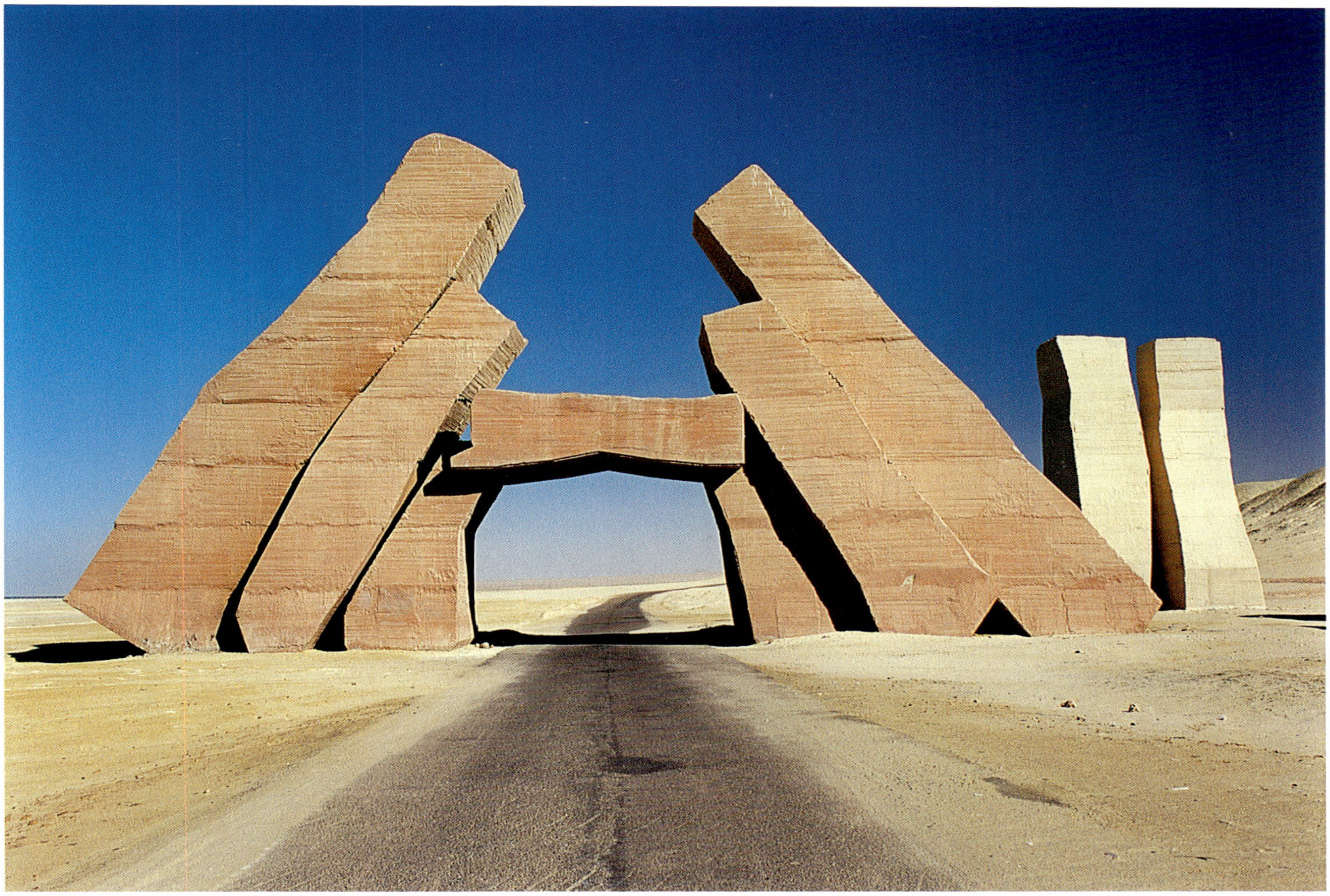

*An empty road between the craggy mountains, Sinai*

*The main entrance to the Ras Muhammad National Park, Sinai*

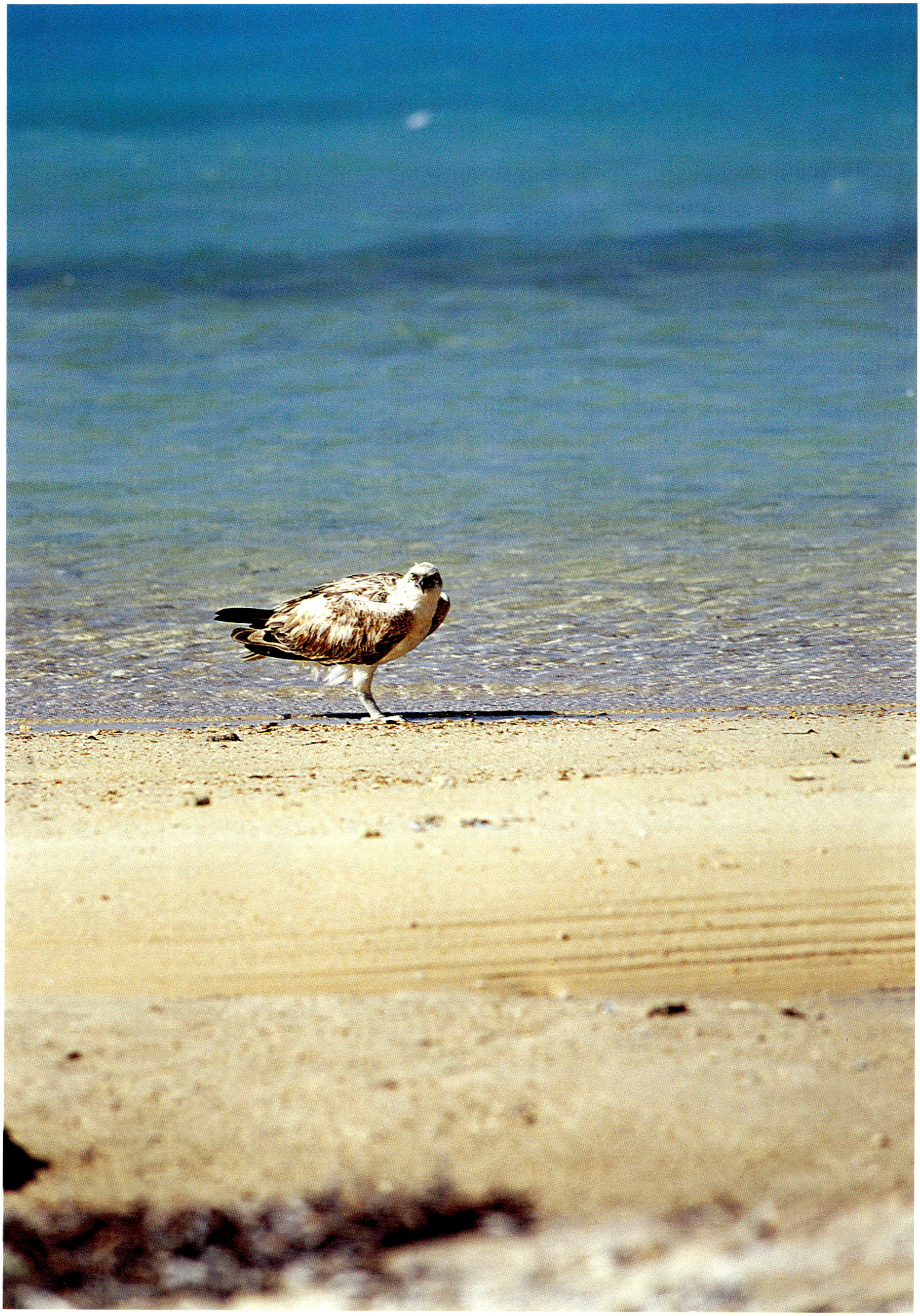

*A solitary osprey on the silent beach, Ras Muhammad, Sinai*

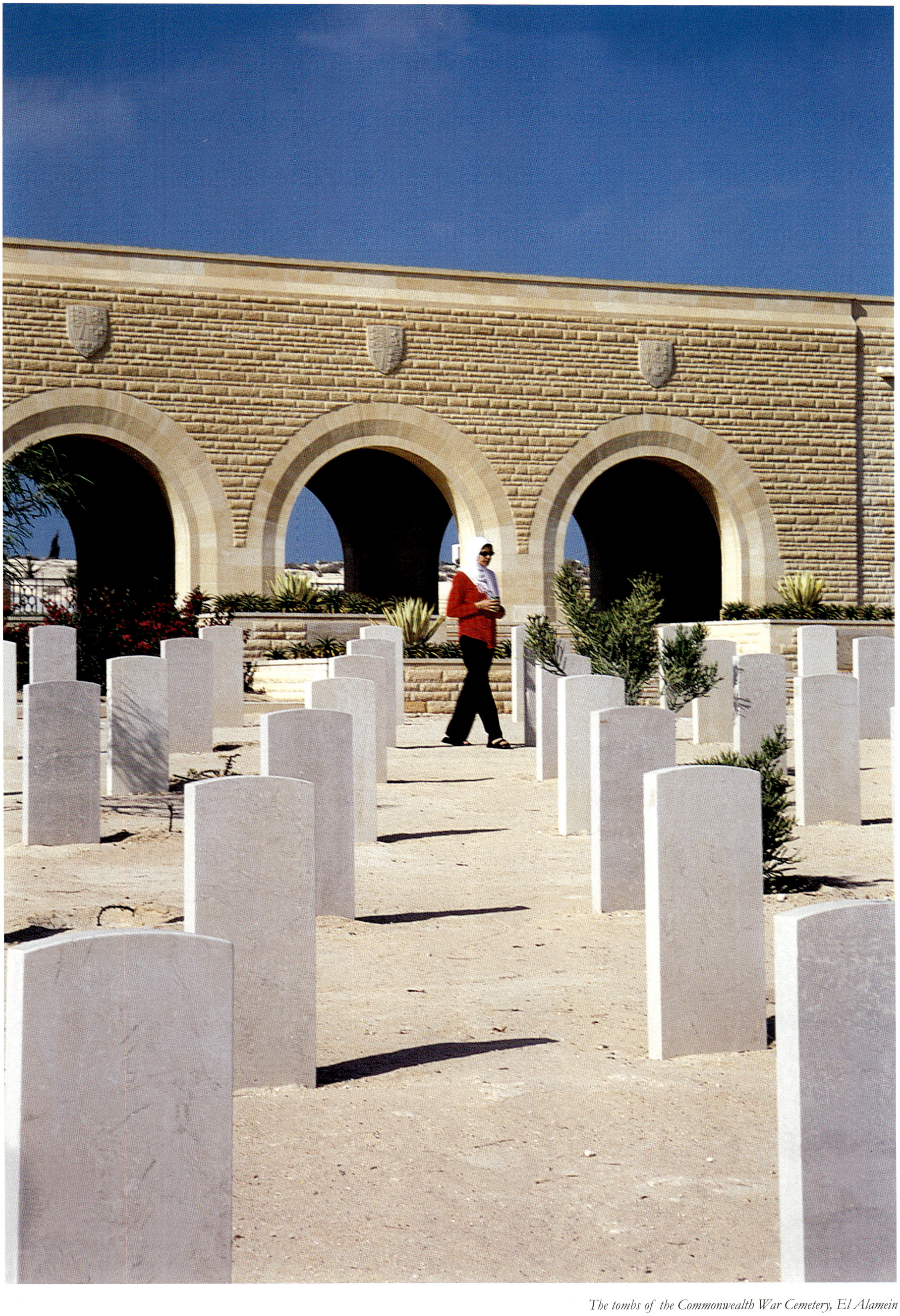

*The tombs of the Commonwealth War Cemetery, El Alamein*

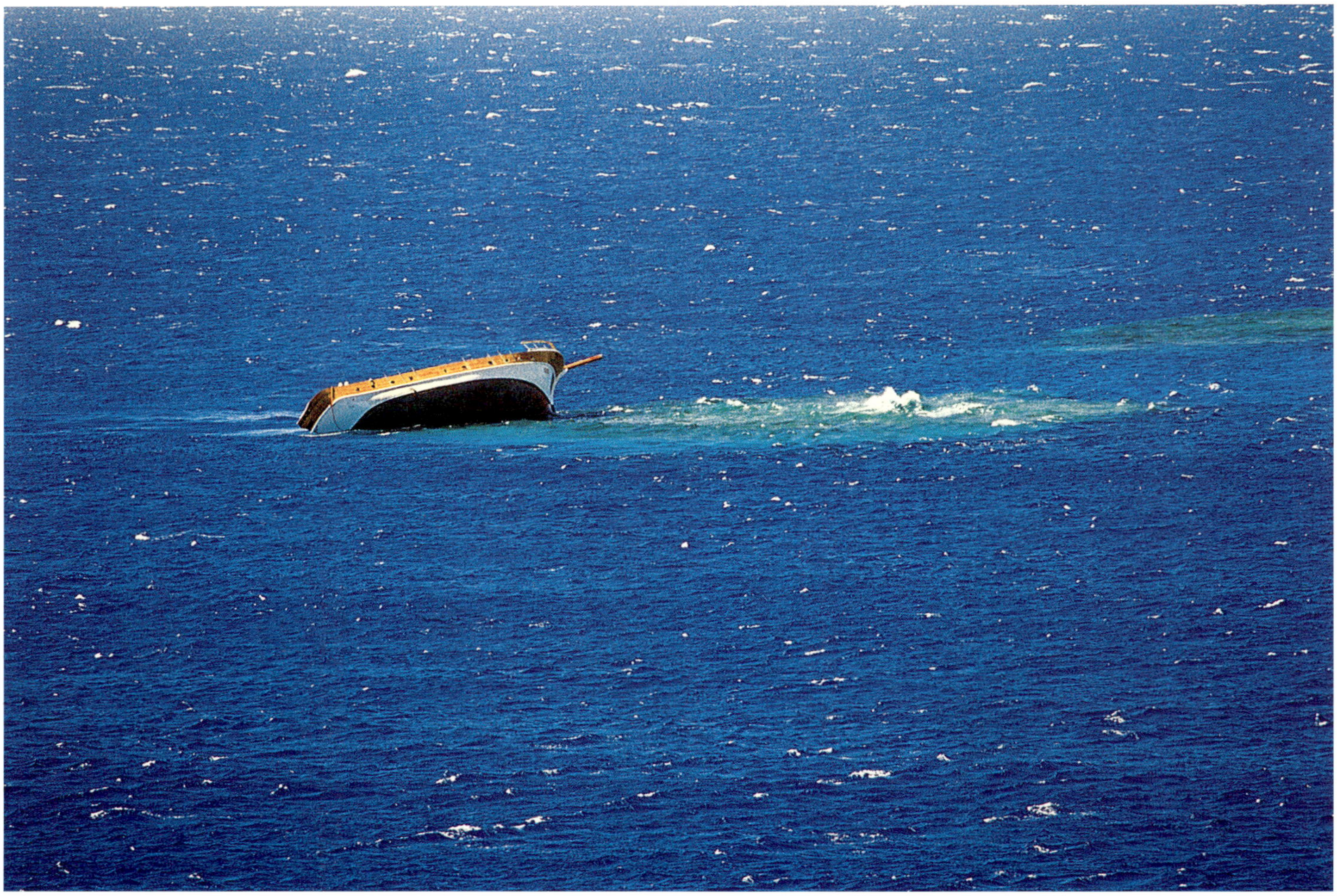

*A shipwreck in the Red Sea, Ras Muhammad, Sinai*

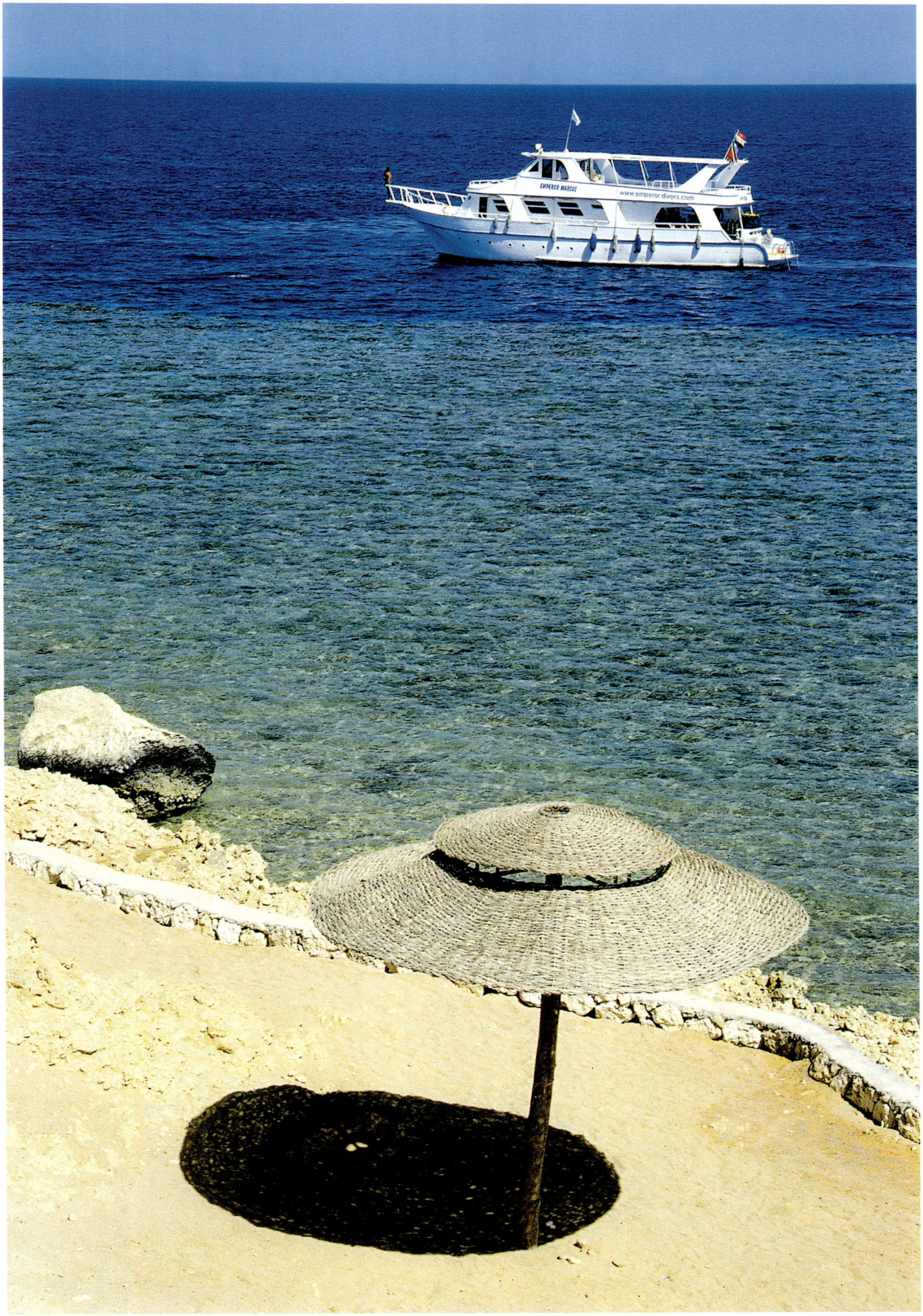


*A silent beach, Sharm al-Sheikh*

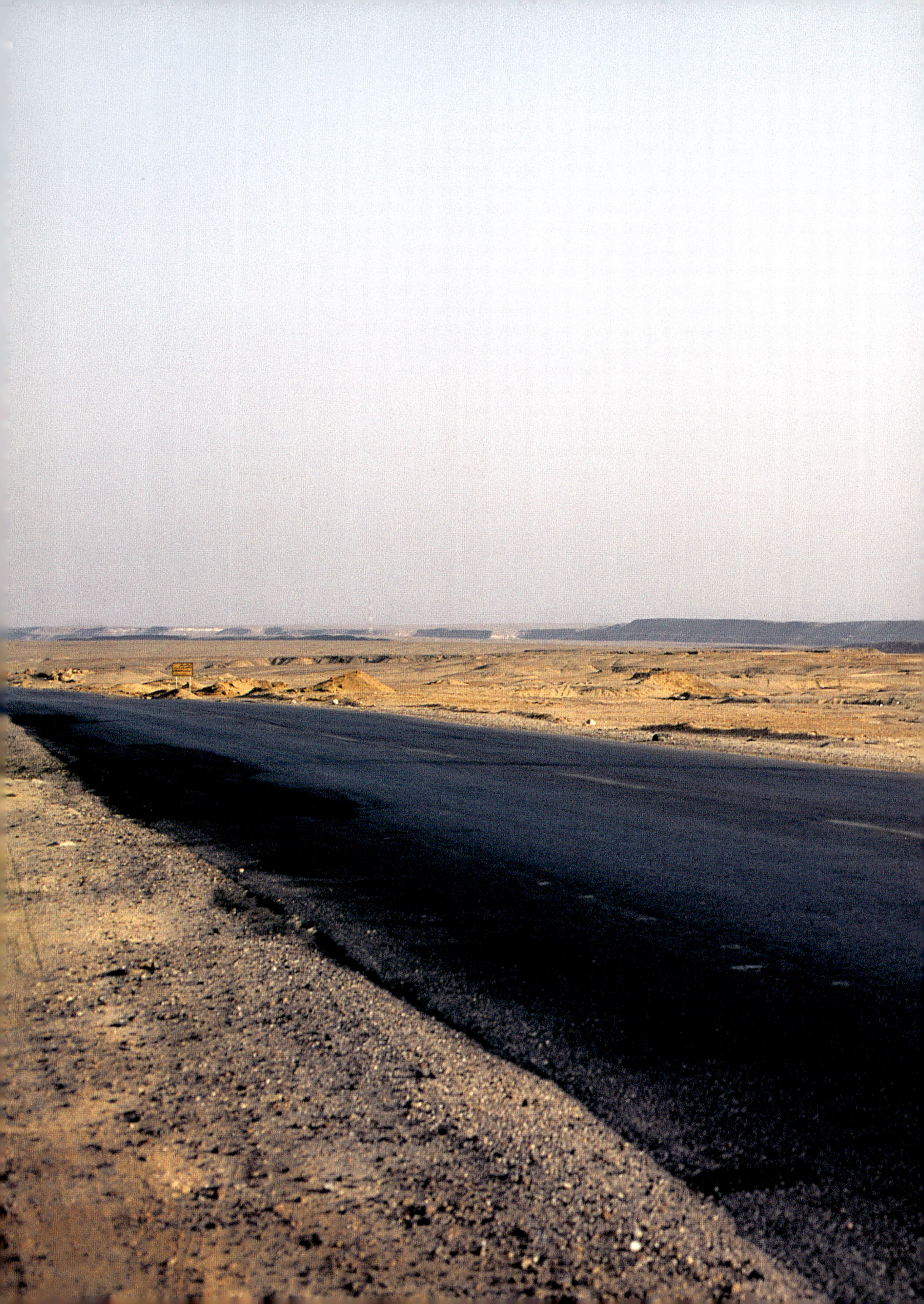

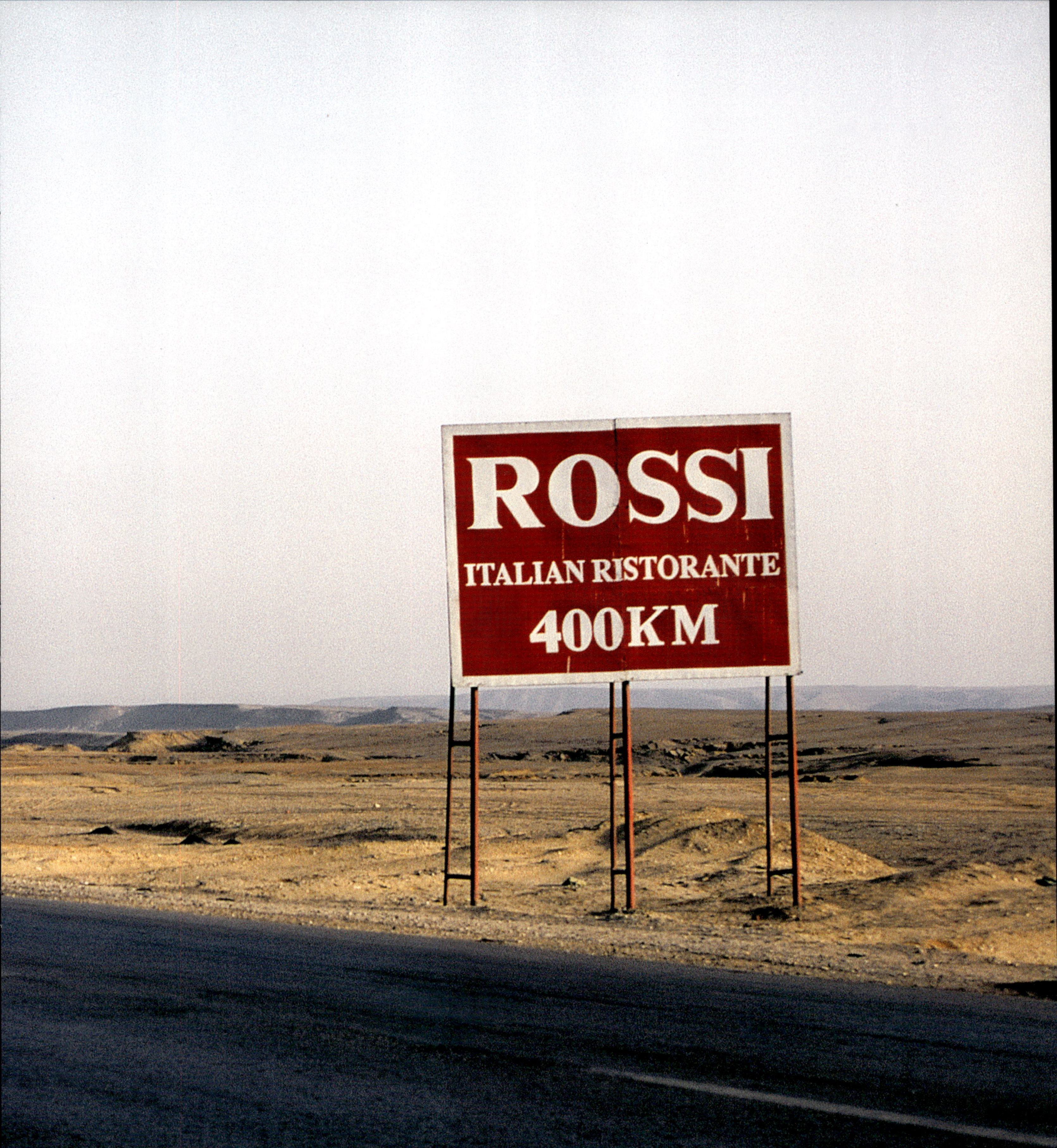
ROSSI
ITALIAN RISTORANTE
400KM

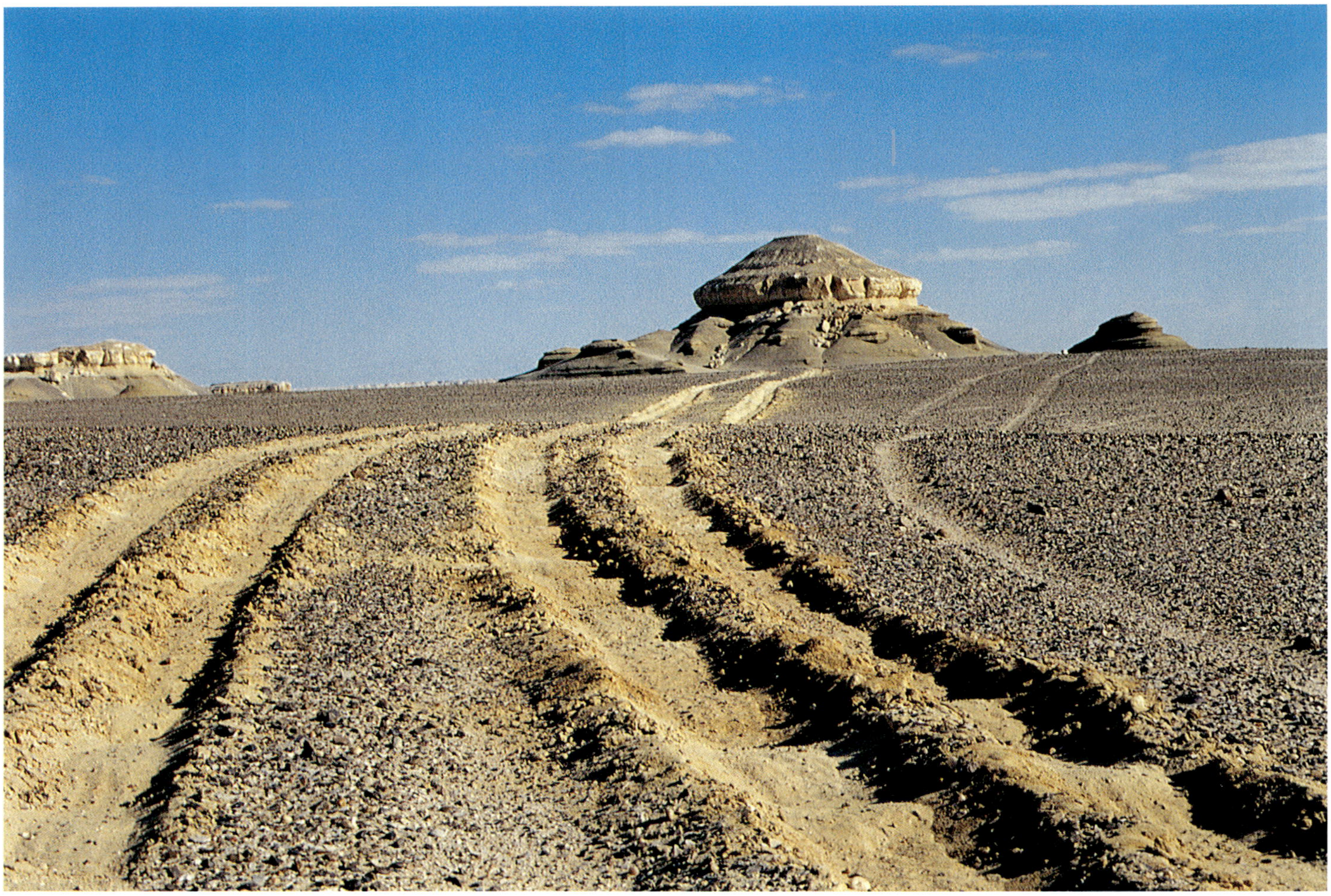

*Previous page: On the road to Ain Sukhna, east coast*

*Four-by-four tire tracks on the sand, Western Desert*

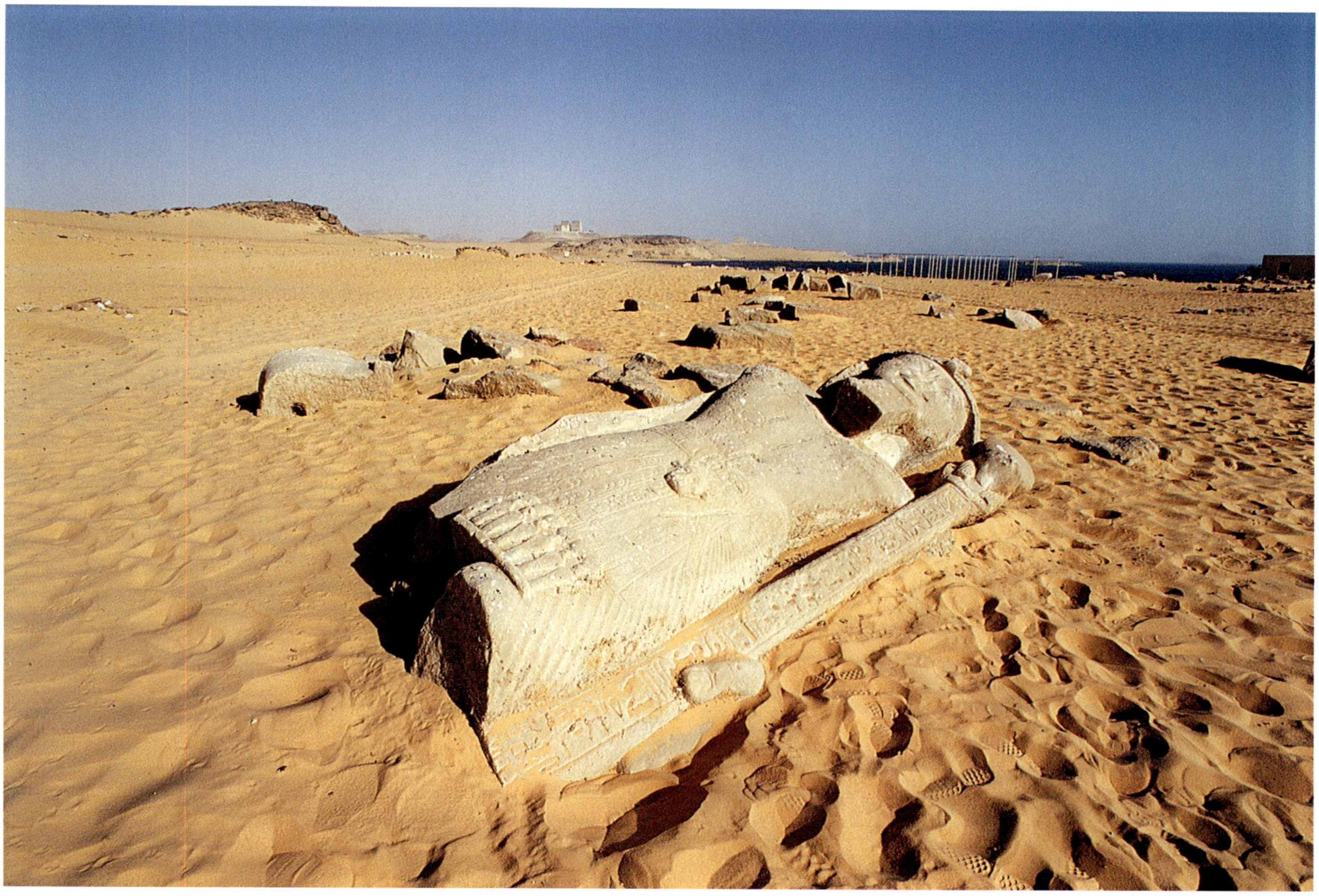

*A solitary piece of history on the sand, Lake Nasser*

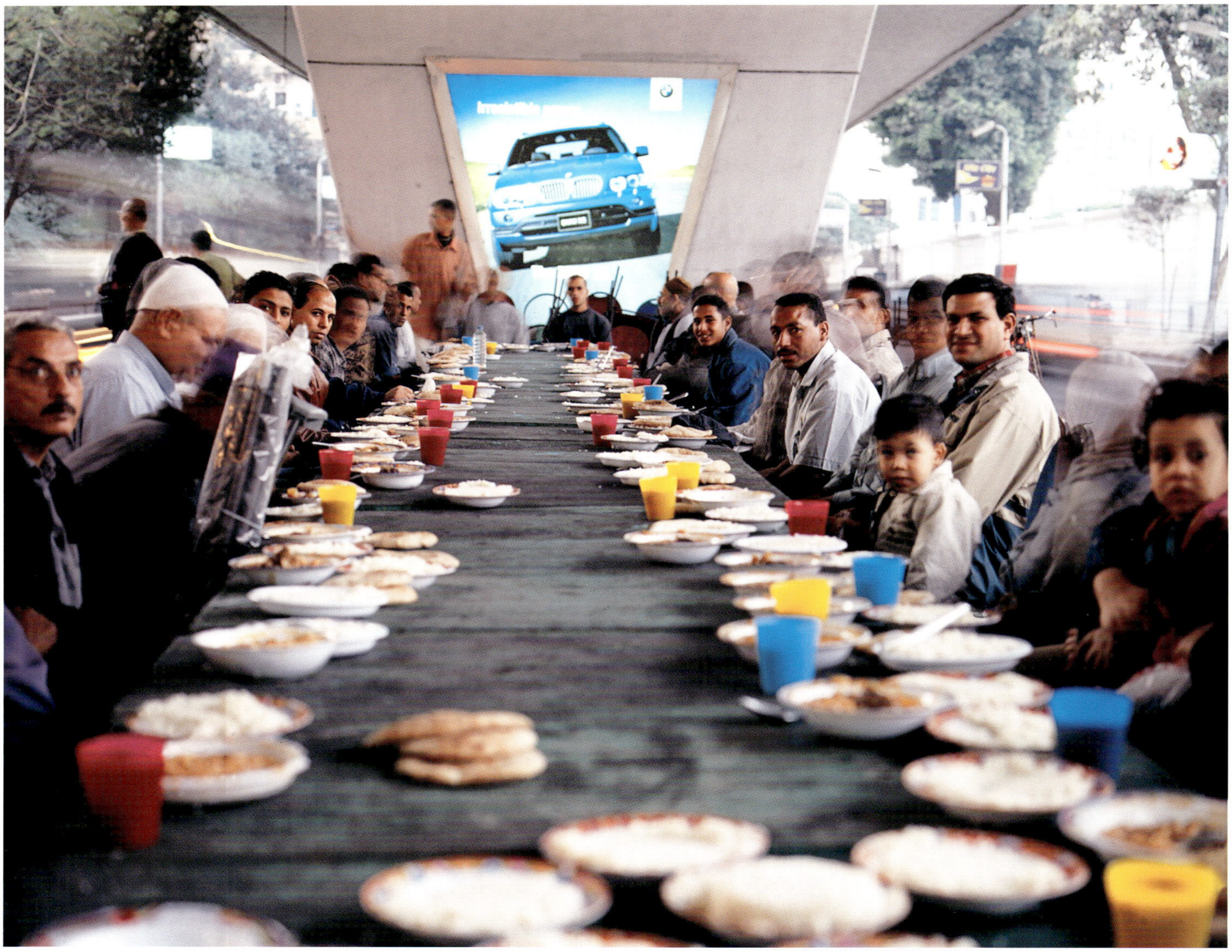

*Waiting for the* iftar *meal, the moment when the food can be consumed during* Ramadan, *Cairo*

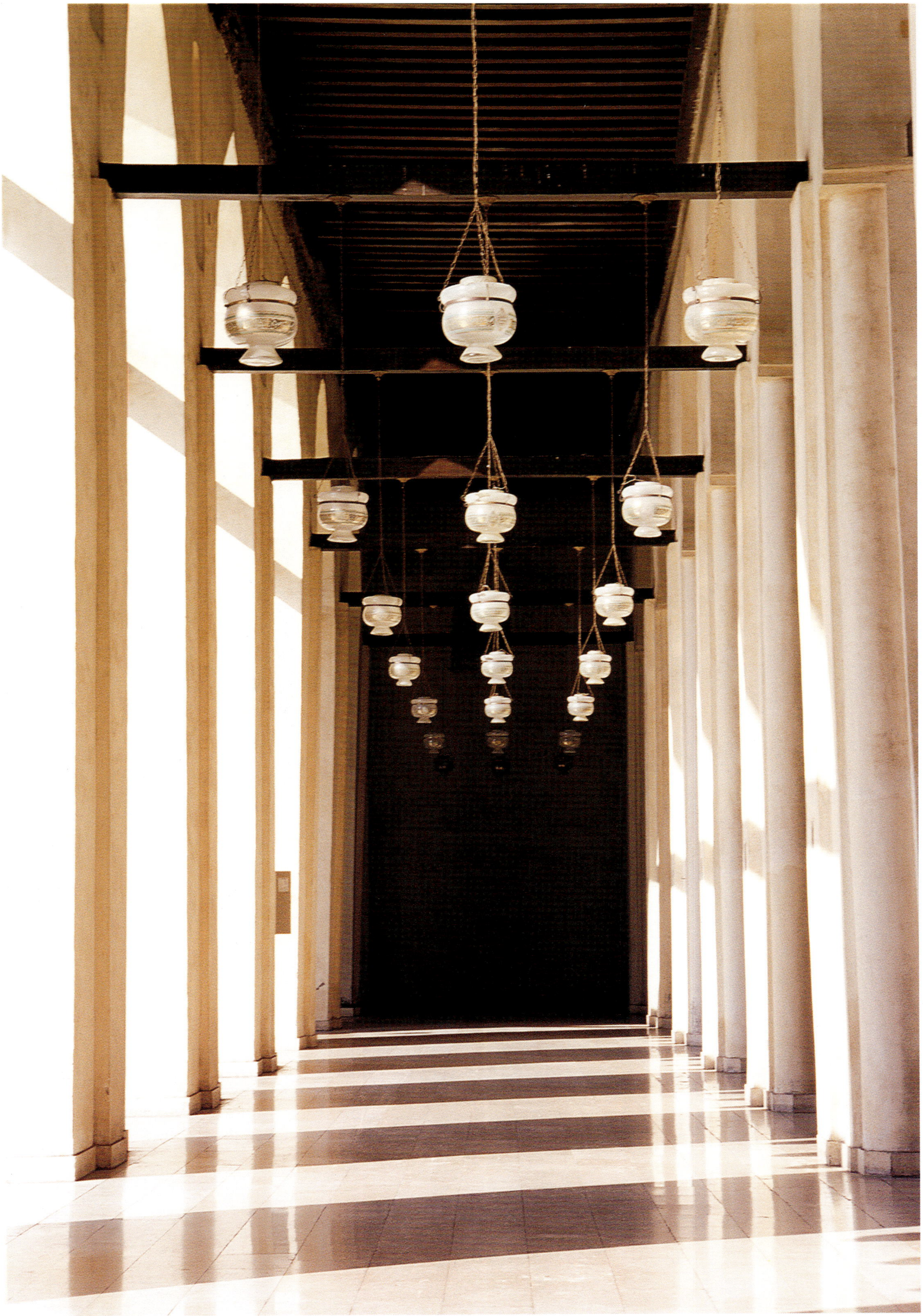

*The glorious al-Hakim Mosque enhances the quiet old Islamic quarter of Cairo*

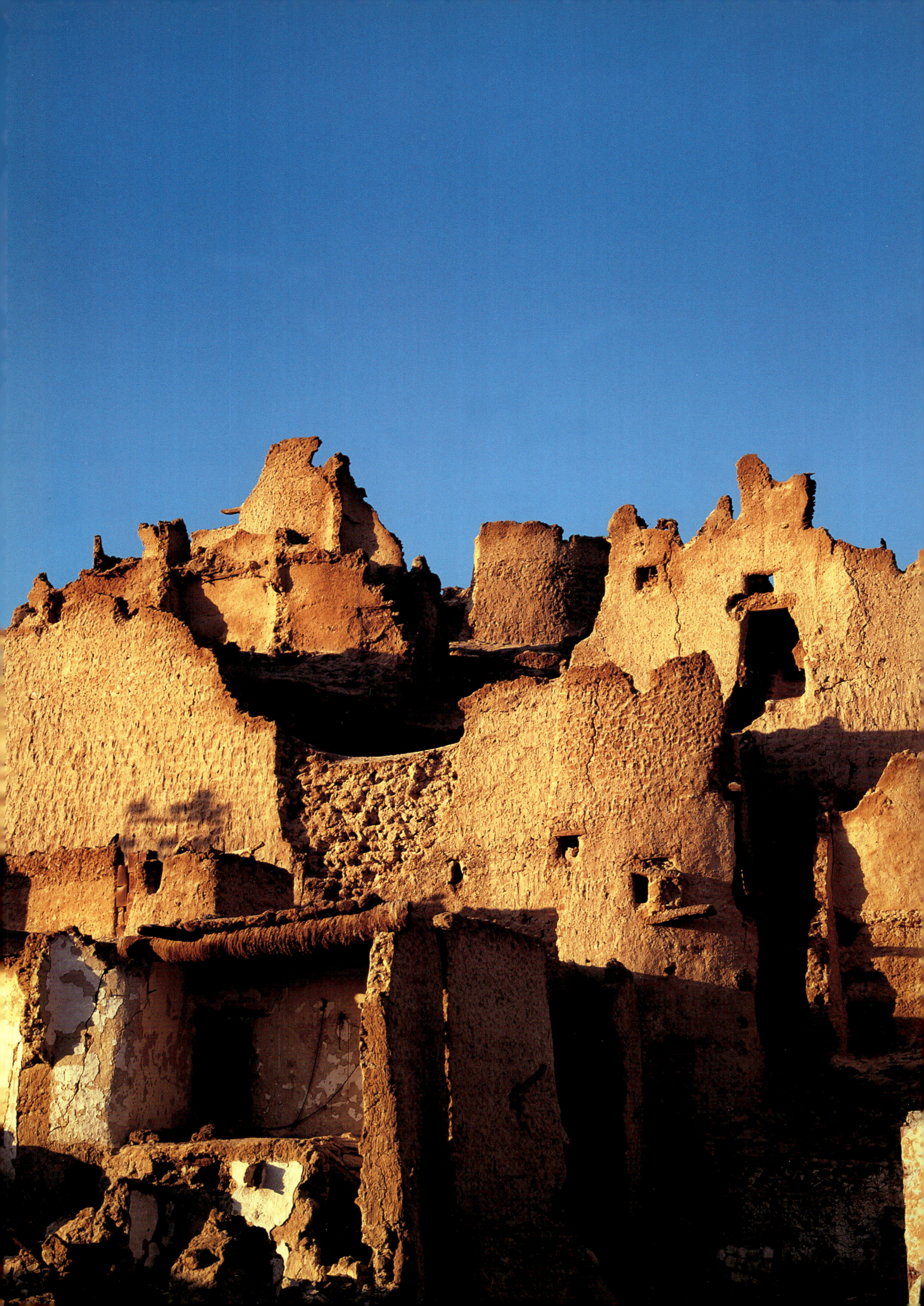

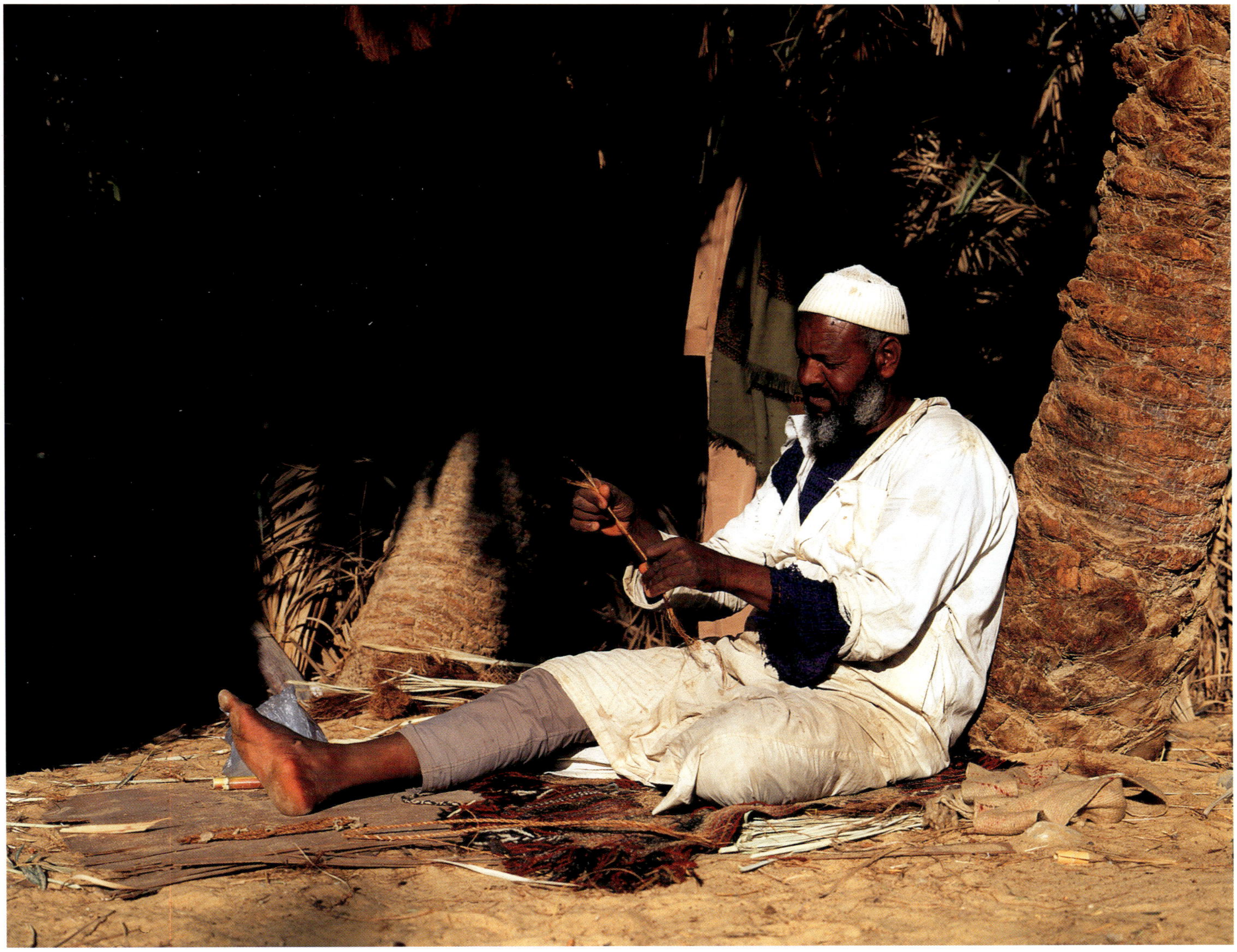

*Shali, the old part of Siwa town*

*A man working in the quiet, Siwa Oasis*

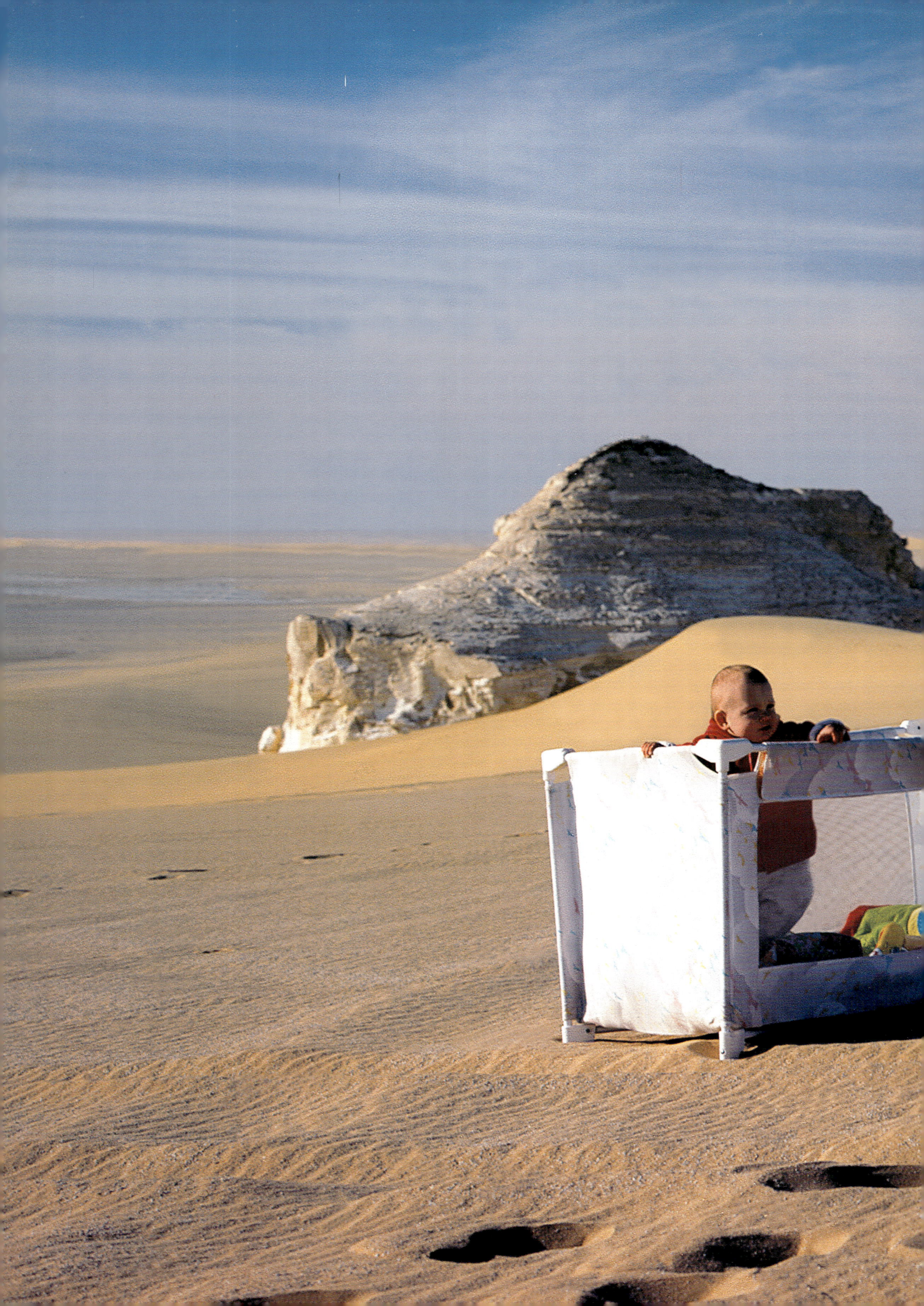

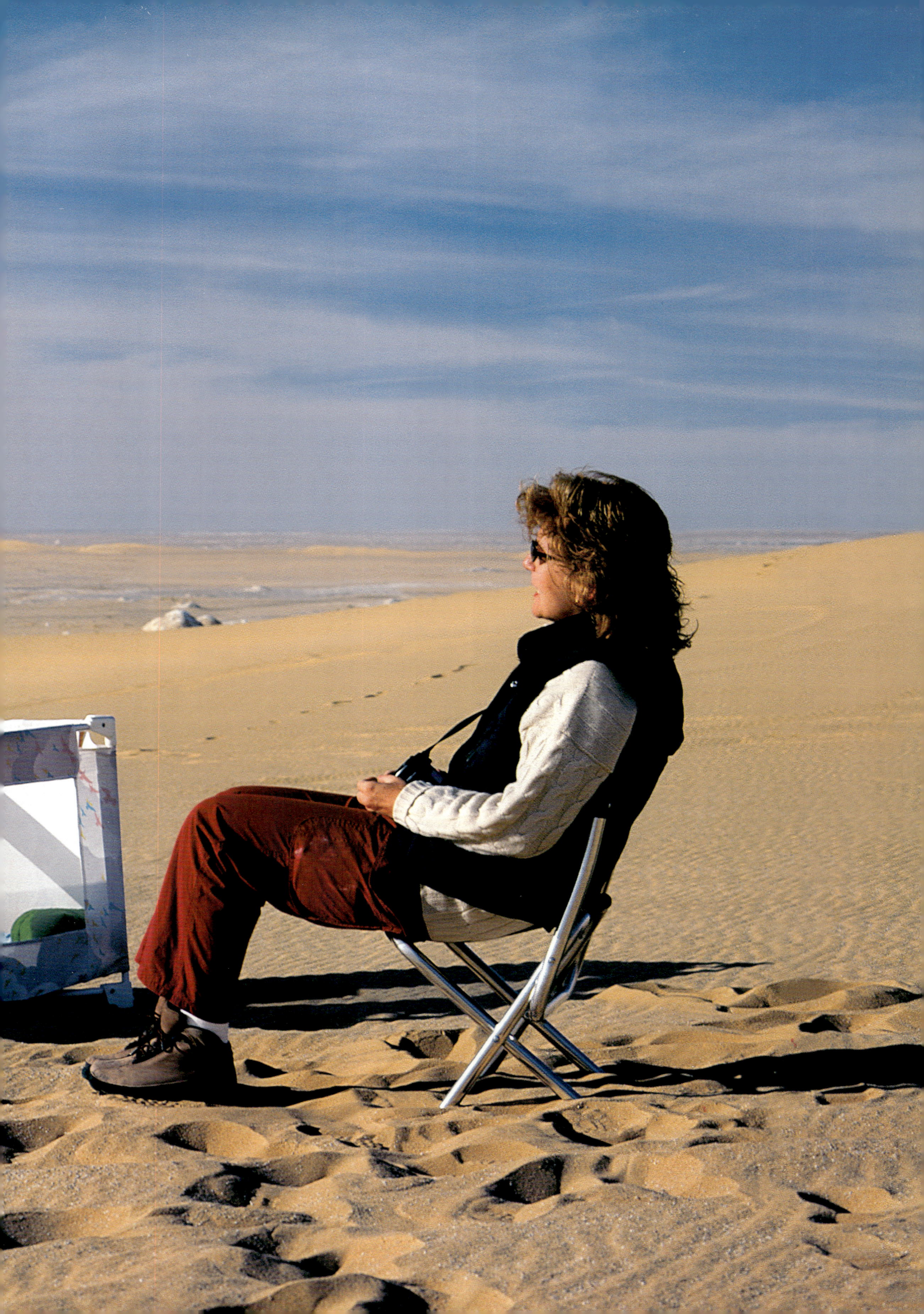

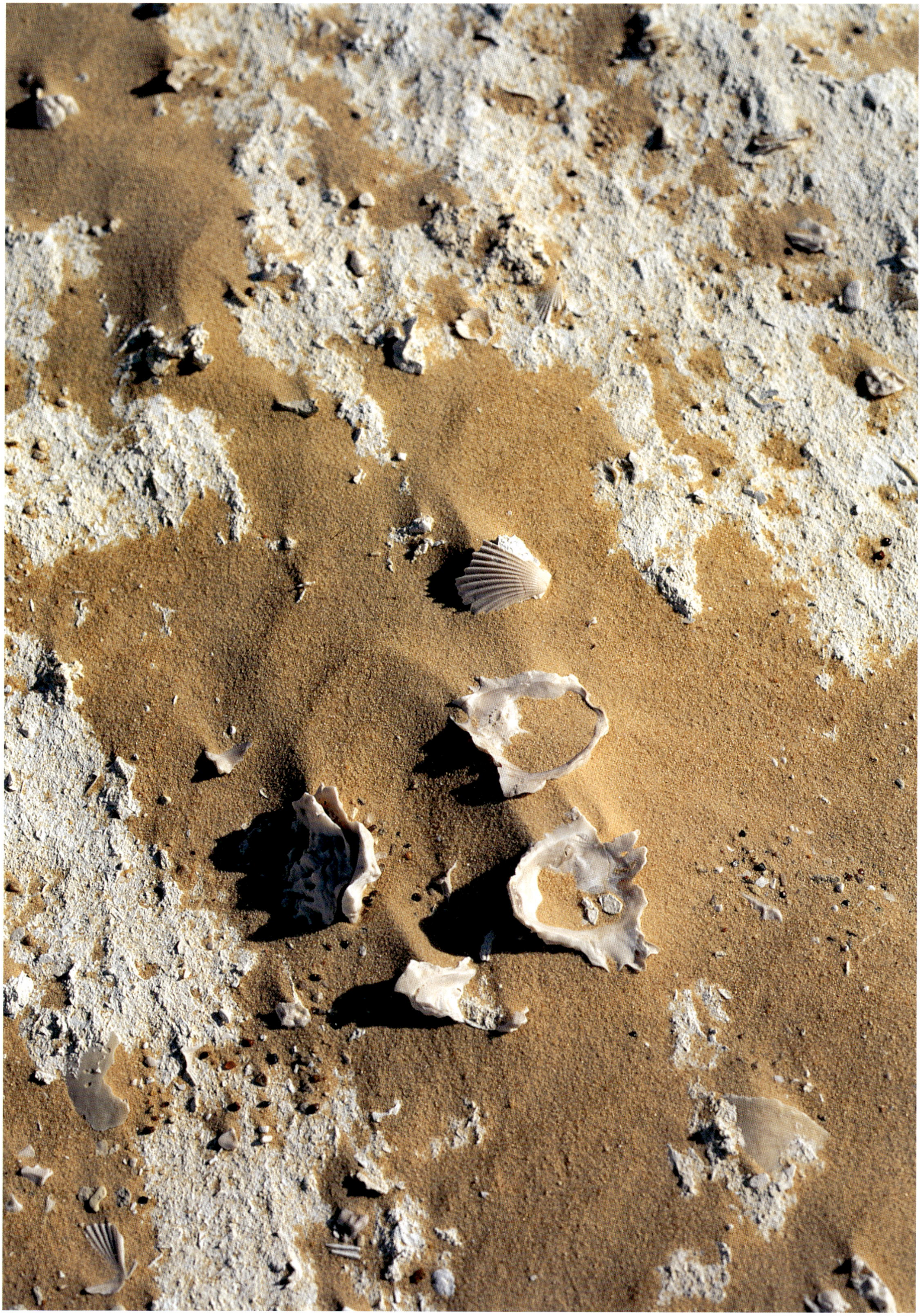

*Previous page: Early morning in the Western Desert*

*Shells millions of years old, scattered across the desert sand, Western Desert*

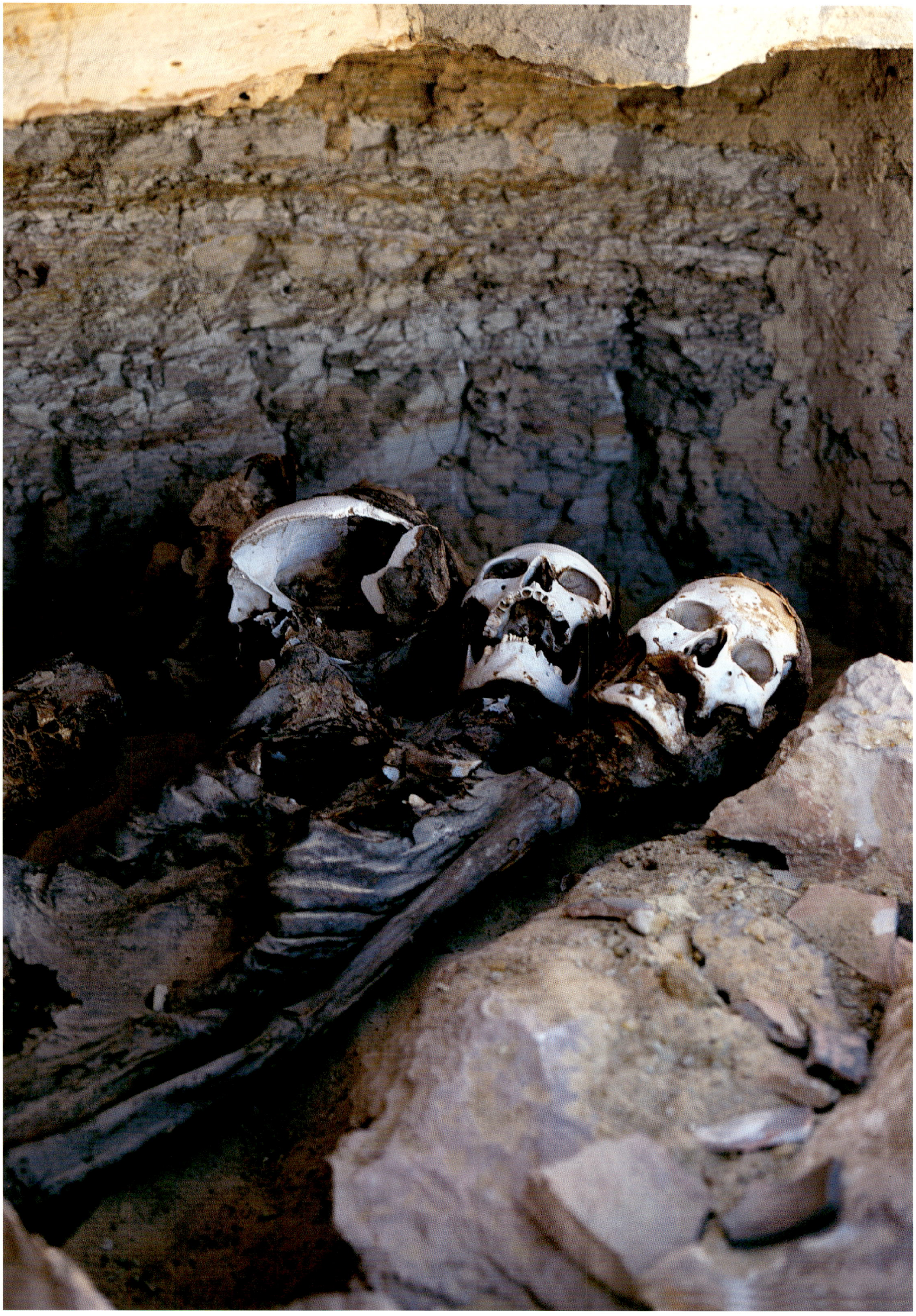

*A recently discovered tomb in the Western Desert*

## Amr Shannon

*Desert guide*

"Straight lines are nice, but restricted! Out there in the desert, you just have an open space and you can do whatever you want to do—no restrictions whatsoever," says Amr Shannon, an Egyptian desert guide who worked as an artist until September 1974, when some of his friends convinced him to turn his passion for the desert into a real job.

While it is sometimes hard to translate art into money, Shannon found the right compromise. "I have a job that inspires me all the time. I think that the desert is one way of feeling art. It suits my fiery nature," says Shannon, who studied fine art and painting in Egypt and Italy.

Shannon has been traveling through the Egyptian deserts since he was ten, and for a while he wondered whether it was better to leave the desert to itself. "I always say that I don't like to abuse a talent or prostitute a talent," Shannon explains. "But my friends convinced me. They said that I could introduce these solitary places to others and at the same time benefit."

Admittedly, not having a standard job with regular income is sometimes hard in this country. "In Egypt it is a little difficult to explain yourself," he confides. "People look at me as a crazy man: still jumping into my car, packing, wearing jeans, sharing an adventurous spirit with younger friends, not married until I was 52. This is unusual here!" he says with a smile.

But Shannon gets to leave behind the questions and comments and head for nature's silence. "The desert is a beautiful sound that you cannot experience in your normal life—sounds and voices that you've never heard before," he says. "The silence is in any place and at any time, but far from people." He points out that human beings tend to make noise in order to feel safe and comfortable, but he finds the silence of the dunes' curves to hold endless possibilities. "It is not a state," he explains, "but a doorway to another place, where better silence is."

But even in such a peaceful place there are still elements that disturb your vision and upset your mind. The Egyptian desert is not always well preserved. "Would you open a supermarket and put things in the window, and then leave the place without anyone taking care of it?" Shannon asks. "I am not expecting anything from this generation. If the power were in my hands I would start educating the children!"

Shannon used to spend most of his time out in the desert, heading back to Cairo less than three days per month. "I did not have to adapt to anyone or anything until three years ago, when I found the right woman to marry." Now he works with his wife: he prepares their two vehicles, the equipment, and the maps, while she takes care of the food and drinks they need for each trip they are leading.

Generally people's first reaction to the empty expanse of the desert is fear. "There is the sweet fear and the black fear," he says. "The first kind is when it is nice to be afraid, knowing that something can happen but you are safe; the second kind is bad, because it kills you. It is my job to understand this fear and to make my group feel safe."

The emotions that Shannon has while in this silent land are difficult to explain in words. "Whenever man is close to nature he starts producing wonderful things. Greek mythology is a good example of this," the desert lover says. "When I put my foot on the sand it pushes me back as if I put the right key in the right lock."

His favorite places are in the Western Desert: the huge dunes of the Great Sand Sea, the surreal rock formations of the Valley of the Whales, the shells scattered across the White Desert. He even sees a metaphor for human life in sand dunes: they start small and then grow, venturing out, acquiring different colors and shades. The softest dune is the most dangerous, just as with human beings!

"Different colors have different vibrations," he explains. "These vibrations reach your energy's sources, making you able to simply find yourself." Shannon thinks that humans waste their time and money trying to suit others in order to be accepted. "In the desert you understand that you don't need to do all this. You are who you are. You are a natural element."

*S. D.*

*Amr Shannon, desert guide*

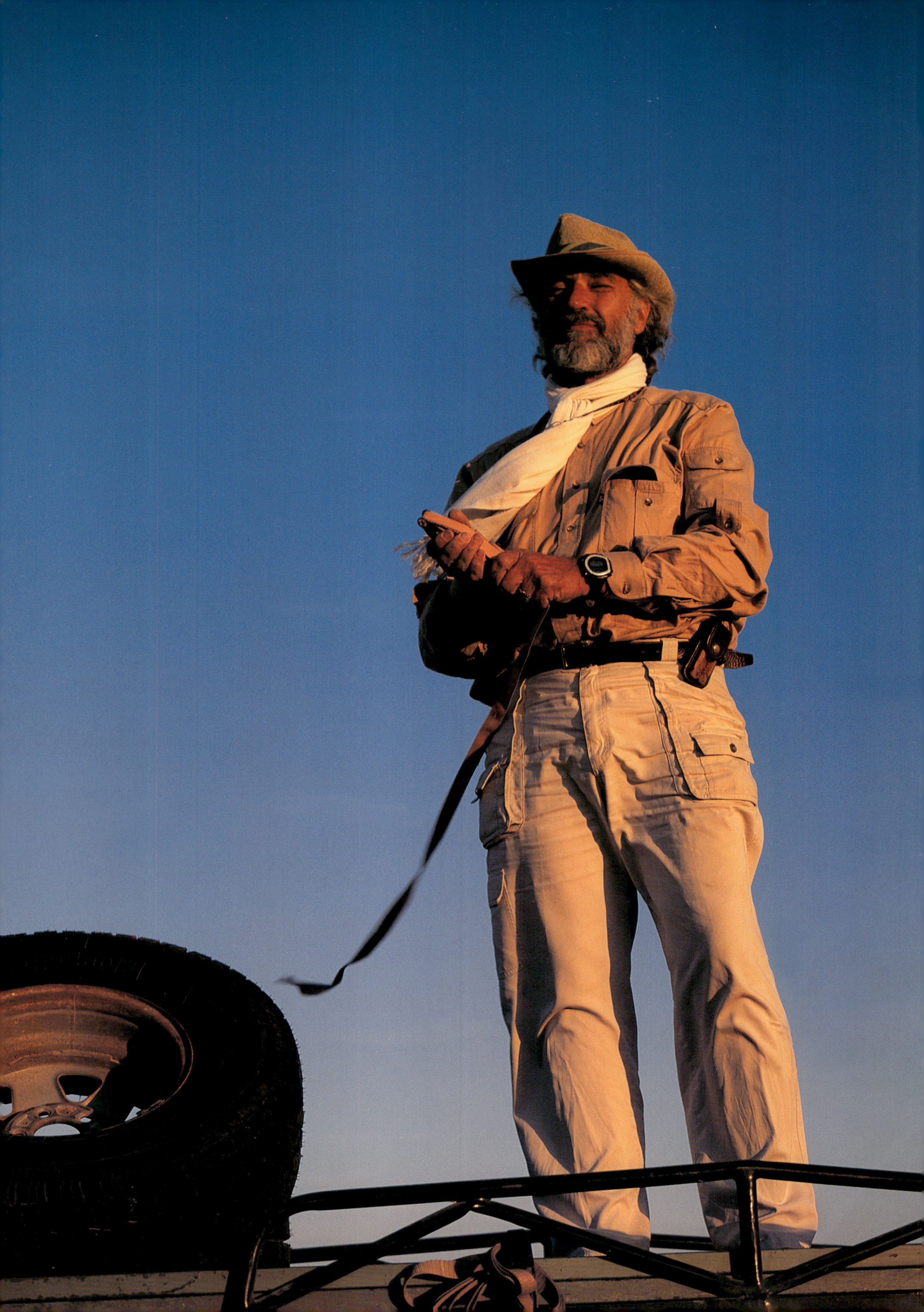

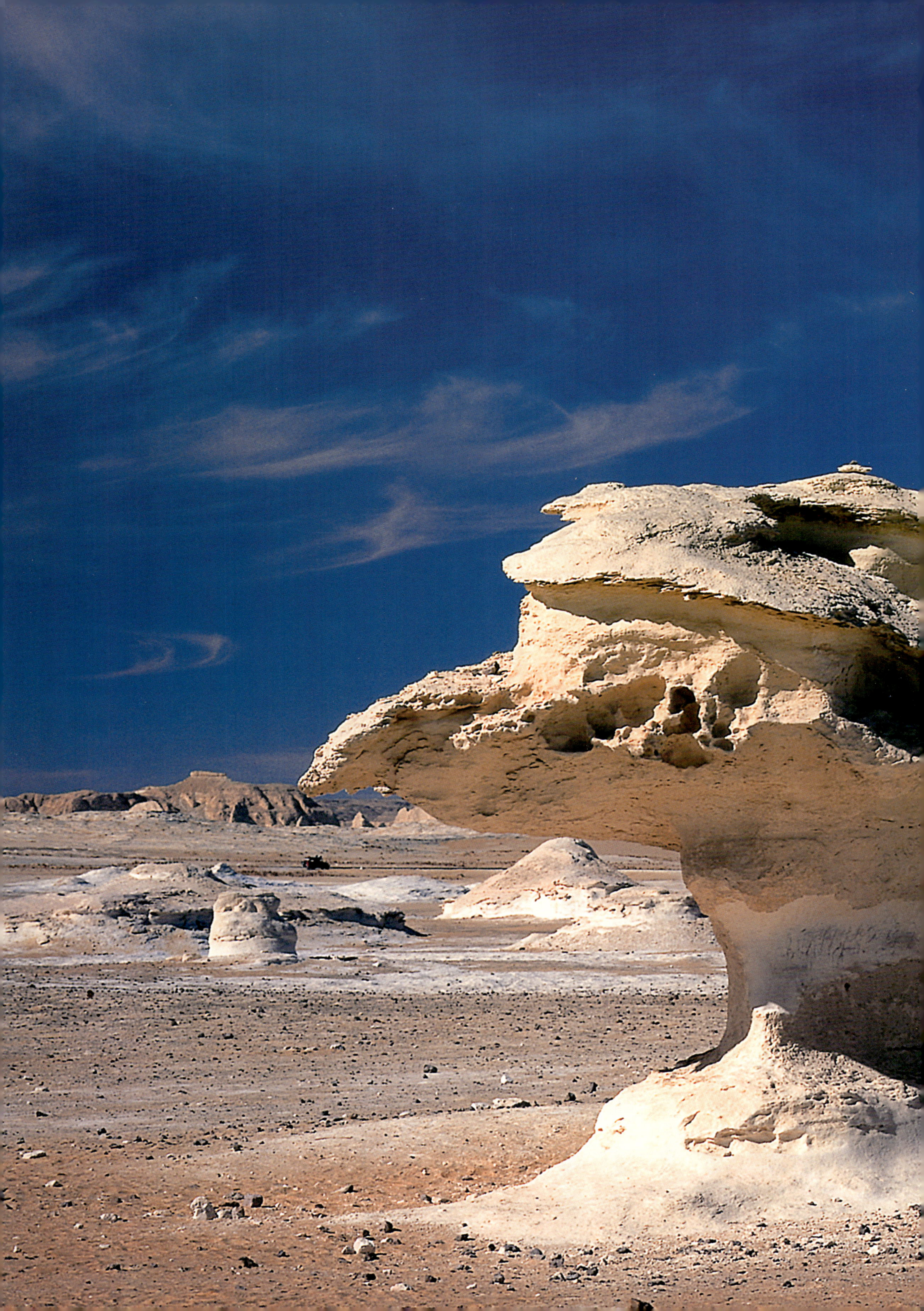

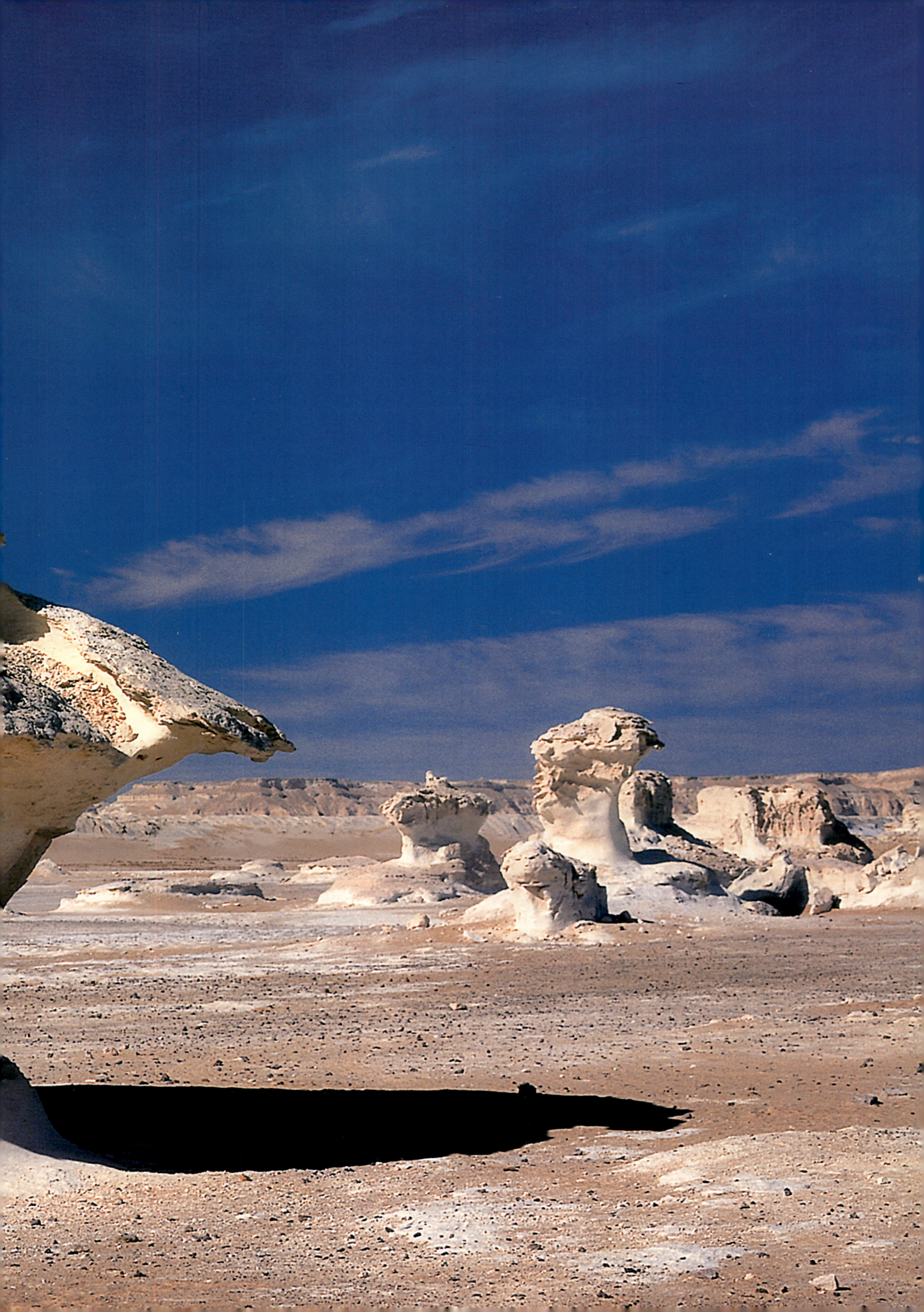

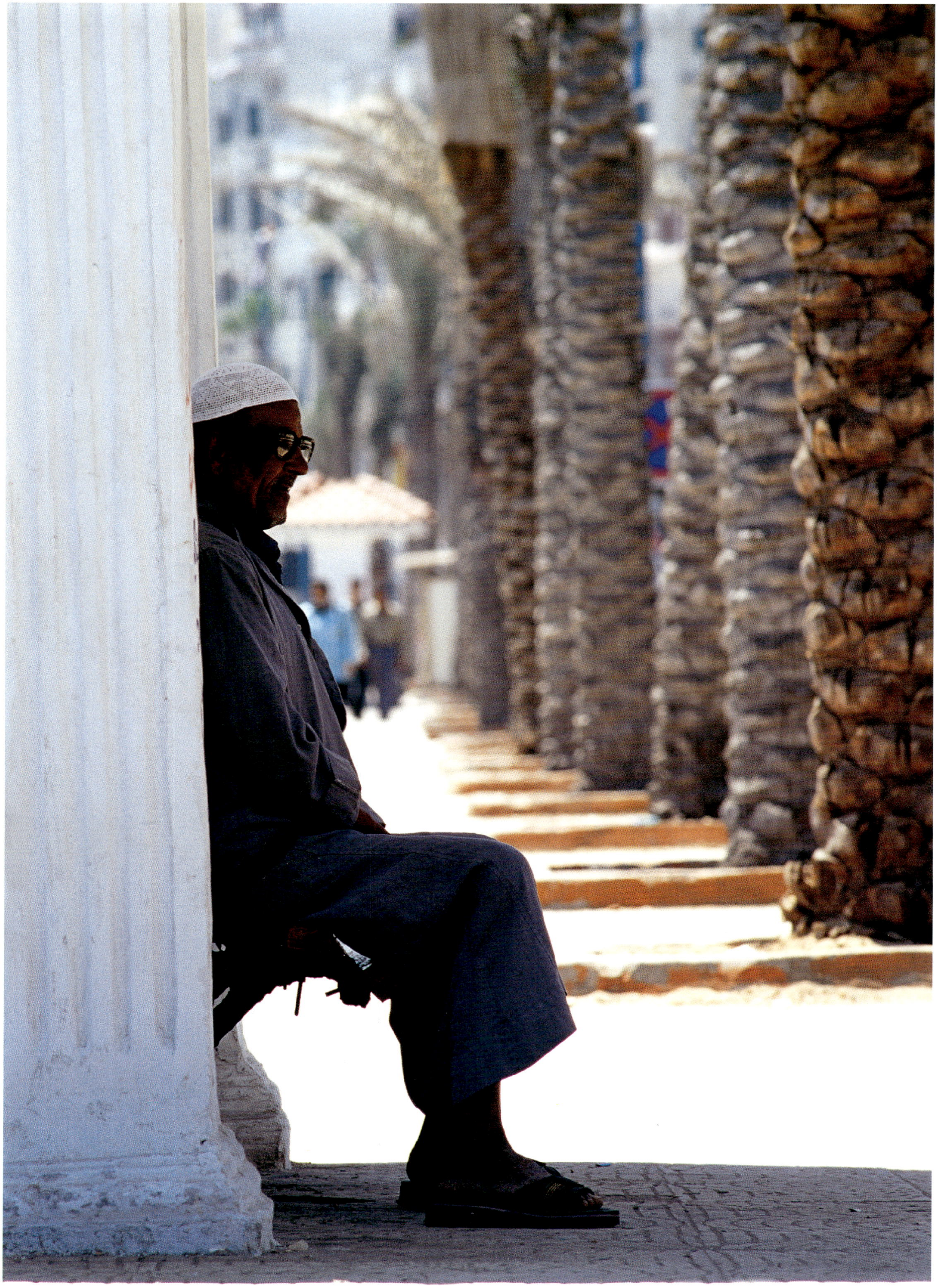

*Previous page: White Desert rock formation, Western Desert*

*Waiting for a bus, Alexandria*

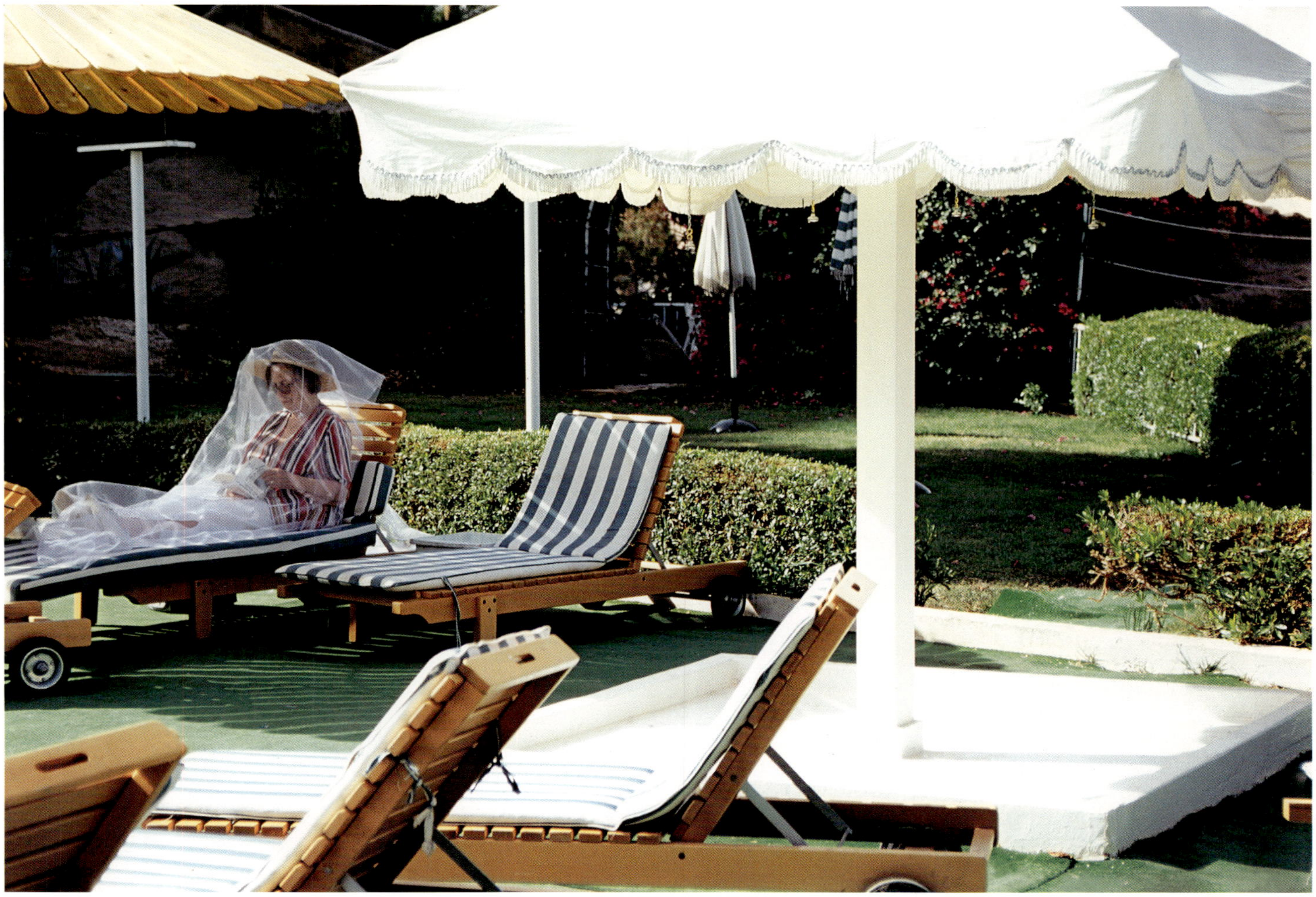

*Reading in the garden of the Old Cataract Hotel, Aswan*

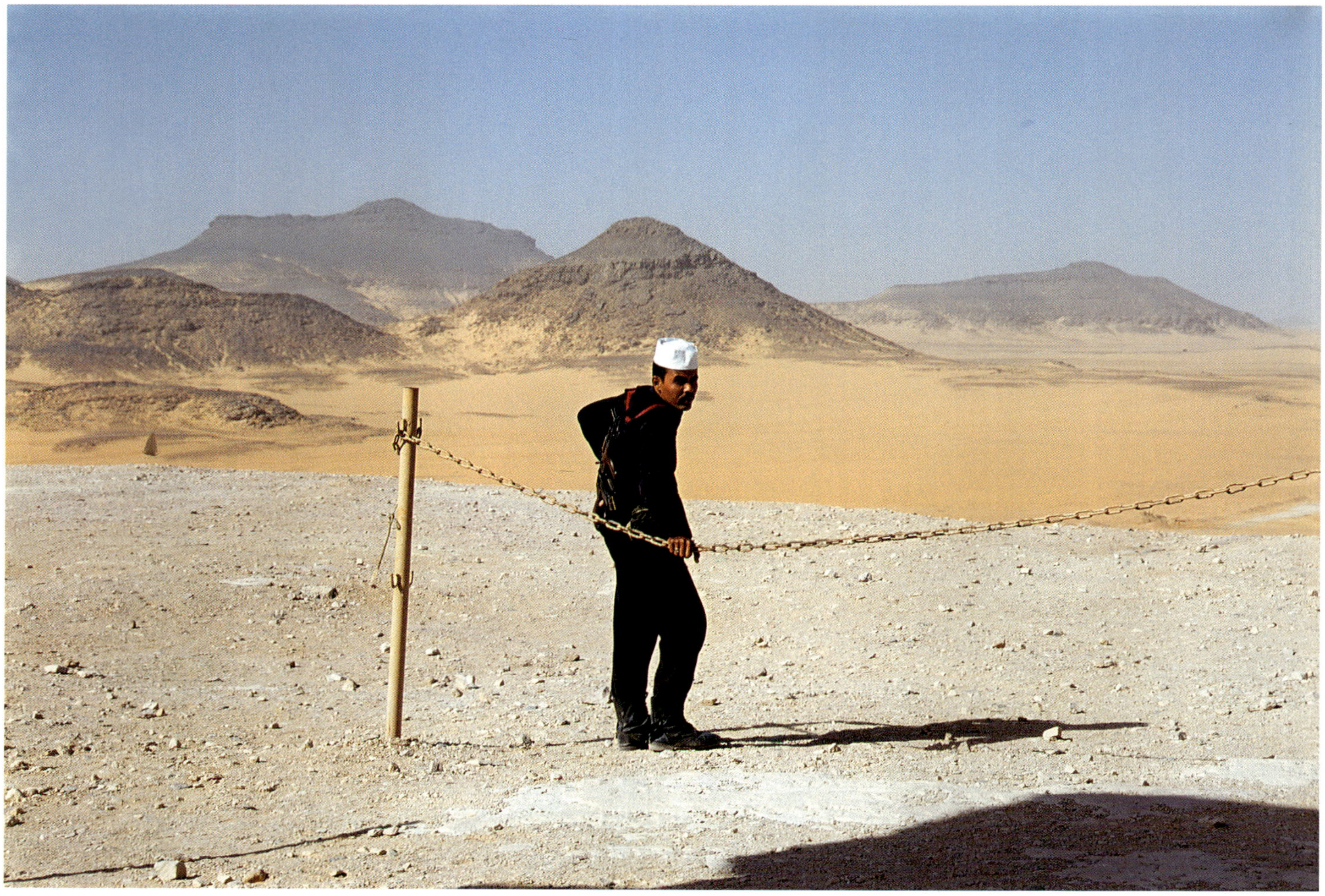

*A tourist policeman, Lake Nasser*

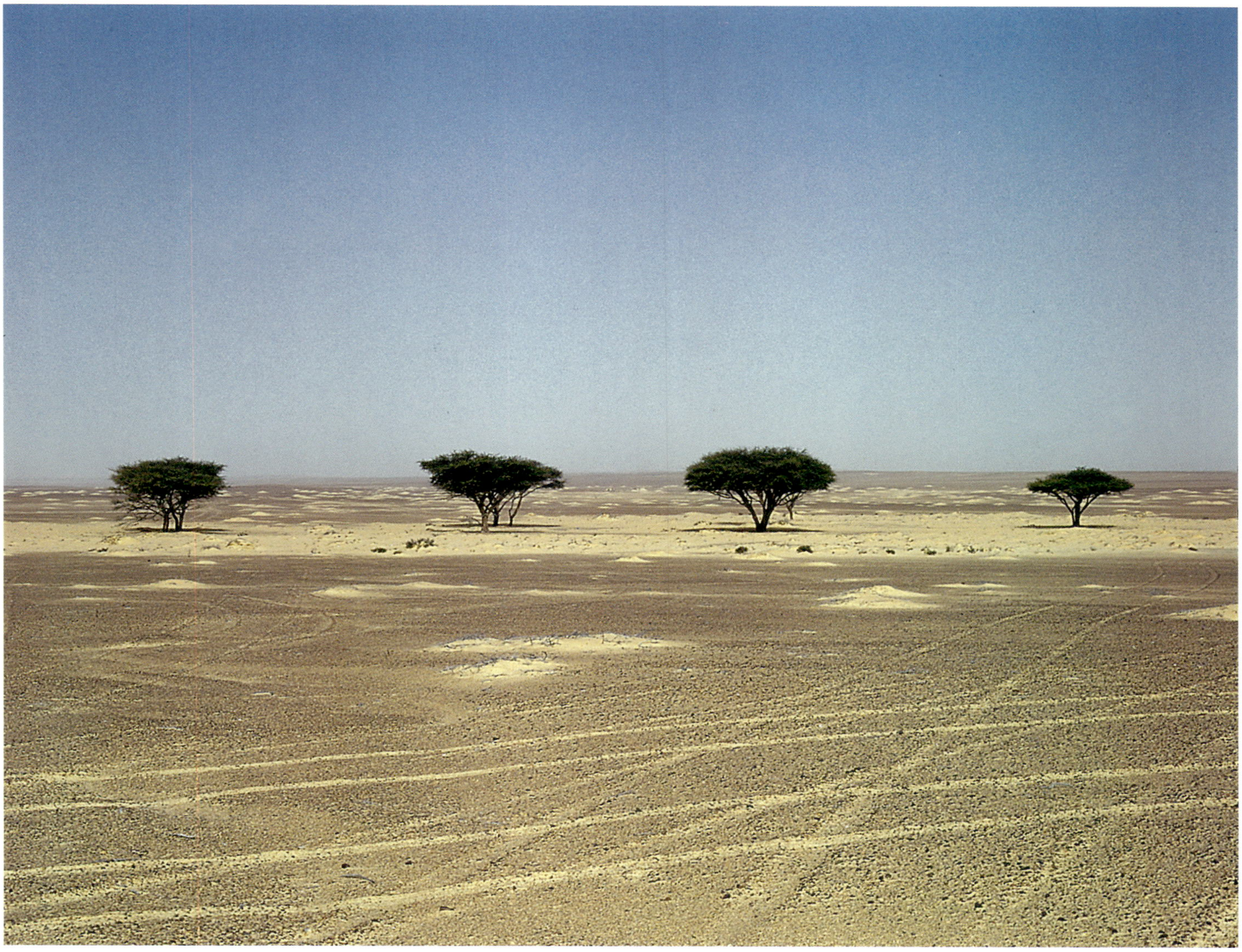

*Lonely trees in the Western Desert*

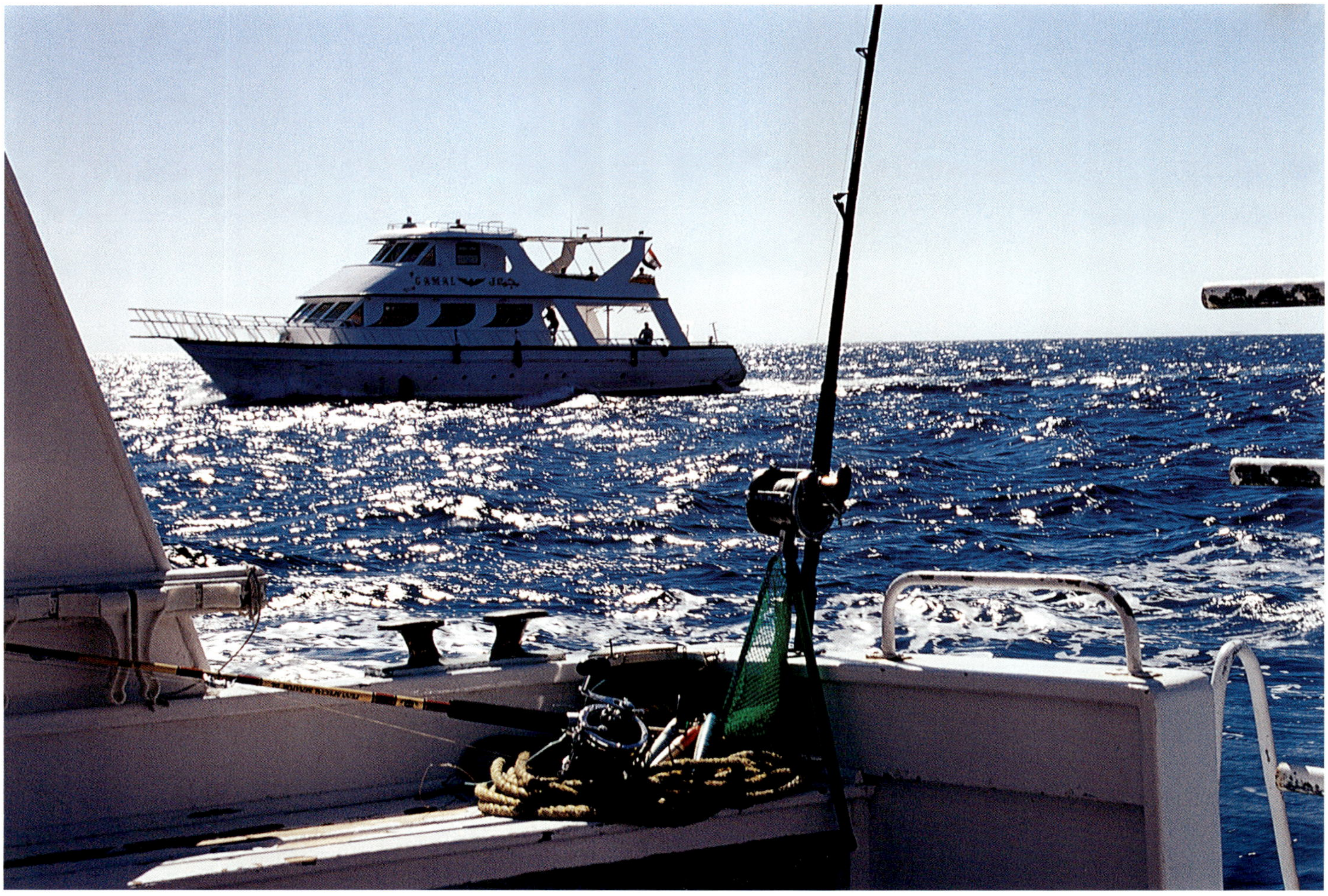

*Deep-sea fishing in the Red Sea, Sharm al-Sheikh*

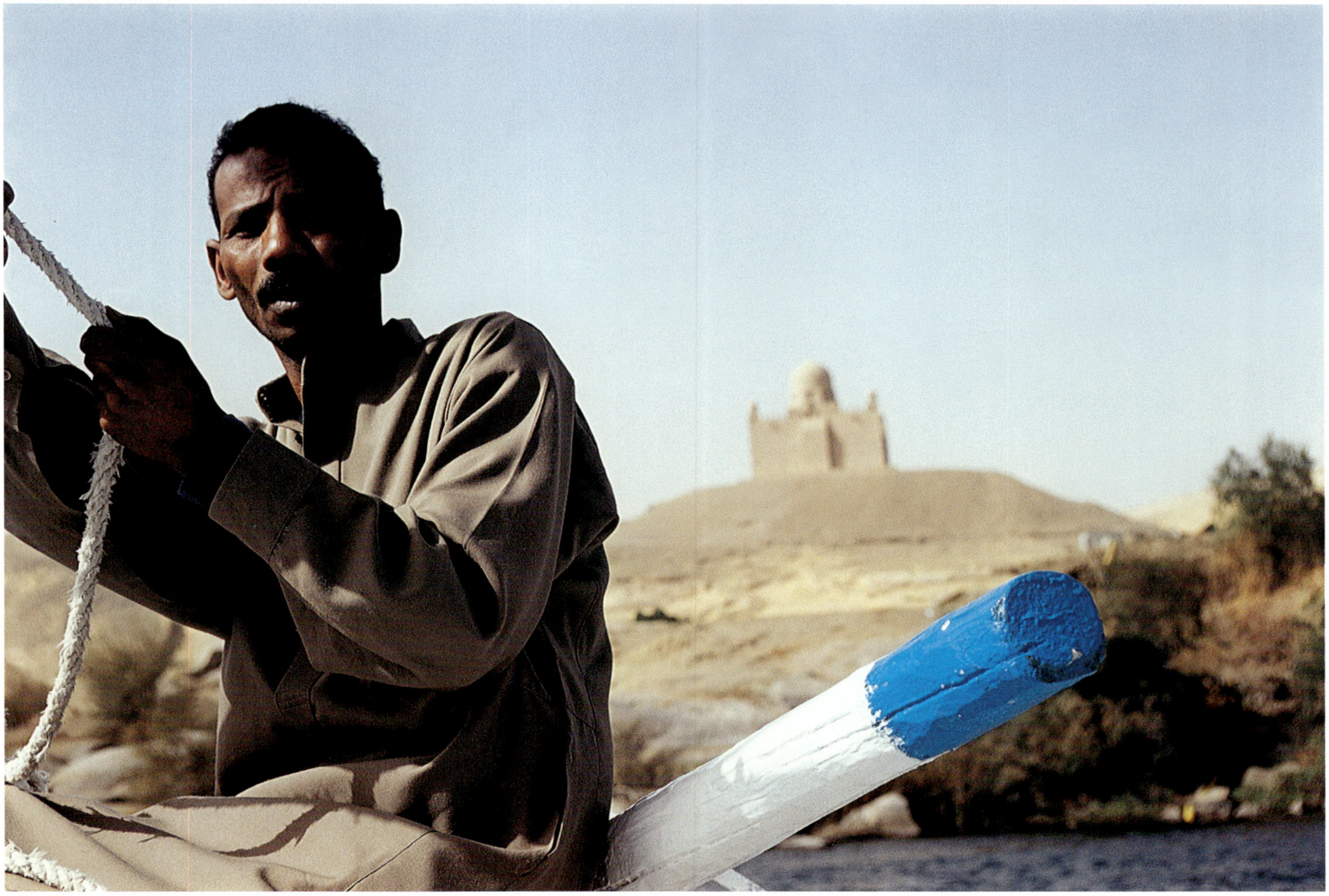

*A felucca owner, Aswan*

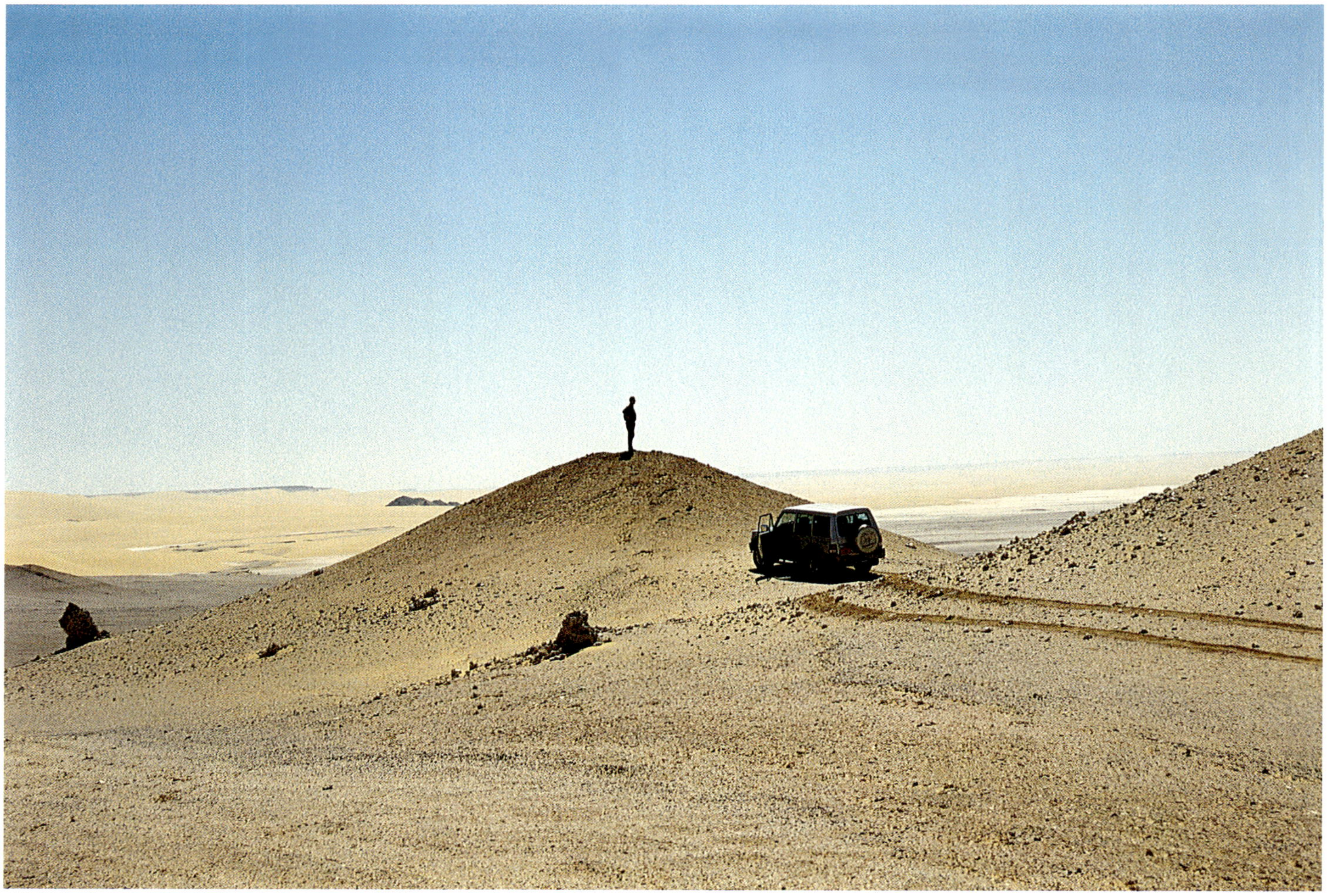

*A moment of reflection while exploring the Western Desert*

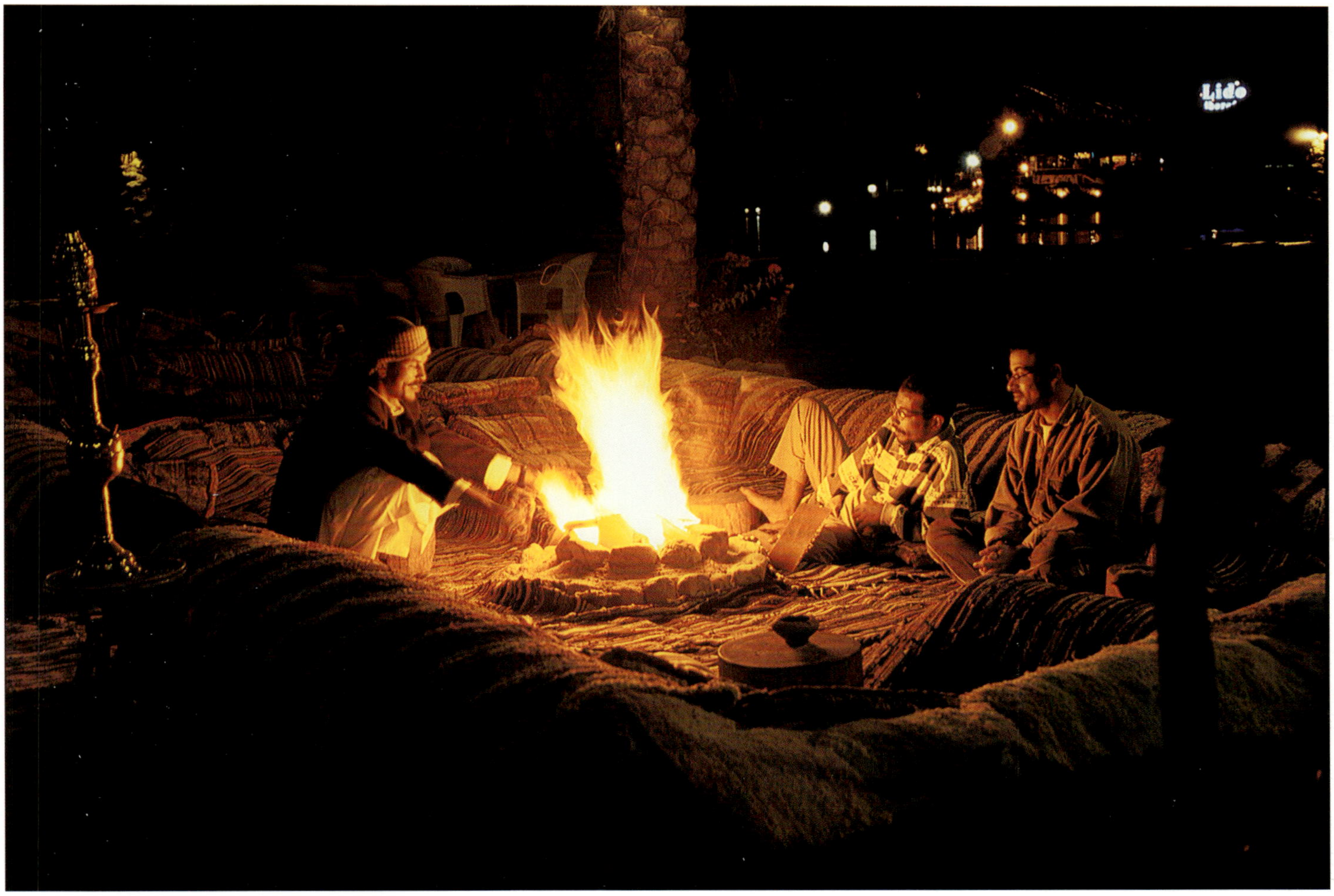


*A traditional café, Sharm al-Sheikh*

*Next page: Sunset in Sinai*

# Movement

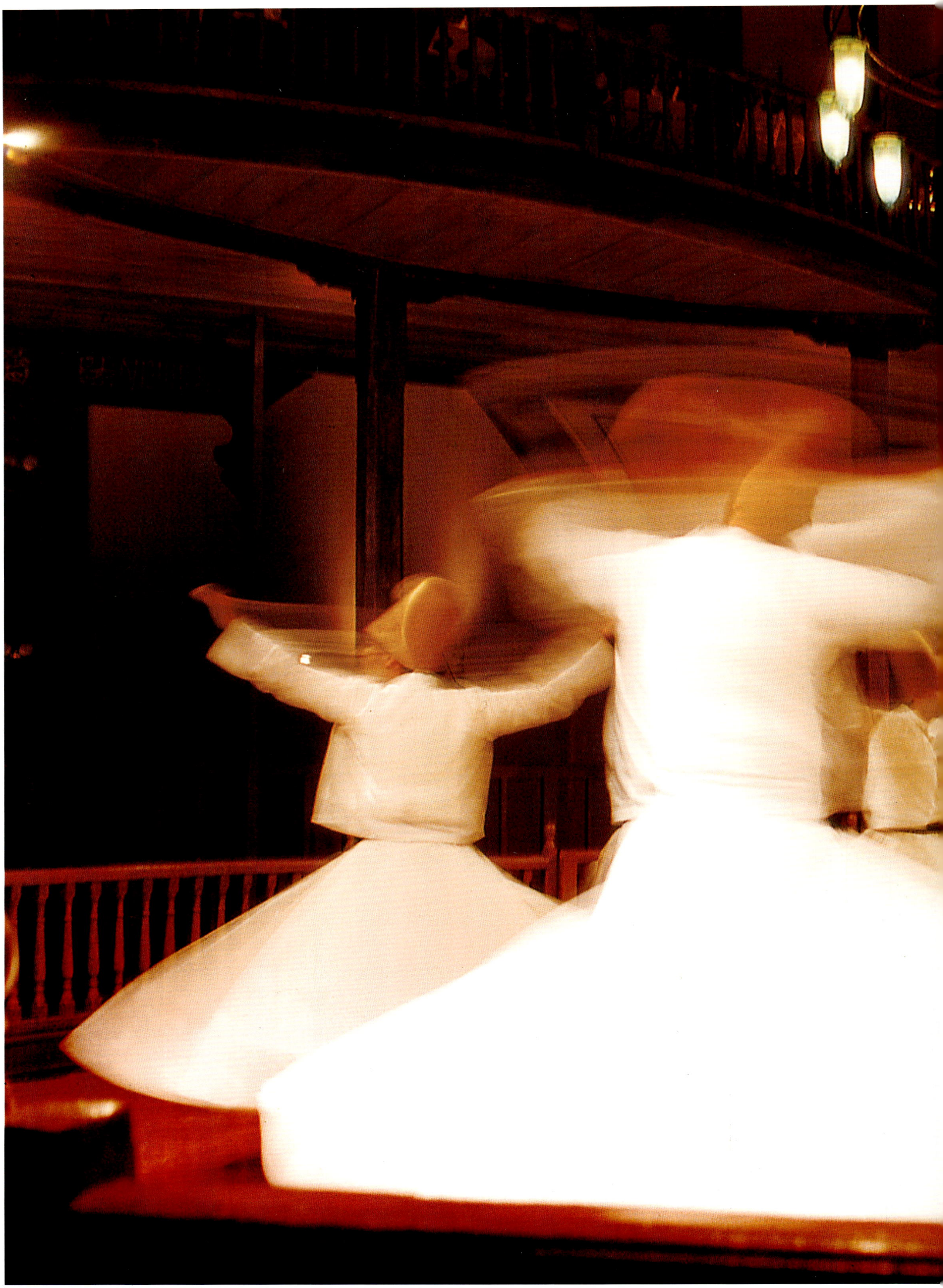

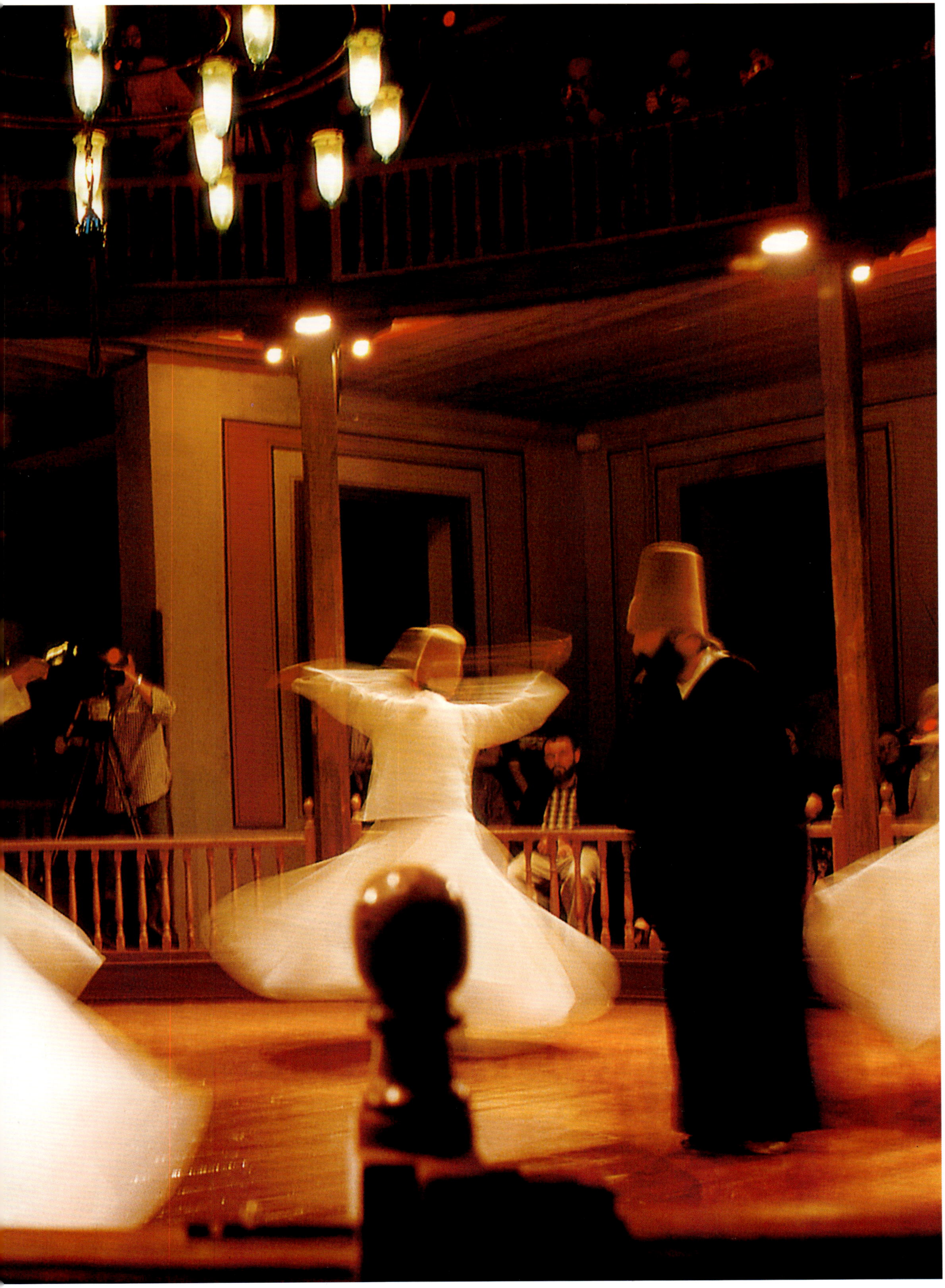

*Dervish performers at the* samakhana, *Islamic Cairo*

The Nile is one of the few rivers in the world that flows north. Perhaps the restlessness and determination of this stream of water has an affect on the people who live next to it.

Or maybe the seemingly ceaseless movement that characterizes present-day Egypt can be traced back to all the caravan routes that once passed through the country. The trade routes of this region are the oldest in Africa. For example, the Forty Days' Road connects Asyut, south of Cairo, to a province of Sudan, a journey of 1,721 kilometers. Merchants would ship goods such as ebony, ivory, ostrich feathers, fans, bows, and shields made of fine hides. Today the route is still used by camel traders bringing their animals to markets around Cairo. From the west, traders would lead long trains of camels and donkeys laden with spices and some of the best dates in the world. Egypt was connected to Mesopotamia—present-day Iraq—by routes that ran through Damascus or Petra. The city of Alexandria—founded by Alexander the Great, who pushed his conquering army across enormous distances—was once a major port, taking in goods and passengers from Europe and the whole world. When the Suez Canal was built by Ferdinand de Lesseps and opened in 1869, linking the Mediterranean and the Red Sea, it utterly transformed the passage to India and Asia from the west. In the fiscal year 2002–03, more than 14,600 ships and tankers used the canal—and this is a low yearly figure.

Today, the natural world still maintains an influence on the movement of the Egyptian people. During the holy month of Ramadan, the cycle of the sun determines the day's activities. People wake before dawn to have a meal, and then fast for the remainder of the daylight. Then during the two hours before sunset, great masses of people are on the move, hustling to get home in time for *iftar*, the meal that breaks the fast.

But mostly the incessant activity of present-day Egypt is the result of the very human pursuits of work and fun. The energetic process of making a living can be seen everywhere in the country, and it is often not hidden behind the cool façade of high-tech office buildings. People mend elaborately patterned carpets, sew tassels and trims for curtains, hawk newspapers on busy street corners, bake piles of bread, and sweep the ever-dusty streets. Tourists on their missions to see the famous sights rush past shops that stay open late into the night. Artists take in the swirl of Cairo and then create paintings, plays, and novels. Horseback riding is a surprisingly popular form of recreation, as is (of course) soccer. For desert safaris, people drive sturdy, well-equipped cars out into the middle of nowhere to revel in the awe-inspiring landscape.

These days, the old grizzled trading routes might still be used, but only rarely by Bedouins, date merchants, and camel traders. Their movement has been replaced by the endless trucks and trains on Egypt's roads, and the airplanes that fly in and out of Cairo Airport at all hours of the day, every day.

*T. E.*

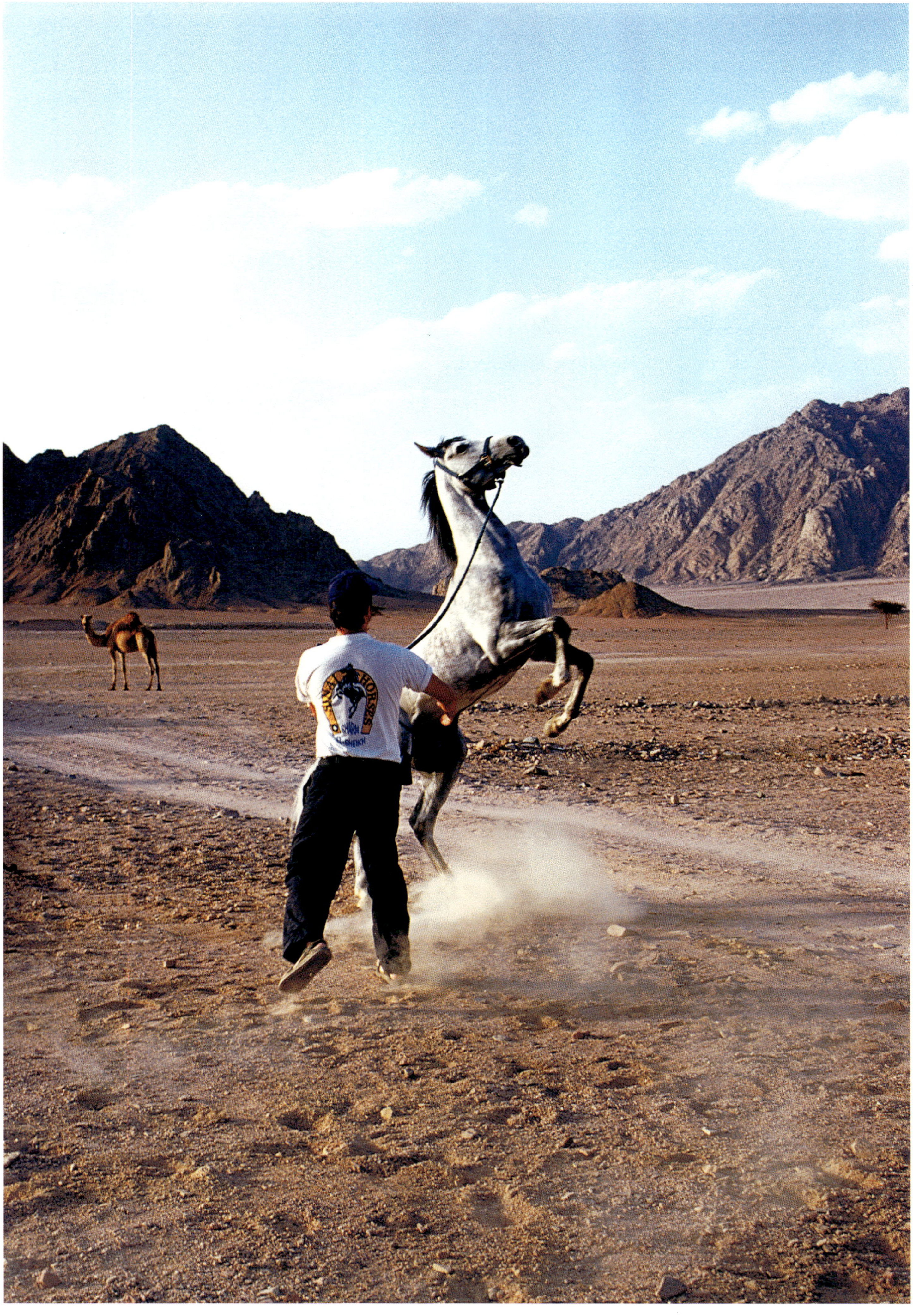

*At a private horse ranch in Wadi Kansour, Sinai*

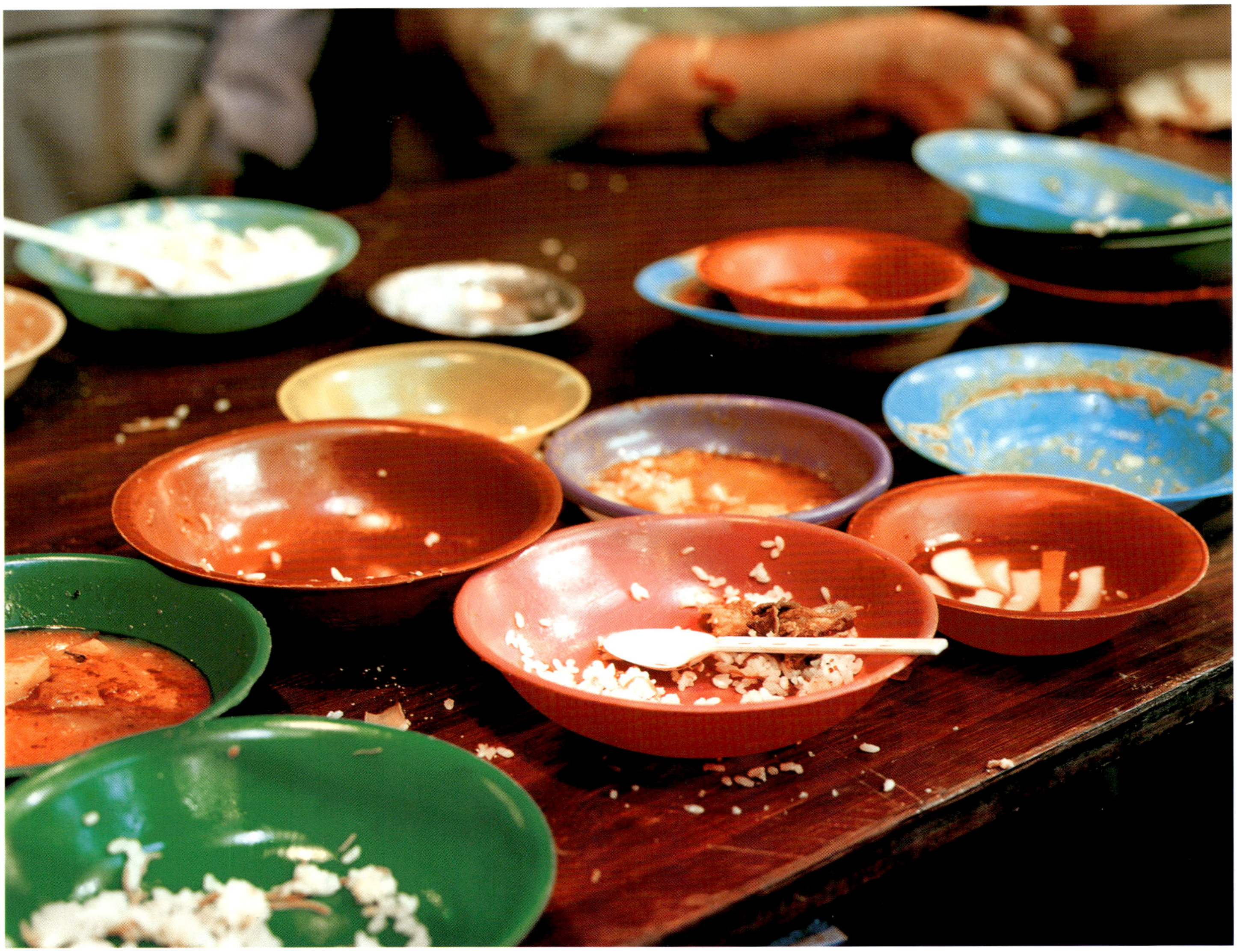

*Colorful dishes used for the* iftar *meal during* Ramadan

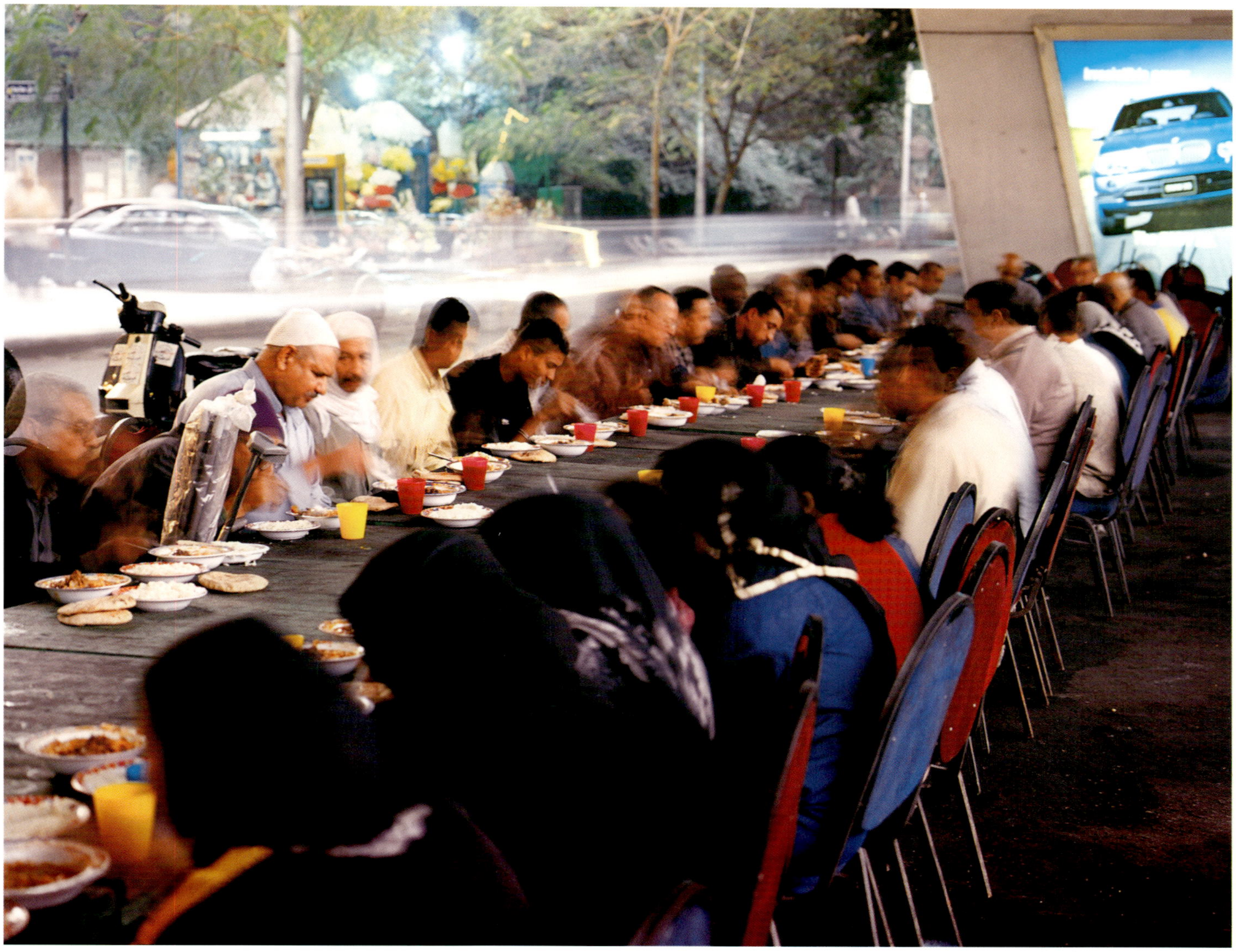

*The public* iftar *meal, Zamalek, Cairo*

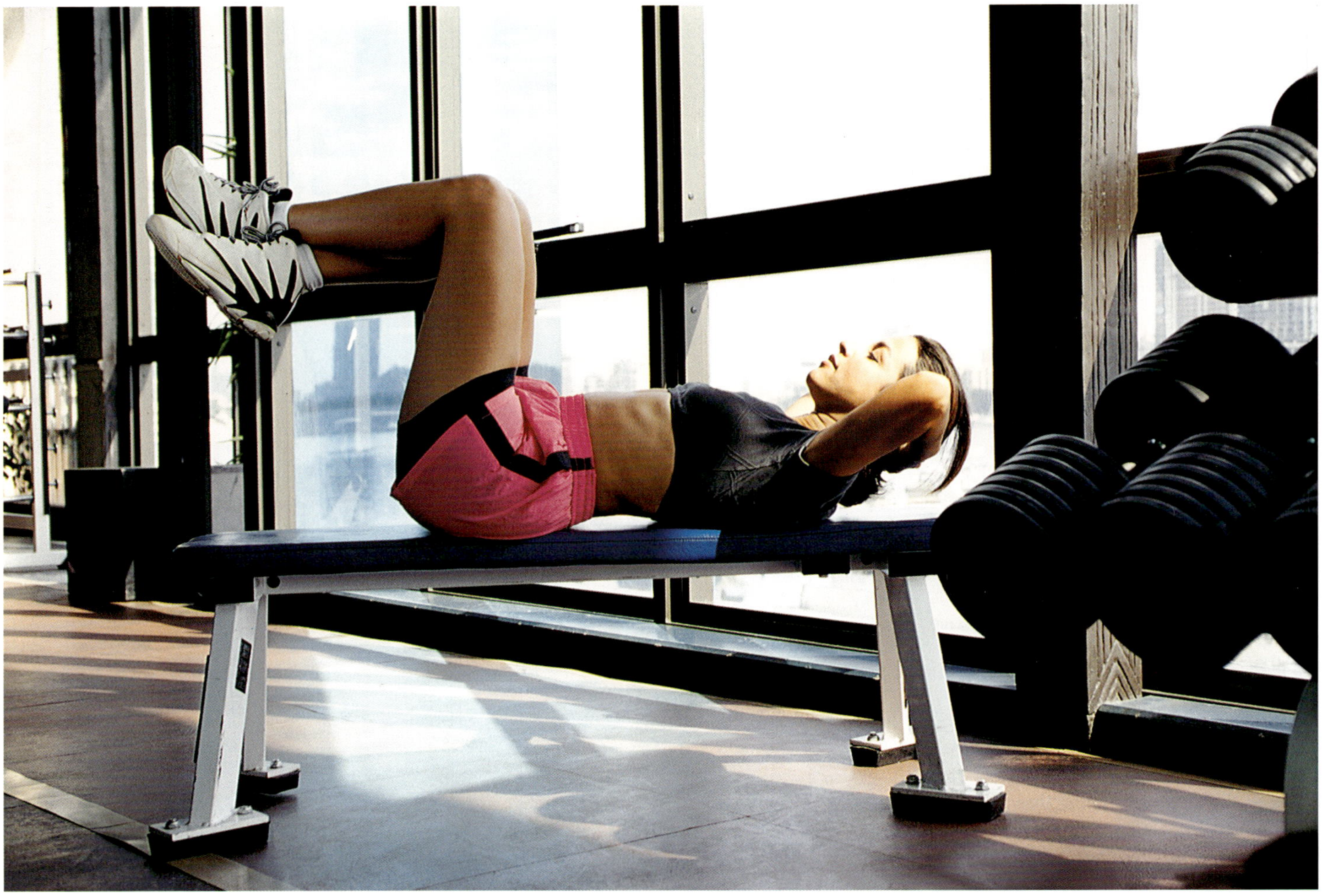

*In a Cairo gym*

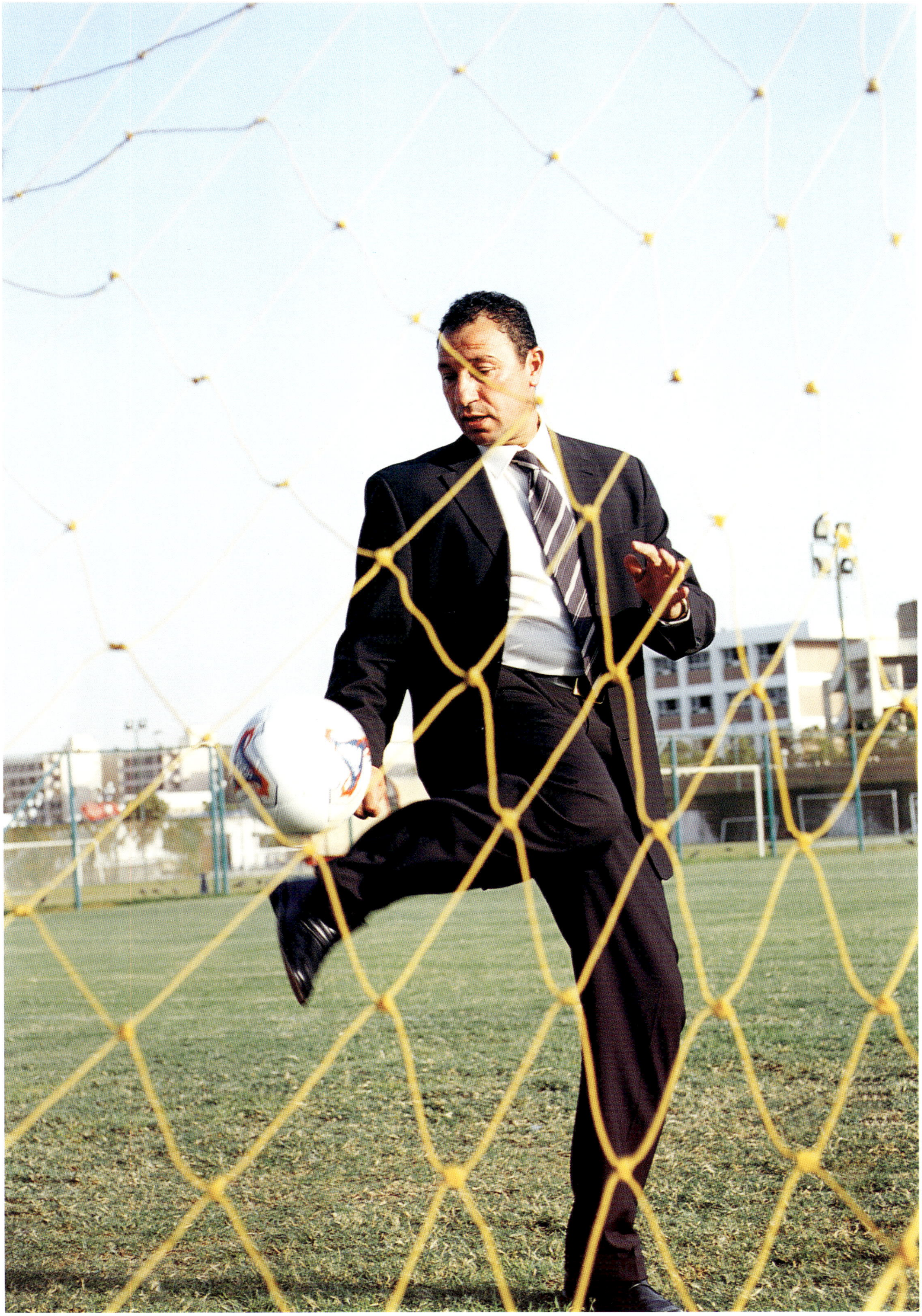

*Mahmoud al-Khatib, the most popular Egyptian soccer player in the 1980s*

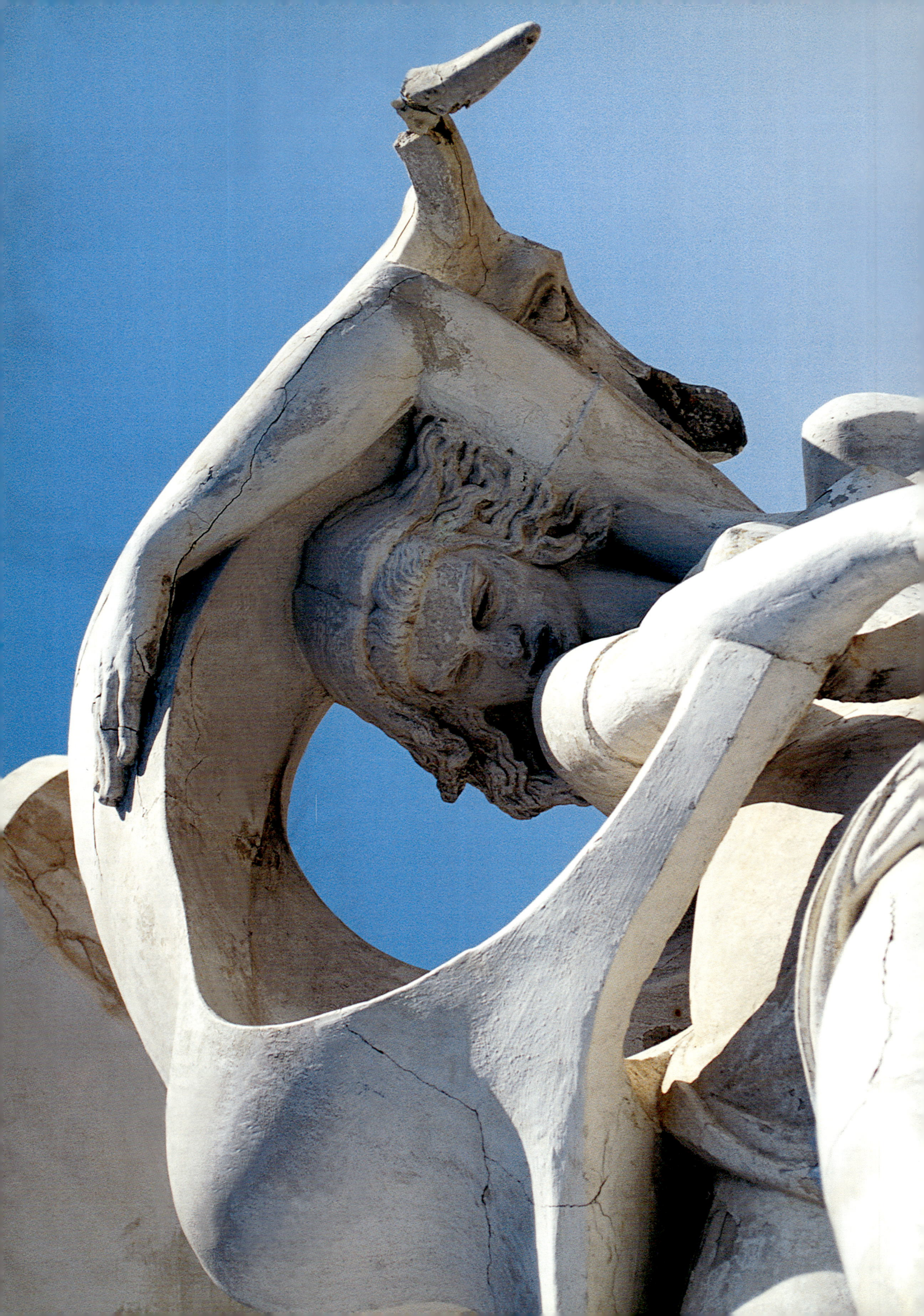

## William Wells

*Gallery owner*

Art gallery owner William Wells cannot help but remark on Egypt's generosity. The country has consistently offered him more than he knows what to do with.

Born in Britain, he first came to Egypt in 1985 as a painter planning to stay for a year or two. "But I discovered that Egypt is not one of those places where you can just say, okay, I'm going to come here, I'm going to do this one thing, and I'm going to leave," he says. What he found instead were "so many opportunities and distractions."

These opportunities included a year he spent living with Bedouins, documenting a village near the Libyan border. Eventually, as he became more and more involved in working with aid foundations, he moved away from doing his own art, and he traveled around other Middle East countries.

The whole time, though, he had an idea: to open up a gallery in Cairo similar to one he had set up in London—a place with exhibition areas as well as studio spaces, where artists could be nurtured, challenged, and promoted.

In 1998 he came back to Egypt. "And I realized there was so much happening that I had missed," he says. He discovered a younger generation of artists, people who had been exposed to the internet and satellite television and had traveled abroad. "There was energy everywhere," enthuses Wells.

This gave him the impetus to open the Townhouse Gallery at the end of a small downtown Cairo lane. Once again, Egypt offered its abundances. "I was expecting to lose money the first few years," explains Wells. His plan was to use that period to familiarize himself with the country's artists and their work. "But I was taken by surprise. Within the first year we were forced to open up another floor of the building. The needs were far greater than we had ever anticipated."

The gallery concentrated on helping artists create portfolios, letting them be part of the decisions about how to display their work, and getting artists into exhibitions outside Egypt. In the process, Townhouse Gallery grew—it opened an annex across the alley—and became a vital part of the Cairo arts scene.

What is particularly remarkable about the gallery, though, is its welcoming atmosphere. "By the very nature of the space, the whole concept is that you can walk in off the street," says Wells. "There's no sense that you have to pass any security. The gallery is run and maintained by the people in the lane. And the gallery houses prayer spaces, so people in the lane pray in the gallery five times a day."

Wells finds that the chaos of Cairo comes through in the art that's produced in the city. "If you go to shows, you're going to find that noise, that chaos that keeps this city alive. And," he adds with a smile, "which is difficult to live with."

*T. E.*

*A sculpture on the Corniche, Alexandria*

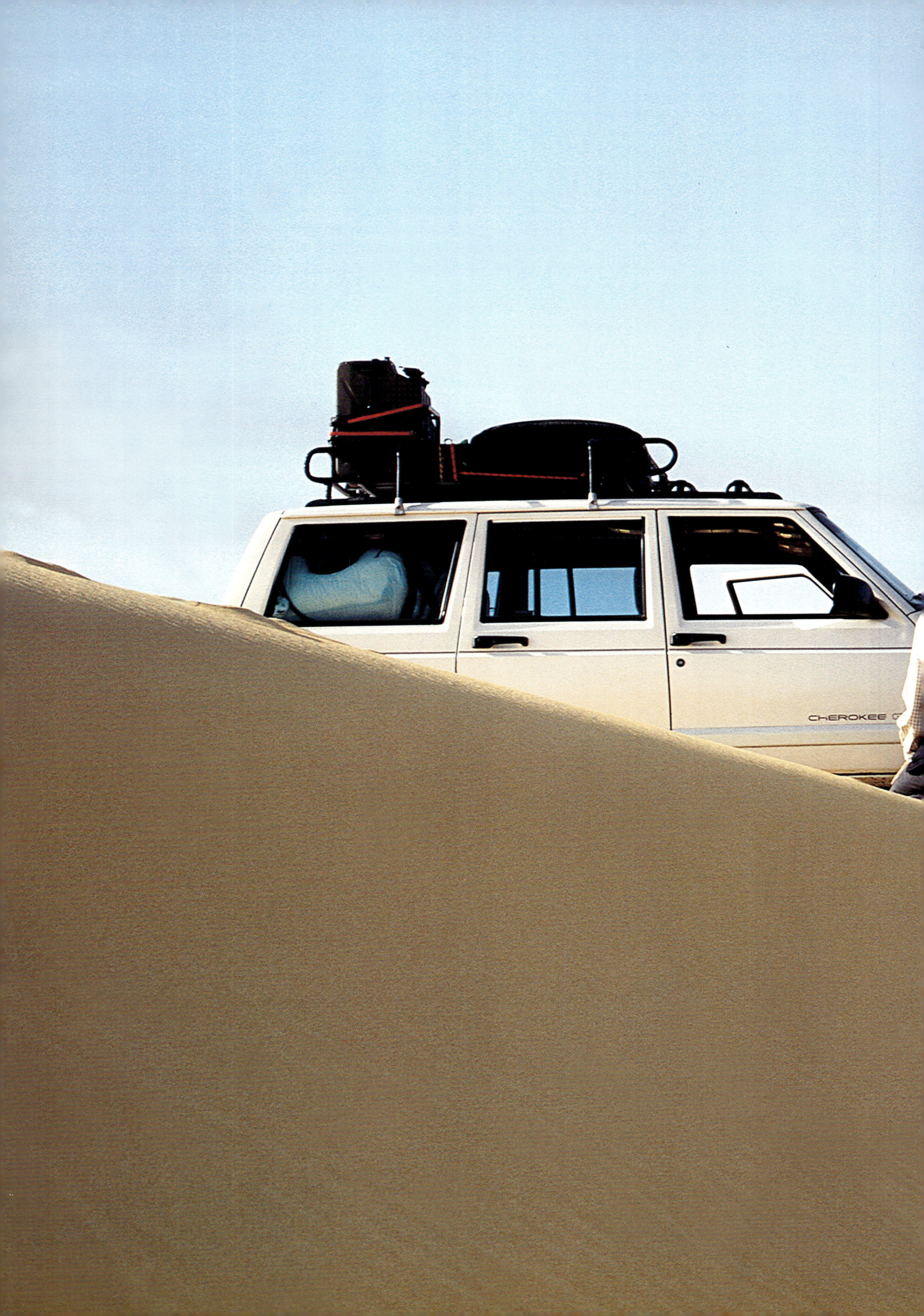
CHEROKEE

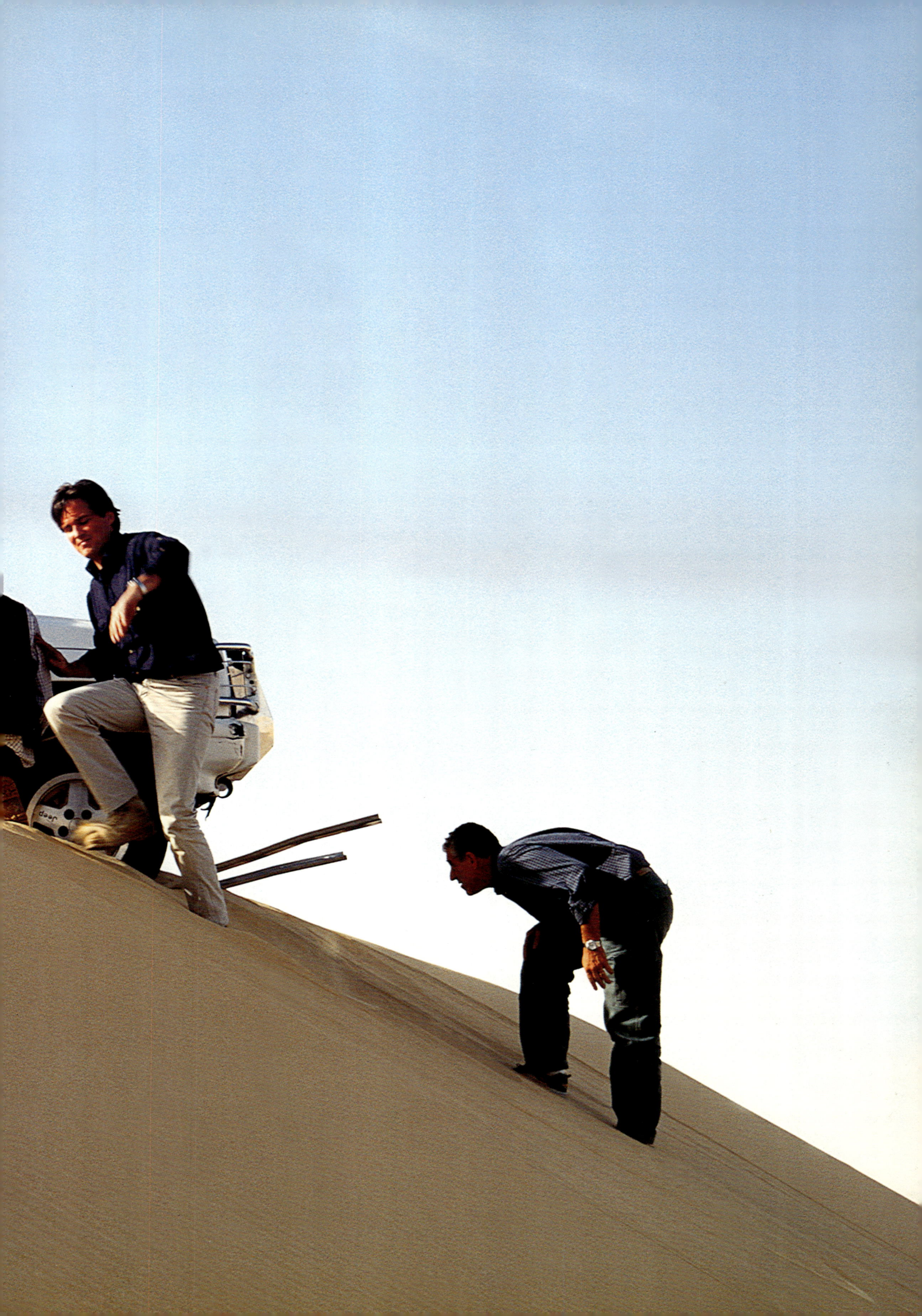

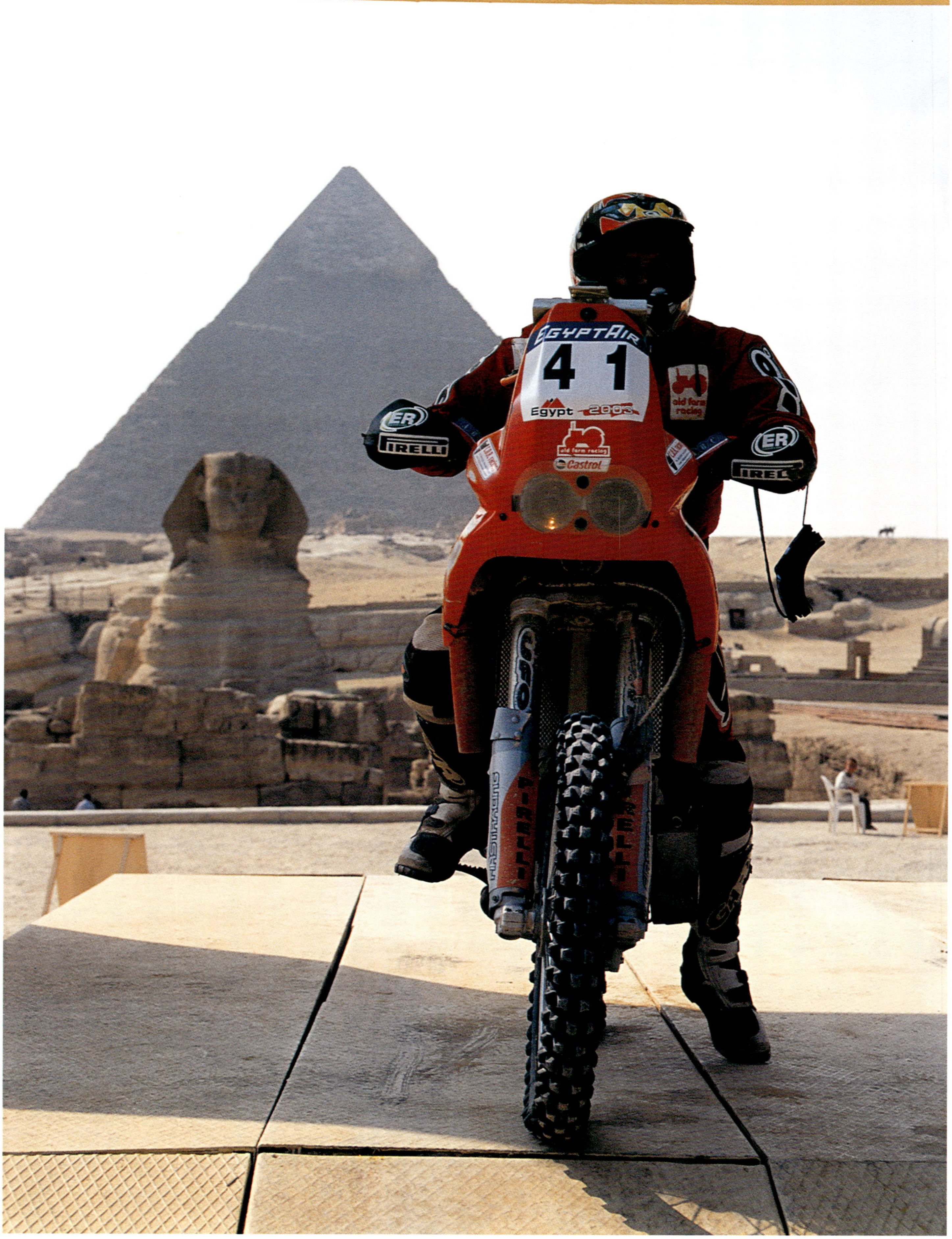


*Previous page: Stuck in a dune, Wadi al-Rayyan*

*Rally of Egypt 2003, the Pyramids, Cairo*

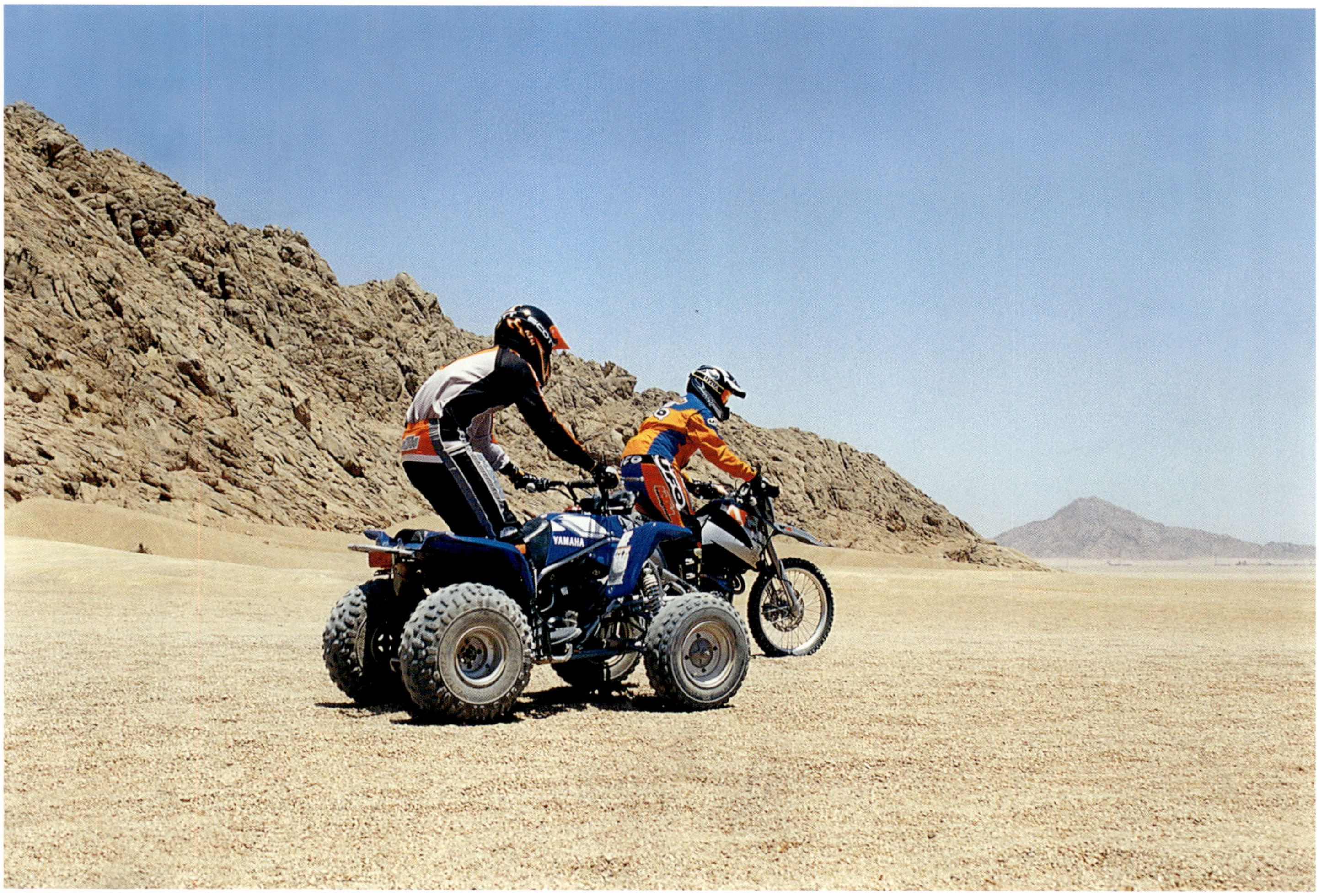


*Quad riders in the desert, Sinai*

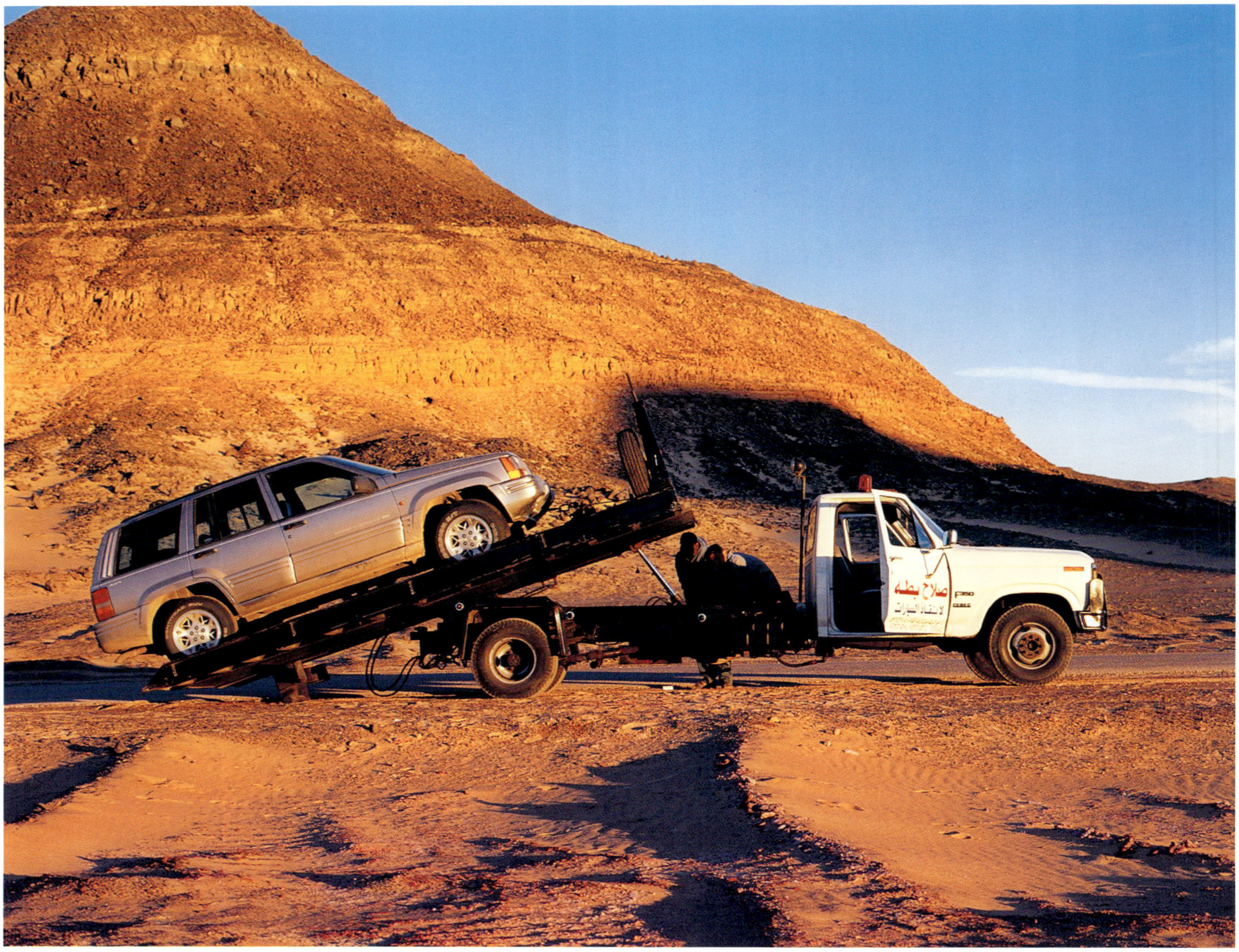

*A not uncommon occurrence after a desert safari*

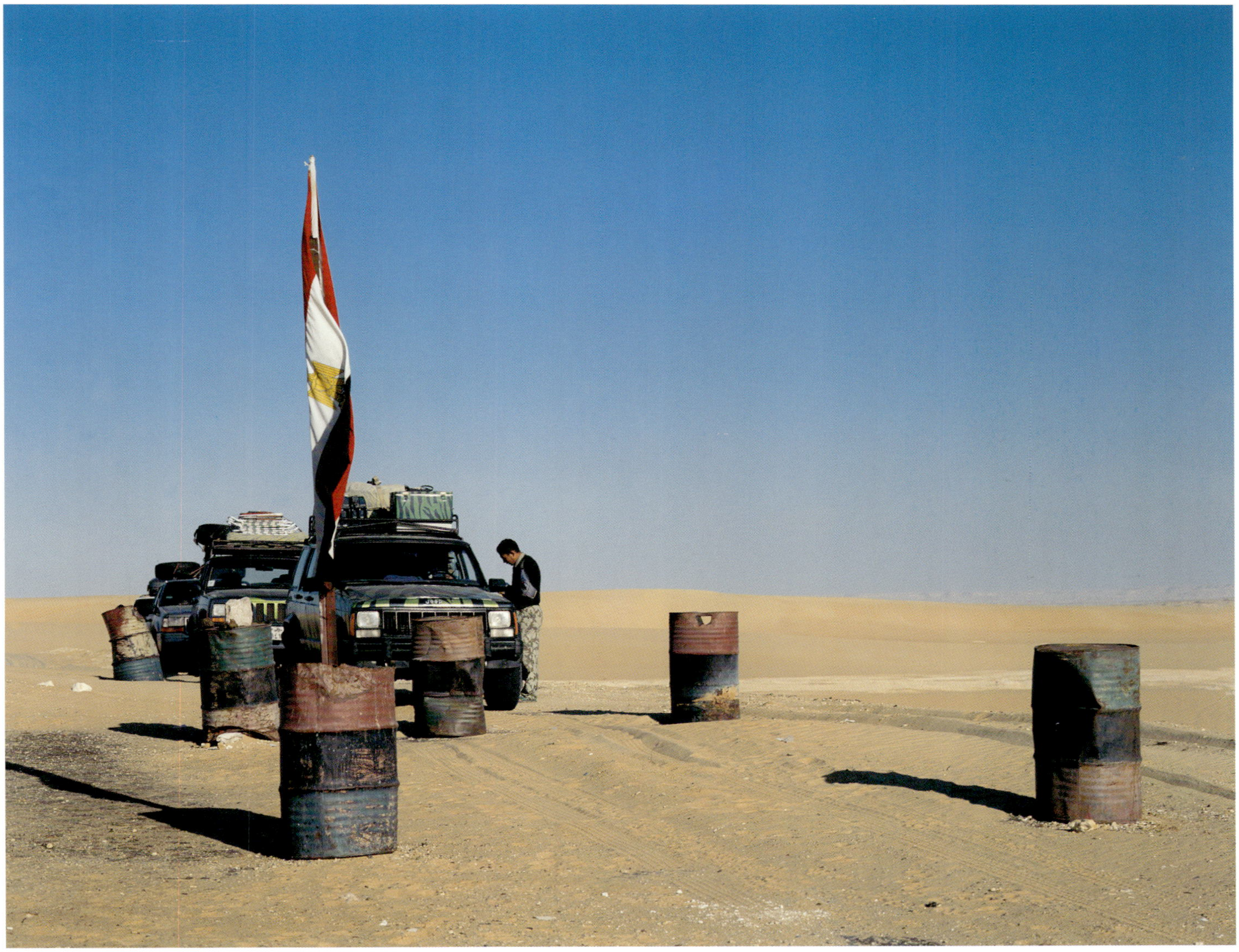

*A desert checkpoint, Siwa*

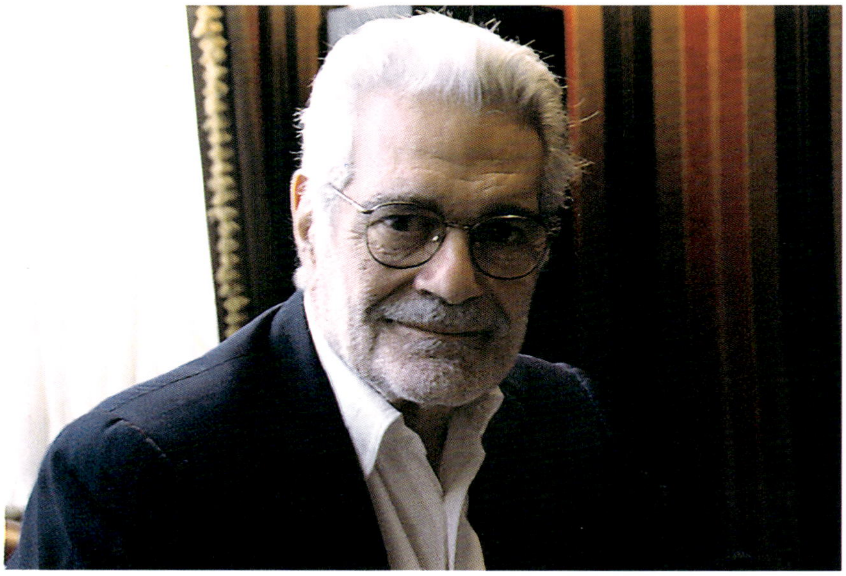

*Omar Sharif, actor*

## Omar Sharif

*Actor*

"In life you always try to advance second by second. The movement is a forward movement, not a backward movement," says actor Omar Sharif, over a cup of coffee at the bar of Royal Monceau Hotel in Paris, where he lives.

He has good memories of his childhood in Egypt. "I am a very lucky person. My adolescence was extremely happy. I had wonderful parents and a very good education." But his expression becomes melancholy when he talks about the time when he left his family to become an actor in Hollywood. "I was married to a woman I loved. We had a child, a nice home, and we were very happy. I was planning to have more children. I was in paradise! Suddenly life took a turn for me. Maybe my life would have been happier if I had moved backward and gone back to Egypt." He never found another woman he loved, and he has lived alone, in a hotel room, since 1968.

When Hollywood discovered him, he was simply asked whether he spoke English and wanted to make a test for a film. "I said yes," remembers Sharif, "and suddenly I became a star."

"Coming from Cairo, it was a cultural shock," he admits. "I arrived in the States in the early 1960s, during the sexual revolution. The girls were all fighting to take me to bed. Of course this period had an influence on me. That was my past. It is finished. The result is what I am now."

This sentiment exemplifies the world-famous actor. He does not care to analyze himself and does not want anybody else to. He combines a powerful look with an apathetic expression, making a visitor somehow feel invisible. "I like not to know myself," he declares. "The less I know about myself, the happier I am, because I love to surprise myself!"

Sharif never plans his future and does not want to think of his past. "I am totally concentrated in the present. That's why I become very passionate when I talk to someone. I put all my concentration, all my passion into what I do in the moment that I do it."

When prompted to describe his childhood, though, Sharif fondly remembers growing up in a multicultural society. His family was rich, but they were not cut off from the rest of society. "I love the poor people in the streets, the ones I consider the real Egyptians. I know them well. They always look happy, although they have nothing to eat, nothing to wear, and no place to live." During his student years he shared experiences with Muslims, Christians, and Jews.

But he now has no desire to return to Egypt. "I became an international actor. It is very difficult to leave all this and go back to making Egyptian movies." And while he considers himself Egyptian, he is not limited to this: "My heart, my feelings, and my emotions are oriental, not necessarily only Egyptian." His identity is even broader: "I have an oriental heart and an occidental mind," he explains.

He does admit that he misses certain aspects of Egypt. "The hugging, crying, laughing, and loving is what I miss when I stay a long time in Europe. The human warmth I have is there only because I am Egyptian!" Nevertheless, his cosmopolitan outlook makes it difficult for him to think about returning to his homeland. "The reason why I don't go to Egypt a lot is that when I go there I miss going to the theater, to the opera, to the concerts. I miss having an intellectual discussion. Egyptians talk about very frivolous things—it is rare to have a cultural conversation there!" One example of this lack of cultural movement is the exclusive, closed-off area of Qattamiya, just outside Cairo, where his son lives with his family. "I find Qattamiya a disgusting place. Everybody goes and stays only with each other in the evenings. They meet the same people every night. They are living in the golden towers over there, where there is no movement. They are segregating themselves. I feel sorry that my grandson should be brought up in a place where he will never see any of the Egyptian poor with his own eyes."

Now, instead of going to Cairo, he wants his family to come to see him in France. "This way they will open their minds!"

As for the film industry, Sharif has observed that the audience has changed and, as a result, the cinema has deteriorated. Older people do not go to the cinemas, preferring to watch movies at home. "The young instead go to the cinemas because they don't want to stay at home with their parents," he notes. "Films are now made for young people: action or guns or science fiction are the most popular ones." What has been lost is the concern for art. "American cinema is a matter of money and people, not of talent."

He feels that in Egypt the problem is even worse. "The rich people don't go to the cinema. They bring a video home. Only the poor go, because they don't have videos. The audience that watches Egyptian movies at the cinema is totally ignorant." It is a sad decline, because just a few decades ago Egypt created the highest quality films in the Arab world.

The film industry transformed Sharif—and, in a way, his fellow countrymen were carried along. "In Egypt I am very famous because I became famous abroad," says the actor. "Egyptians are proud of me because of that. When I kissed Sophia Loren it is like they all kissed Sophia Loren!"

*S. D.*

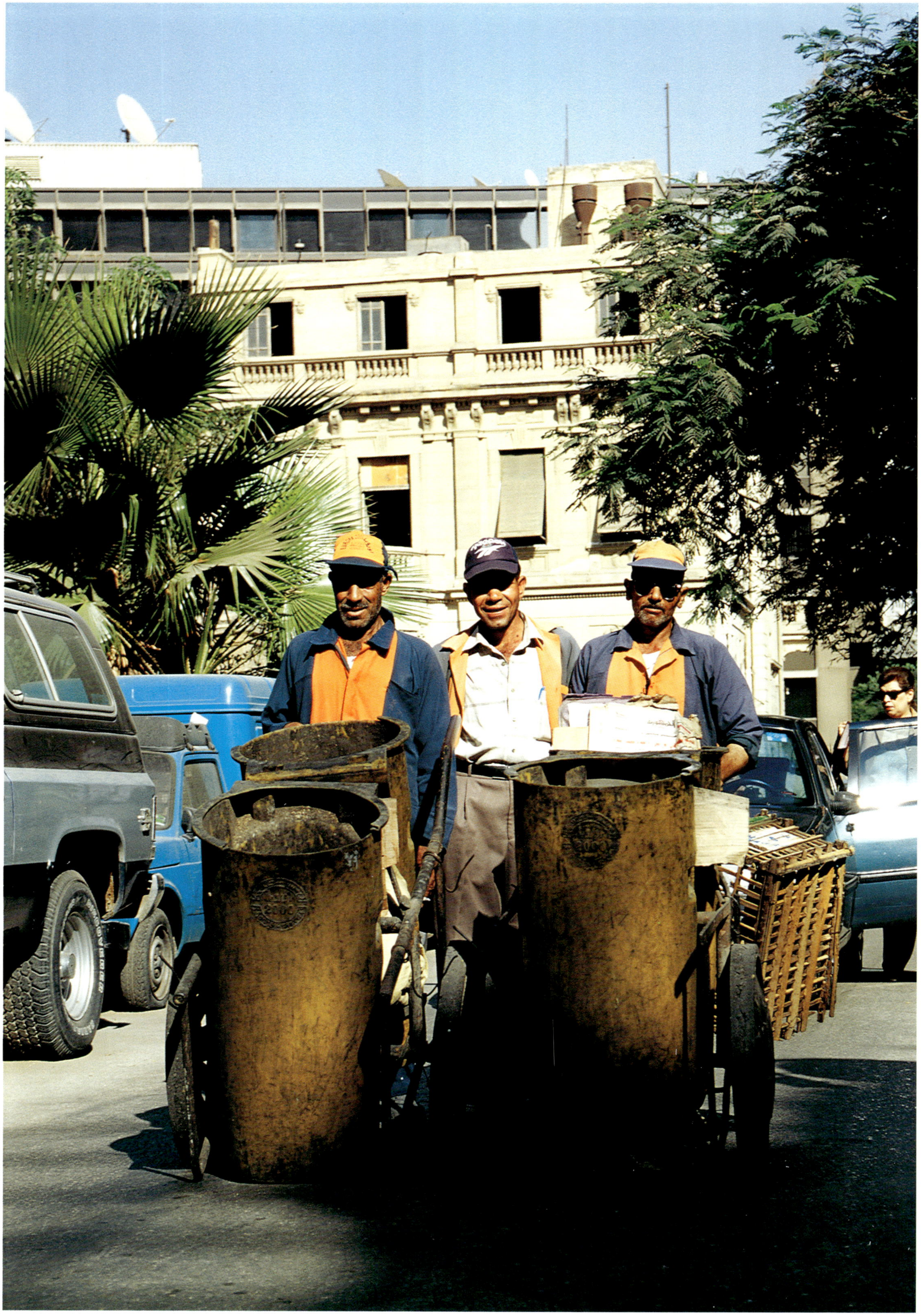

*Street sweepers, Garden City, Cairo*

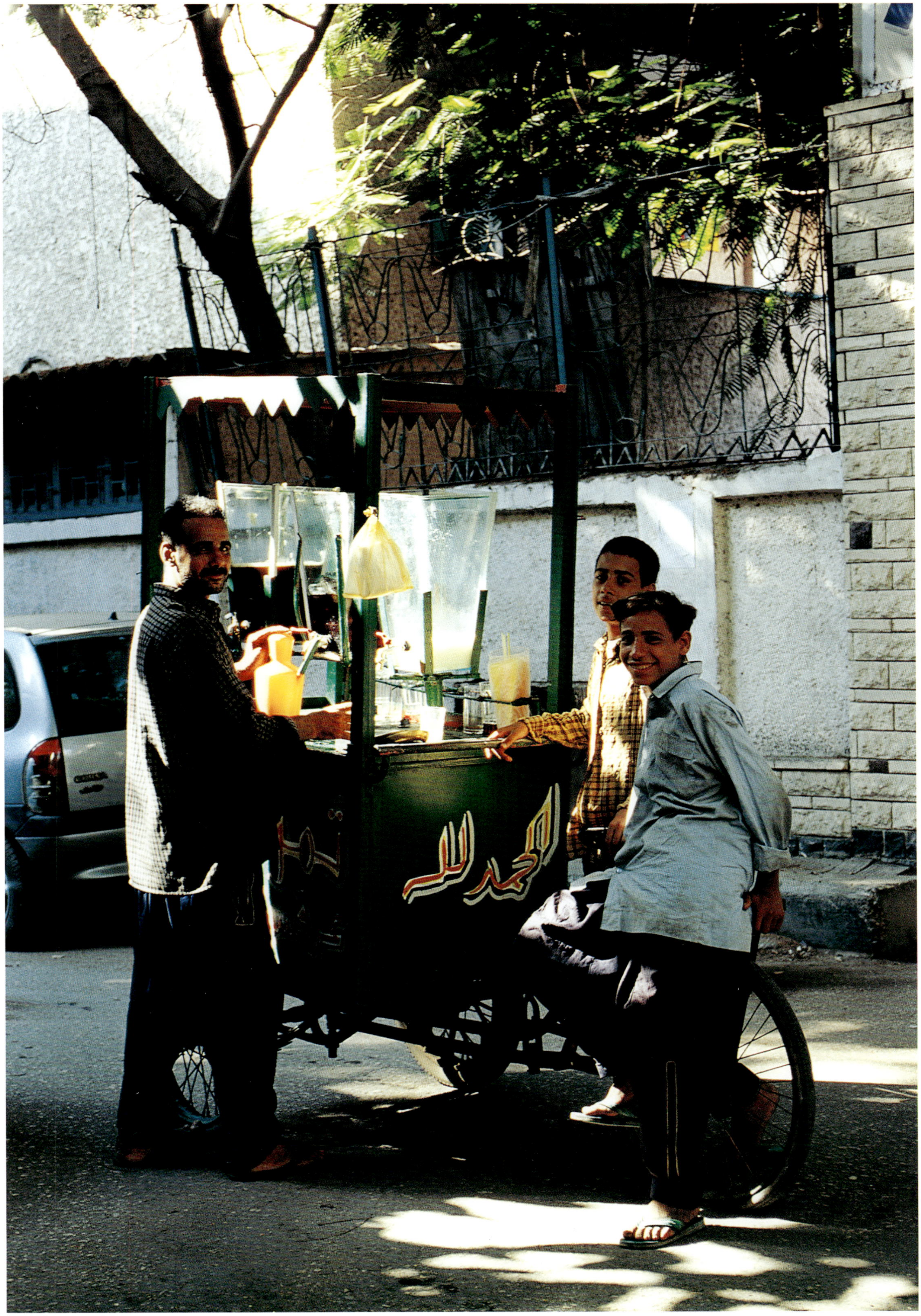


*Street vendors, Zamalek, Cairo*

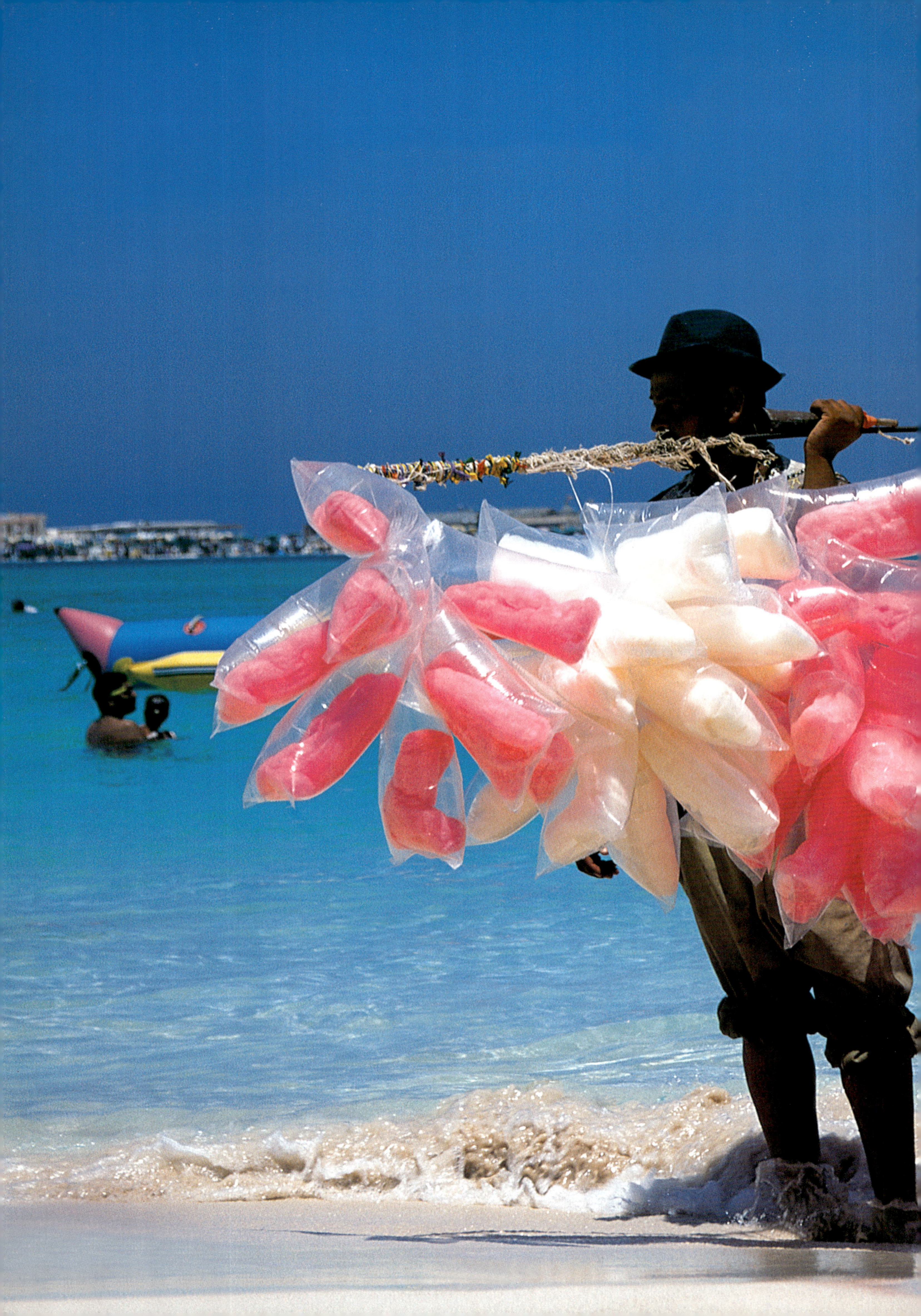

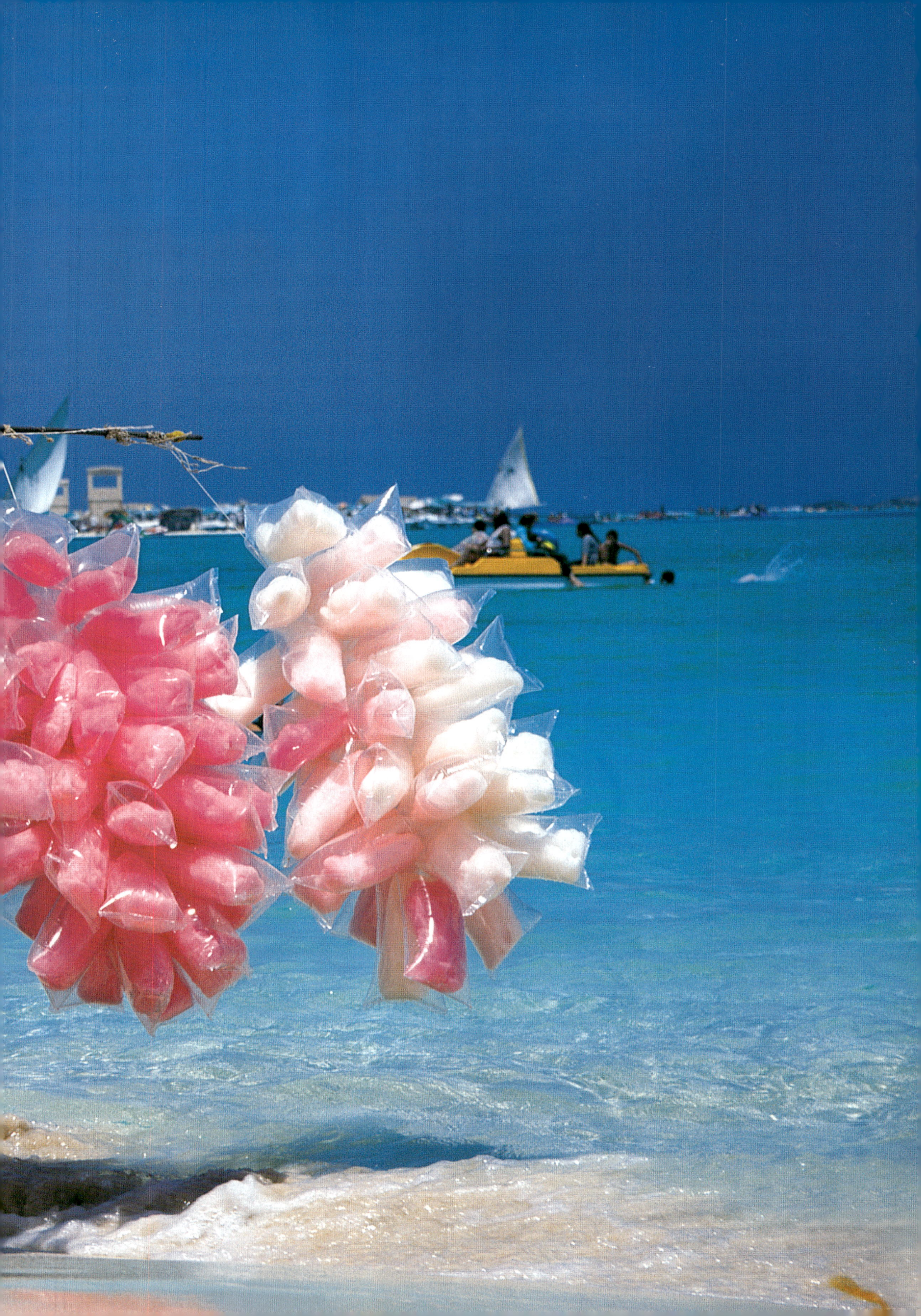

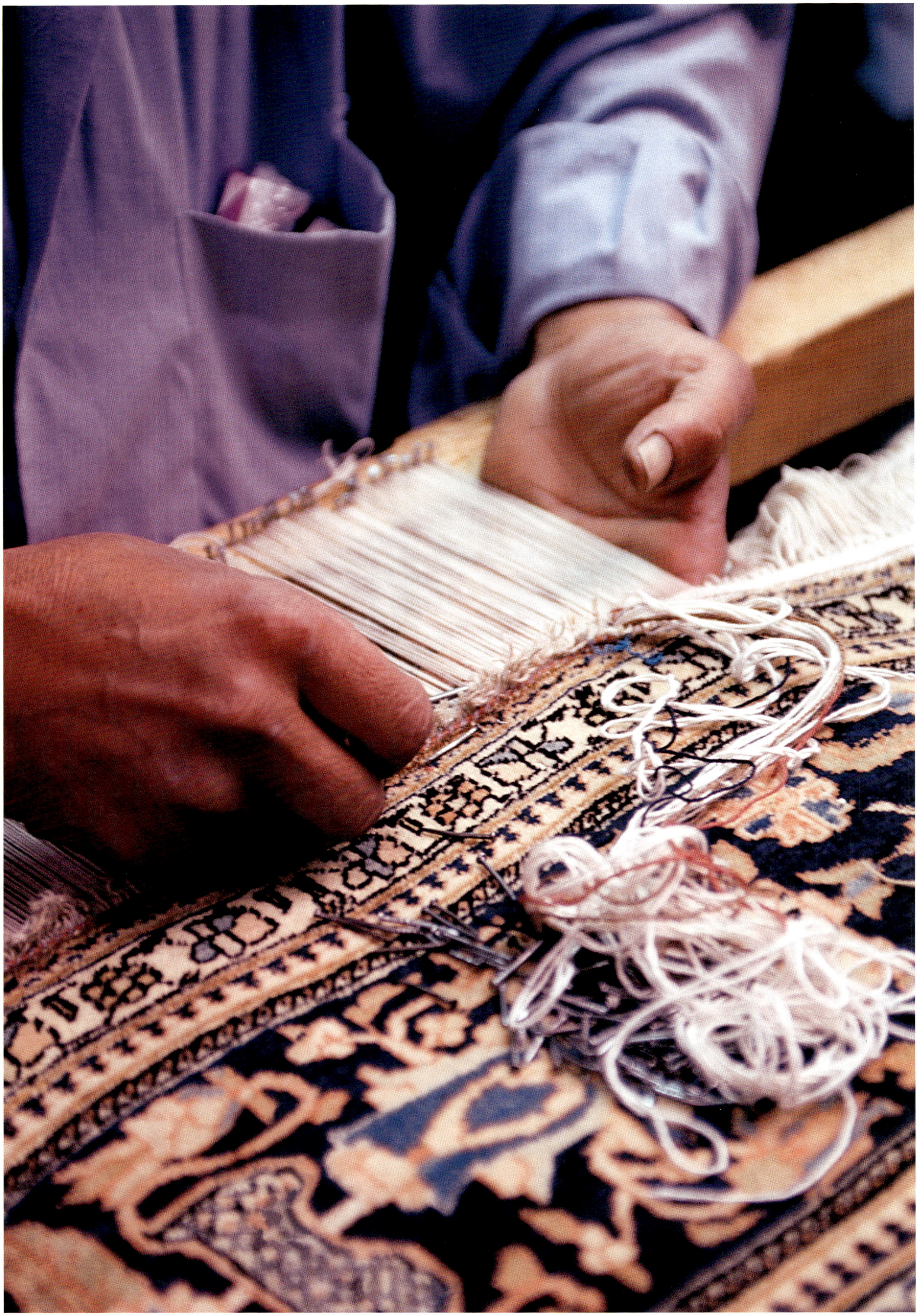

*Previous page: Cotton candy vendor, Marsa Matruh*

*Carpet mender, Cairo*

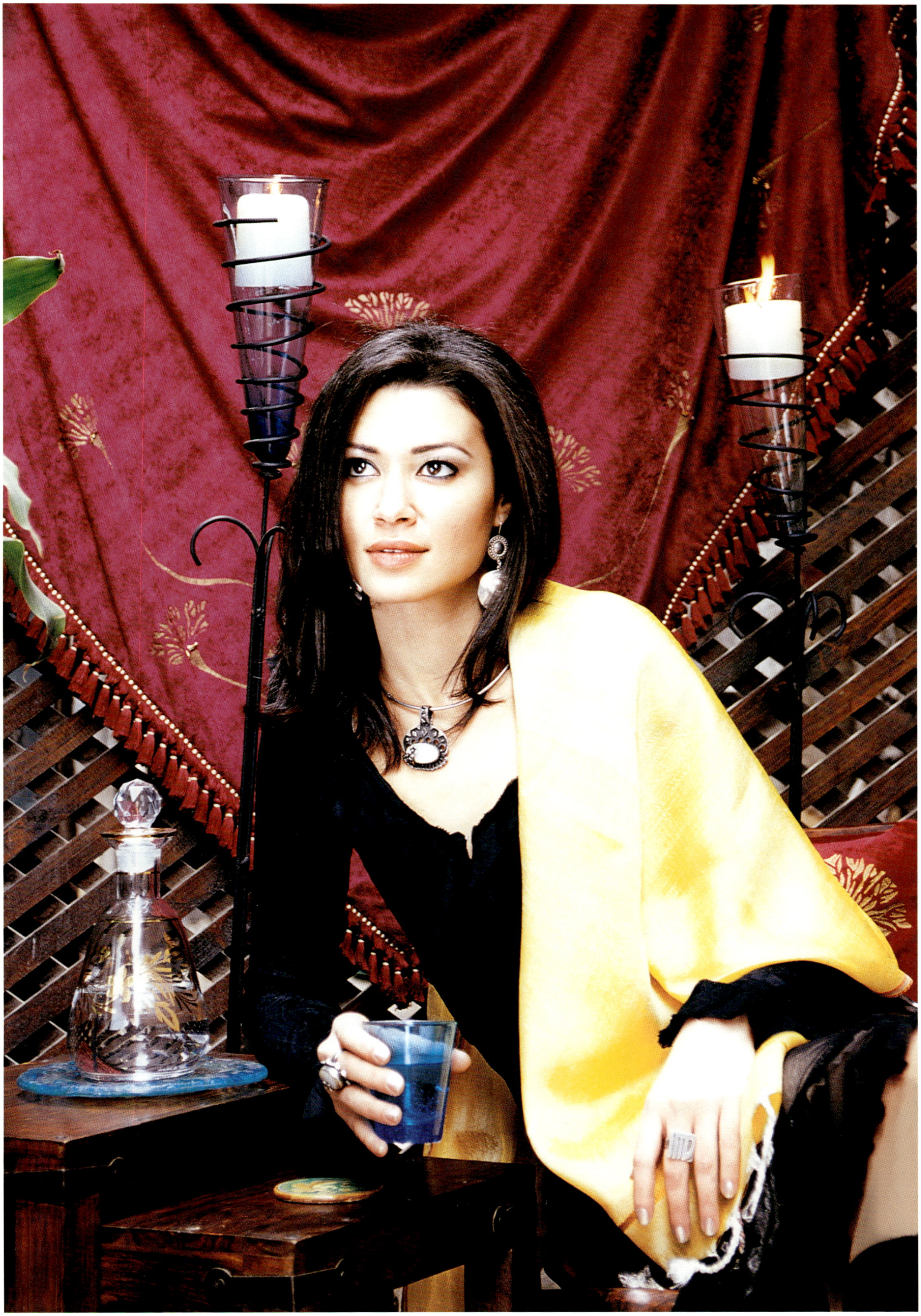

*Arwa Gouda, Egyptian model*

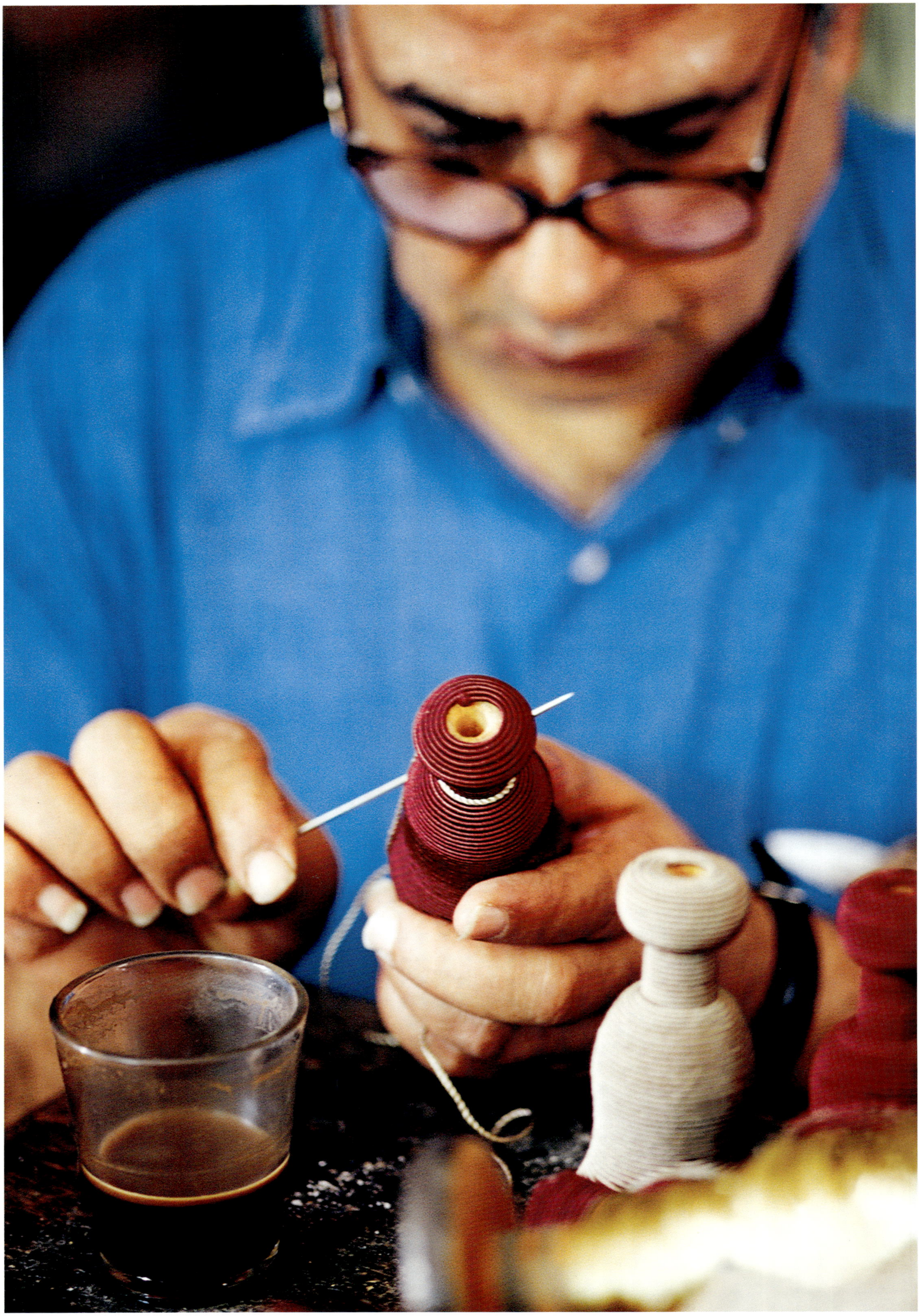

*An artisan sewing tassels and trims for curtains, Cairo*

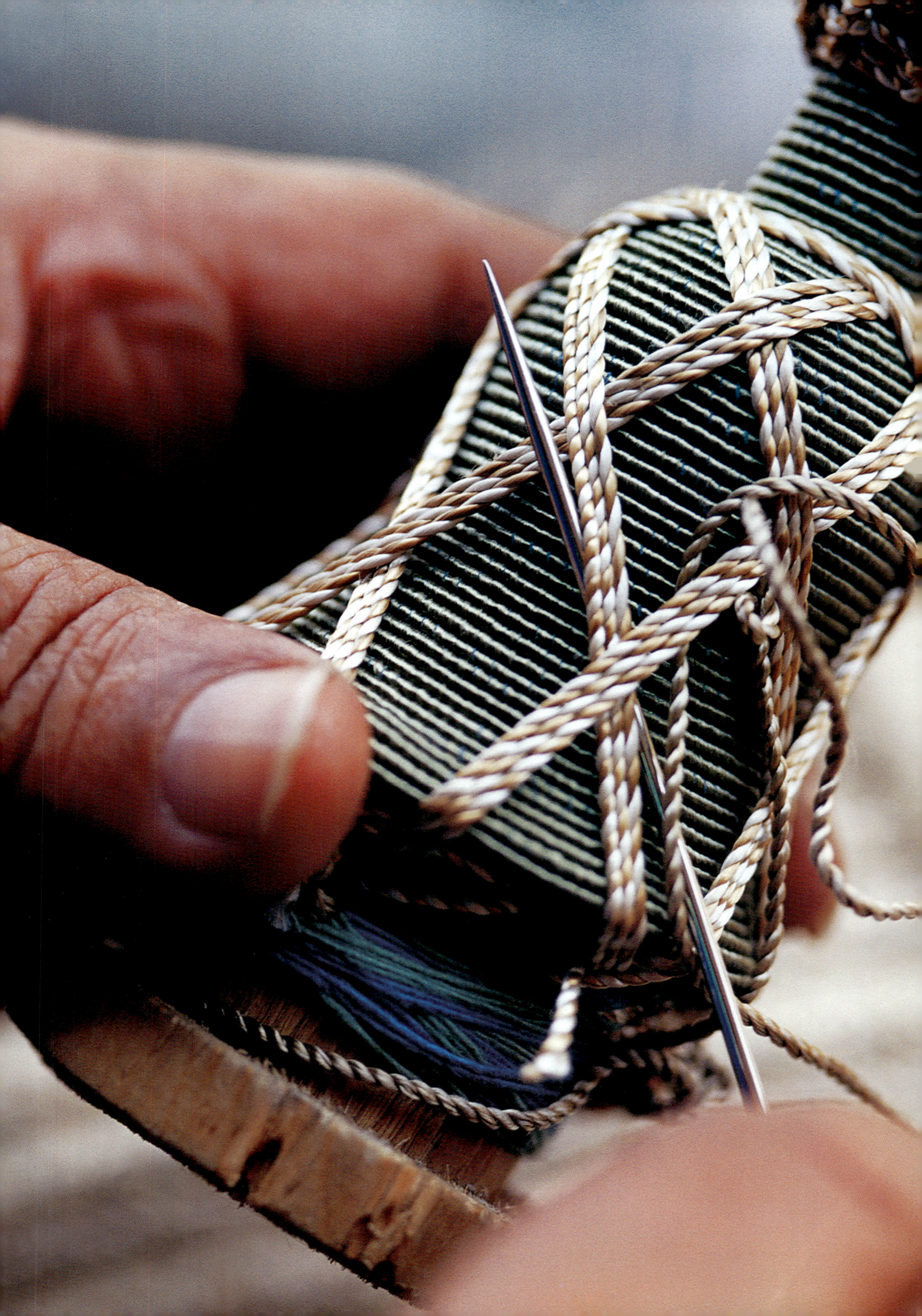

## Maha Awad

*Television presenter and stylist*

Television presenter and stylist Maha Awad knows what it is like to be in the public eye in Egypt. As host of several programs, including *Studio One*, an international music show, she has interviewed Shakira, Marc Anthony, and other world-famous musicians. She has also worked as a stylist on music videos by Egypt's hottest singers, such as Amr Diab and Hakim.

Along with her successful career, she has an outsider's perspective on her country: Awad was born in Egypt but lived in Los Angeles from age seven until she graduated from UCLA. When she returned to Egypt, she realized that so many aspects of the country she left as a child were complicated and hidden. "Things here are not what they appear on the surface," she explains, "and it takes a long time to understand all the different layers. Because every time you think you know something, you peel off another layer and you realize that there's more."

Although Awad works in the entertainment world, where image is highly important, she laments that the culture is overly concerned with keeping up appearances in a different kind of way. "There are a lot of images that people try to maintain," she says of social life, "while things underneath are so tumultuous. People in their twenties and thirties are very confused. We are not what our parents used to be—where everything is straightforward, everyone knew what a man does and what a woman does, the politics that govern relationships and marriage and so forth. We're no longer that, because we're too open to the rest of the world, but we're also not the west."

Awad shakes her head when considering the predicament of young Egyptian men and women. "There are just thousands of conflicted people walking around here," she laughs. When asked if there are any outlets for young people to talk about the difficulties, she responds, "I think they need more than conversation and dialogue. I think they need therapy! I do! I think that everyone here from the age of 25 to 38 or so needs interpersonal relationship therapy."

In Egypt, the conservative elements of society still frown upon people going out on dates, and what are known as 'living-room marriages' still occur regularly, where the couple conducts their entire engagement in their parents' houses. As a result, men and women must struggle against different kinds of pressures. "For example," says Awad, "the hip, liberal, well-traveled guys don't feel like they can marry in the traditional way, meaning someone they hardly know or someone who fits the trophy-bride image. But on the other hand they still have that whole Middle Eastern male thing inside them, and if it gets to a point where it crosses the line too far, then it's hard for them to accept. If she's too hip or too cool or too independent, they still have problems with it." Women are also trying to process confusing signals. "Through the media we get so many influences now from the western world, but at the same time we're still here. We can't change the religious background, we can't change this and that."

For Egyptians, the large amount of western images is still a fairly new phenomenon. "Egypt has developed a lot in the past ten years since I've been here," notes Awad. "I remember when I first got here there was maybe one place to go out, something like two TV channels—just much less of everything. People had satellite dishes, but there wasn't Showtime or anything like that. If you really think about it, all this was developed in the past decade. Especially in my field—it has grown exponentially in the past ten years."

Awad's career has grown, too—she is currently involved with six different television programs. The media expansion that she's witnessed shows no signs of stopping, which means that Egyptians will continue to be exposed to even more various influences. From what she has seen, Awad thinks the younger people in Egypt are a source of optimism. "They have gotten beyond the inner conflicts," she says. Then she pauses and adds, "Although we'll see, when it comes to them getting married."

*T. E.*

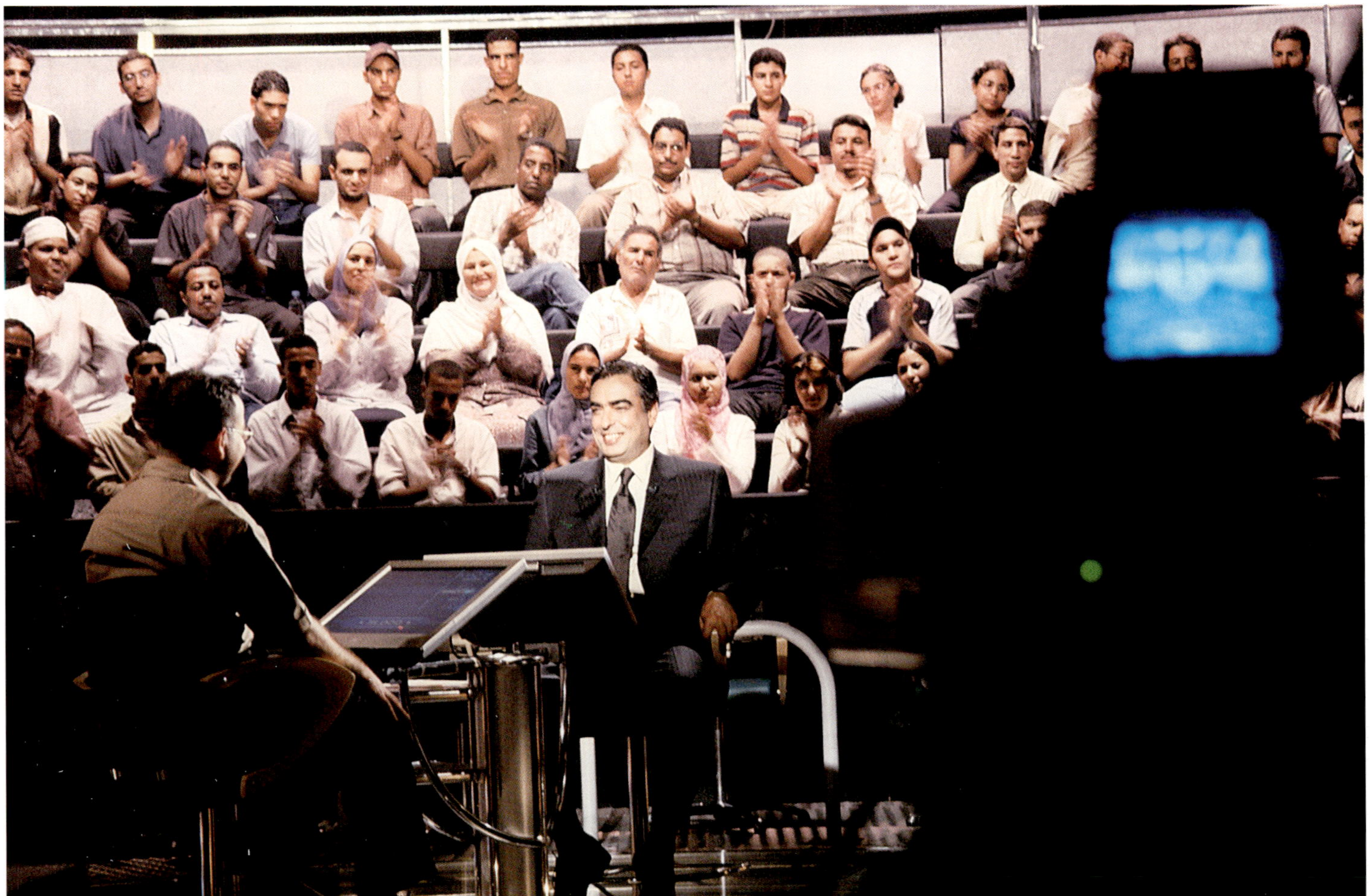

*George Kerdahi during the television show 'Who Will Win the Million?'*

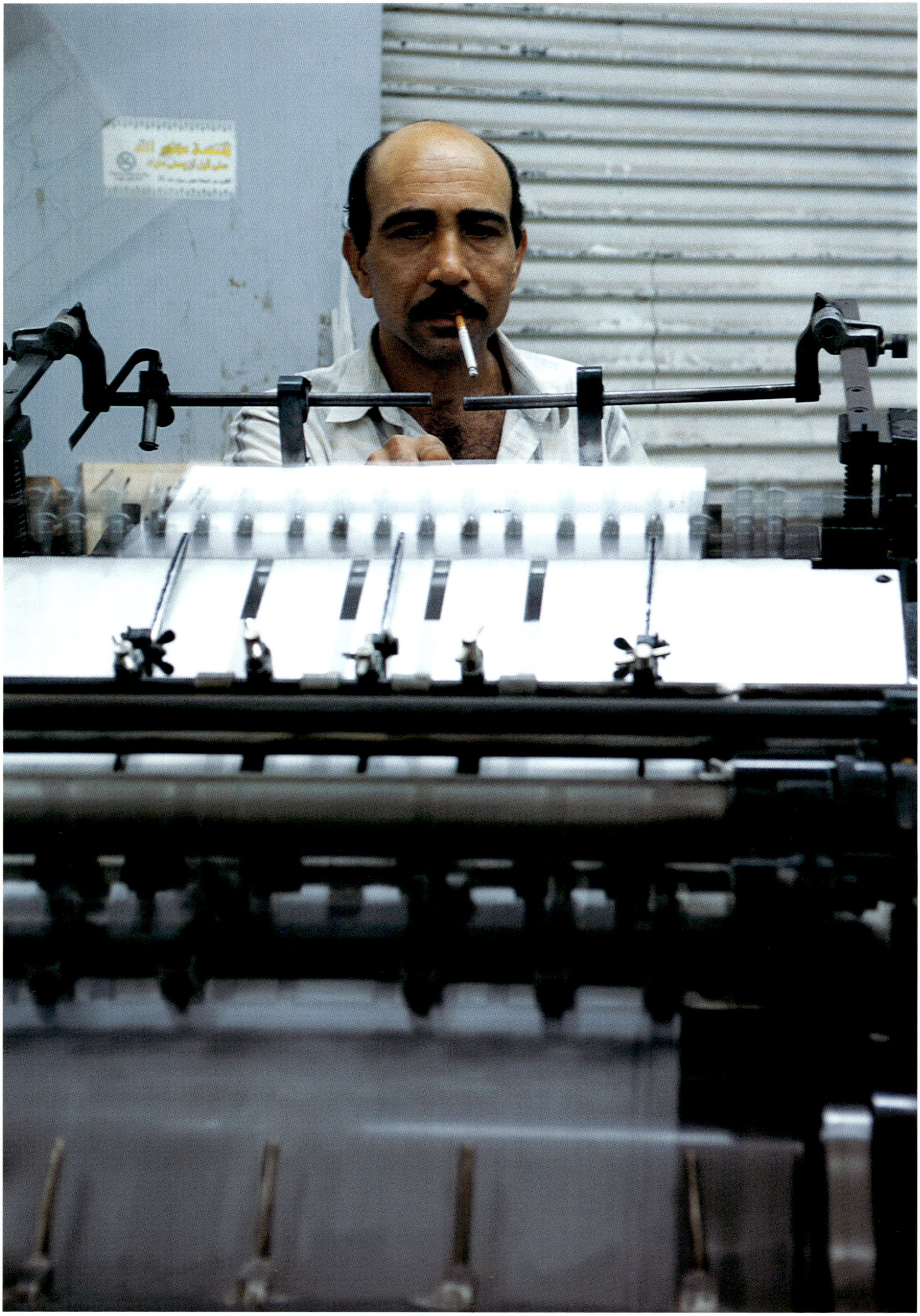

*A printer, Cairo*

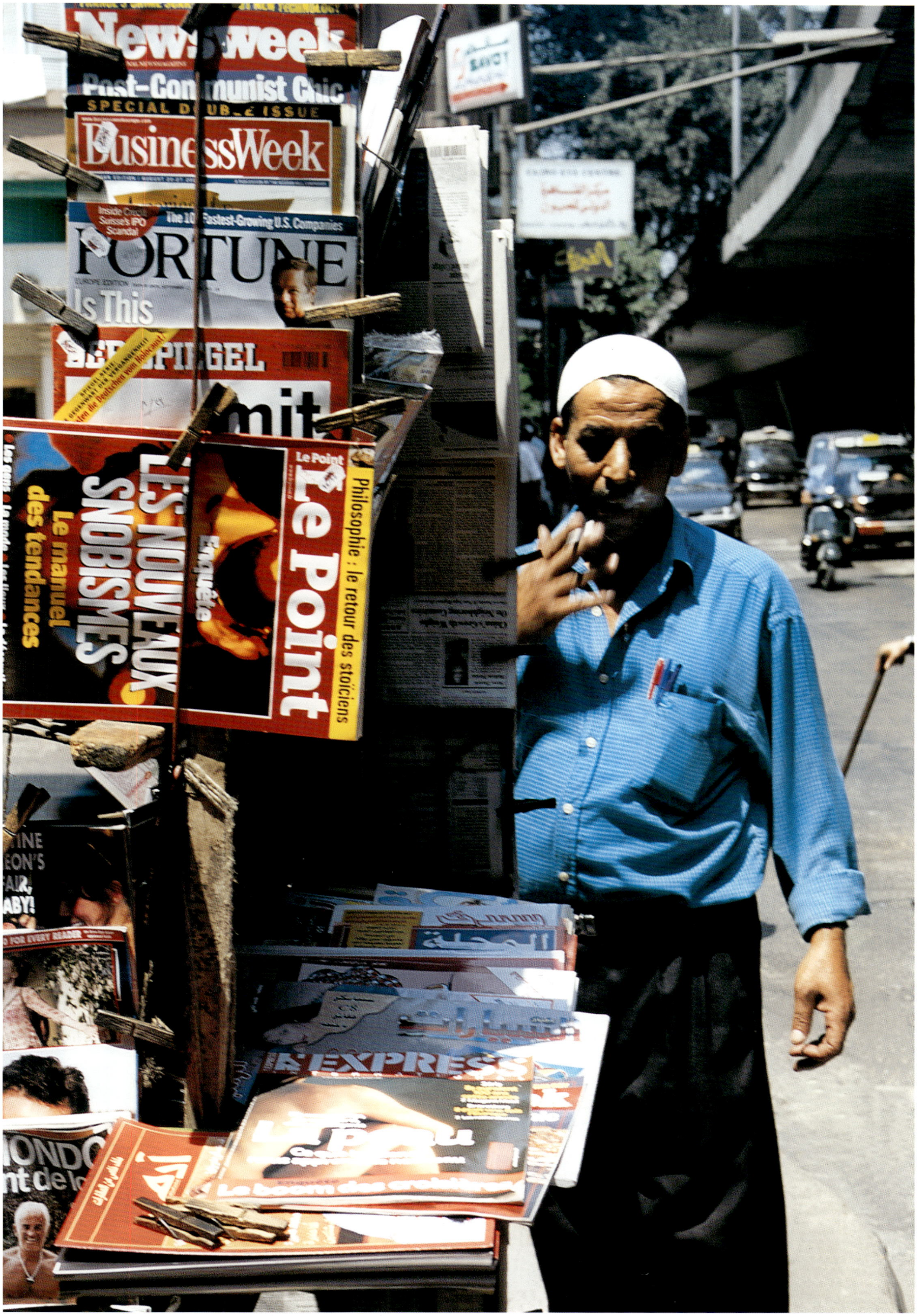


*News vendor, Cairo*

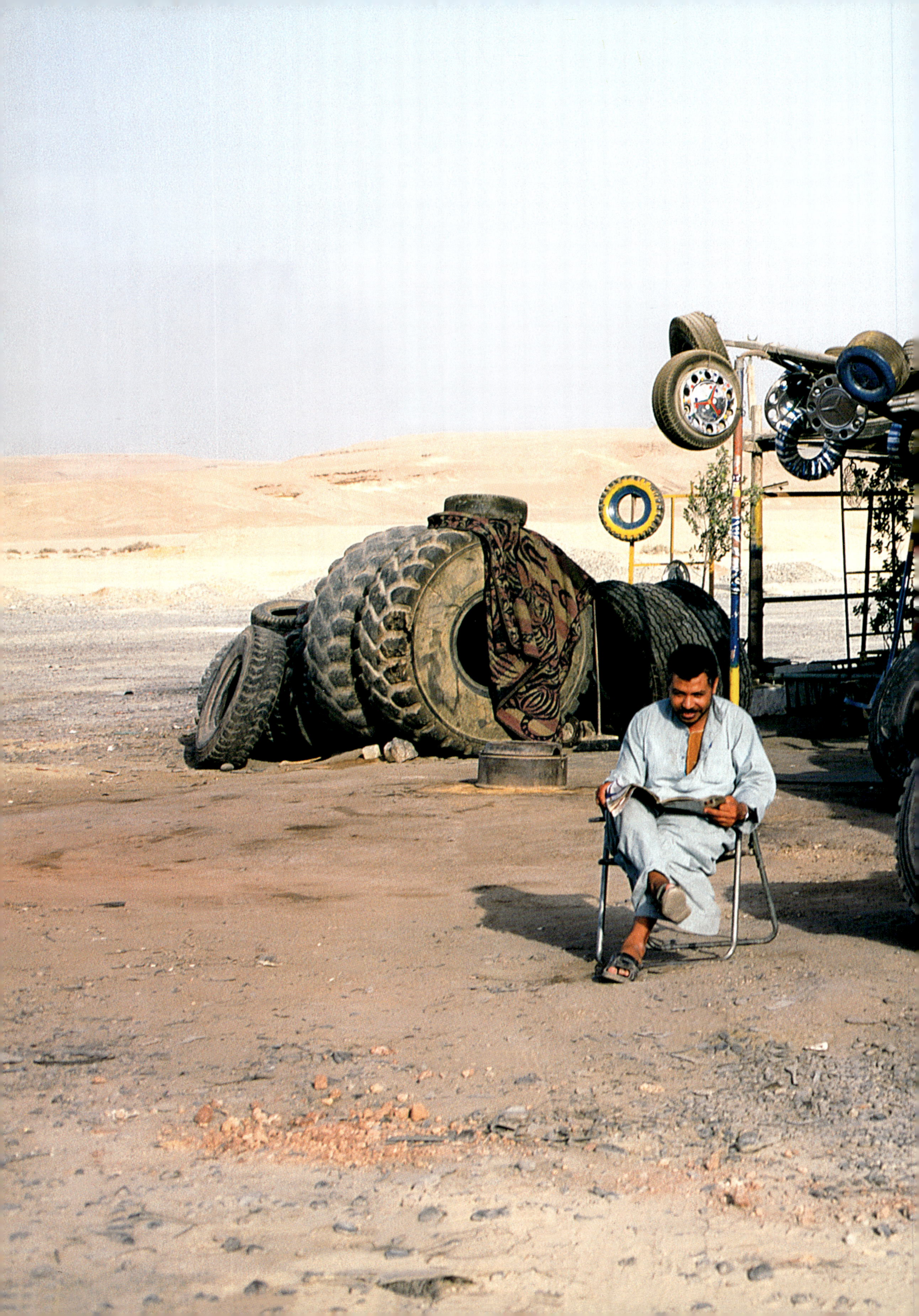

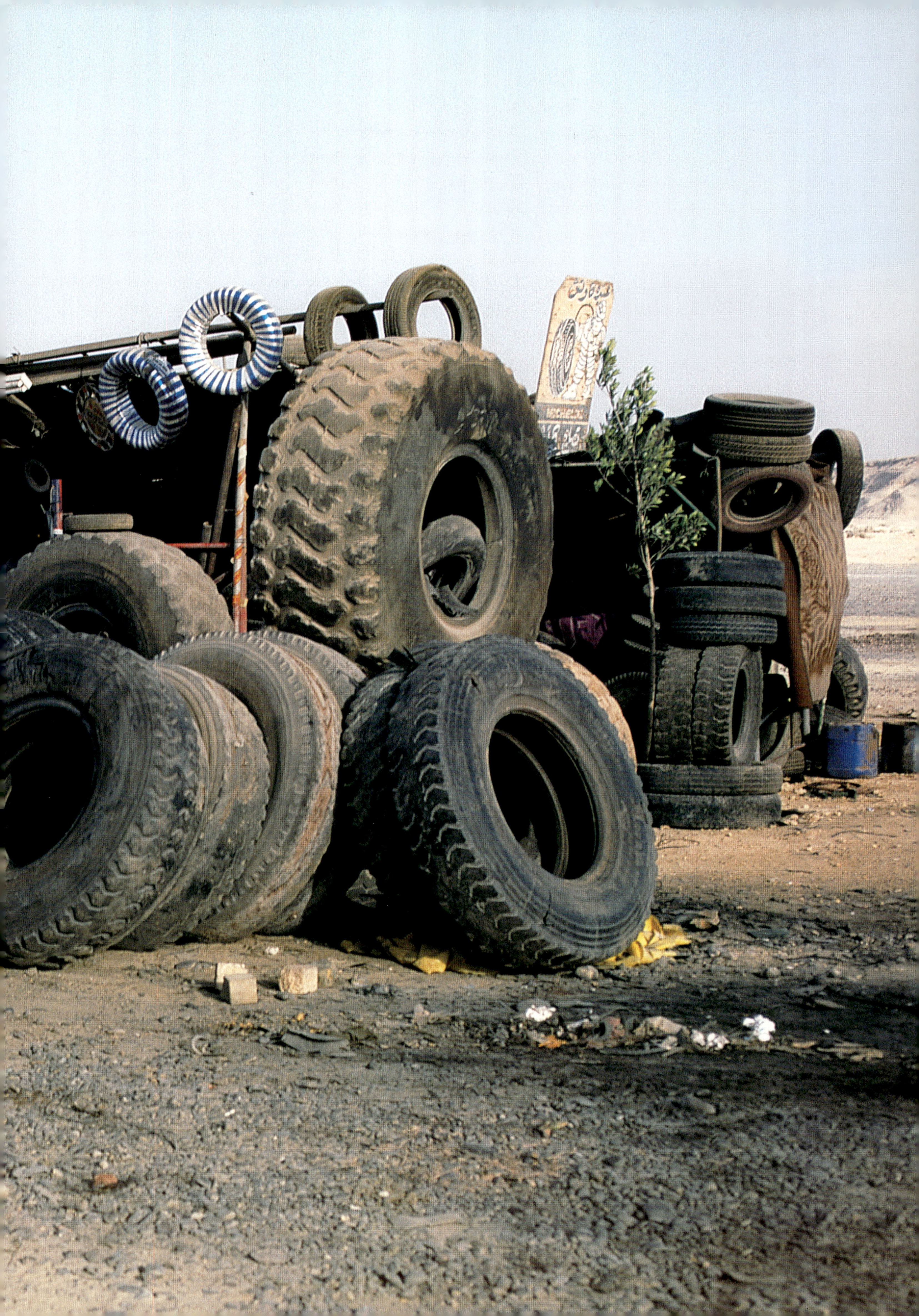

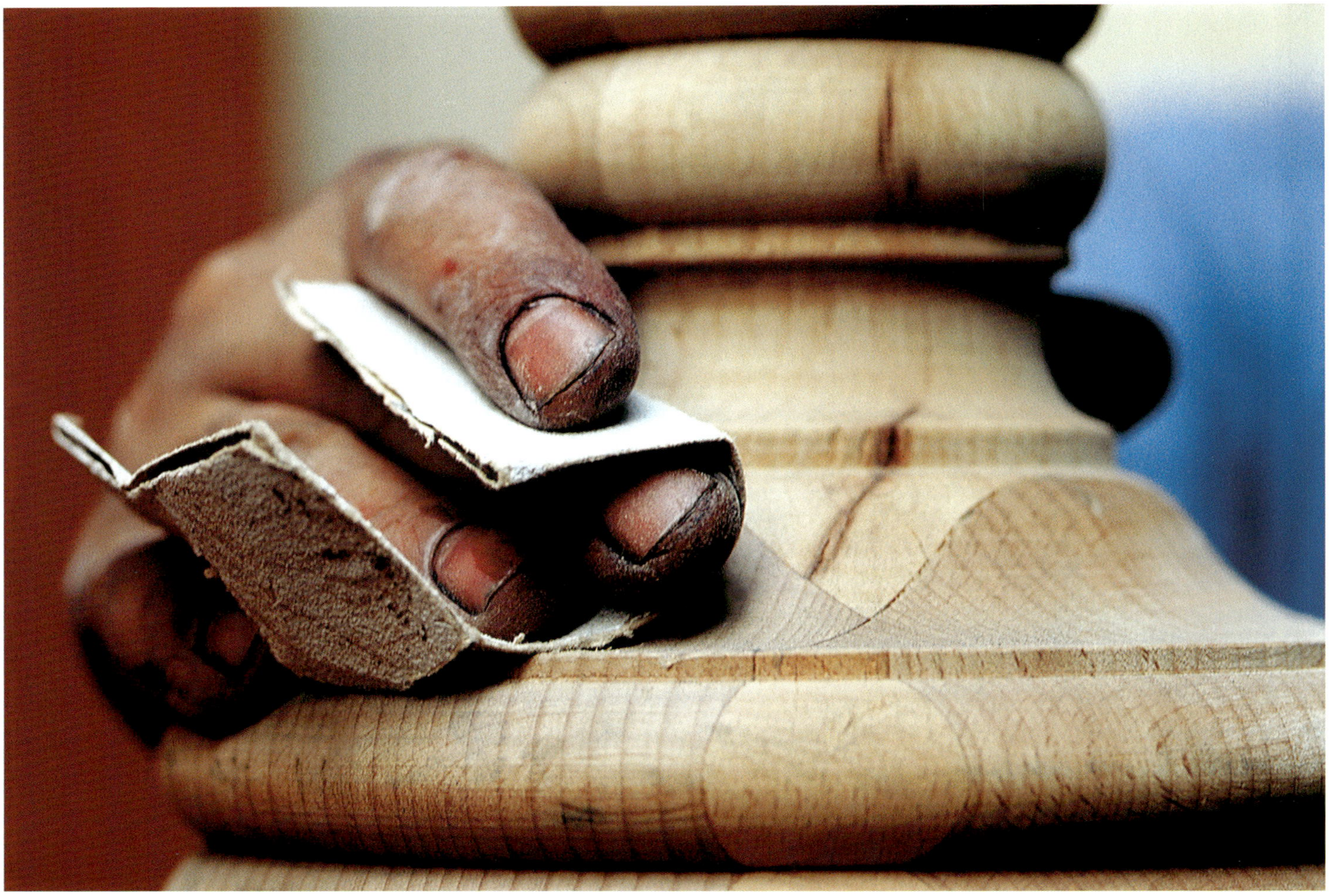

*Previous page: Tire vendor, east coast*

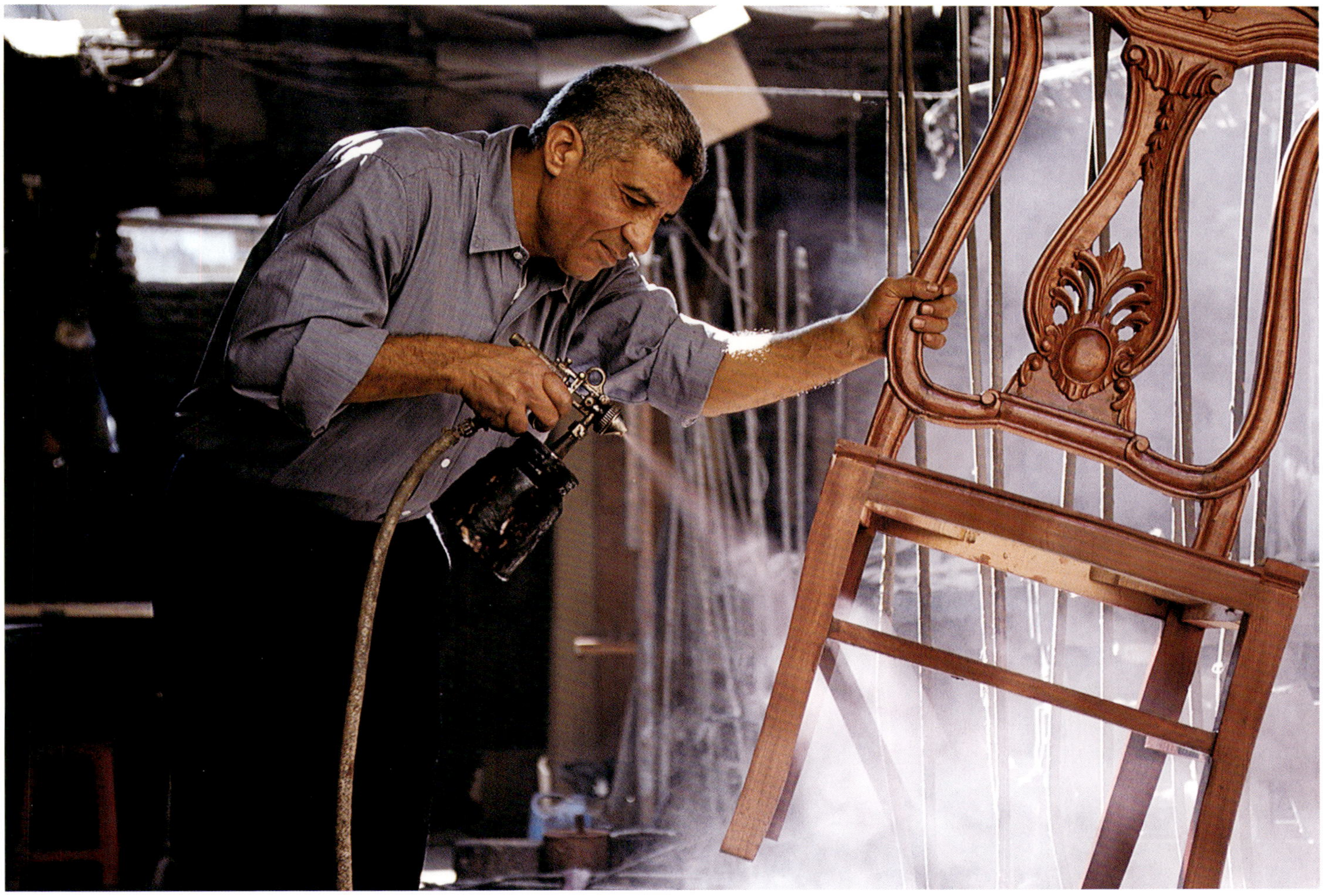

*A joiner at work, Cairo*

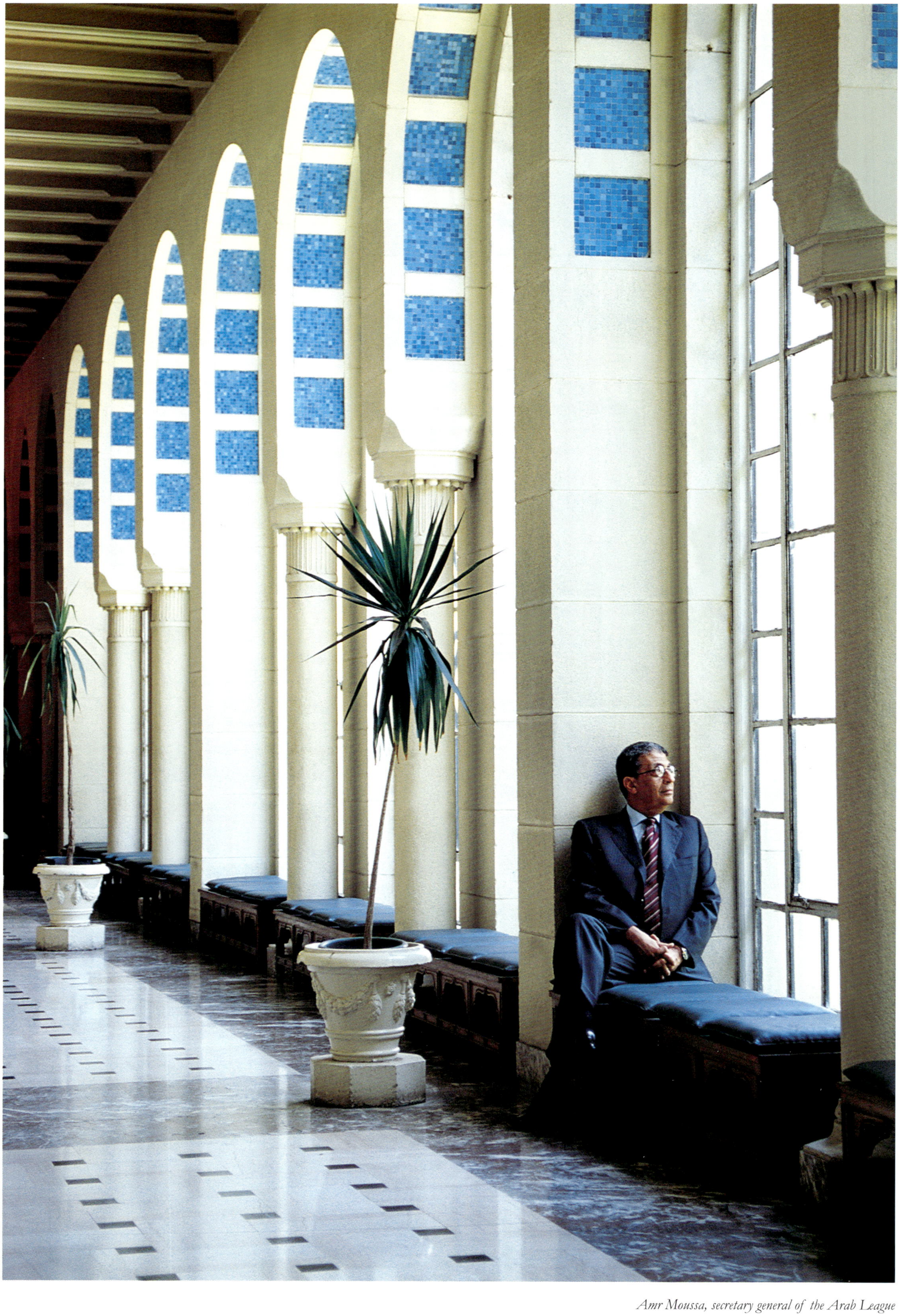

*Amr Moussa, secretary general of the Arab League*

## Amr Moussa

*Secretary general of the Arab League*

"There is a lot of terrain to walk until one can really say, 'Here I am, departing, leaving my culture behind,'" says Amr Moussa, the secretary general of the Arab League. Then he notes the difficult paradox that comes with change. "Egyptian society must cross, must go, must walk, must change and move on, without necessarily sacrifying the basic dimension of its culture."

Moussa's advice for Egyptians is not to be afraid, and to move ahead. "There is always room for change, and all of us—in Egypt and in the other Islamic countries—feel that we have to change," he says.

But progress should not come at the hands of western countries that see the Middle East as a mysterious place that needs to be improved. "I am uncomfortable with the word 'western.' I accept the generic sense of it, but I have my reservations." After all, he notes, political positions vary greatly among western societies—between the United States and Europe, for example, and even among the European countries themselves. "I would like to say to 'westerners' that, first of all, the Arab world is not their enemy. But secondly, that doesn't mean that the Arab world should be considered simply a source of fortune. And thirdly, it could very well be their friend."

Moussa sees extensive distortion of the image of Arab culture and the Arab way of thinking. "I wish that this stereotype would come to an end," he says adamantly. For a start, most people do not have a complete picture of Egypt. "Many western countries have not really discovered Egypt. It is not only what you see in Luxor, Aswan, Cairo, and Sharm al-Sheikh. Egypt is everything: present, past, and future. It is spiritual and it is factual, it is poverty and it is richness. There are so many contradictions one should notice. You can see the bones that pull Egypt to live with its past and other forces that push this country to live with the future. Even its culture is much more diverse than most people realize. As much as we are Arabs, or Muslims, in the majority, or Africans, we are also Mediterranean, and we have a special relationship with Europe."

Egypt was once the home of numerous French, British, Italians, and Greeks, most of whom left the country in 1960s, after the Revolution. The current generation is more likely to come only for a week, to scuba-dive somewhere. "They have a superficial vision of this country," Moussa says. "They may not know Egypt the way the previous generation did."

At the same time, Egyptians can be suspicious of the west. For example, some Egyptian families have spoken out against the reduction of religion classes in schools, blaming this on the influence of America, and reacting by sending their children to classes in mosques.

Egypt has a very long history, Moussa points out, and a very strong life in the present. "We also have our policies and interests!" But that does not mean that certain kinds of help would not be welcome, such as in the areas of science and technology. "This is what would quickly create change, a change that has to serve society itself but can improve only with our approval," says Moussa. "What tarnishes the attempts at change is this kind of interference: 'You have to change and we'll tell you how to change, and to change first when it comes to Islam.'" Moussa thinks that the way the 'west' has dealt with the matter is counterproductive. "The cultural class in Egypt has not been enriched and irrigated lately, and is now in a state of frustration because of the conflict with western societies. The right strategy for these improvements could be more cooperation based on dialogue."

What would Moussa wish for Egypt? "I want to see Egypt promoting cultural relations, because Egypt can do a lot in projecting the cultural dimension of its life. Human development also needs to be underlined and promoted." Both the west and Egypt must keep in mind their shared past; Egyptian culture is actually the foundation of western—and particularly Mediterranean—culture.

As for religion, "There is no problem between Muslims, Christians, and Jews," he declares. "The problem stands in politics." Then what is the cause of the increasing religious radicalism of some groups? "The main reason brings us to politics," Moussa says simply. "It is Palestine."

Of course there are many signs of western culture in Egypt, such as McDonald's, Coca-Cola, and KFC. "Are these the symbols of western countries?" Moussa asks with a smile. "Western food and western policy are two different things. Disagreeing with American policy on the question of Palestine, for example, is something that needs to be analyzed in a different context. One has nothing to do with the other, even though I know that some people are boycotting the hamburger."

Egypt has always played the part of the mediator between the western and the Arab countries. After September 11, its role became more difficult. "Egypt in the past was the bridge, because it was the most modern Arab country," says Moussa. "Now I don't think the west needs a bridge of communication between its society and any part of the Arab world. But on the sensitive issue of the clash of civilizations, Egypt can play a very important role, together with two or three other Arab countries."

Is Egypt moving on? "I believe it is," answers Moussa confidently. "It is the nature of things to move on."

*S. D.*

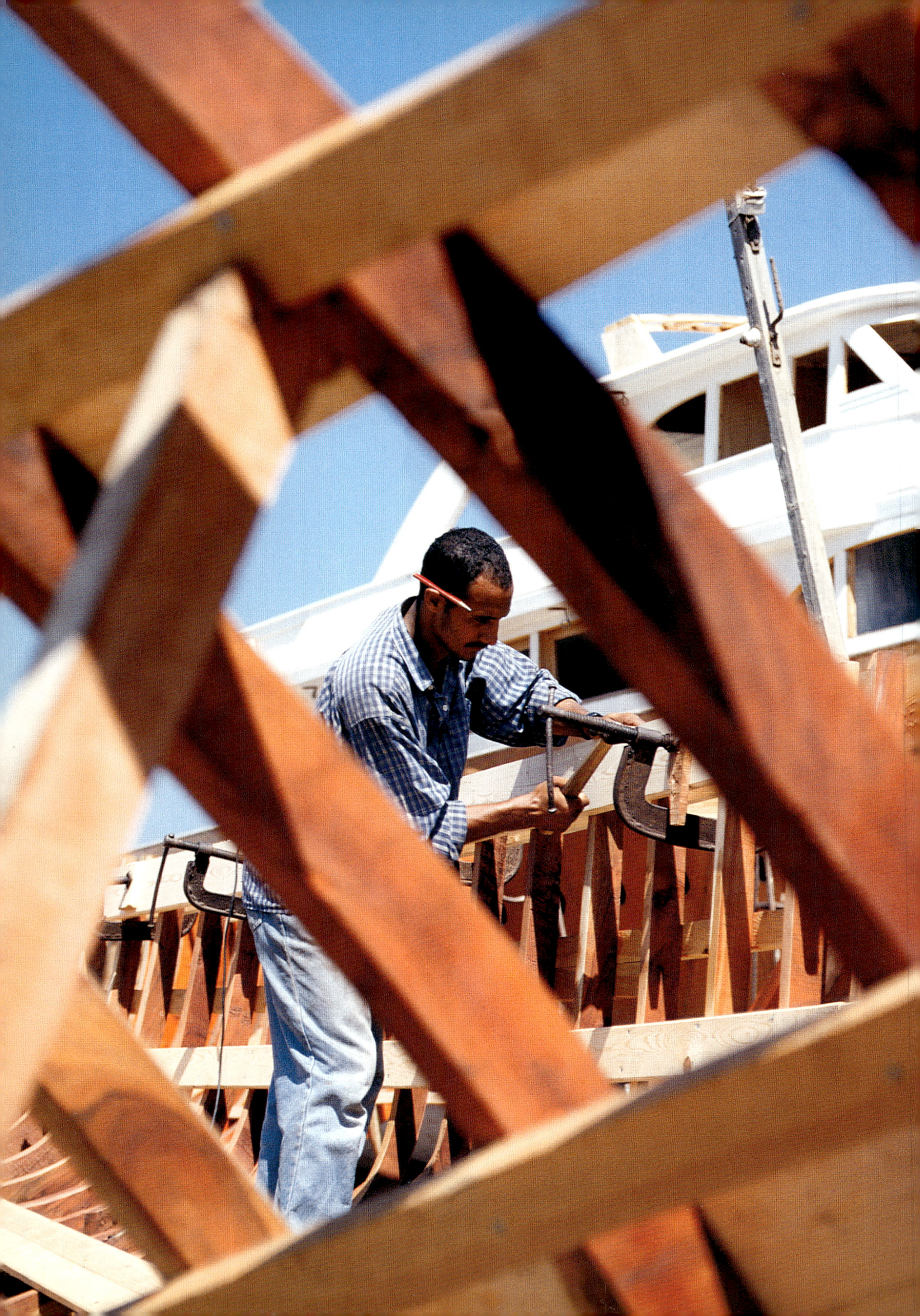

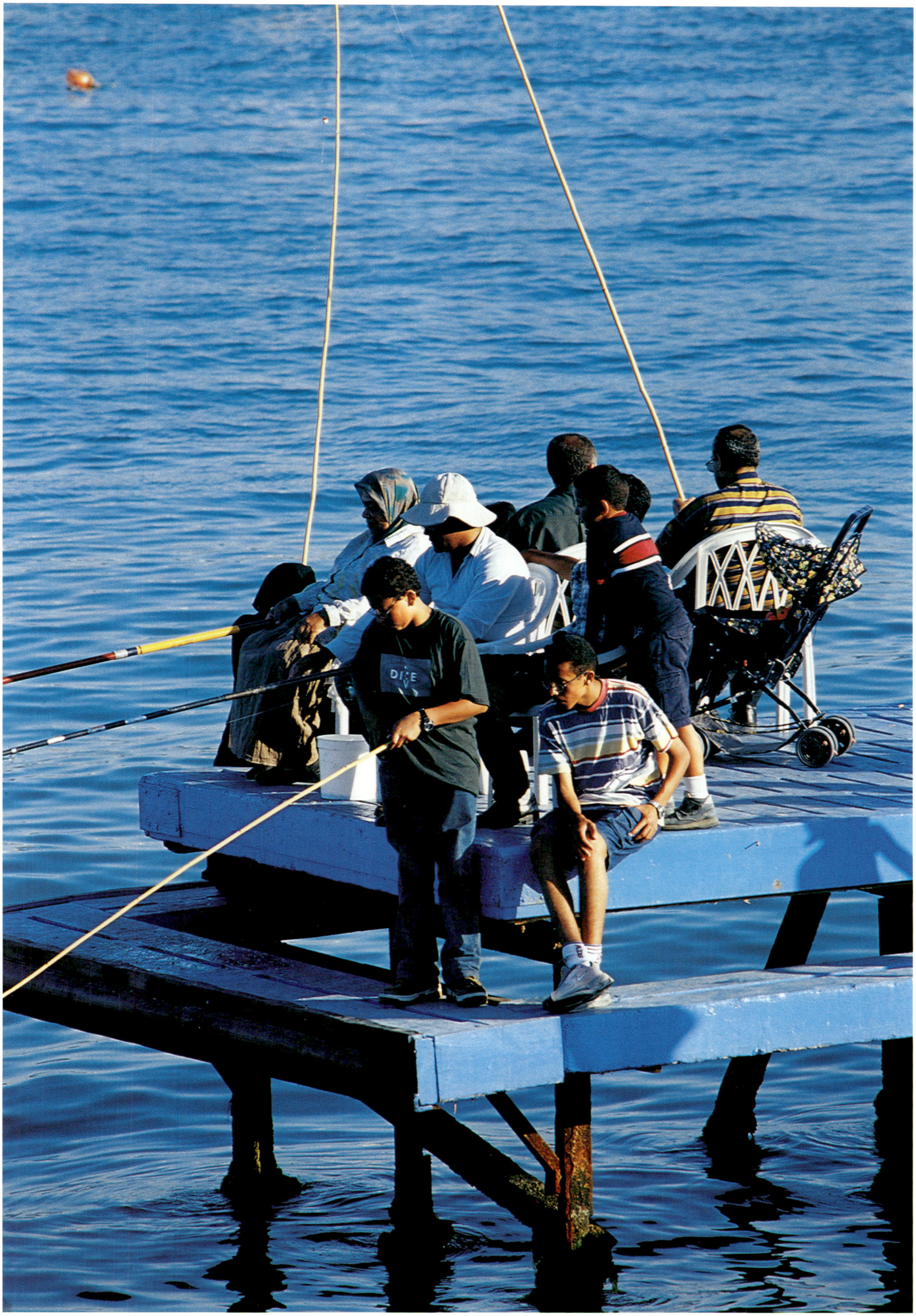

*Boat maker, Alexandria*

*Amateur fishermen, Alexandria*

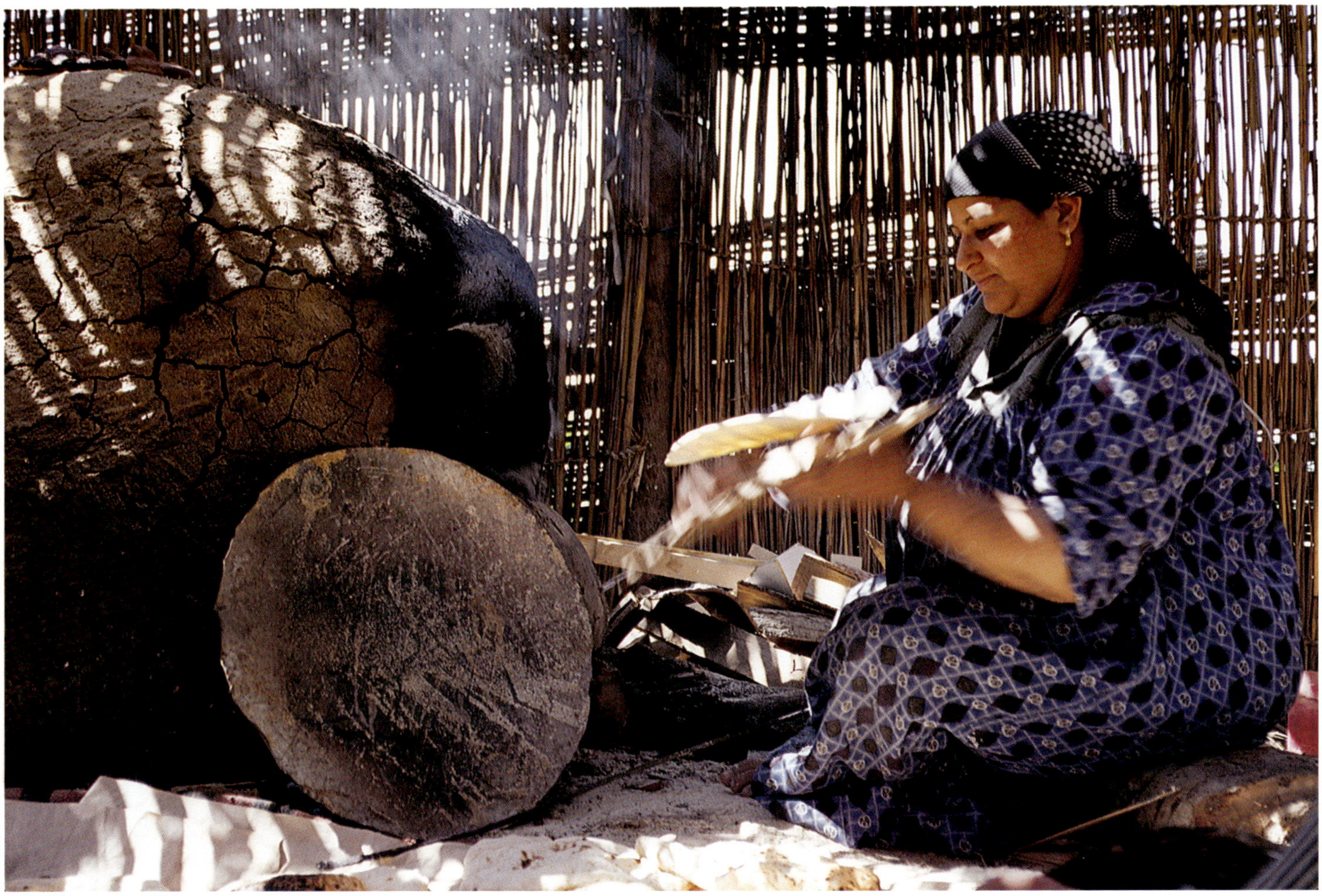

*Making bread, Saqqara*

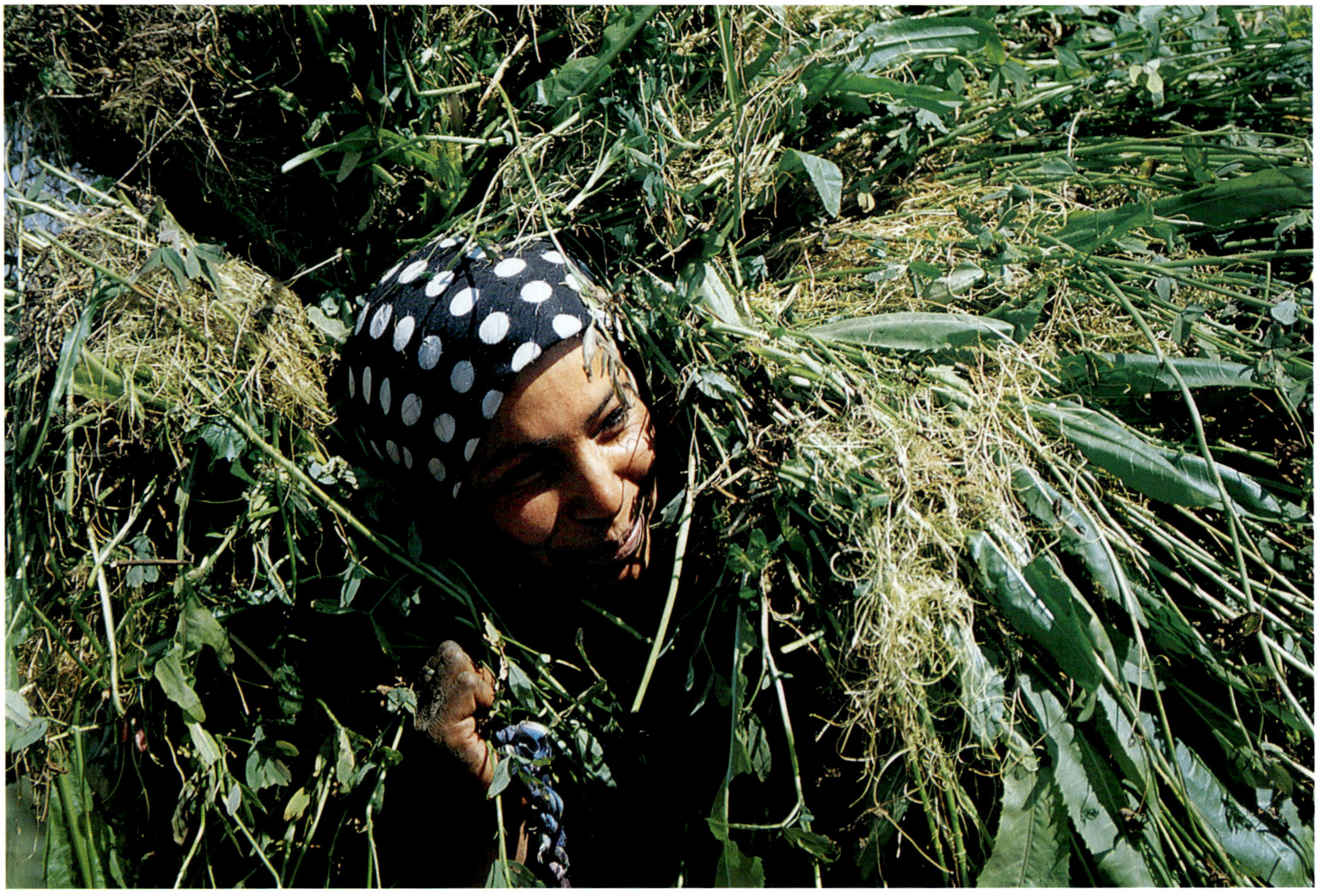

*Farm worker, Saqqara*

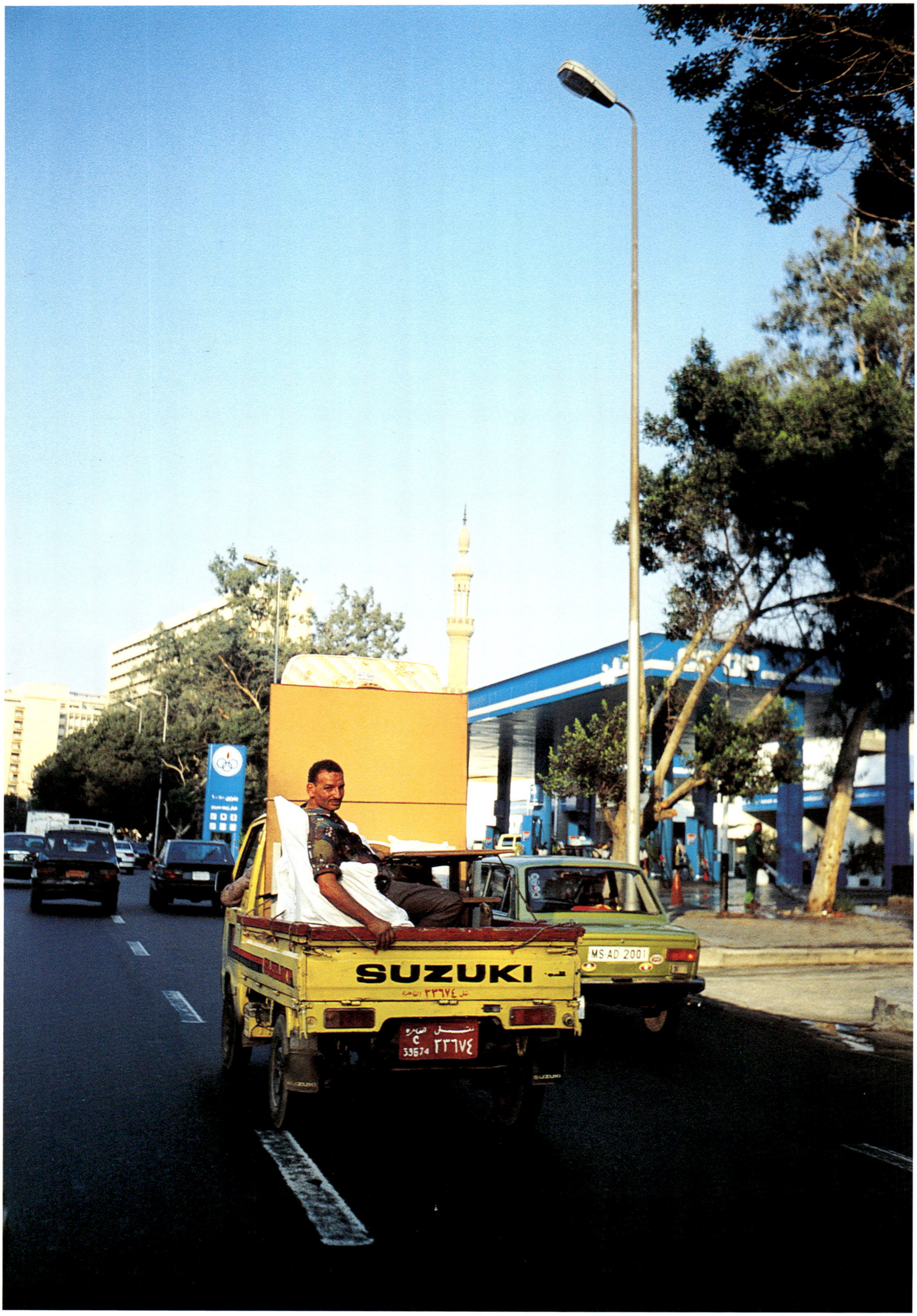

*On the road to Heliopolis, Cairo*

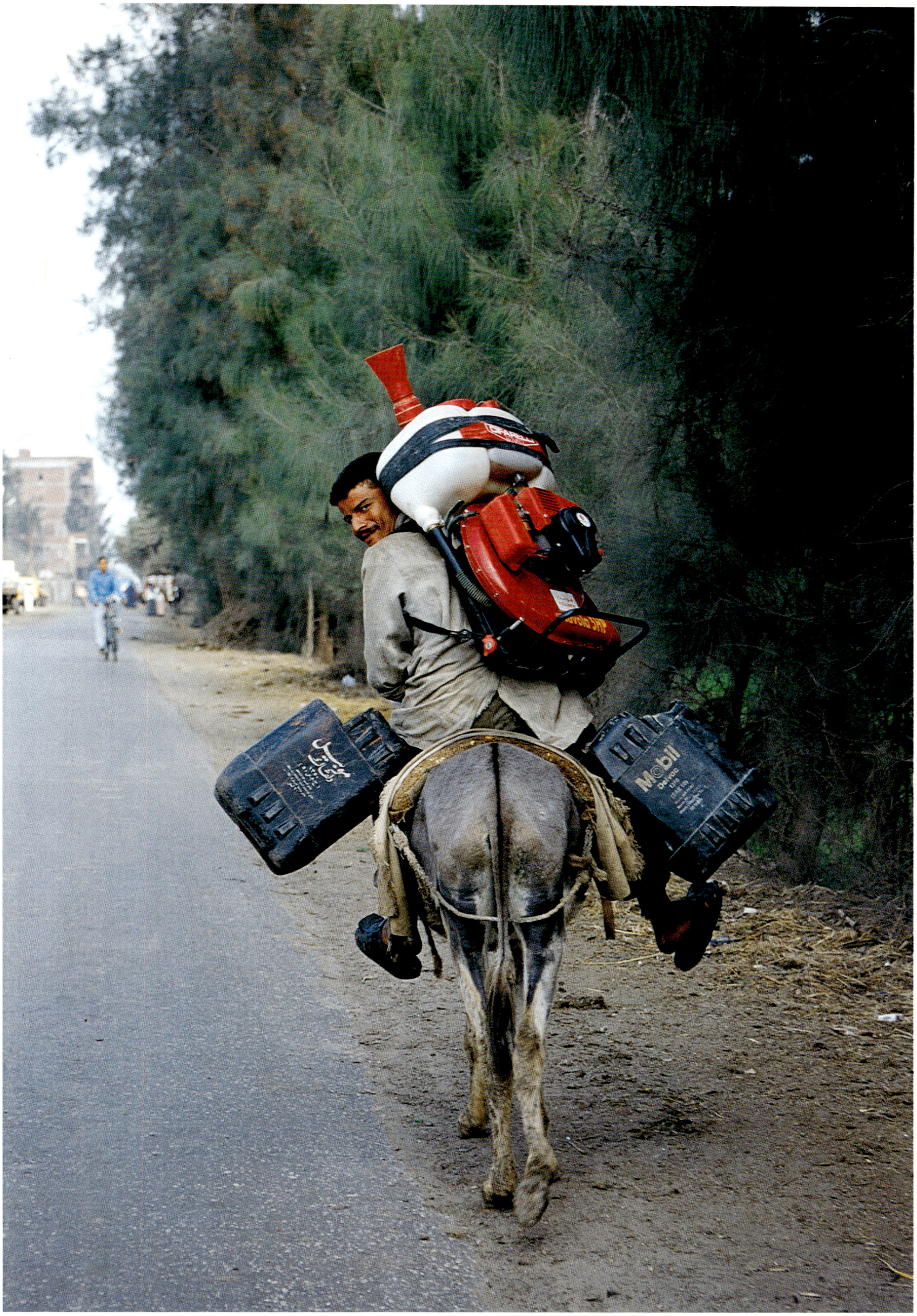


*On the road to Damietta*

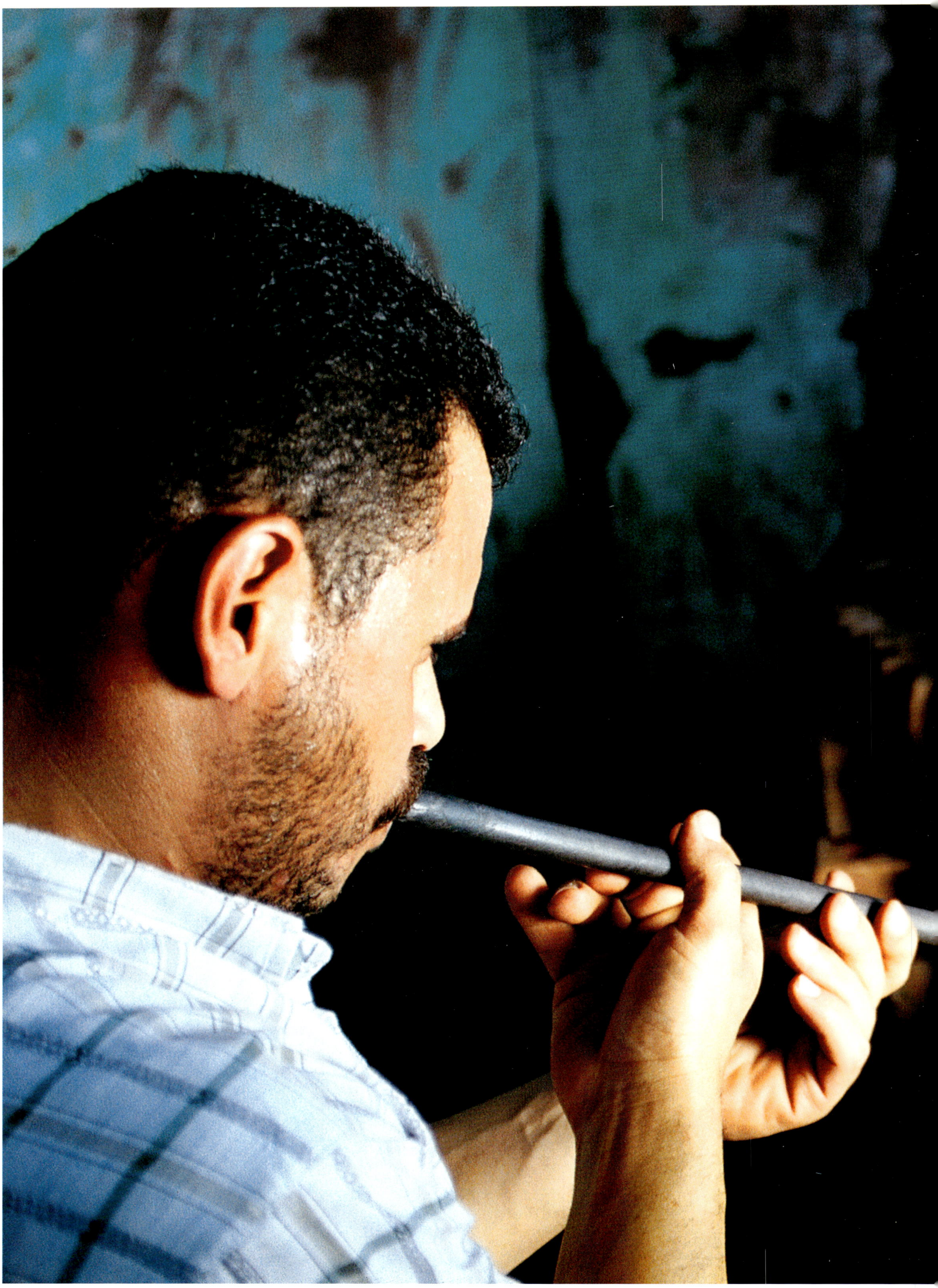

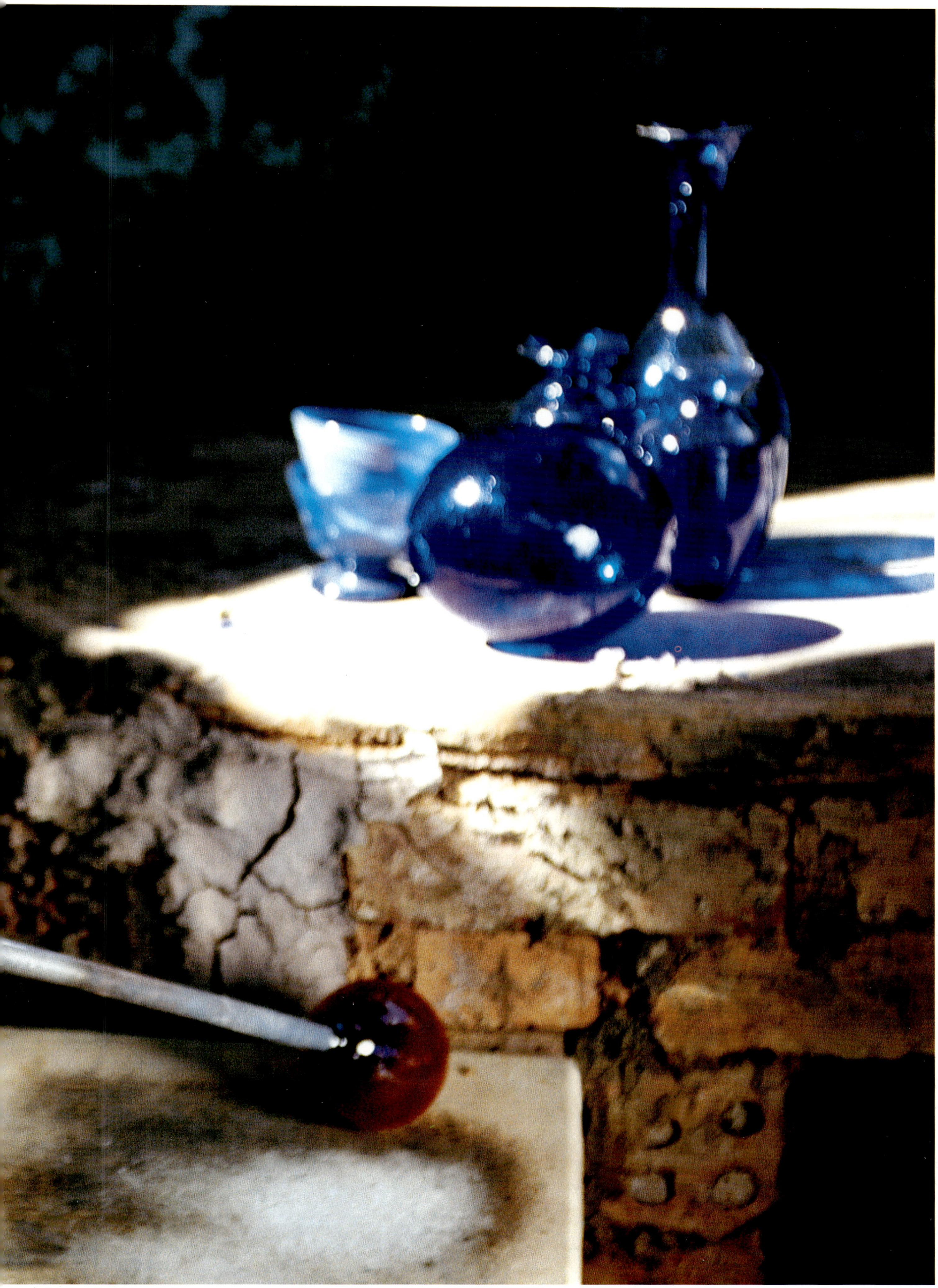

*Glass blower, Beni Suef*

## Umberto Vergine

*General manager of IEOC (Eni) in Egypt*

Umberto Vergine first came to Egypt in November 1999 from West Africa, where he was working and living with his family. The contrast was immediate. "Cairo Airport was clean," he says. "The streets didn't have holes. But the number of people out on the streets was even greater than what I was used to." The first day ended in a pleasant hotel on the Corniche, with a striking view of the Nile.

At the time, Vergine, an Italian, was the general manager of one of the two operating companies through which Eni works in partnership with the Egyptian Petroleum Corporation. "I left the country eighteen months later," he explains. "I came back in October 2002 and I hope to stay at least two years, and leave within four." He is now the general manager of the Egyptian branch of IEOC, also part of the Eni Group, which manages all oil and gas exploration and production activities in the country.

Vergine quickly noticed a particular way of approaching business. "In any field, Egyptians work hard to find an area of common dialogue, a sort of compromise. It is what I call the 'Khan al-Khalili,'" he says, referring to Cairo's large bazaar, "the art of haggling!"

As for social interactions, he felt a strong sense of friendship, which is not often part of other countries' cultures. "What also surprised me is the class-conscious point of view of this diverse society." And the levels of background, education, and culture are extremely varied. "Compared to other countries it is easier here to meet people who studied and worked abroad," notes Vergine.

After returning to Egypt, he is still able to find interesting aspects of the country, especially in the professional field. "The country changed, but I changed as well. Perhaps I became less open," he points out.

"The present economic crisis has a strong impact on the society, creating enormous limits in terms of freedom," he observes. The need for money is getting stronger, and poorer Egyptians are ready to give up their pride and self-respect to get any kind of job in order to meet their daily needs.

Nonetheless, the country's atmosphere is still the same. "This is not a country of big changes, but a place with continuity, where the cosmopolitan culture is very strong, as well as the wish to look beyond its borders. Egyptians are drawn to a Mediterranean dimension more than a Middle Eastern one."

Is Egypt able to ride the wave? "Because of the language problem it is difficult for me to access to information and therefore to understand the domestic politics," he says. "But I feel that the country is constantly exploiting the opportunities offered by international politics, as well as playing an important role in public opinion, while achieving economic stability." Vergine explains that improvements such as the attraction of foreigner investment, industrial development, the sharing of investments in the bordering countries, and the new business partnerships are simply a result of all this. "It is a movement that comes from the foreign politics, not from the domestic side."

Eni considers Egypt the most important country in which it operates abroad, not only because of its fifty years' partnership with the country, which has given the company its privileged position among its competitors, but also because of its high rate of production. "Egypt is a mature country, where the prospects of new discoveries are becoming lower as the research activity has become very intensive," says Vergine. "We have a competitive company in a saturated market."

Is Eni's competitiveness affected by the Egyptian companies it works with? "Yes, possibly," answers Vergine. "We sometimes have to work with local companies subject to bureaucracy and to governmental rules. For example, these companies are sometimes too overloaded and therefore unable to give us the attention that we need."

What is Eni's future in Egypt? "We are waiting for the recovery of the national economy," explains Vergine, "as well as for a swing in the strategies of government politics."

As for his personal experience, Vergine is aware of the good and the bad aspects of being an expatriate. "In a foreign country you have the advantage of comparing yourself with a different culture. This could be problematic, but in the end, living far from your normal routine is extremely stimulating." The bad side is being far from family and friends. "Here my family and I live a kind of artificial life, as we know it is temporary," Vergine explains. "It is very important to be able to balance what you are doing here with what you will do when you go back home."

*S. D.*

*Trimming a date palm in Zamalek, Cairo*

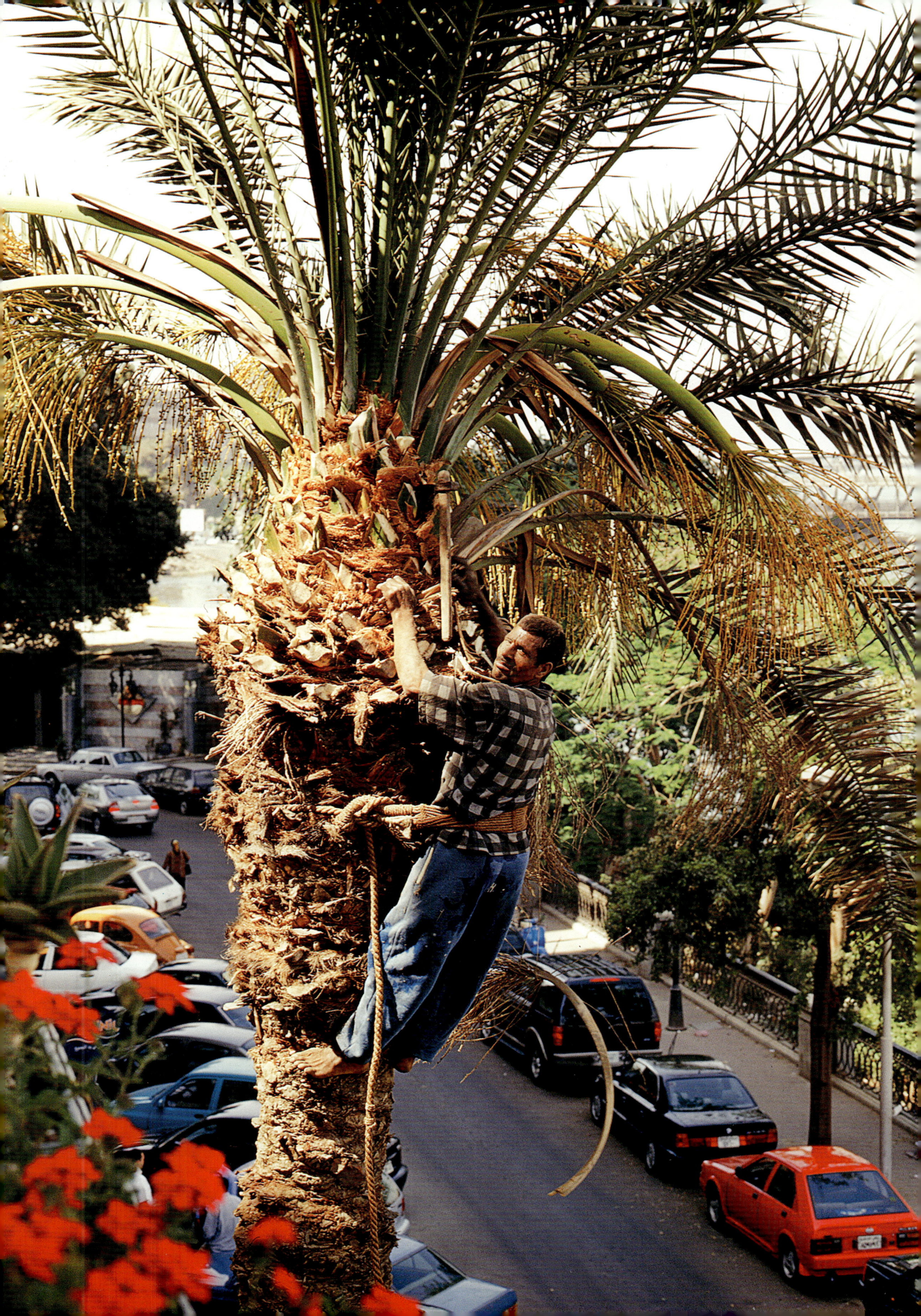

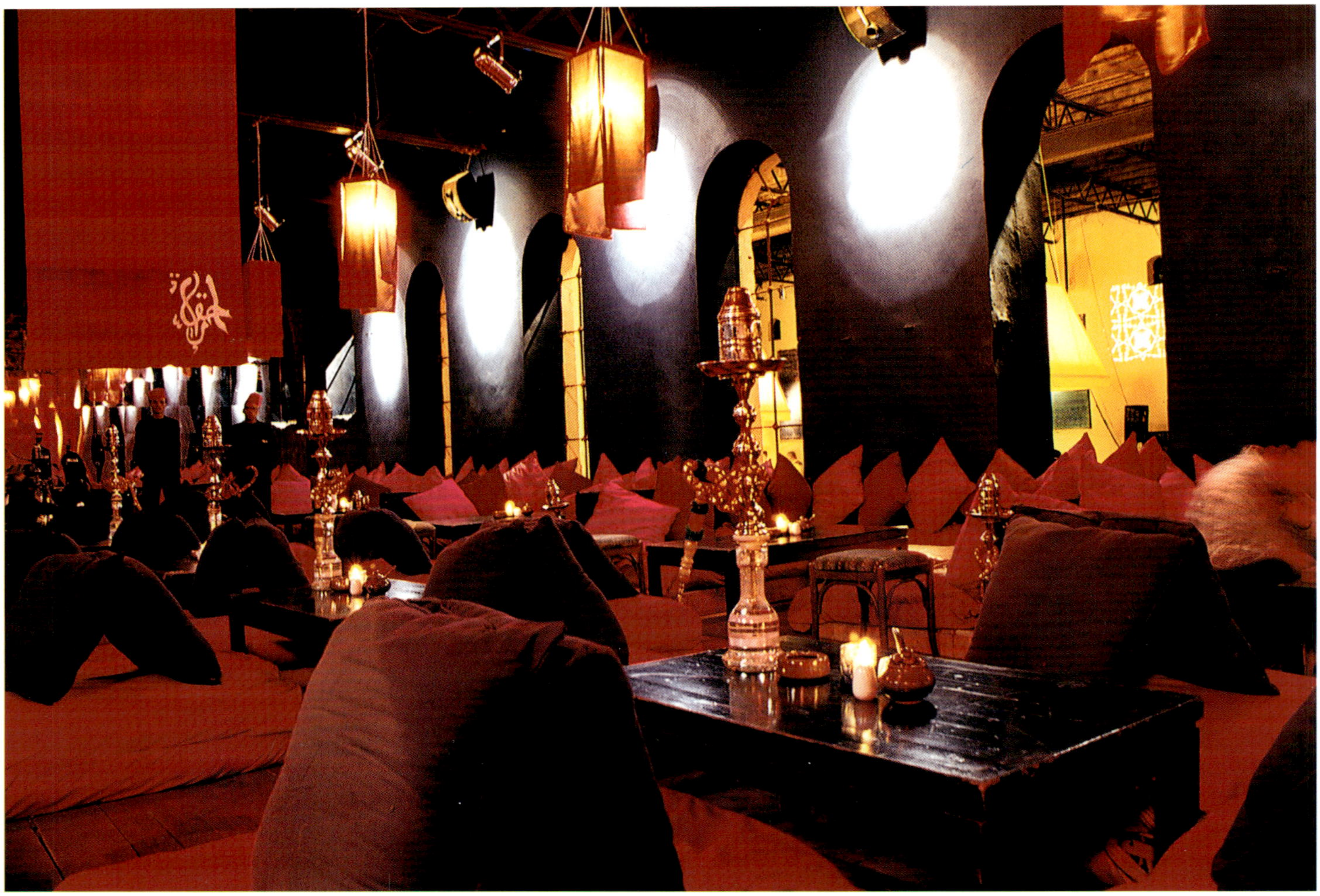

*A Ramadan tent, Cairo*

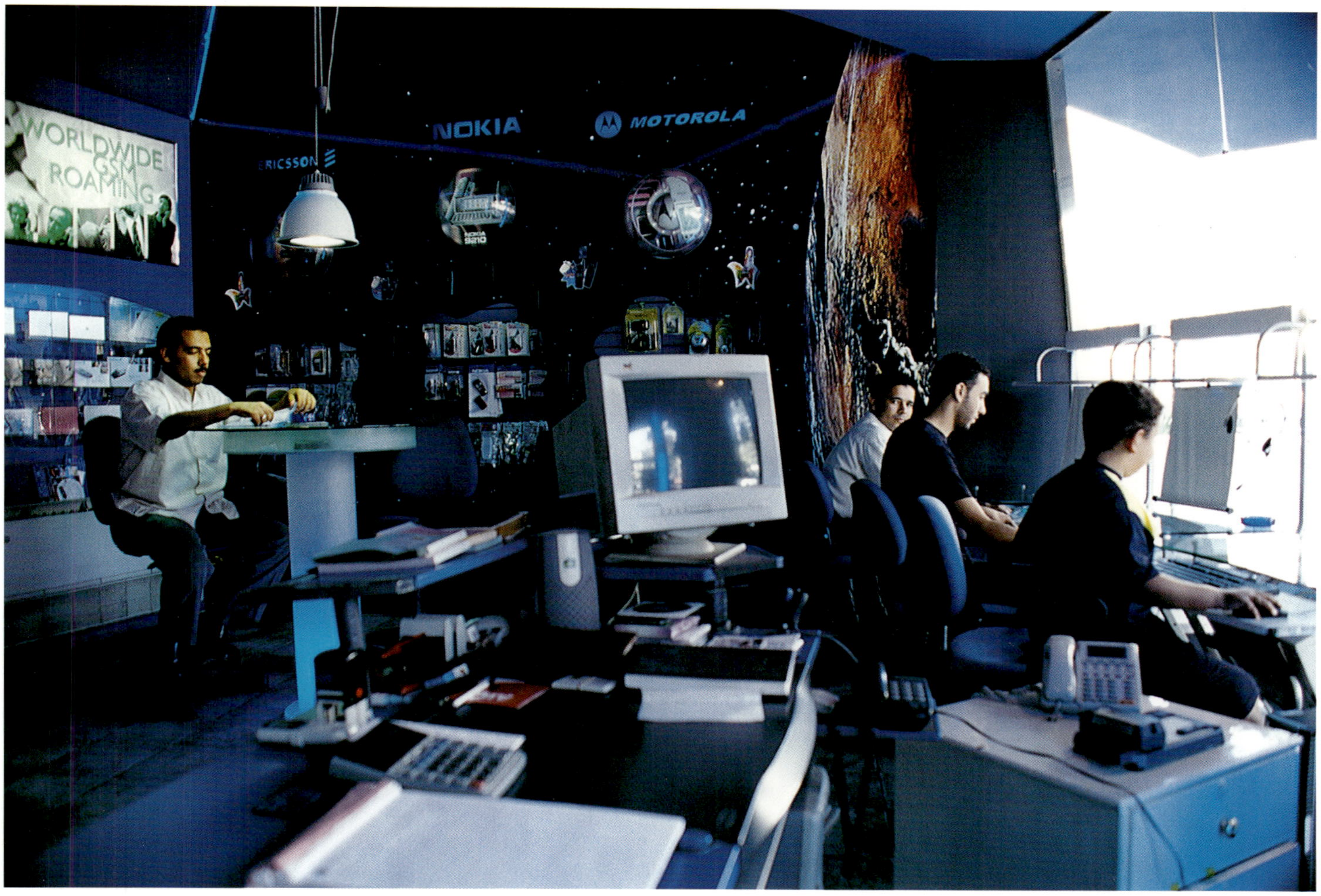


*An internet café, Cairo*

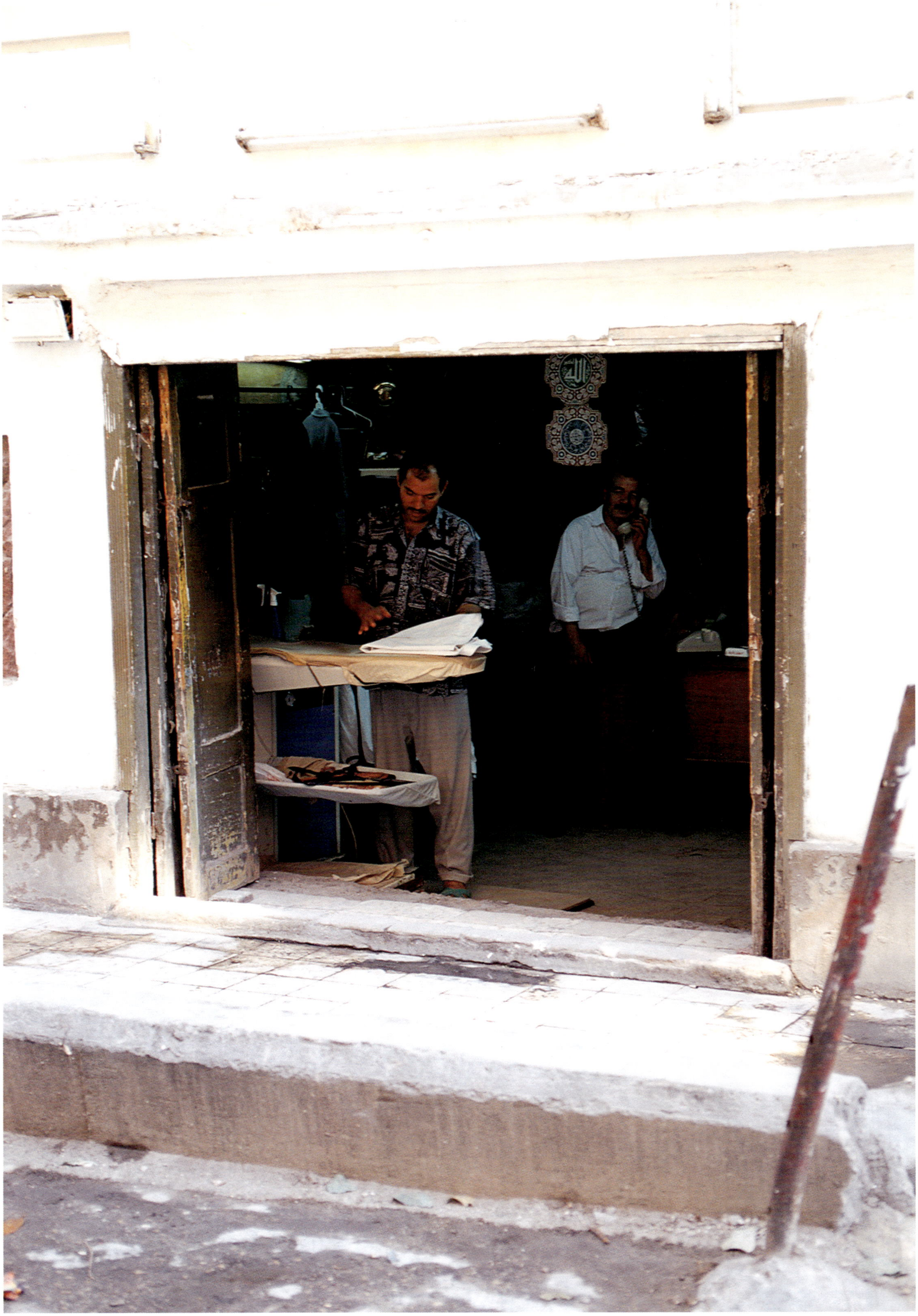

*A local* makwagi *(ironing man), Zamalek, Cairo*

*A local* bawwab *(porter), Garden City, Cairo*

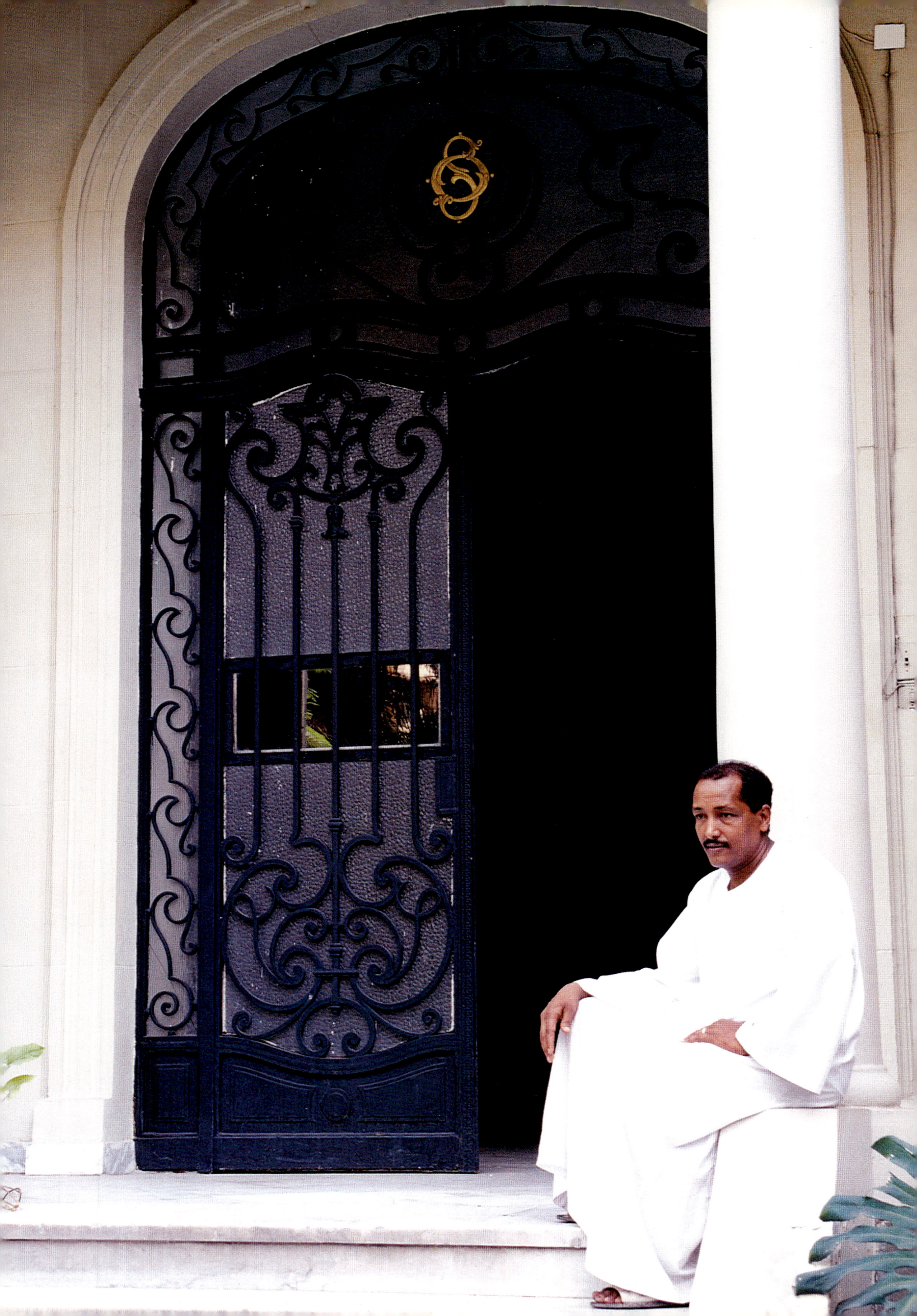

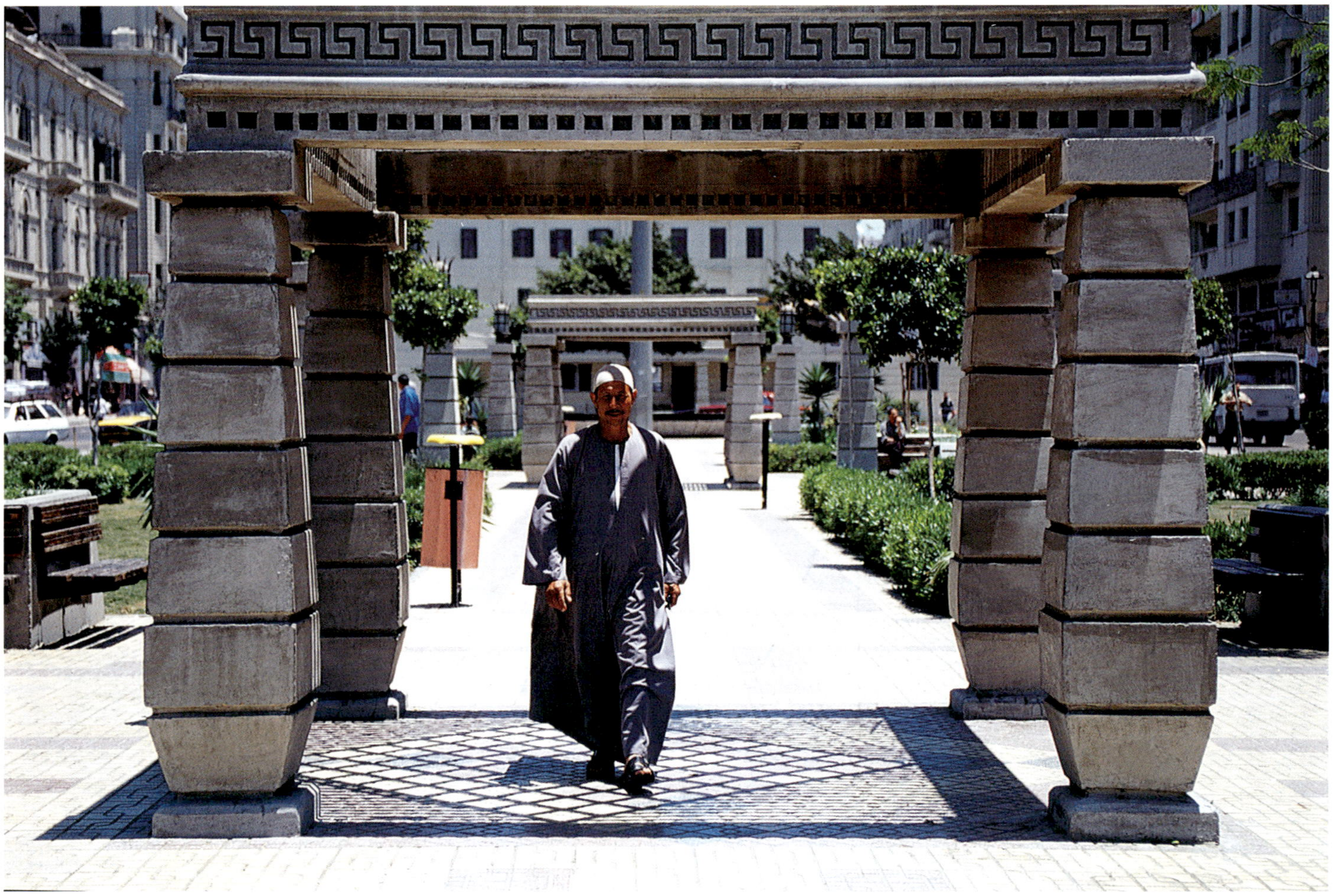

*Midan 'Urabi, Alexandria*

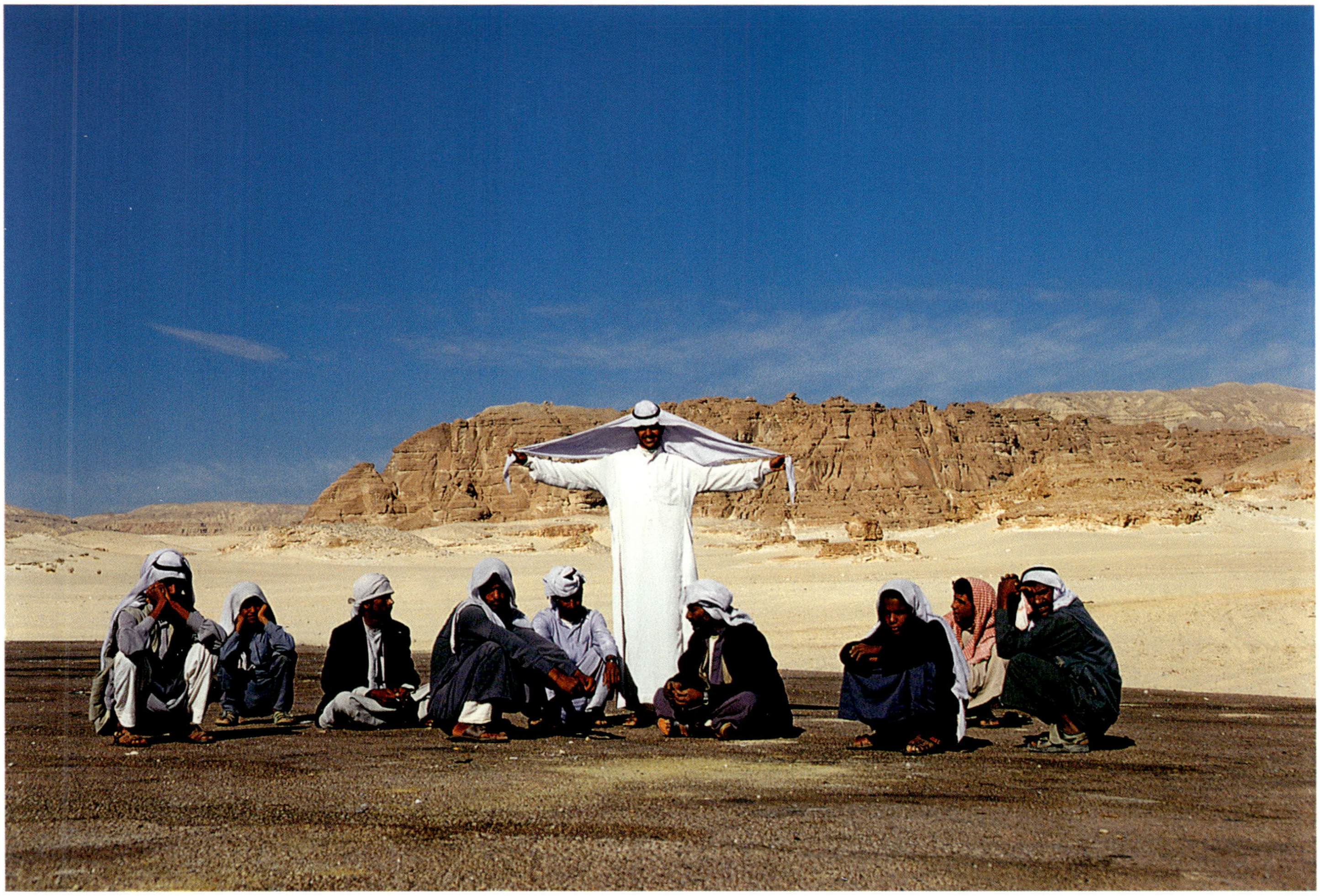

*Bedouins on the road to St. Catherine, Sinai*

## Norbert Schiller

*Photographer*

"I arrived in Egypt in February 1978. I didn't really choose it," says the half-American, half-Austrian photographer Norbert Schiller, who has been living and working in Cairo for a quarter of his life. He is on the verge of ending his Egypt chapter: after traveling to Iraq to document the aftermath of the 2003 war for the European Press Agency, he and his family are relocating to Lebanon, but he continues to visit Egypt regularly.

Schiller first came to Cairo with some people he met in Greece, who aroused his curiosity through their enthusiasm for Egypt. "I arrived in Cairo at 11:30 at night from Athens. What amazed me was that it was midnight and downtown was completely packed. They say that New York is a city that never sleeps. My first impression of Cairo was of a city that never slept," Schiller remembers.

His memories from that period are very vivid. "The noise at that time was to me a source of life. The smells were beautiful, and even the garbage in the street was unique in a very special way. It wasn't in the form of plastic bags, like it is today."

Schiller can trace his life's progression as it relates to Egypt. "My past was that of an adventurer, exploring every nook and cranny the country had to offer." Then around 1990 there came a change: he came back to Egypt after a three-year break. "I returned a different person. I had a job and I was married. I grew as a person, husband, and father."

When he imagines visiting Egypt in the future, he is cautiously optimistic. "I hope that I have left in time to be able to return on visits and be able to find only what I love about the country." But he is not sure if this is possible. Initially he had the impression that everything was for the better in Egypt, but as time wore on, he began to see failure, such as the neglect of the environment. Admittedly Schiller thinks that too much damage has already been done. "As Cairo grew it began to lose its little-big-city identity. Suddenly quiet neighborhood streets became thoroughfares. Trees were knocked down to make room for mosques or ugly apartment complexes or shopping malls, and the noise became a sort of frustration. The sad thing about people living in areas with too much noise is that they cannot appreciate quiet," Schiller says. "Cairo was unable to balance what is considered modern and the beauty that had been prevalent over the ages. Basically, Cairo couldn't handle growth well."

But Schiller is not the kind of man to give up. Married to a Lebanese woman and father of two children, he is ready to move on, holding on to the memories and no longer fighting the system. And on the whole, the country has treated him well. "Egypt is good to foreigners. With a small amount of money you can have a good standard of life here. Travelers are treated like kings, it's easy and cheap to get a resident's visa, there are decent places and restaurants to go to." Schiller looks at Egypt as a kind of sponge: "It takes all this abuse—and you can saturate it. People can come, can abuse it, and can leave. In many ways you can start a good life here. That's why Cairo attracts foreigners."

But there is also the down side: "The kind of life you live here is hard to leave!" says Schiller, who knows foreigners who have claimed many times that they are leaving the country and have never left. "It is one of those countries that makes it very easy to live, and in a way this is bad, because it's not the greatest and cleanest place to stay."

Schiller learned a great deal about Egyptian culture by working as English teacher and interacting with the students. Once he asked them to write about their ideal kind of woman or man. He found that the young men had very similar ideas about what they wanted. "The twenty male students gave me the exact same answer: good mother, good Muslim, and good homemaker to look after me." The young women, though, were quite different. "It is amazing what goes on inside women's heads. They have much more variety of thoughts and many more opinions. They feel uncomfortable talking about these things to other Egyptians, but with foreigners they feel safe."

Working as photographer in Egypt has not always been easy. "Here you learn to work with the system," Schiller says. He worked out how to get what he wanted by negotiating, but the process often involved a certain amount of abuse. "When they see a foreigner with a camera shooting, there is always a lot of reaction. They think you are looking at the bad side of Egypt," he explains. "I always have this philosophy: I do what I do, I never stay—I shoot and leave!"

*S. D.*

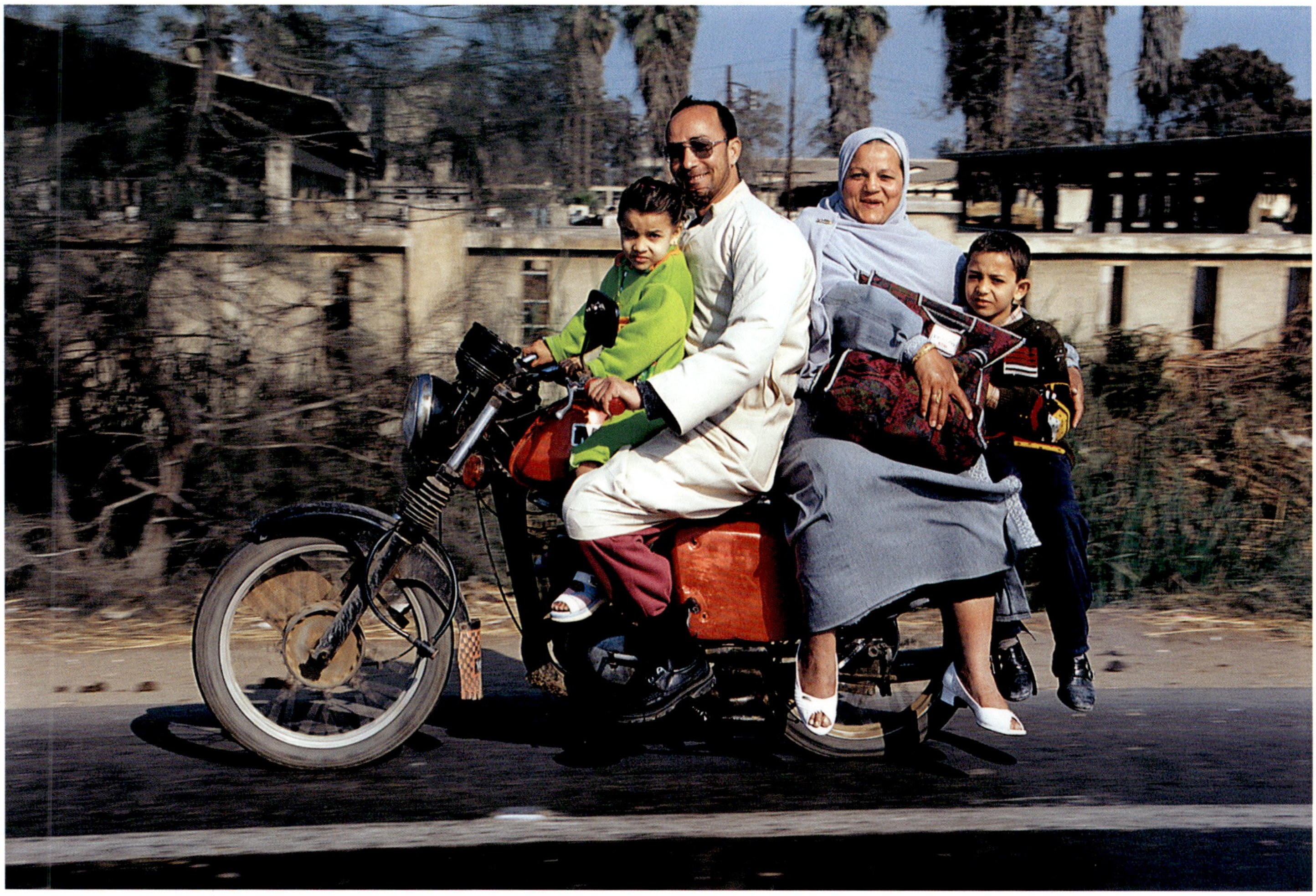

*A family on a motorbike, Damietta*

# Spirit

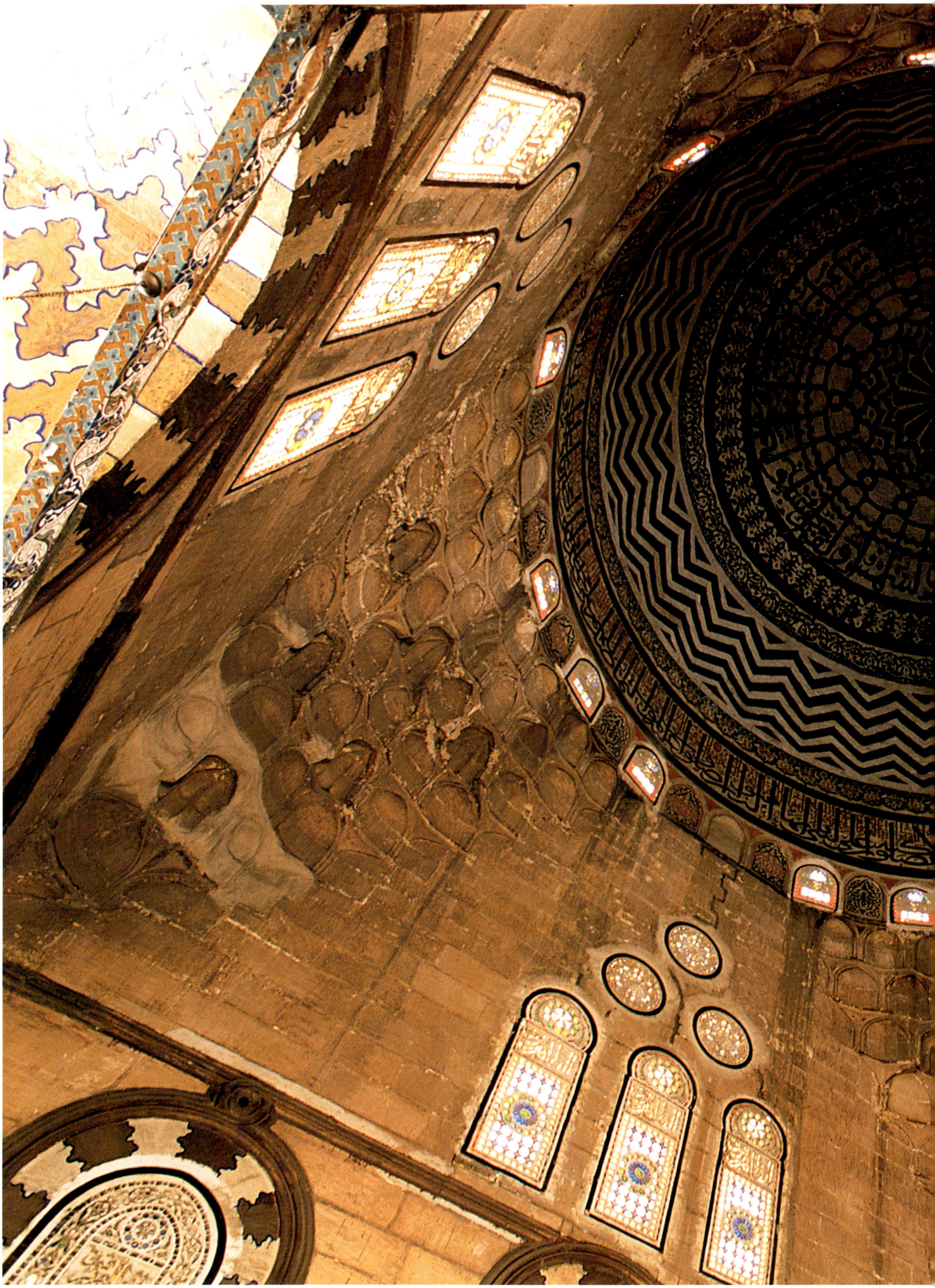

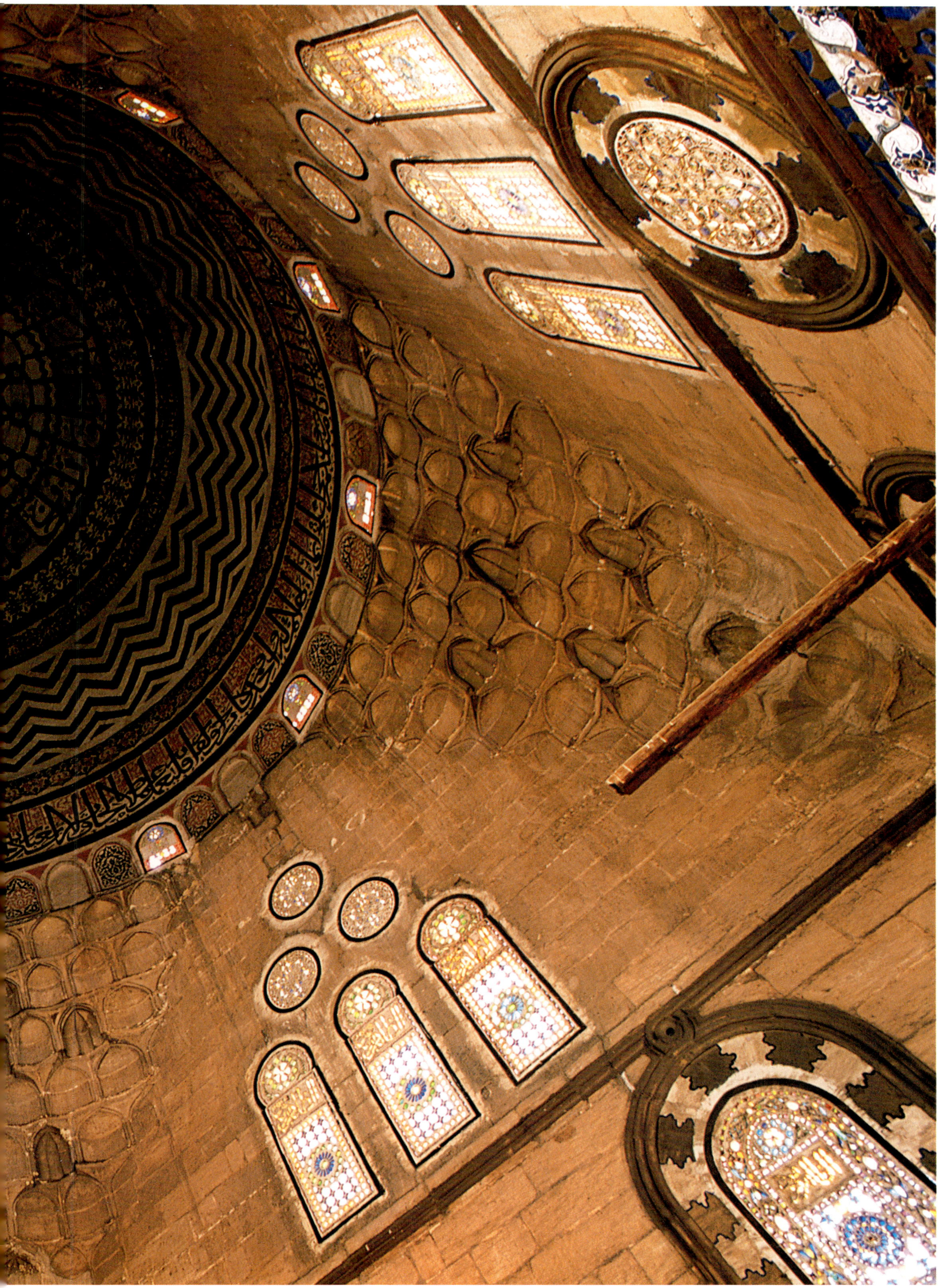

*One of the stone domes of the Sultan Farag Ibn Barquq Mosque (1411 A.D.), City of the Dead, Cairo*

One of the main reasons people are drawn to Egypt, touched by it, and fall in love with it, has to do with what can only be called the country's spirit. After all, almost all the immense structures that survive from pharaonic times were created because of the ancient Egyptians' concern for their spirits, the part of them that did not die.

Hieroglyphs, cut deep into the stone to make sure they would not be erased, praised the rulers of the sky. Several of the world's current-day major religions converge in Egypt, causing the spirit of the country to grow even stronger. In the Old Testament, the chosen people were enslaved in Egypt, eventually traveling across the parted Red Sea. The time of the Israelites' exile in the country even offered a lesson in kindness: "Love ye therefore the stranger," says the Book of Deuteronomy, "for ye were strangers in the land of Egypt." Early followers of Jesus made their way to Egypt to spread the word—legend says that the apostle Matthew preached in Egypt, and to avoid persecution in Rome, and at the Lord's direction, both Peter and Mark went to Egypt.

Certain places in the desert are dotted with caves where Christian hermits and monks spent their lives in prayer and contemplation. A handful of monasteries are still active in the country's less-traveled parts, and St. Catherine's Monastery nestles among the Sinai mountains, where Moses received the Ten Commandments, the bedrock of Christian moral behavior. In the old Coptic section of Cairo, a walk through the Christian Hanging Church or the Jewish synagogue can put a visitor in touch with the religious spirit that flowed through Egypt hundreds of years ago.

It did not take long for the followers of the Prophet Muhammad to bring Islam to Egypt. Just a few short years after Muhammad died, one of his generals conquered Egypt and immediately introduced Islam to the country.

Nonetheless, it took several centuries for Islam to reach south to Nubia and west to the outposts of civilization near present-day Libya, such as Siwa Oasis. In the Sufi sect of Islam, imported from Turkey, followers experience a mystical connection with God through chanting, music, and twirling, one palm turned upward, toward heaven.

Nobel prize–winning author Naguib Mahfouz says the spirit of the Egyptian people is defined by patience.

Whether standing inside the ancient tombs or in the medieval mosques, a person can easily learn a spiritual lesson from Egypt: how the world cannot be rushed.

*T. E.*

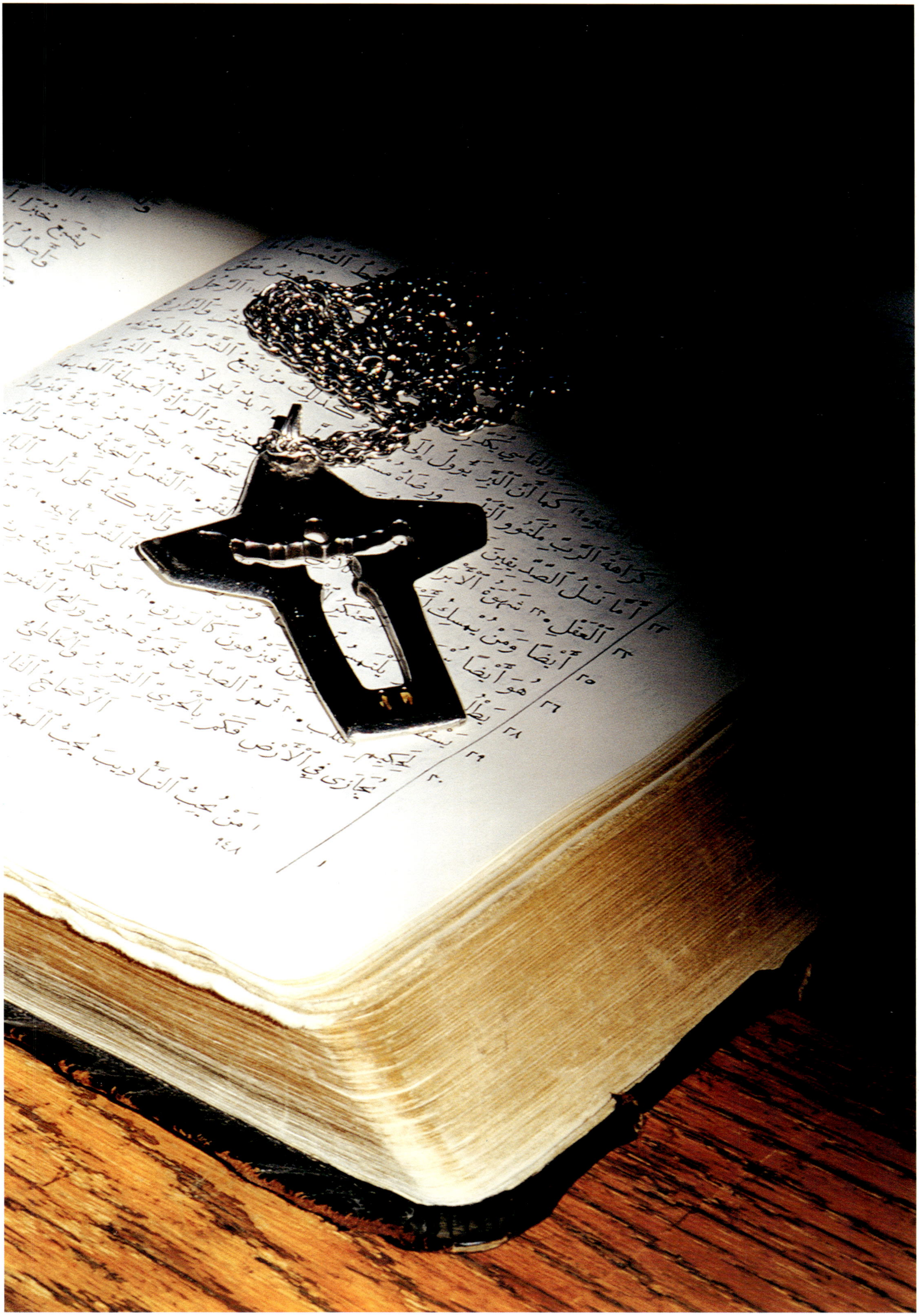

*An Anglican cross*

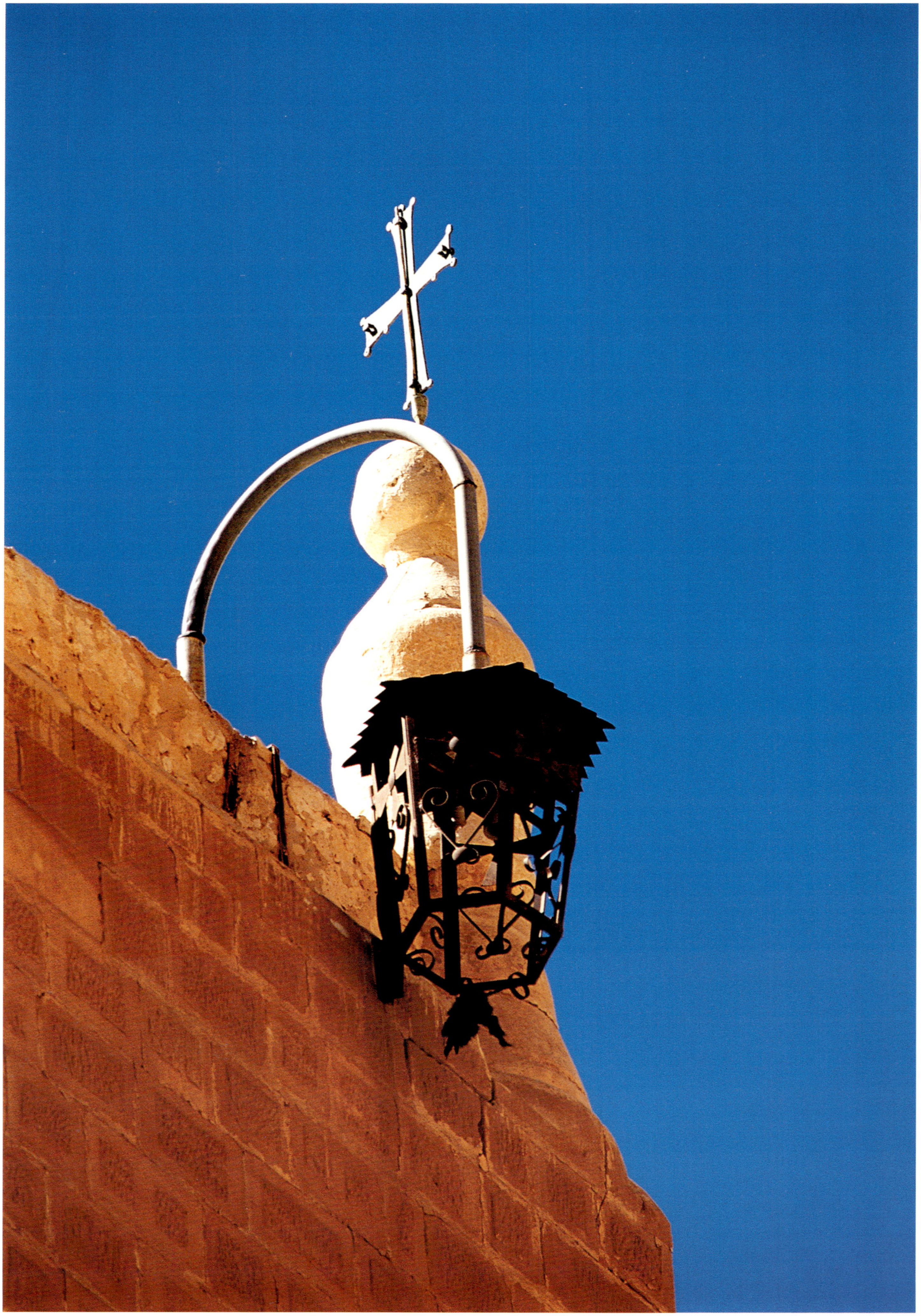

*St. Catherine's Monastery, Sinai*

*The Mausoleum of Muhammad 'Ali Pasha, City of the Dead, Cairo*

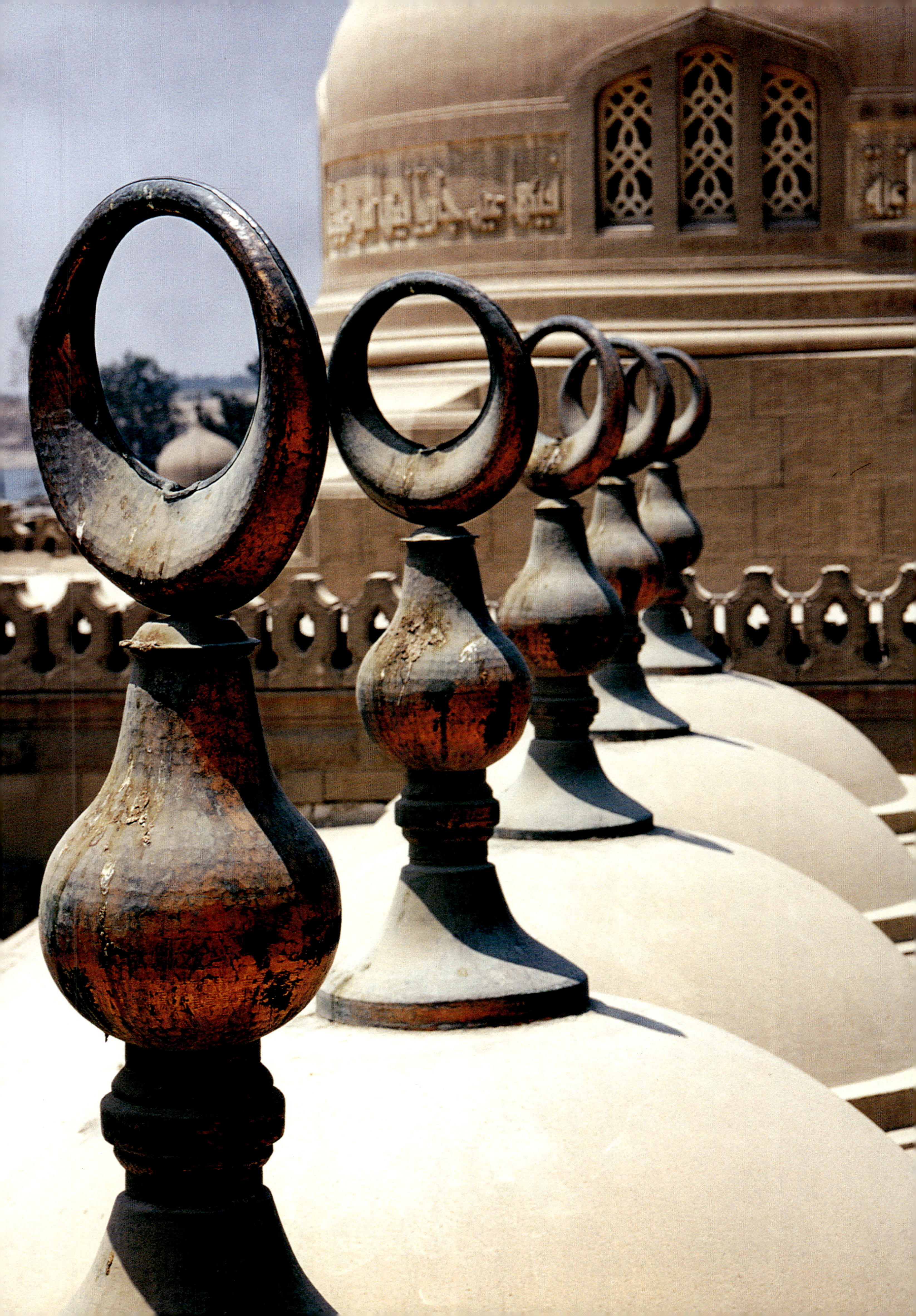

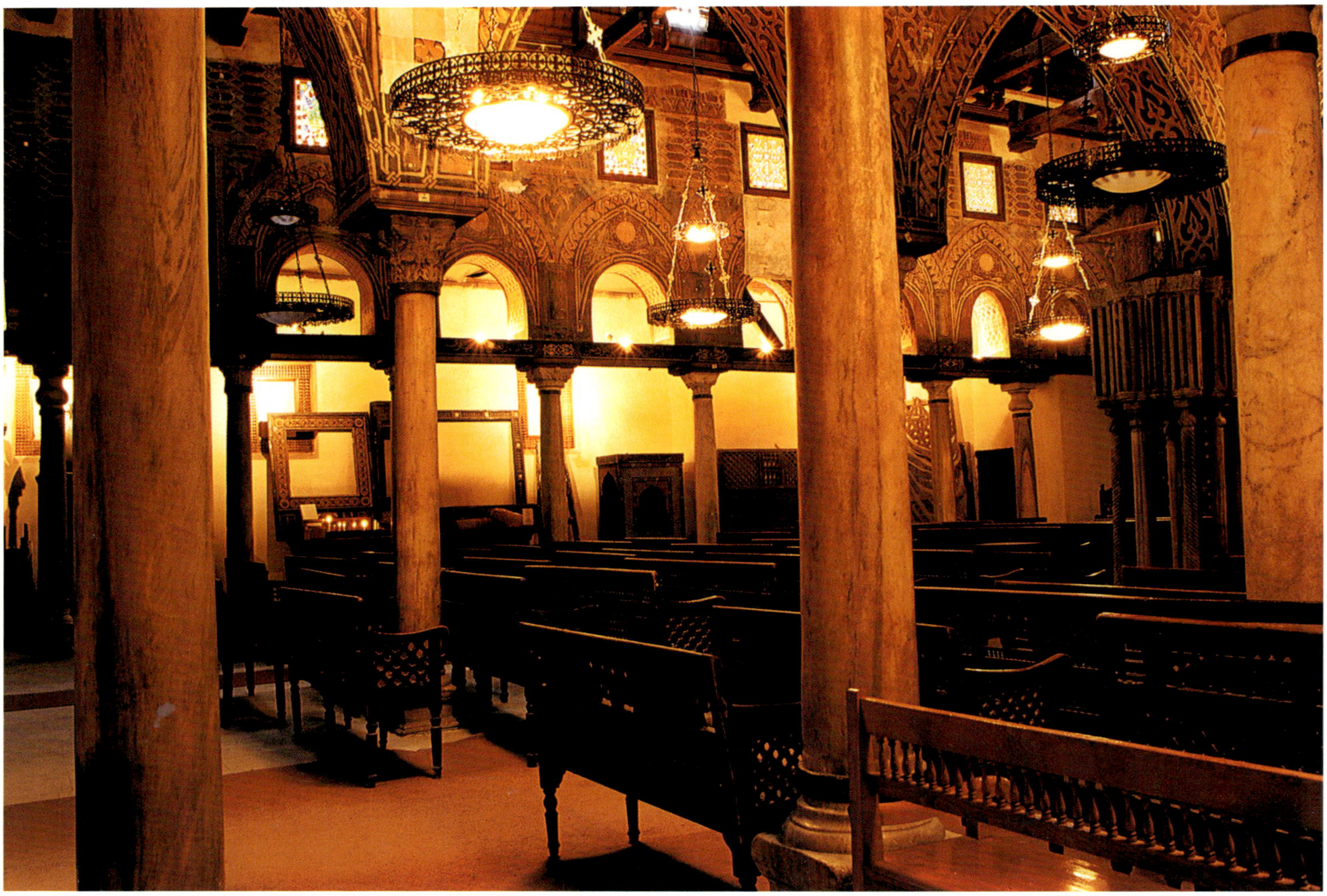

*The Hanging Church, Old Cairo*

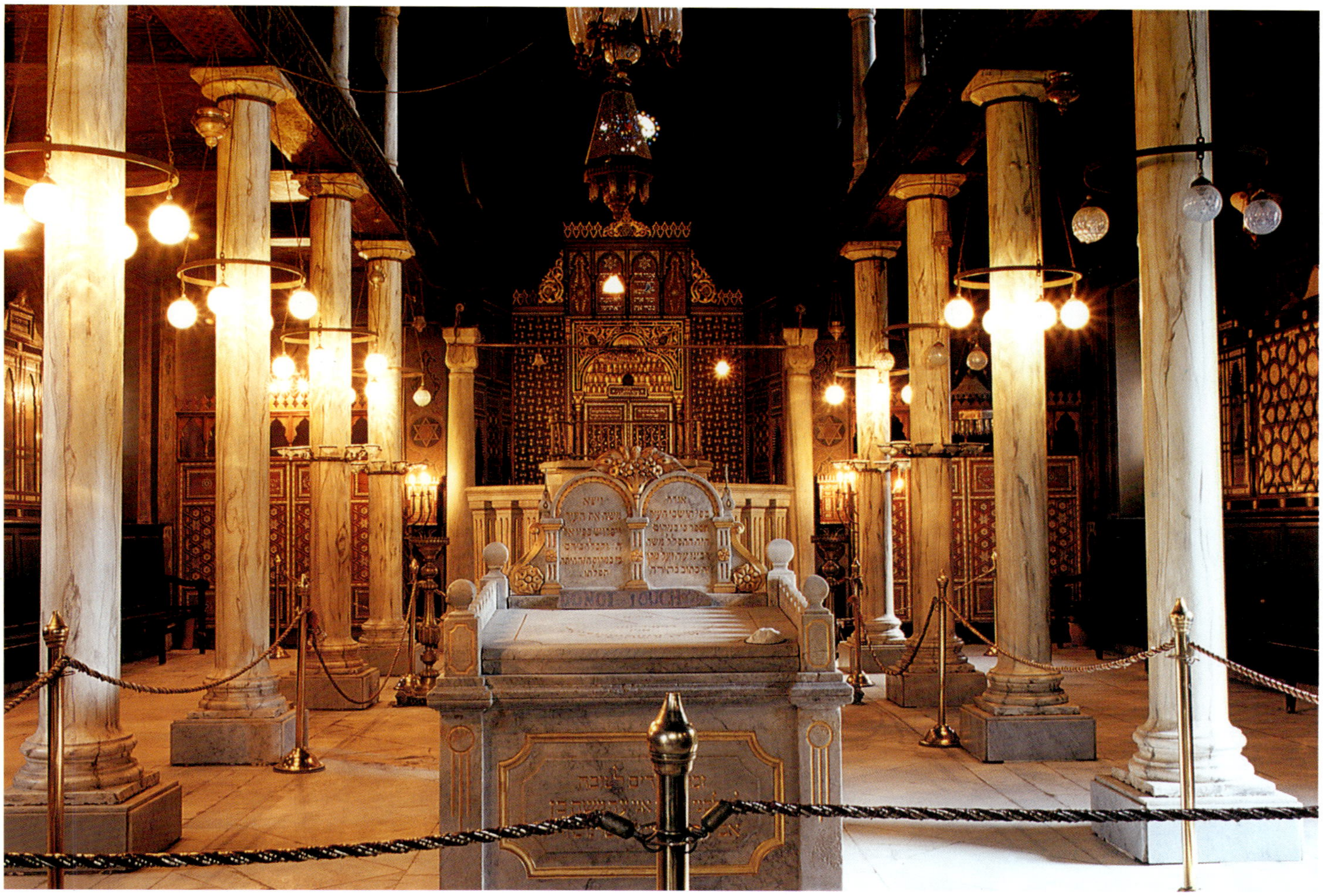

*The Synagogue of Ben Ezra, Old Cairo*

## Naguib Mahfouz

*Writer*

Born in Cairo in 1911, Naguib Mahfouz has witnessed nearly a century of Egypt's development. During this time he has made impressive contributions to his country's cultural life: he has written some three dozen novels as well as several volumes of short stories, many of which have been translated into several languages. In 1988 he was awarded the Nobel prize for literature, the first Arab writer to be so honored.

In Mahfouz's lifetime, enormous changes have occurred, which he has chronicled during his long career. But when asked to identify a constant quality in the spirit of his country, the world-famous author does not hesitate. "The patience of the Egyptian people in the face of catastrophes," he says.

He has had to face tragedies of his own. His 1959 novel *Children of the Alley* was denounced by religious leaders as blasphemous and banned in Egypt. In 1994 he was stabbed in the neck by two Egyptian Islamic militants, who disapproved of his writings.

He is, though, a devout follower of Islam who is deeply concerned about his country. "We are at the gates of times that may be very dangerous—God only knows how dangerous," he says. "The current economic crisis has reached extreme degrees." He wonders about Egypt's future role in the world. "It is hard to tell how globalization will affect us," he admits. "We must go through it. Are we going to develop like the rest of the world? And at the same time keep what makes us special—our roots and our traditions?" What does he consider foremost among those traditions? "Religion," he declares. "Also the parts of our behavior patterns and heritage that have remained throughout the years in the region, such as the literary classics like *A Thousand and One Nights*."

Mahfouz is most famous for his major work, a set of three novels known as *The Cairo Trilogy*. They depict the life of family over three generations from World War I to the 1950s, when King Farouk was overthrown. As with most of his stories, *The Cairo Trilogy* is set in the densely populated old quarters of Cairo, such as the Gamaliya district where he grew up. One of his novels, *Midaq Alley*, follows the mostly tragic fates of the people living and working on a tiny, poor Cairo street. Mahfouz has unflinchingly depicted the difficulties faced by ordinary Egyptians; thus, when asked what advice he would give to a young writer, his answer is not surprising: "To be honest with himself and the subject he is dealing with. To be open to all cultures and all times."

Although Mahfouz's hearing and sight now are both very weak, he still gathers with friends and admirers every Monday night at a Cairo hotel to talk about literature and politics, and he continues to write a weekly newspaper column.

In his Nobel prize acceptance speech, Mahfouz said that he was the son of two civilizations, the pharaonic and the Islamic. He then told a story of how after one victorious battle against Byzantium, the Muslims had given back their prisoners of war in exchange for books of the ancient Greek heritage in philosophy, medicine, and mathematics. "This," he said, "is a testimony of value for the human spirit in its demand for knowledge."

*T. E.*

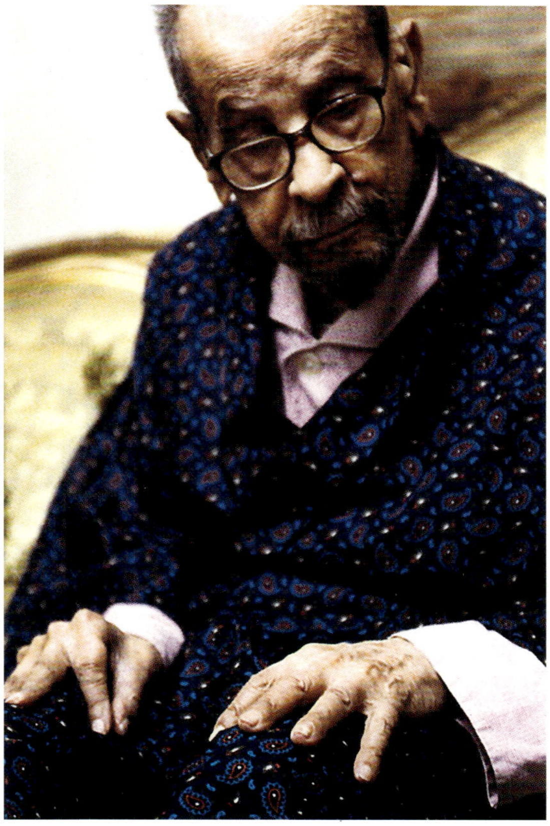

*Naguib Mahfouz, writer*

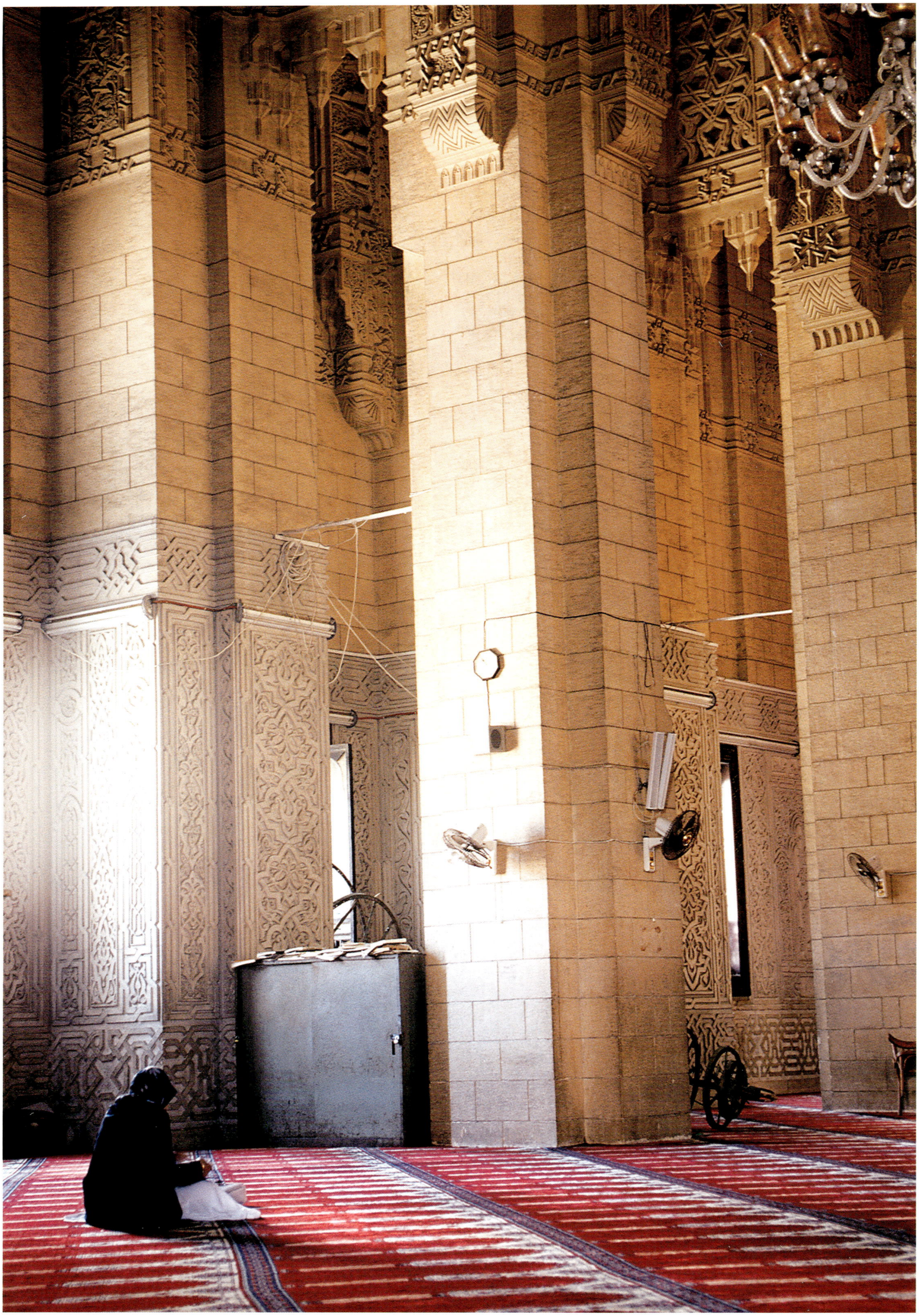

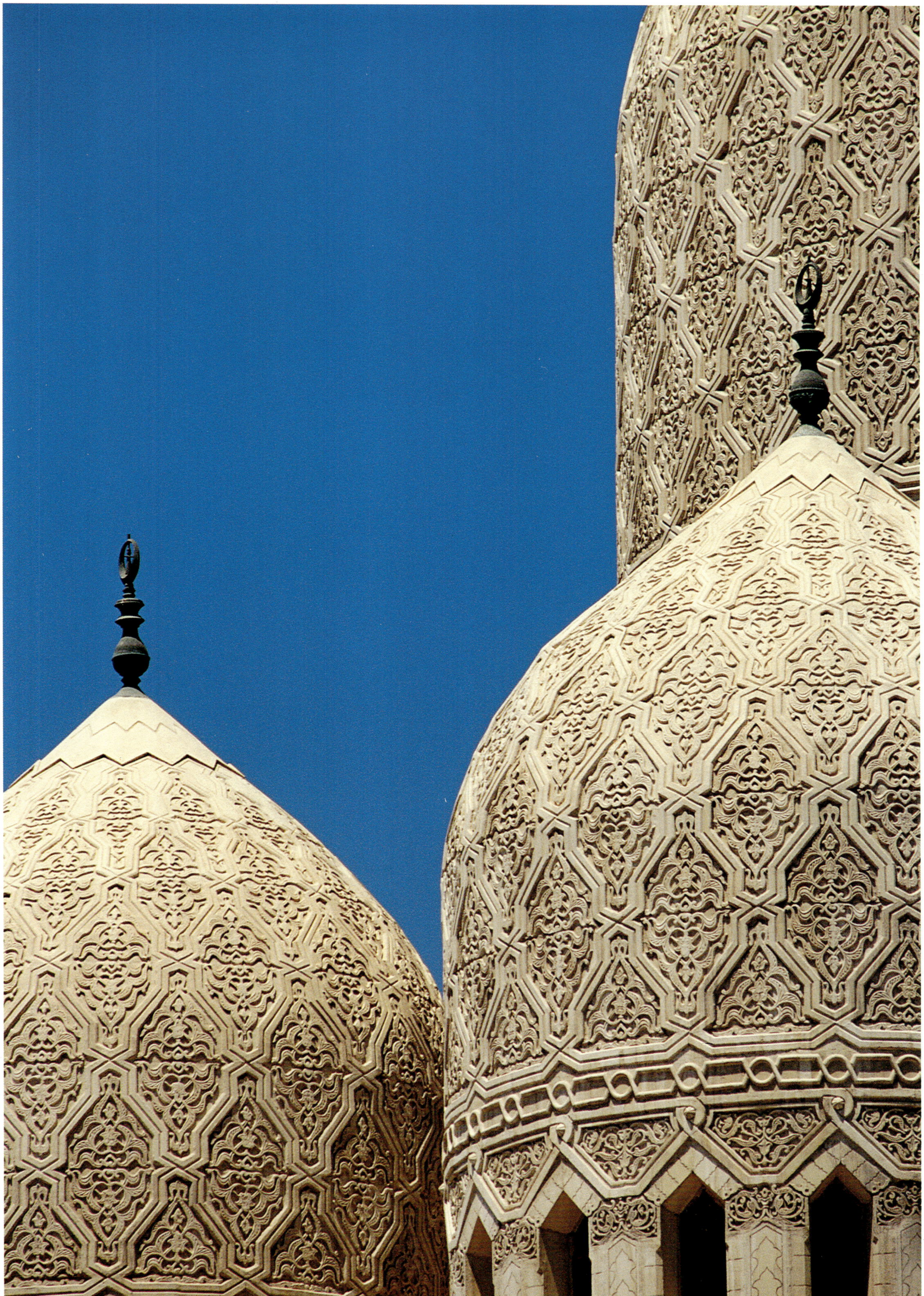

*Al-Mursi Abu al-'Abbas Mosque, Alexandria*

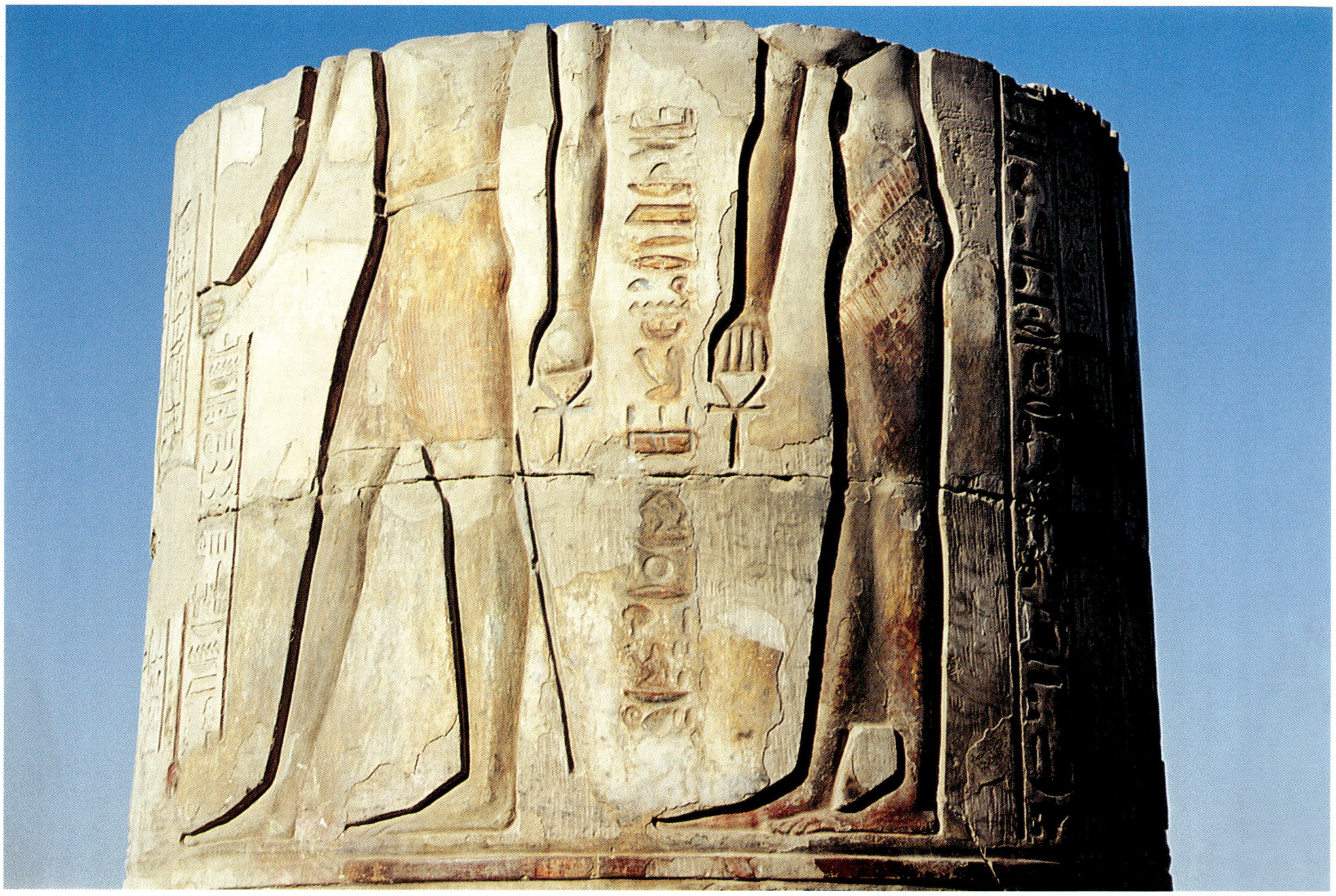

*A broken column at the Temple of Kom Ombo, Aswan*

## Emma Bonino

*Italian politician*

To get into the spirit of Egypt, Emma Bonino chose to learn Arabic. "The knowledge of a language is the most important instrument to know a country and its people, although I was surprised when I realized that language in Egypt is not an identity factor. Middle-class families also speak English and French at home. Their identity does not rest only in Arabic," says the Italian Radical Party politician and member of the European Parliament. "Today I am able to read local newspapers and to follow the local television news. My interest here is mainly political," she confesses.

Bonino visited Egypt for the first time in January 1986 as a tourist. She came back in 1991, after the first Iraq war. In 2001, during her party's election campaign, she received a phone call from some friends, women members of the Tunisian Association of Young Lawyers. They asked her to organize a European Parliament delegation to attend the trial of Nawal El Saadawi, who had been accused of apostasy. Bonino decided to leave in the middle of the campaign and head back to Egypt, where she then met Barbara Ibrahim, whose husband, professor and human rights activist Saad Eddin Ibrahim, had just been arrested.

"It was then that I decided to do something in Egypt," Bonino remembers. She is convinced that the Arab world is totally unknown to most south Europeans. "Only a few of the European Parliament's members know Arabic and therefore have access to local information," she points out. "The Egyptian political class speaks at least English and French. The consequence is that they know us very well, but we don't know them at all!"

"Thinking about what I could practically do here, I decided to change my usual Brussels–Strasbourg–Rome trip into a Brussels–Strasbourg–Cairo one." Well known for her strong character, her campaign for civil and political rights, and her frequent participation in hunger strikes and acts of civil disobedience, Bonino now spends ten days a month in Egypt, and all her vacations.

But she admits, "I can't tell what is the real spirit of the Egyptians. I tried to understand it with the help of locals who became friends, as well as my Arabic teacher. I worked with many non-governmental organizations on the female genital mutilation issue, and I realized that women are the most reactive part of this society. But in general I noticed a resigned spirit, as if it would be useless to move ahead," says Bonino.

"As a European I really think that Europe must place the 'Mediterranean' on the priority list. For political reasons I thought the same about the eastern European countries in the 1980s." Then Bonino wonders, "How can we solve the problem of immigration if we don't know the reasons why people leave their country? The current international answer is inadequate."

For Bonino, the goal is clear. "On this side or on the other side of 'the lake,' we need to understand how to live together."

Egypt certainly stimulated her curiosity. "This is a country at a huge crossroads: it could choose to take the responsibilities and the risks to look ahead, or it could choose the status quo, in which the end result is certainly the failure of the country itself." Bonino feels that part of the Egyptian establishment is aware that the second solution is dangerous, but that the lack of economic reforms and the bureaucracy reinforce the established powers without developing the country. "Egypt is facing an incredible demographic explosion, around 2.7 percent, with a zero economic growth," she explains. "Maybe they don't find the right policies, but at least they talk about it as a real problem."

"Society's three pillars in Egypt are the political-economic class, the religious class, and the military and secret service class," says Bonino. "Religion in Egypt is more of a useful political instrument than a spiritual doctrine." She compares Egypt's present-day situation to a period of Europe's history. "We waited hundreds of years and we had to fight many wars before the discovery of the laity, allowing the government to rule the country and the citizen to choose to pray to the God he wants."

If Bonino were an Egyptian politician she would launch her electoral campaign giving particular attention to civil and political rights, such as the right to associate and the right of free expression.

She has many future projects, one of which is certainly to push Europe to look south. "I would also like to continue this experience, maybe outside Egypt. If I had the chance to choose I would go to Syria—although my masochism has a limit!"

*S. D.*

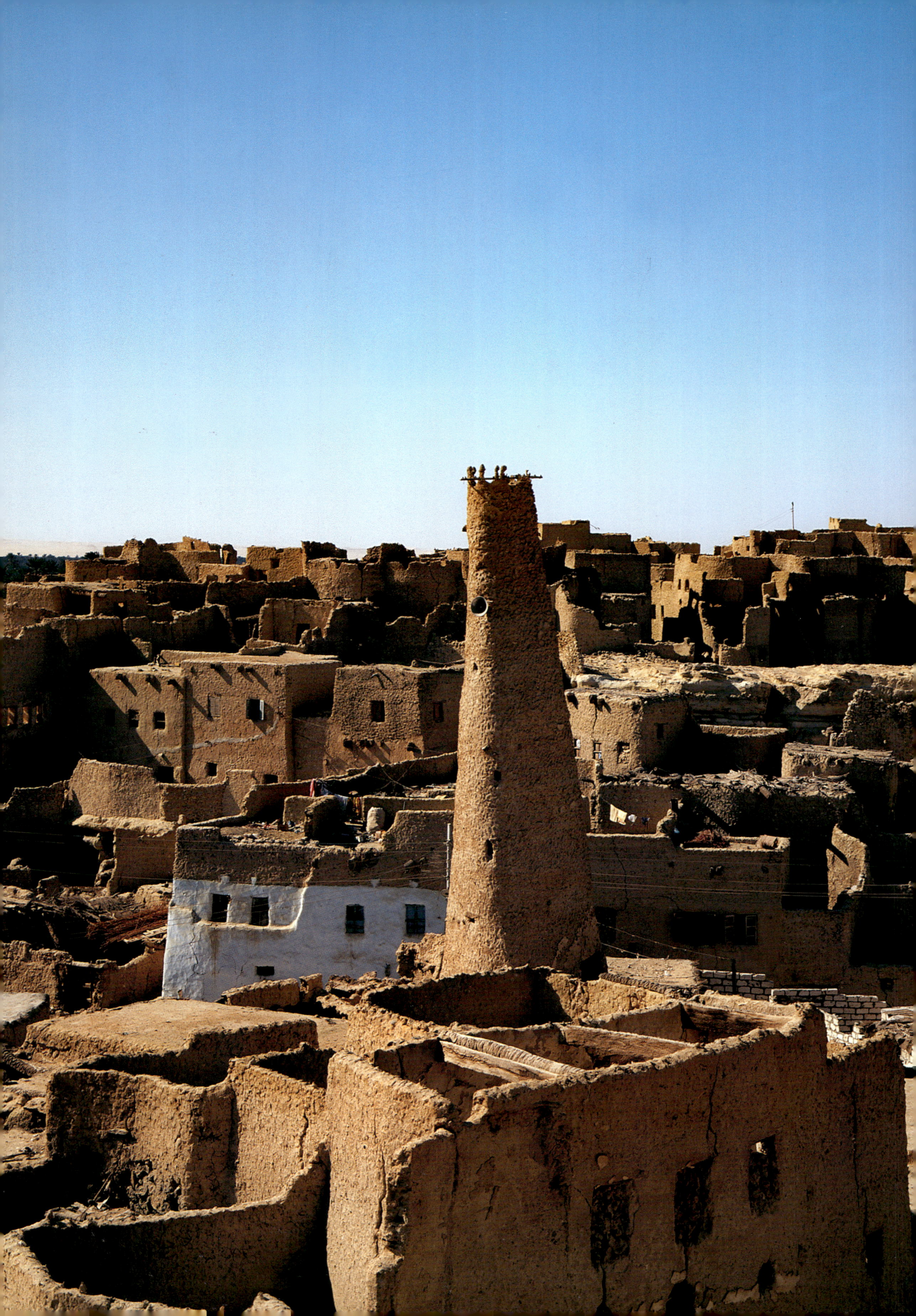

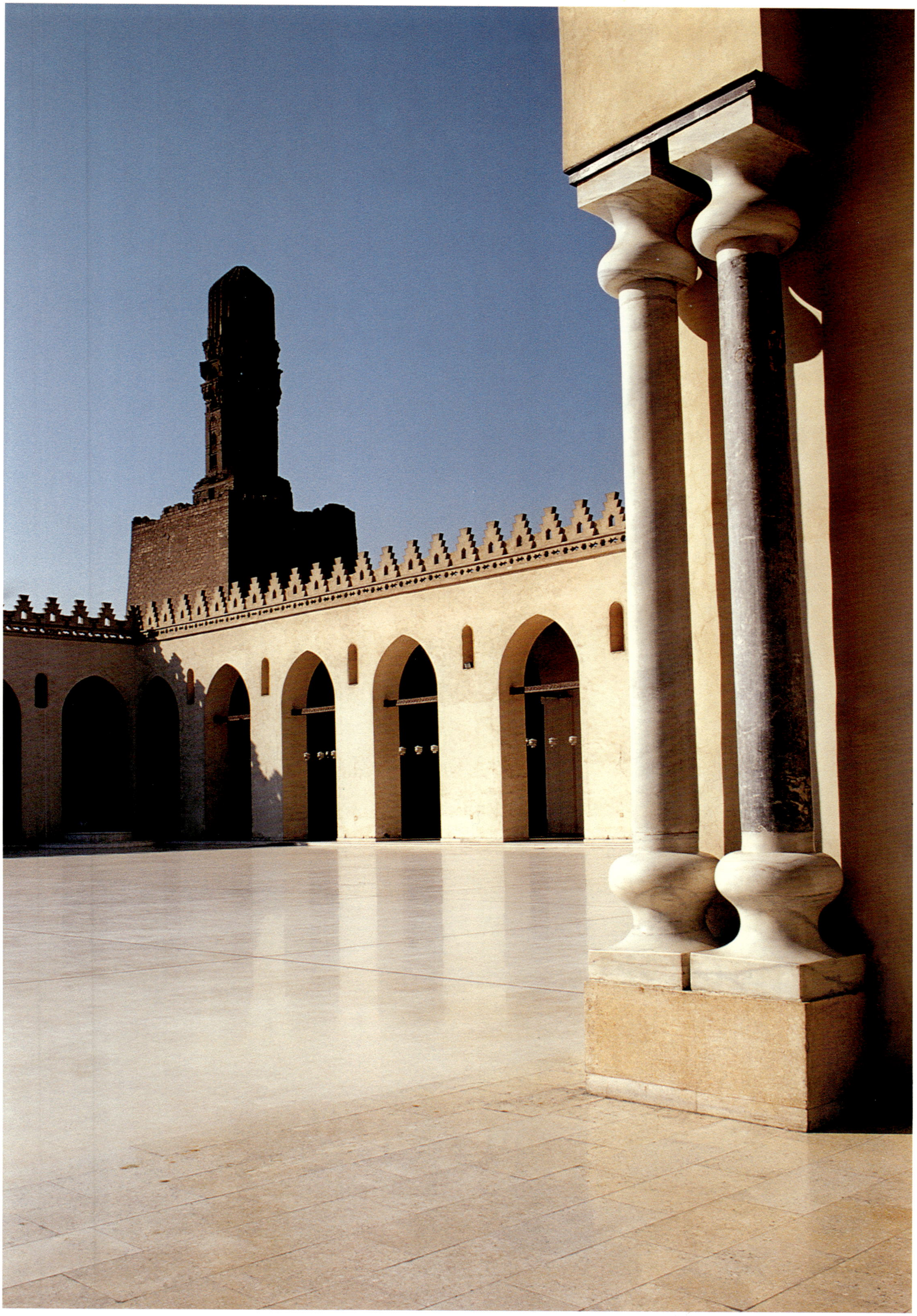

*A mosque in the old town of Siwa*

*The Mosque of al-Hakim, Islamic Cairo*

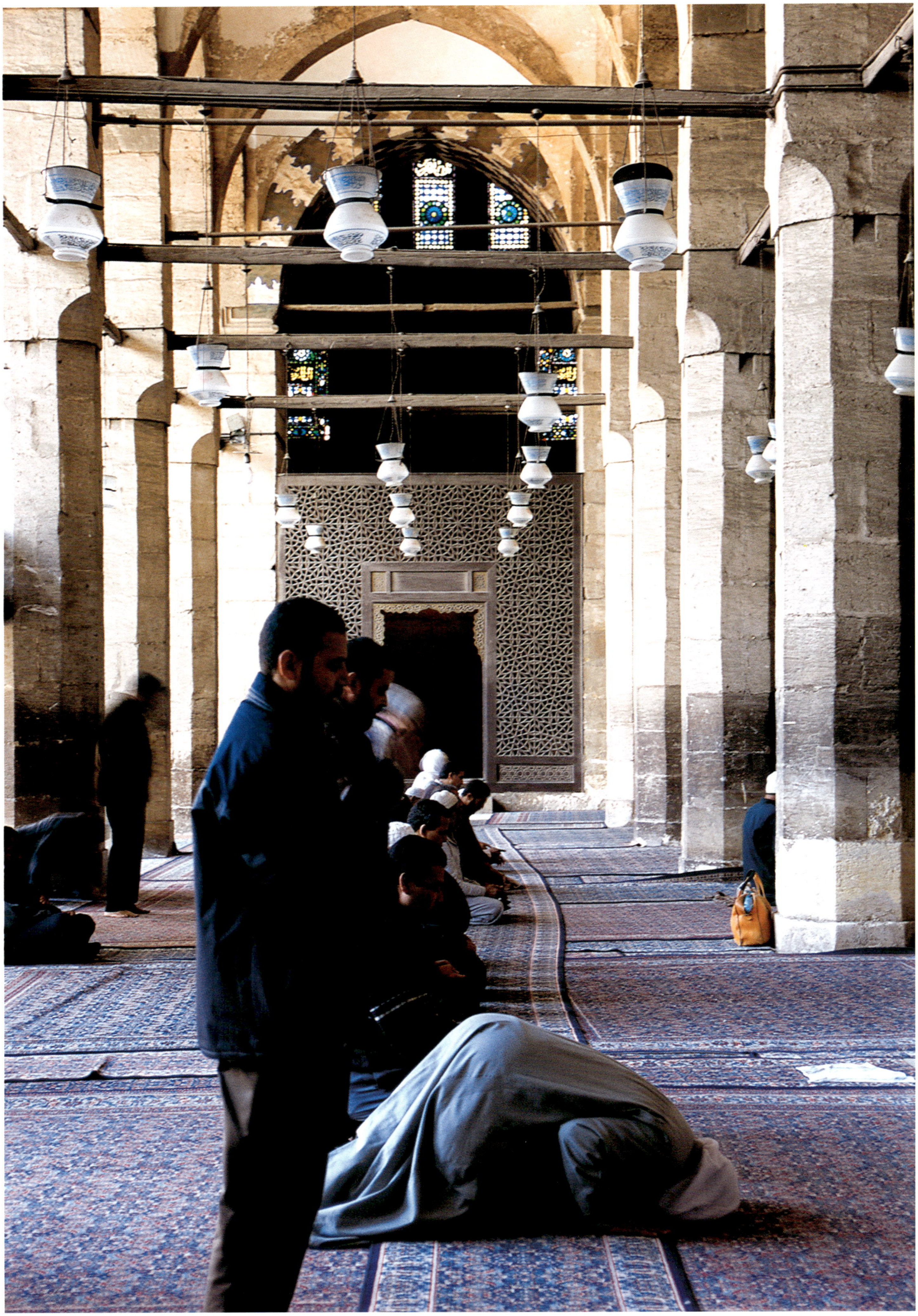

*Prayer time inside the Madrasa–Khanqah of Sultan Barquq, City of the Dead, Cairo*

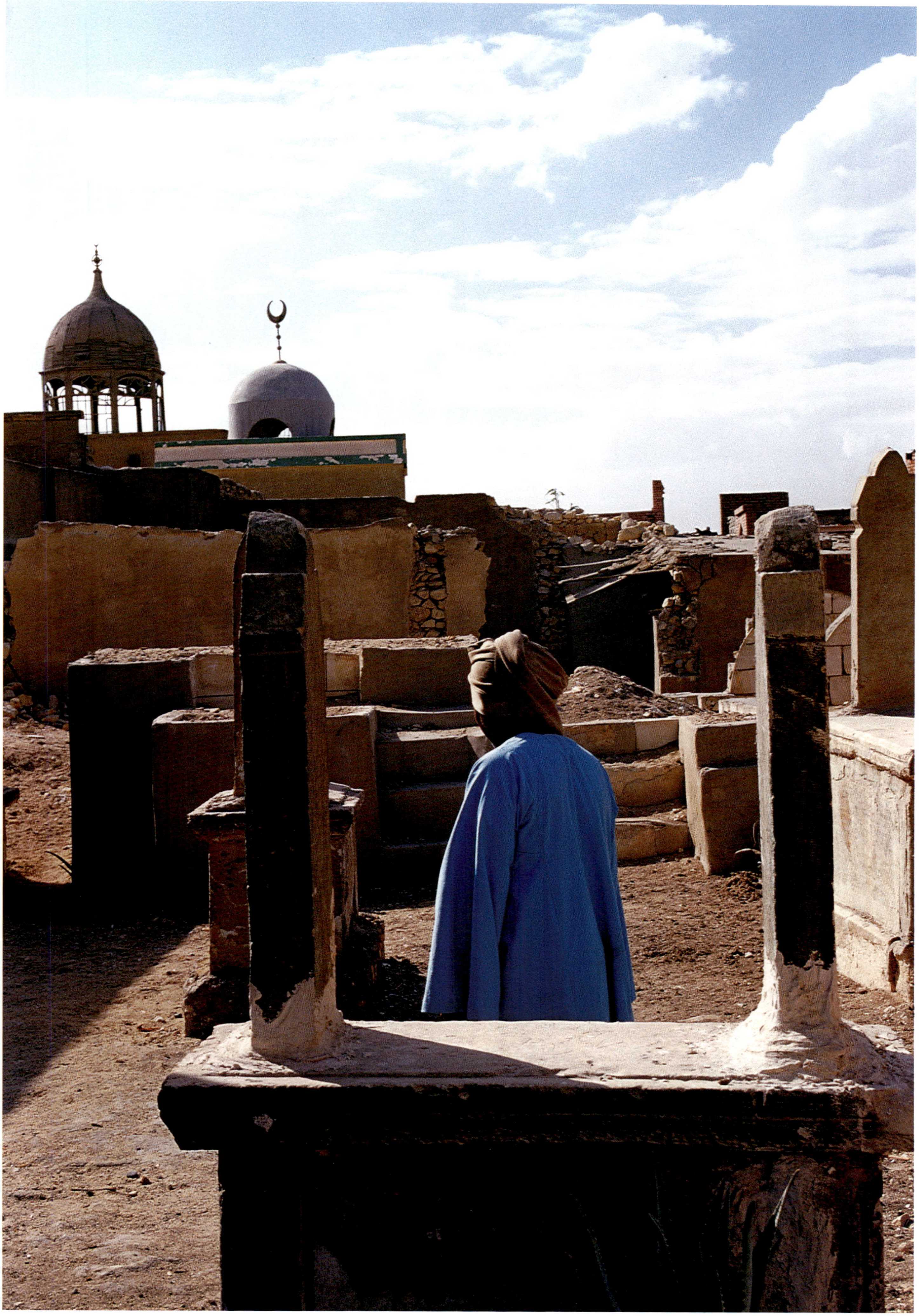

*The City of the Dead, Cairo*

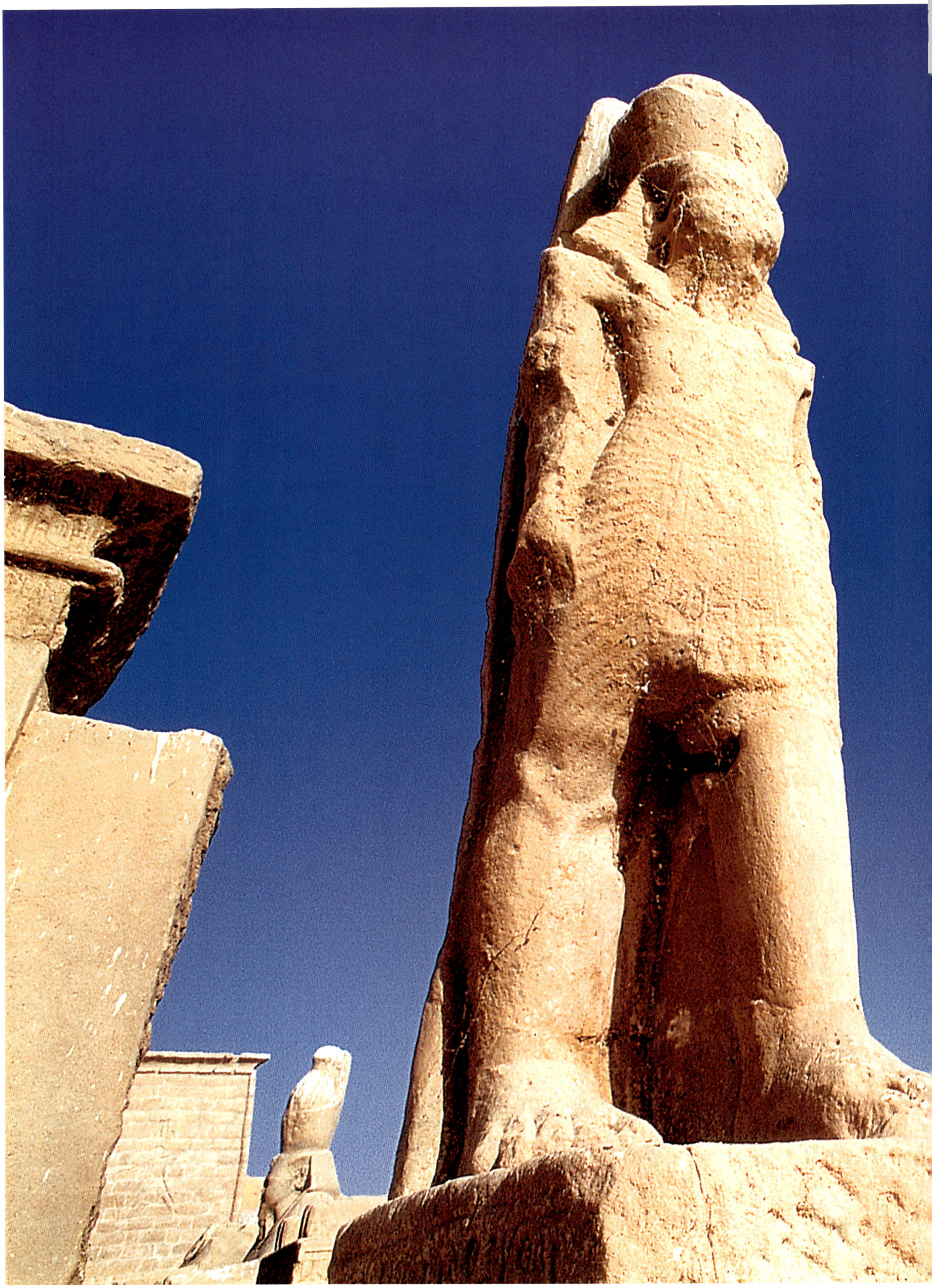

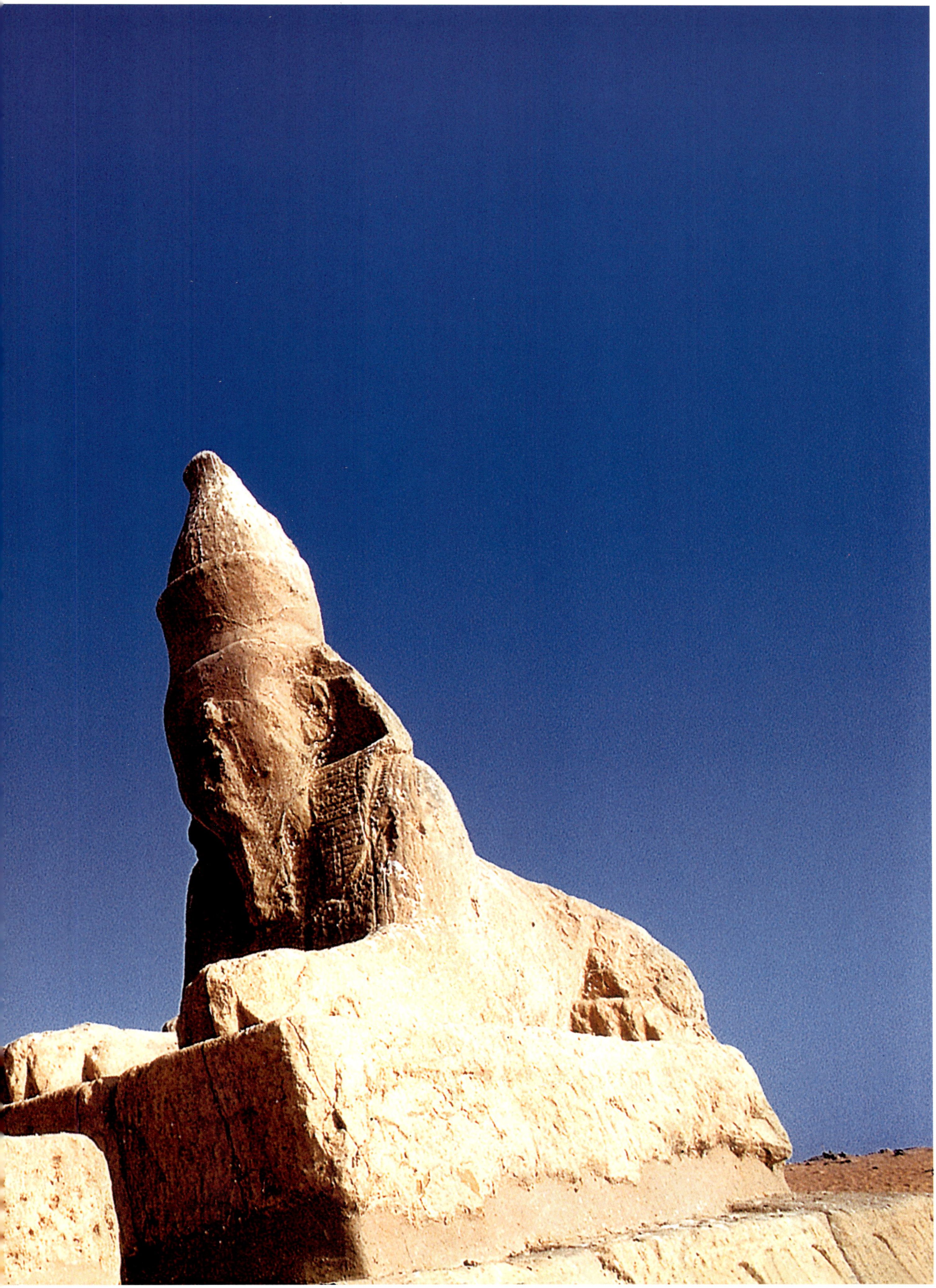

*The entrance to the Temple of Wadi al-Sebua, Lake Nasser*

## Zahi Hawass

*Archaeologist*

"When I was young I found the spirituality of Egypt in the Nile, as I was born in a village facing the river. Things changed when I fell in love with archaeology: the Pyramids and the Sphinx suddenly became spiritual. When I go inside the Pyramids alone I can feel a strong power. It is this power that gives me answers to questions that I never had answers to before," says Dr. Zahi Hawass, secretary general of the Supreme Council of Antiquities and the director of excavations at the Giza Pyramids and Bahariya. "The Pyramids certainly have a spiritual value. If you set your eyes on them and you start thinking about your future and your past, it is simply incredible."

Hawass did not plan to be an archaeologist—and certainly not one of the most recognizable archaeologists in the world. At first he wanted to be a lawyer, but after only a year studying law he felt uncomfortable, so he transferred at random to the Faculty of Arts. "I attended the Archaeology Department without any emotions. At that time archaeology did not touch my heart at all," he says. When he graduated from college and went to the Antiquities Department he looked at the archaeologists there and found them "old, boring, ugly, and lazy," he remembers. He decided not to continue in archaeology, and chose to pursue a diplomatic career.

But he failed the oral exams. "Oral exams need connections," he shrugs. So he returned to the Antiquities Department, and it was only at this point, when he was sent to an excavation in the Delta area, that something magical happened: "I met two men," he says, "Hagg Mohamed and Reis, also known as 'Doctor.' They had huge experience, without any education. One day they told me, 'We need you to come, because we discovered a tomb,' and they began to teach me how to excavate. While using my brush my hand touched something. It was the statue of Isis, the goddess of beauty and love in ancient Egypt!" he says, the excitement still clear in his voice. "When I looked at the eyes of this fantastic piece I was holding, I immediately fell in love with archaeology, the only thing in my life since then." Suddenly he becomes emotional. "The gifts the sand generously give us are magic! When I discover a statue my heart beats fast and my eyes shine, because I know I am the first one holding a piece of art that no one else has seen in 4,500 years. That is a moment that I cannot describe," he says.

Famous for wearing an American hat that once brought him good luck, Hawass has made major discoveries at the tombs of the Pyramid builders and more recently at the Valley of the Golden Mummies in Bahariya Oasis.

His attitude toward his job can be summed up in the advice he gave to some schoolchildren while on a recent visit to America: "First, give your passion to your work. Make from a small job a big job. Second, never waste your time in fighting anyone. Don't lose your energy in fights, but invest it in success."

Hawass's role requires him to balance the rational and the emotional. When discovering something new, which part comes first? "There are three moments," he explains. "Before the discovery I must think hard, therefore the rational part comes first. During the discovery passion comes immediately. After it, professionalism prevails."

Hawass believes that because of his work, Egyptian history is better known to the people of the world—including Egyptians themselves. "When I walk around, people talk to me all the time, they watch me on TV, they ask me questions," he says. "Thanks to the media, I think Egyptians now know more than before, even the poor people."

Egyptians take pride in their history, and yet there are vast differences between ancient Egyptian culture and present-day attitudes. "We have to know that the past is history before religion," says Hawass. "The Egyptians look at the past culture as their heritage. That culture began and ended before modern religion. Egyptians are aware of this evolution and they accept it. If you understand the past you have a good future," he says with determination.

Hawass is busy promoting the future of his country: "I am pushing the new generation. I want the children to visit the museums and the new exhibitions. I want to make everyone in Egypt know that we controlled the world five thousand years ago. If I put this in the heart of every Egyptian, this country will soon progress!"

*S. D.*

*Zahi Hawass, secretary general of the Supreme Council of Antiquities and director of excavations at the Giza Pyramids and Bahariya*

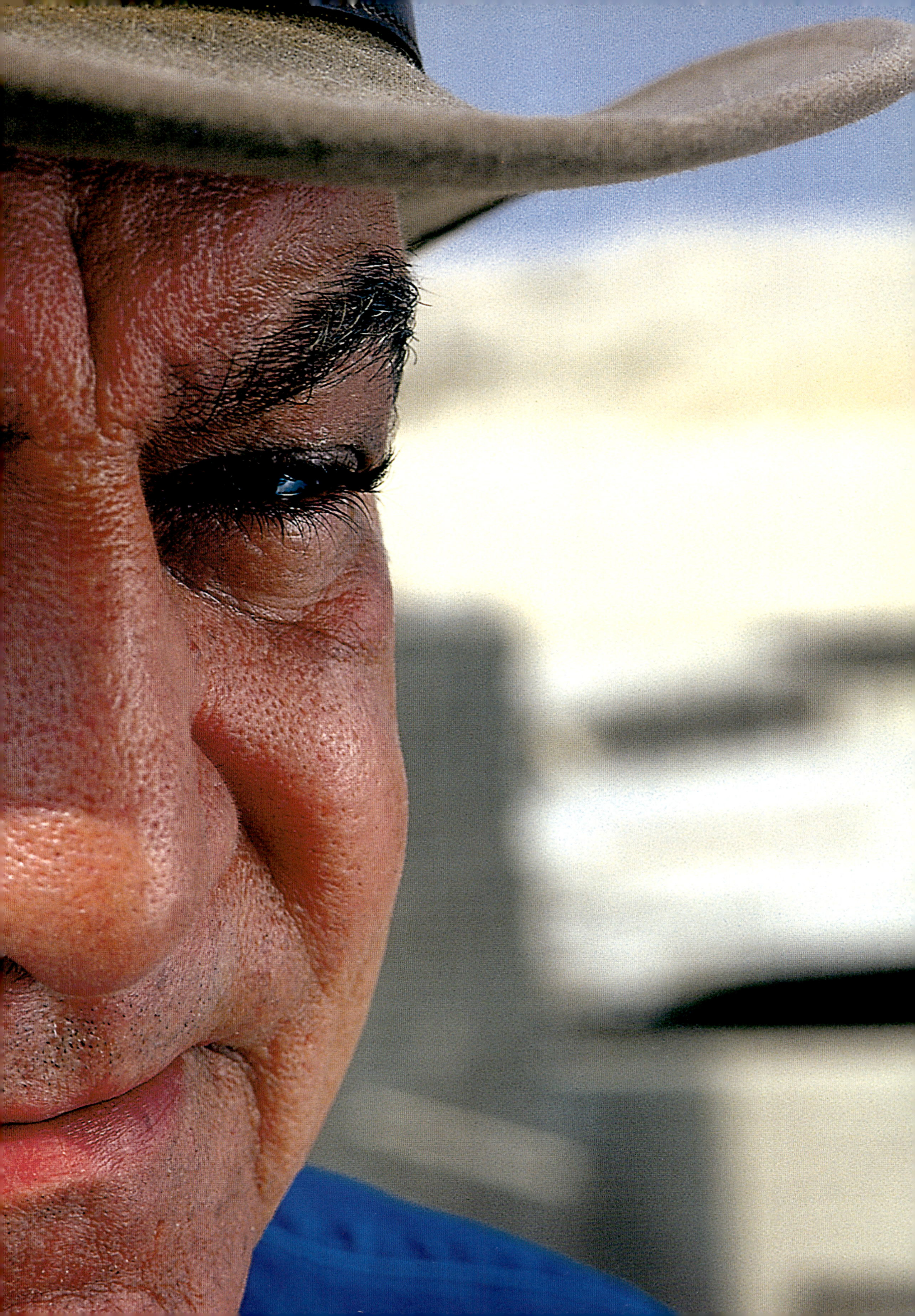

# Past

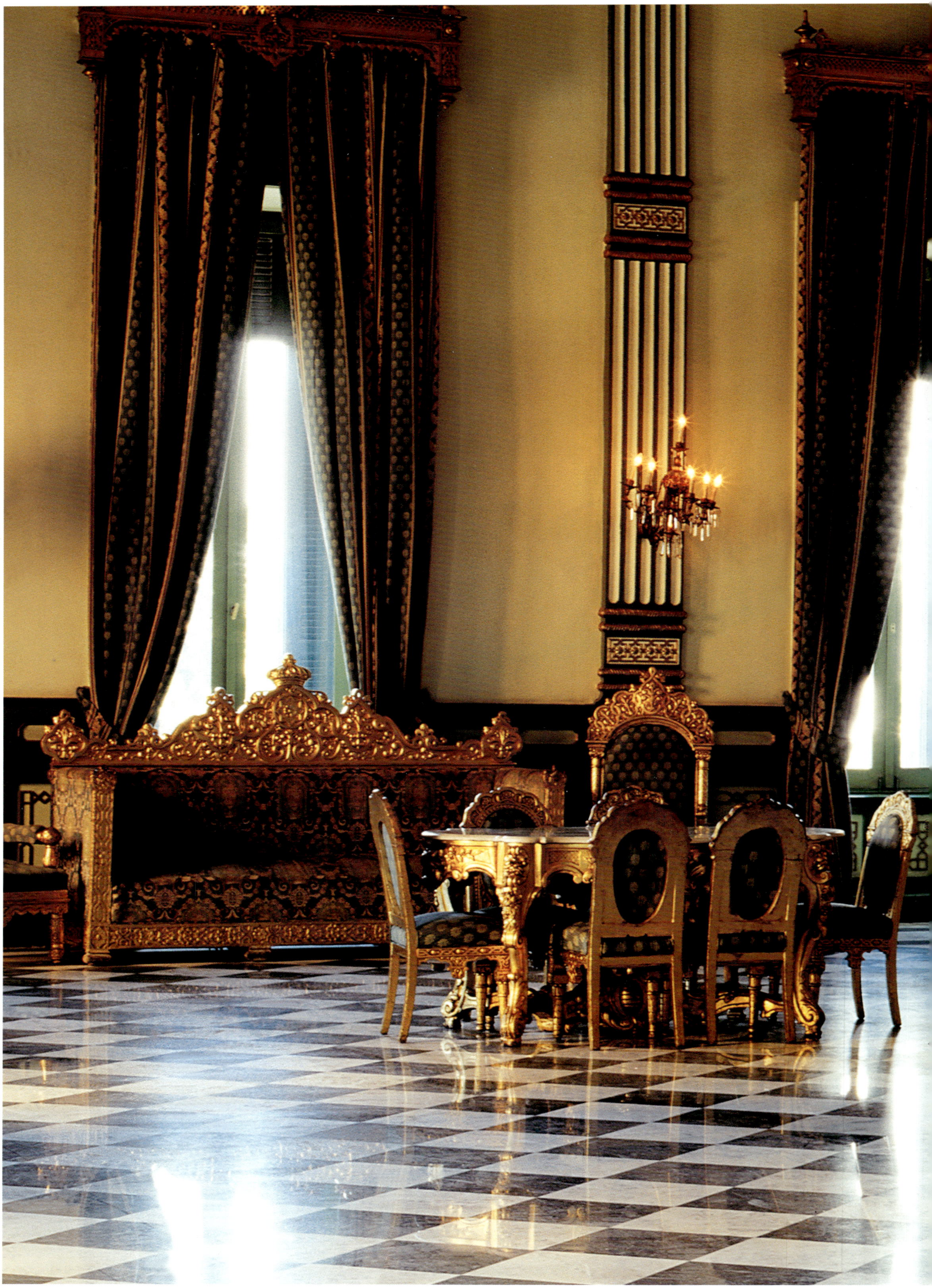

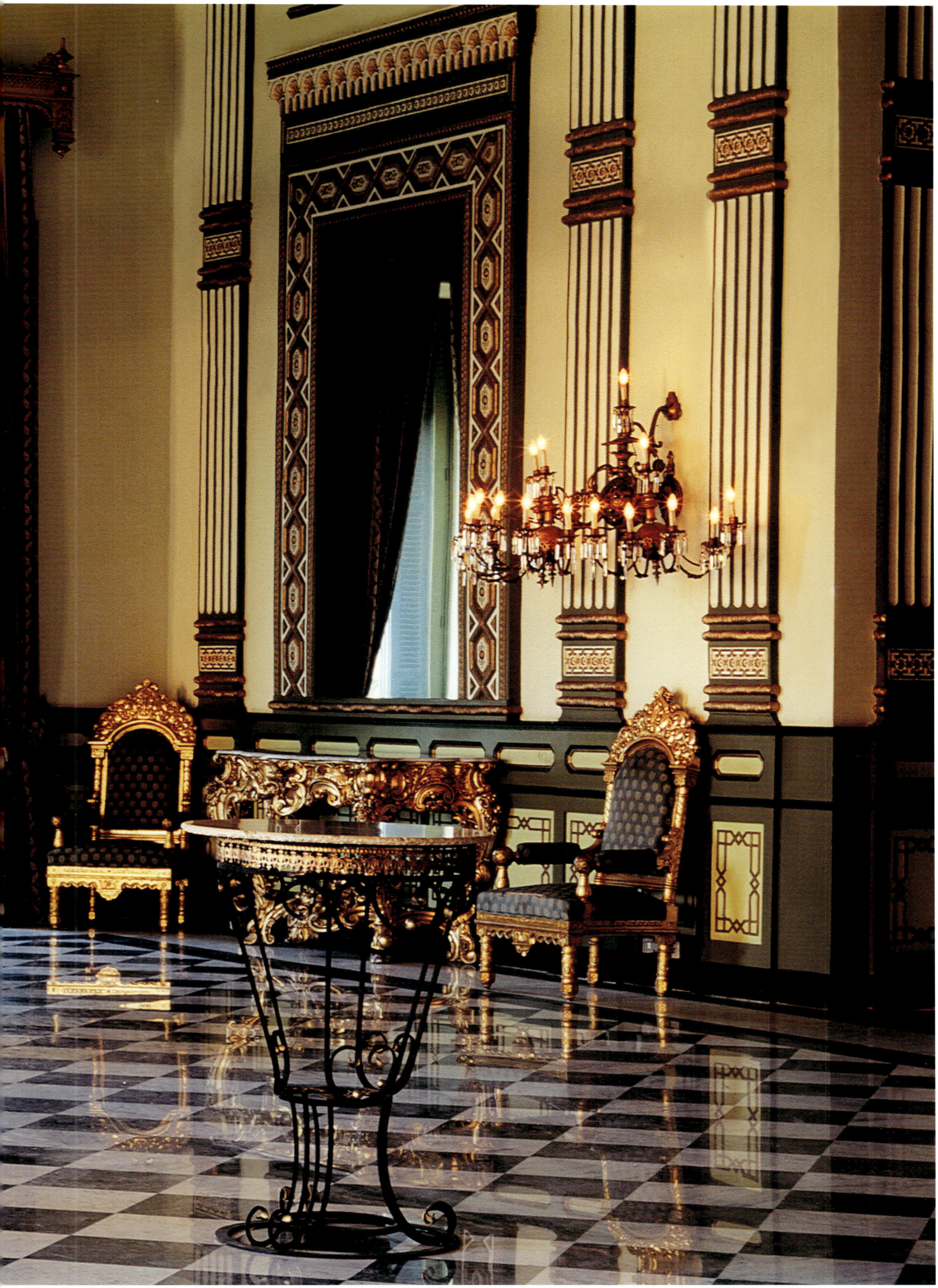

*The Cairo Marriott Hotel*

The two mounted eunuchs with drawn swords were following the royal carriage. The year was 1869, and Major Morgan, an American officer engaged in the Egyptian army, was out riding in Cairo when he passed the carriage, obviously occupied by a lady. Instead of averting his eyes, as a gentleman was expected to do, Morgan gazed inside the carriage and saw a pretty lady, who handed him flowers. In the next moment two outraged eunuchs were pursuing Morgan.

Luckily, Morgan was riding a good horse: the thoroughbred being trained to carry Empress Eugènie when she arrived for the opening ceremonies of the Suez Canal. But the horse was only one of the gifts planned for Eugènie. Khedive Ismail built a whole palace for her—and that palace is now the Cairo Marriott Hotel.

Egypt's past is full of unexpected mixtures: an American soldier pursued by eunuchs, an Ottoman ruler wooing a married French empress, a canal constructed by a French engineer that would soon be operated by the British. For centuries Egypt had been ruled by foreigners—Romans, Mamluks, French, Ottomans, British. Their influence can be seen on just about everything surviving from the time between Alexander the Great and the 1952 Revolution. "Here it was the Greek community, the Cypriot community, the Italian community, the French community," Professor Salah Lamei Mostafa, head of the Center for the Conservation and Preservation of Islamic Cultural Heritage, recalls about his childhood in 1940s Cairo. "I still remember everywhere the shops, the cafés, the restaurants. It was a wonderful time. A really wonderful time. Downtown, it was like Paris."

Today's Cairenes have the British to thank for several of the graciously planned neighbourhoods of Cairo. Areas such as Zamalek, an island in the middle of the Nile, maintain a decaying beauty despite the addition of sleek, trendy clubs and elevated highways. From the sidewalk, oversized entranceways provide glimpses of elegantly engineered vintage elevators wrapped by curved, marble staircases. A handful of restaurants in Cairo and Alexandria still exude a World War II–era charm: a feeling of Paris, yes, mixed with a literary salon, and Casablanca, and Ottoman Empire ornateness. Somehow these places hold off the chaos and buzz of Egypt's thriving, overpopulated metropolises.

When considering the past in Egypt, however, the first things that typically come to mind are not the cities but the antiquities—the immense monuments suddenly rising from the emptiness of the desert and the breathtaking, brightly-painted tombs concealed in the valleys. And there is the desert itself: if you turn your back on the Nile and look across the Western Desert, which occupies two-thirds of Egypt's land, you will of course see the famous Pyramids. But beyond these mythic structures lies Wadi al-Rayyan, which forty million years ago was part of a vast ocean. Now the remains of marine life lie scattered across its sands, including numerous skeletons of ancient whales. Much, much farther across the Western Desert, almost at the border with Libya, near the Great Sand Sea, where a Persian king is thought to have lost an entire army, is Siwa Oasis. Legend has it that Siwa did not see a European from the year 160 until 1792. The Berber-speaking inhabitants practice unique customs and traditions, many of which still remain hidden from the world, outside the march of history.

*T. E.*

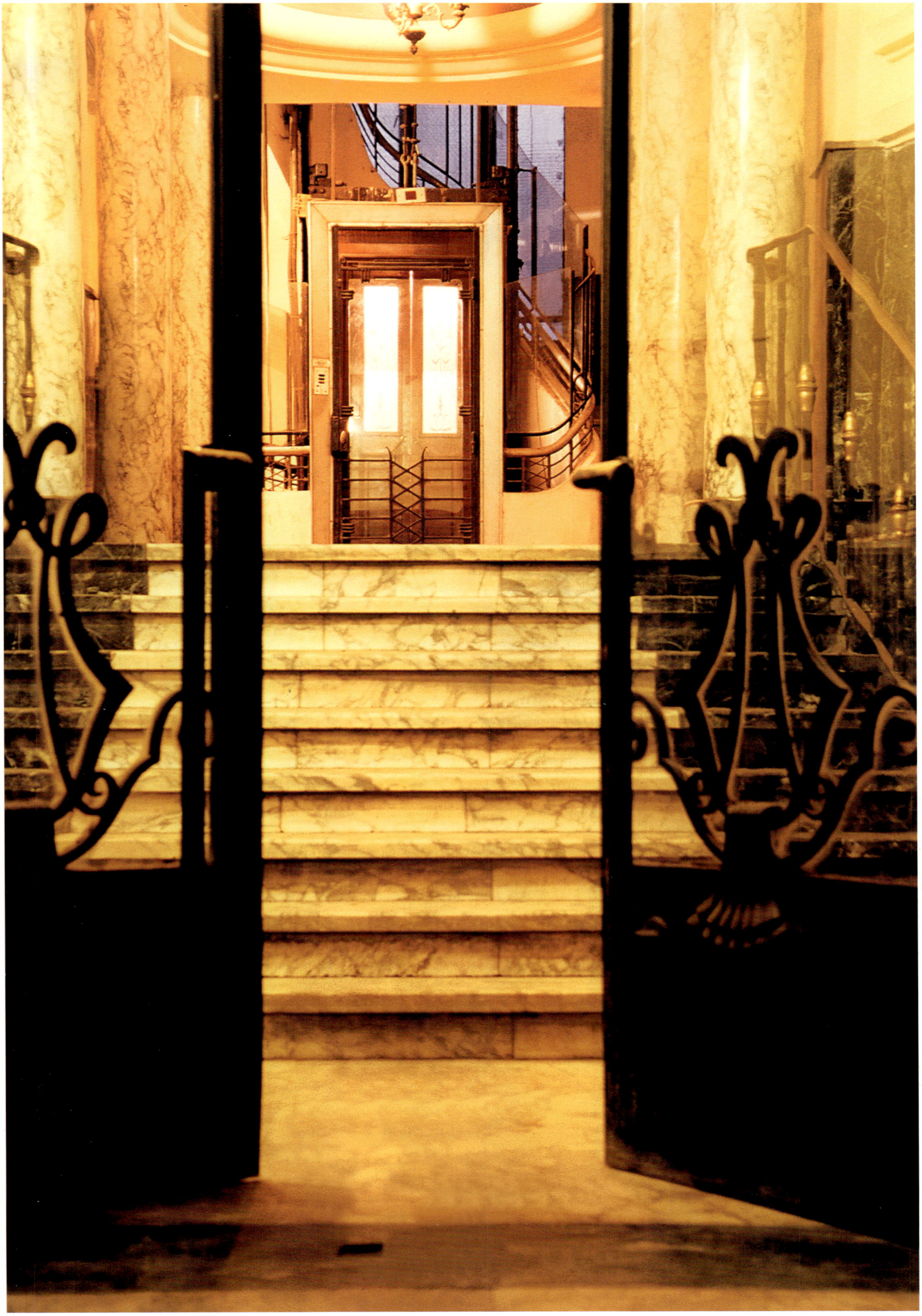

*An elevator in Zamalek, Cairo*

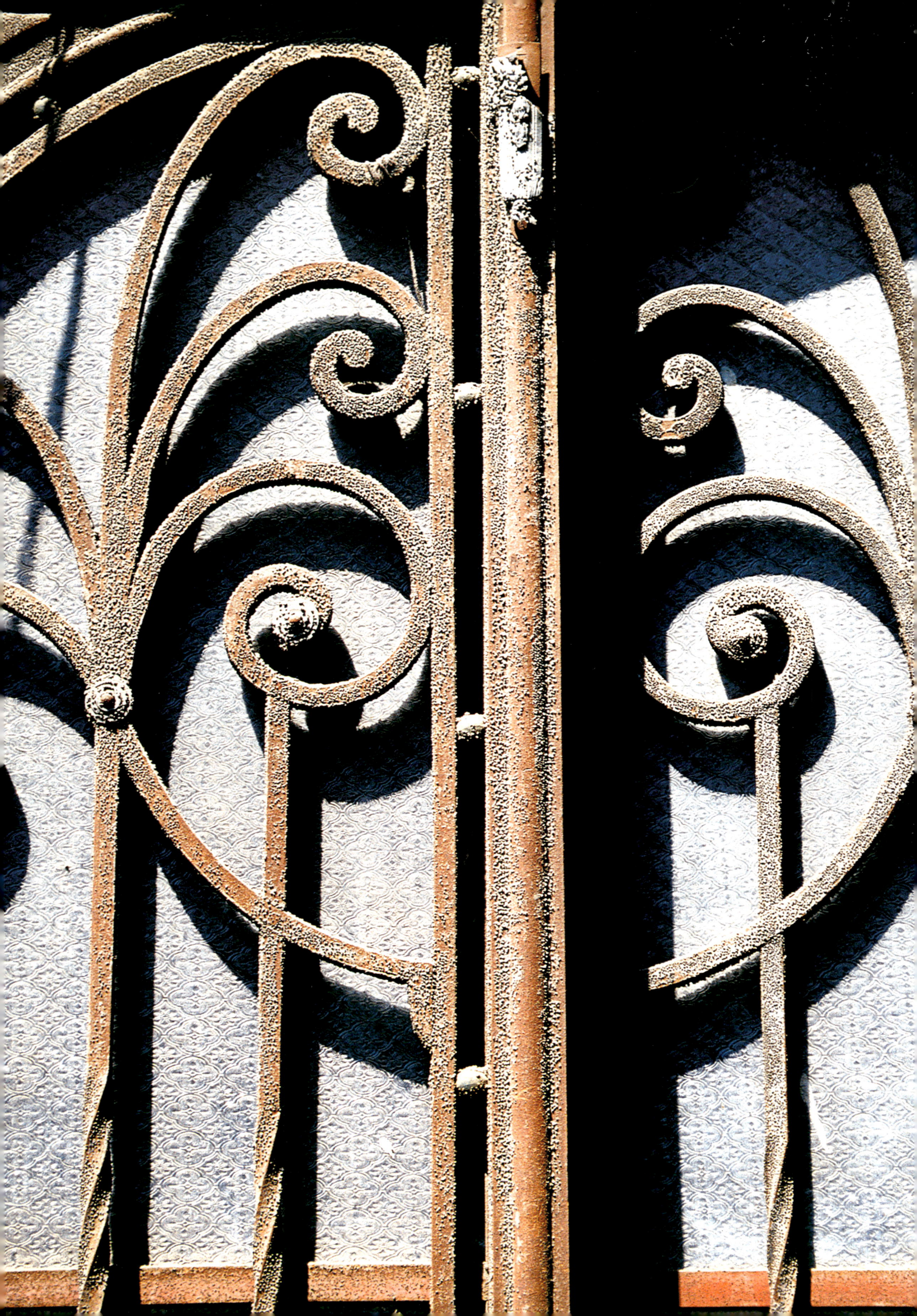

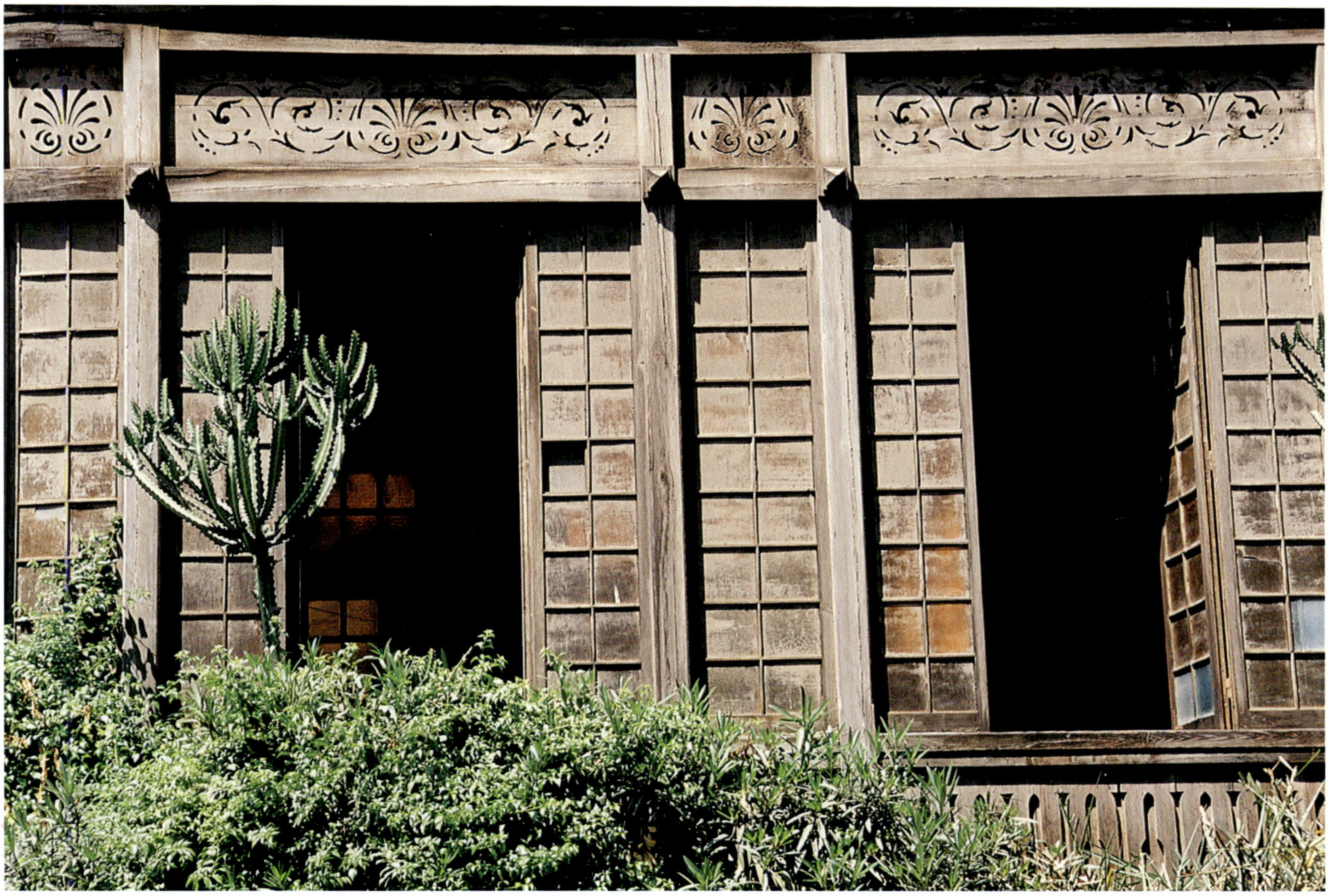

*A door in Garden City, Cairo*

*A private house in Garden City, Cairo*

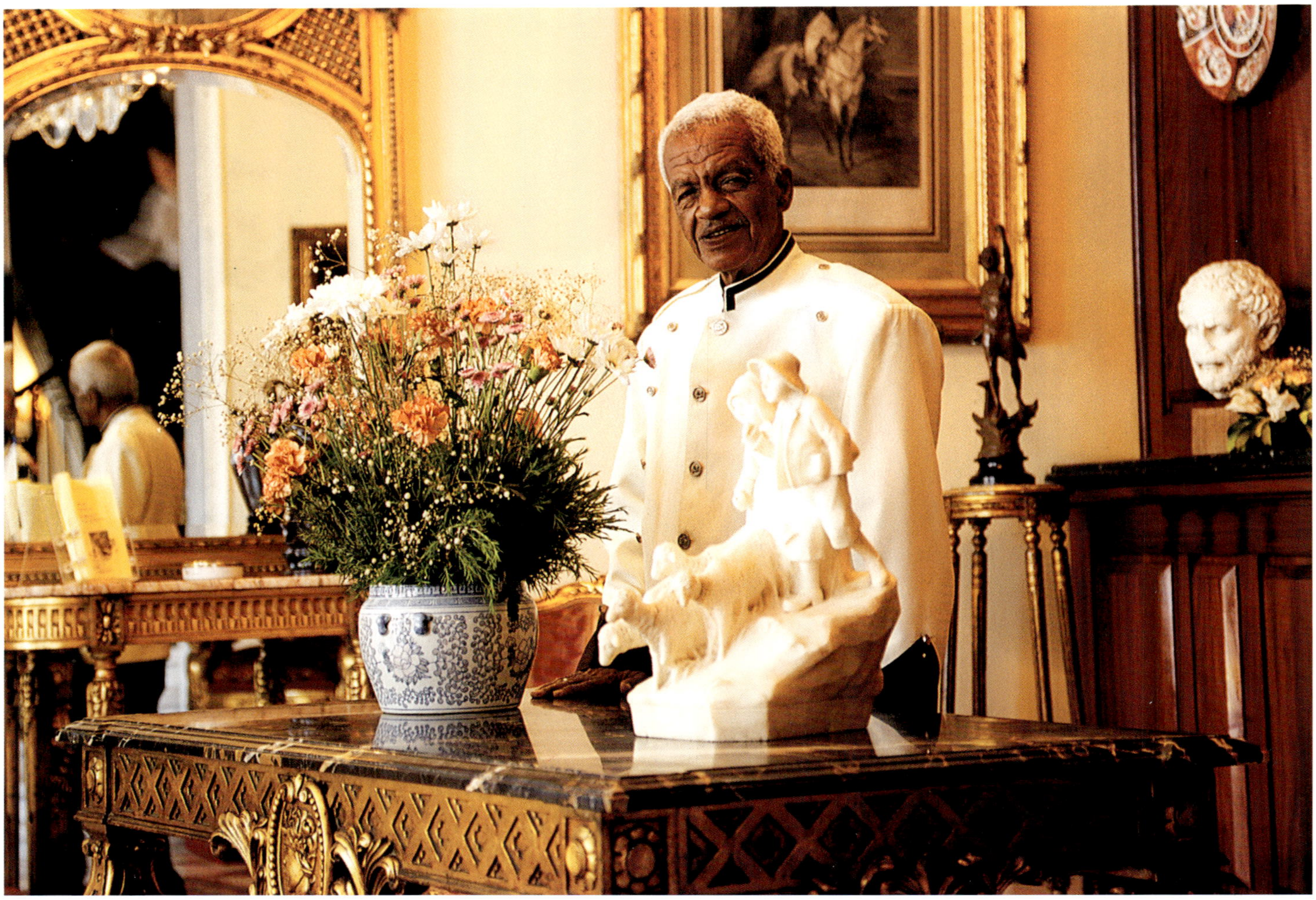

*The barman at the Metropole Hotel, Alexandria*

**Emile Attia**

*Restaurant owner in Alexandria*

"Quickly! Quickly! Move that table, change this glass, light the candles. He's on his way! He'll be here in a minute."

Everybody became suddenly nervous, and in the next moment they were all bowing elegantly, looking down, as if captivated by the color of the floor. A shrill voice broke the silence: "Good evening, Your Majesty," said Panayoti Soulos, the owner of Santa Lucia at that time, now one of the oldest restaurants in Alexandria. "Would you be so kind as to follow me? This is your table, Your Majesty, the one you normally prefer. I will immediately send you our Mostapha, to serve you a cold glass of champagne."

"It was a lovely period, with fantastic memories," says Emile Attia, who in 1993 became Soulos's partner. King Farouk and his wife Farida were regular customers, "and secretly,"—Attia lowers his voice, while a sly smile emerges on his round face accented by large eyeglasses—"on other occasions, his attractive lover." Attia surveys his restaurant. "King Farouk used to sit at that table, next to the big window over there," he points out. "His favorite dish was the *tarama*, a special caviar imported from Greece and puréed with spices and seasonings. We were actually the only place at that time allowed to import caviar. It normally arrived by boat in a big freezer. I remember how difficult it was to plan a menu without even knowing whether or not the caviar was coming."

Attia looks over the black-and-white pictures, hung on the thick walls, that record such a rich history. The old waiter Mostapha El-Saghir, the wooden interior, the bar, the fireplace, and the dance floor are still there today, as they were when Santa Lucia hosted royalty. The sound of music is there, too, but it is different now, as are the faces of the people who sit around a table once reserved for a king.

*S. D.*

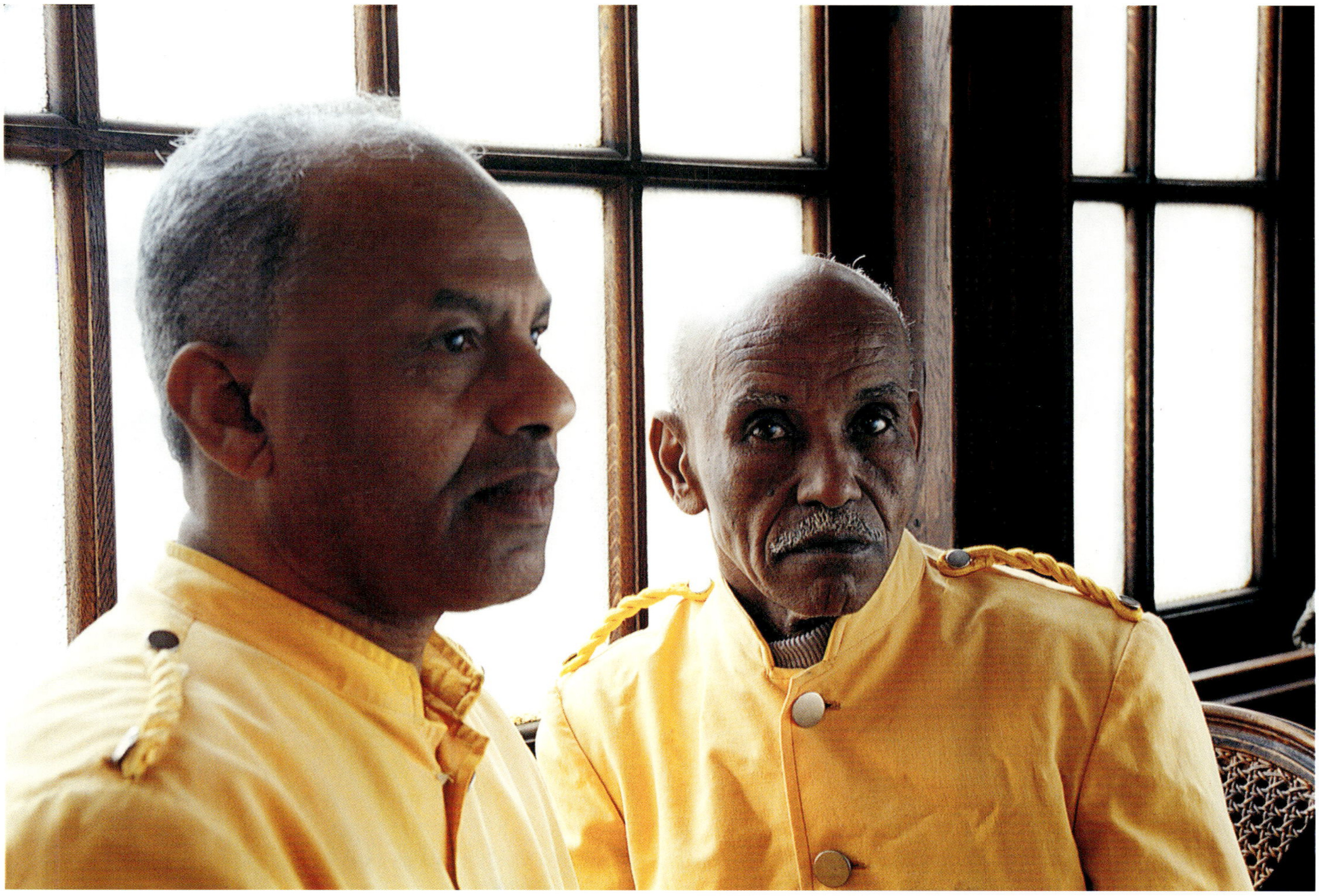

*Waiters at the Santa Lucia Restaurant, Alexandria*

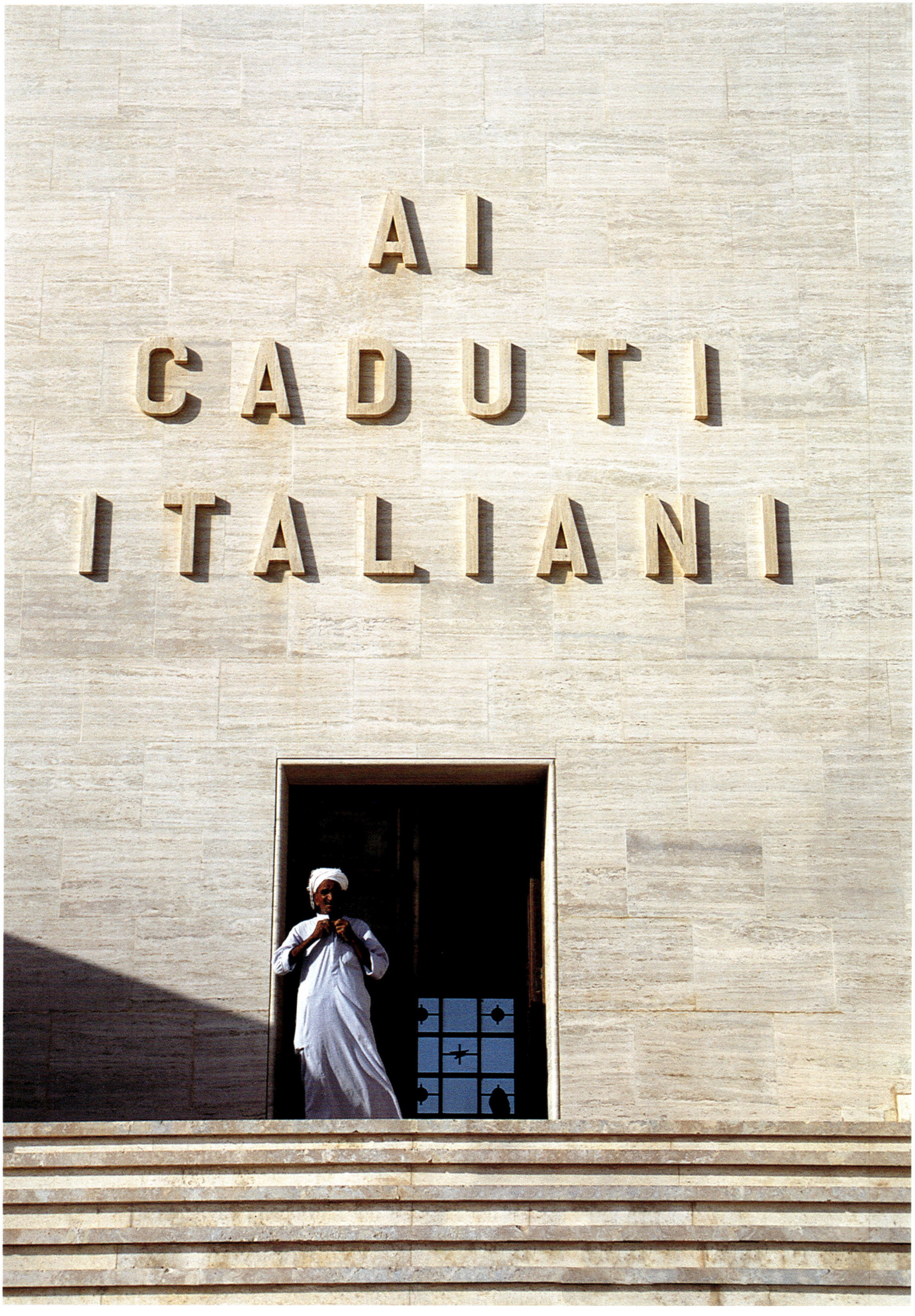


*The Italian sanctuary, El Alamein*

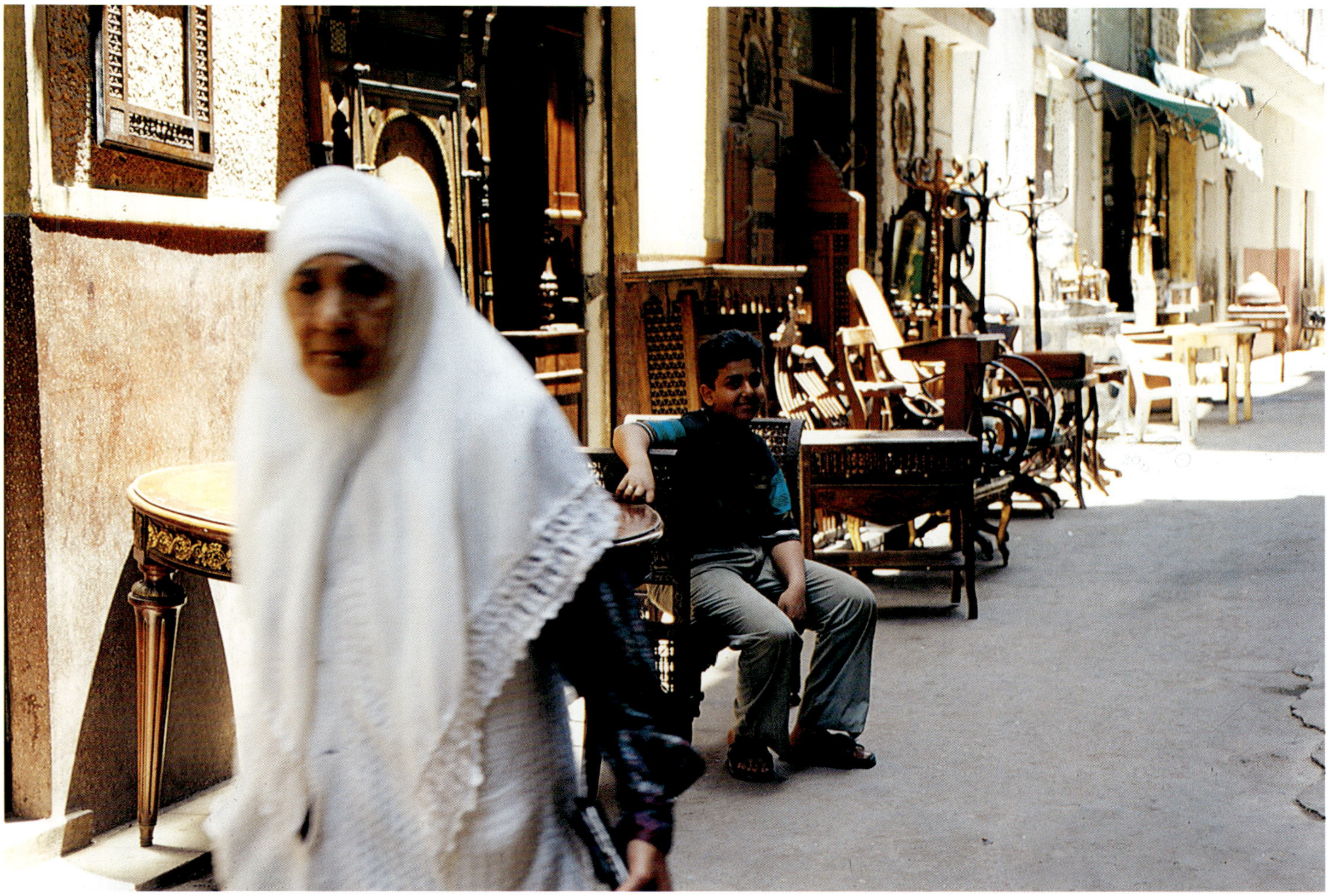

*The old area of al-'Attarin, Alexandria*

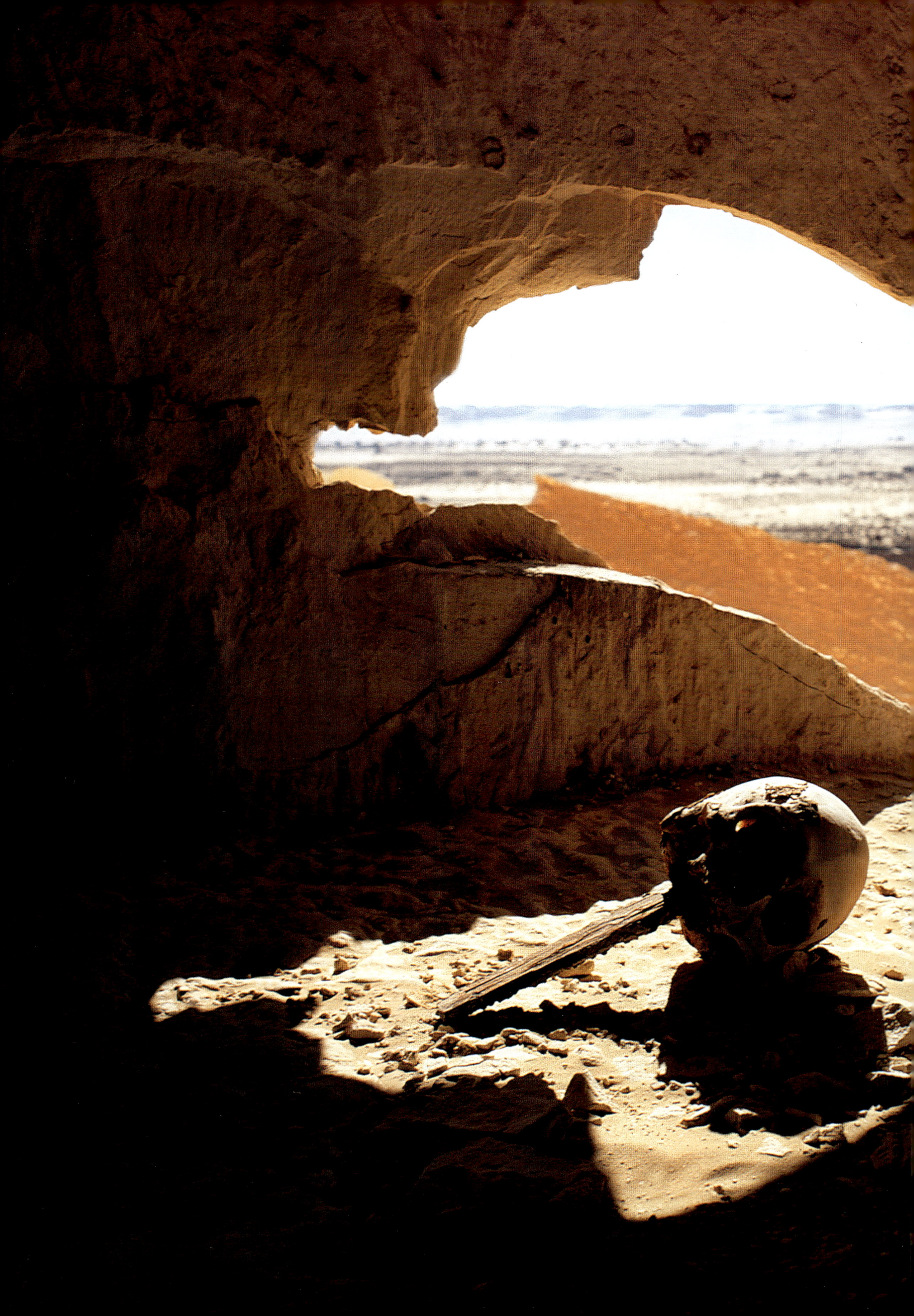

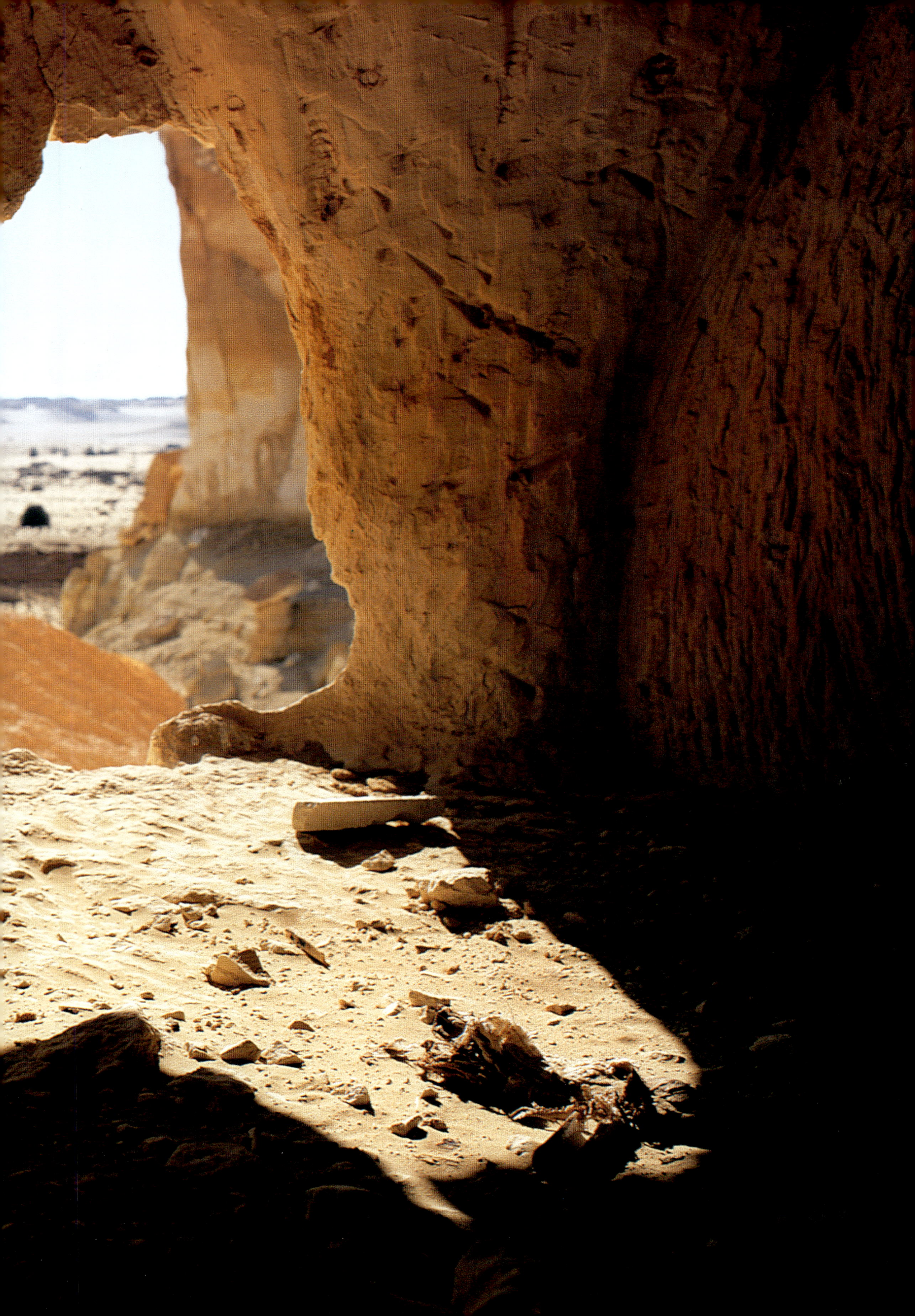

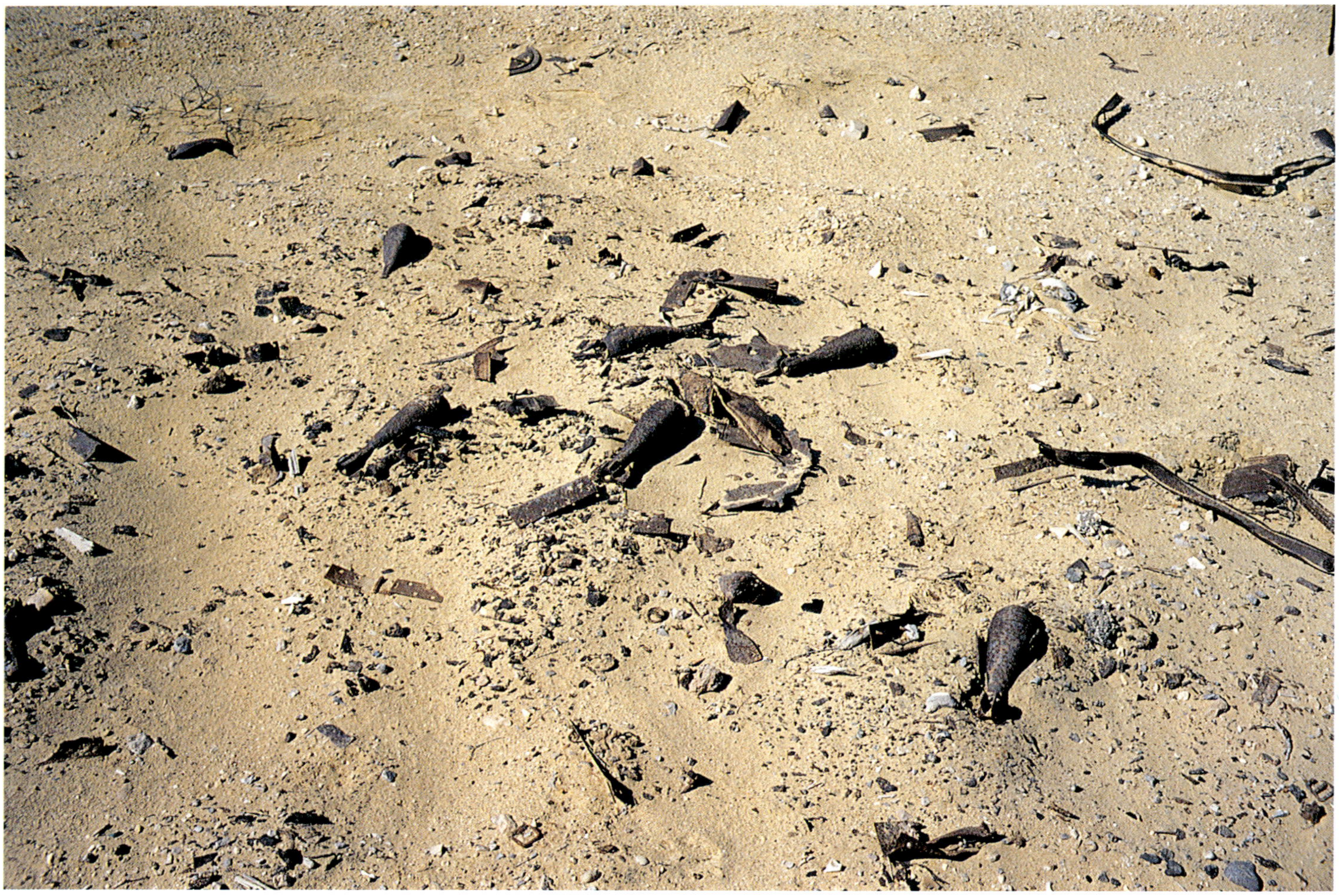

*Previous page: A tomb in the Western Desert*

*Unexploded bombs, Sinai*

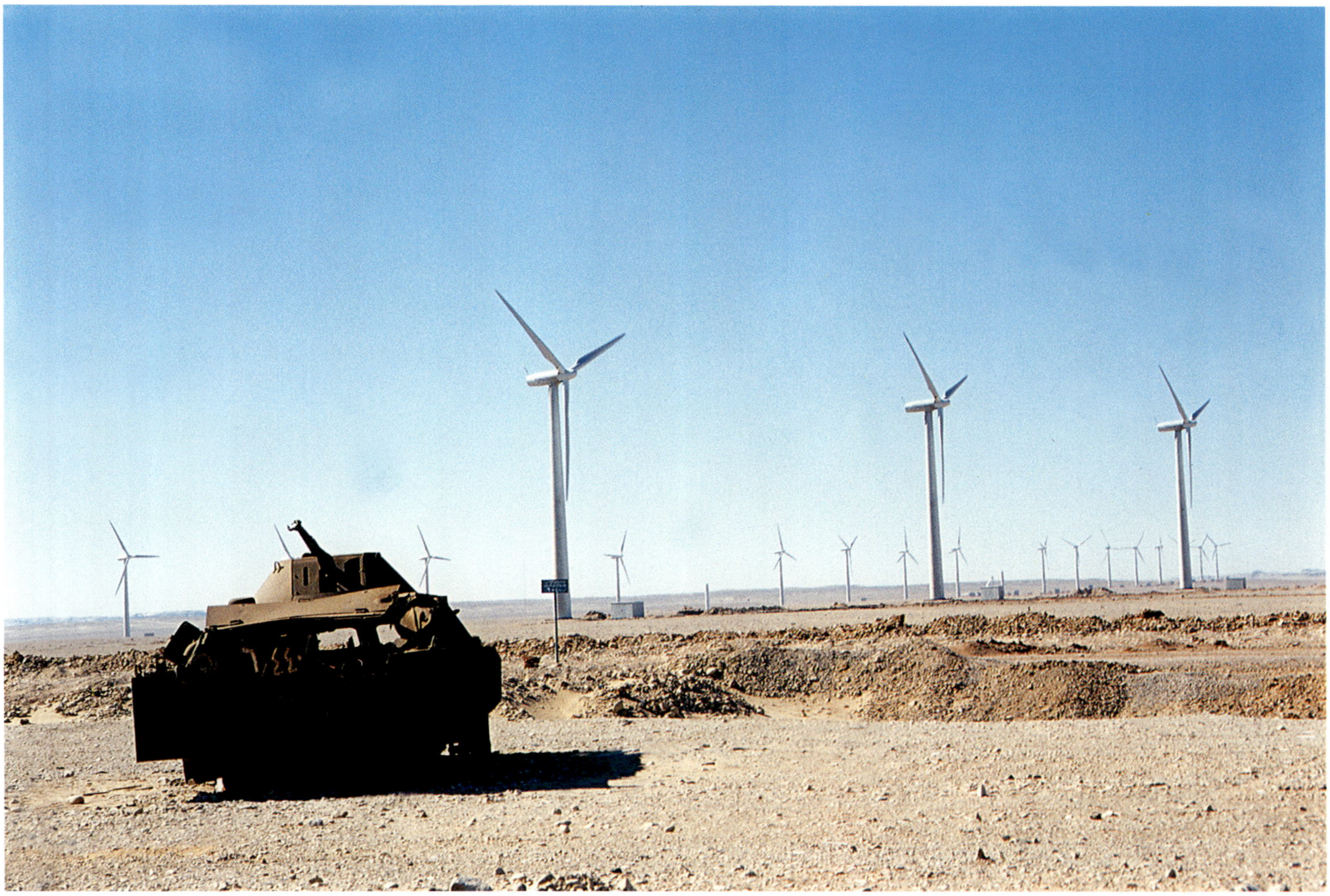

*The remains of a tank on the road to Hurghada*

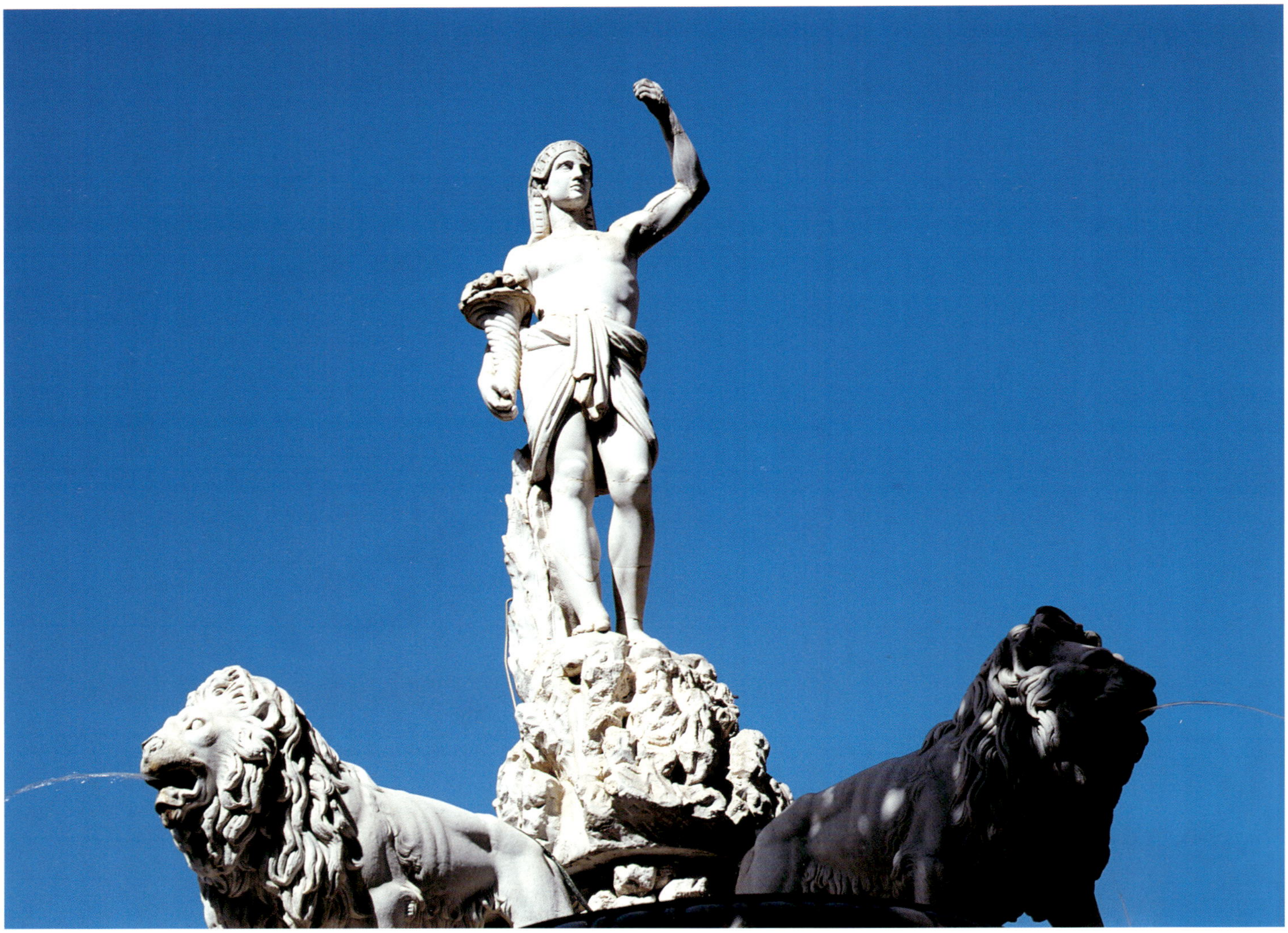

*A fountain in the gardens of the Marriott Hotel, Cairo*

*Statue of Alexander the Great, Alexandria*

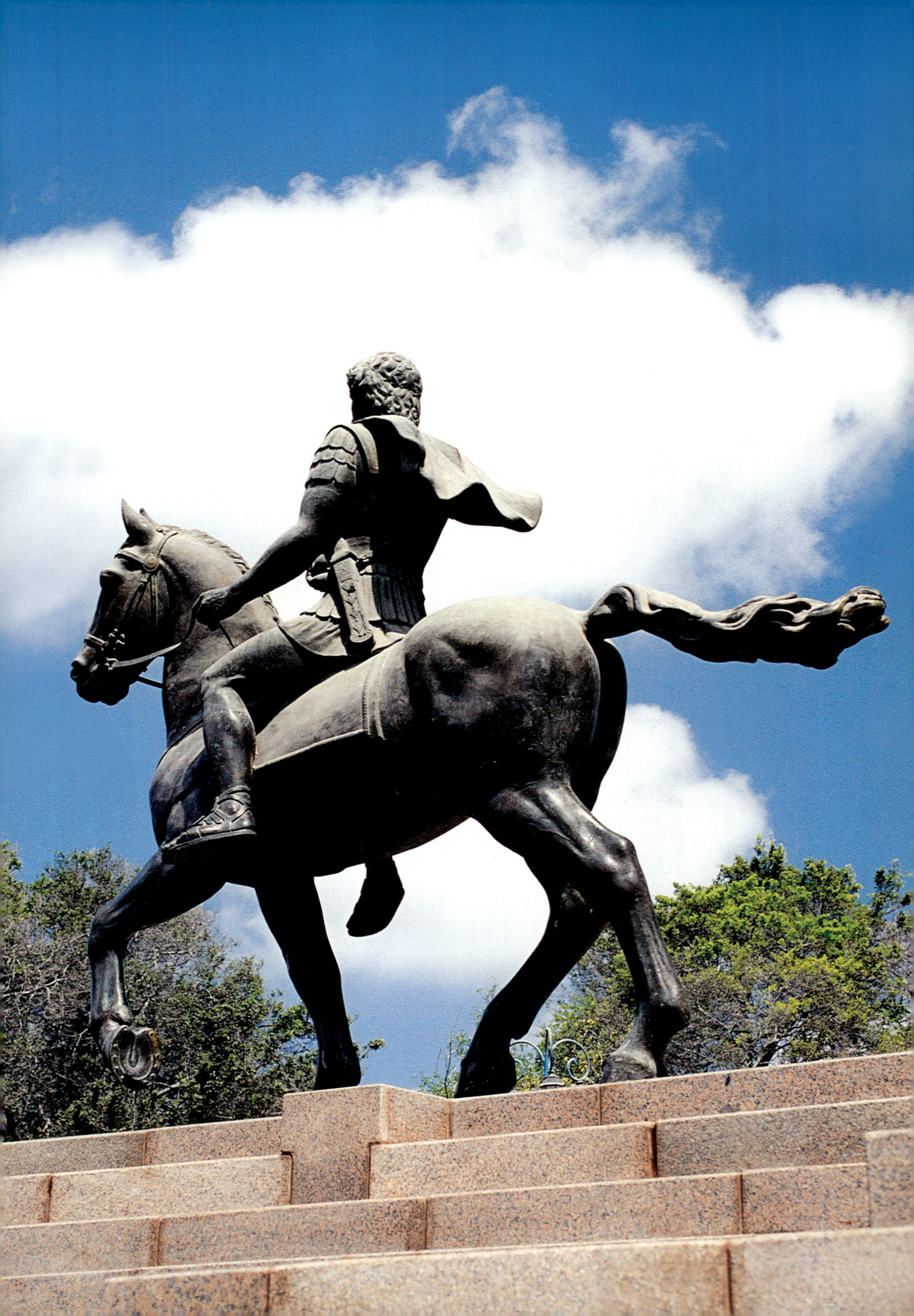

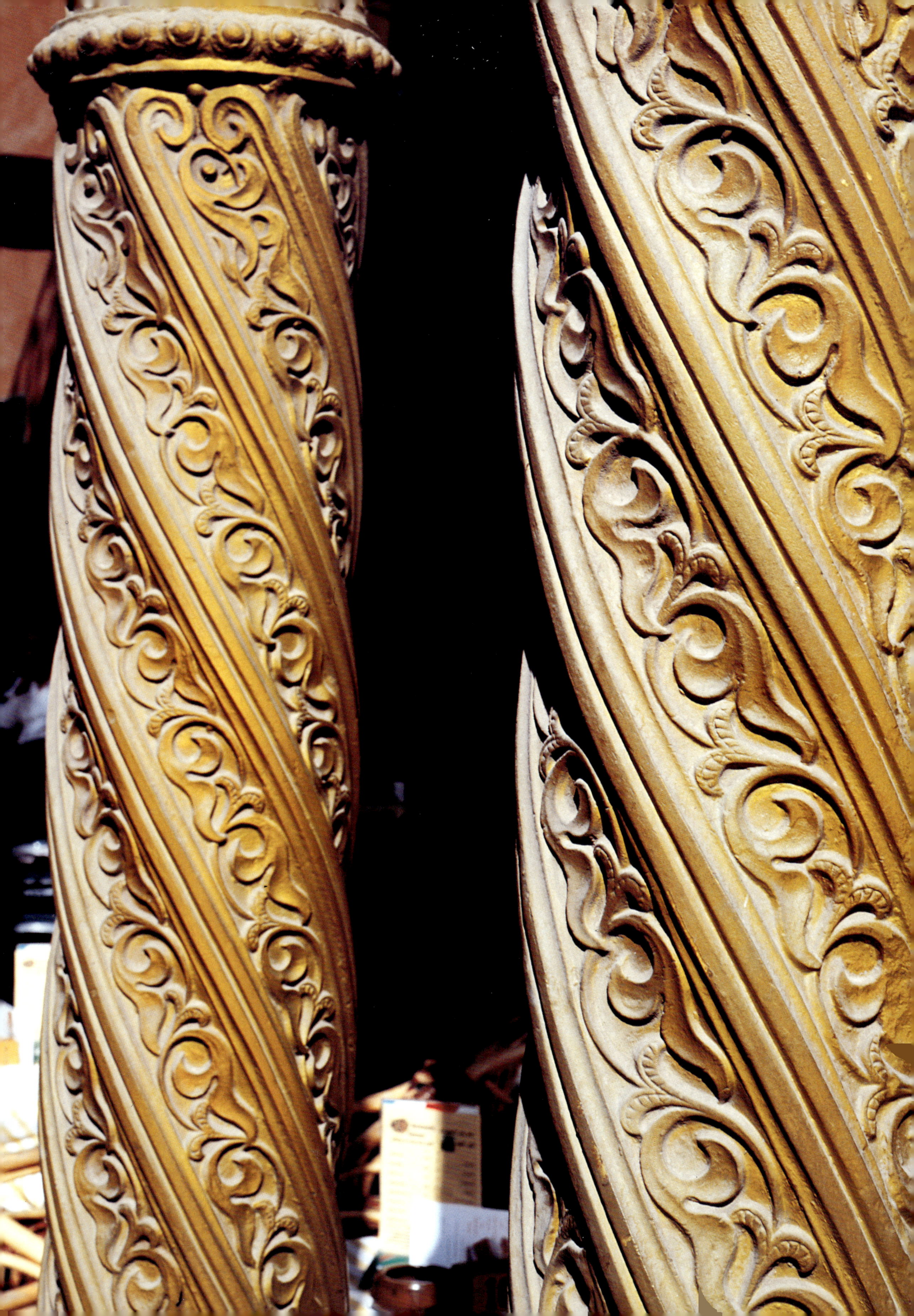

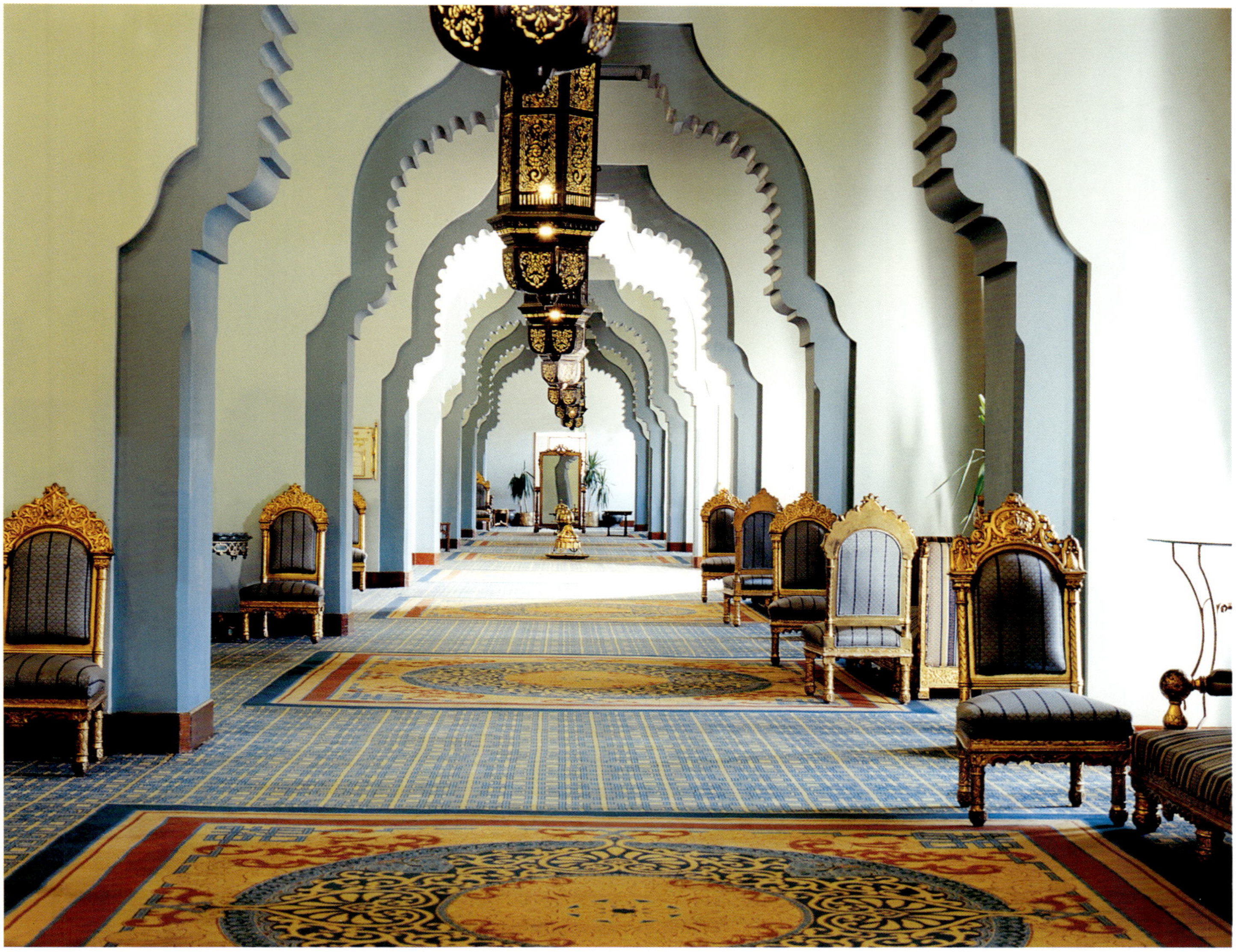

*The Cairo Marriott Hotel*

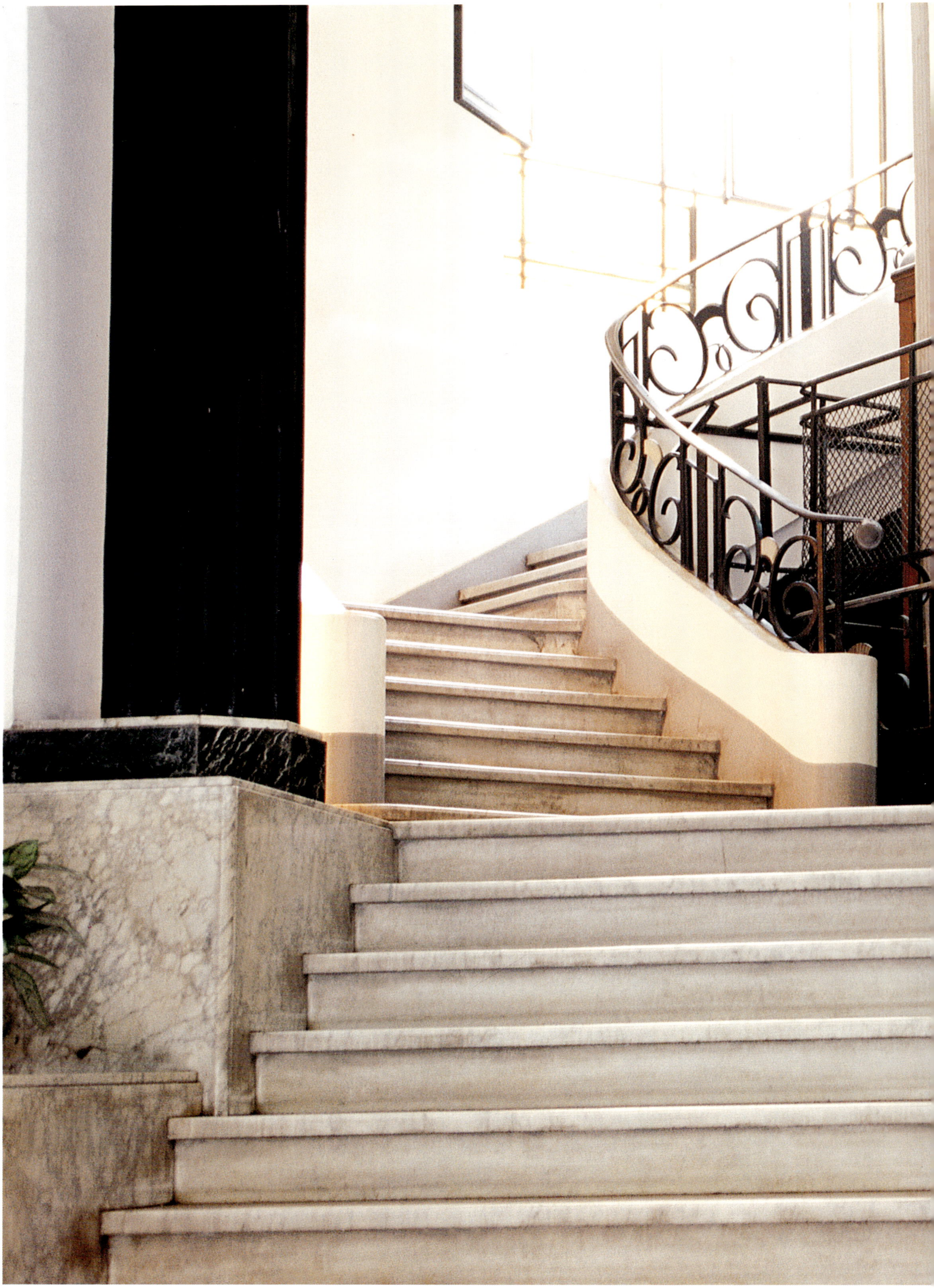

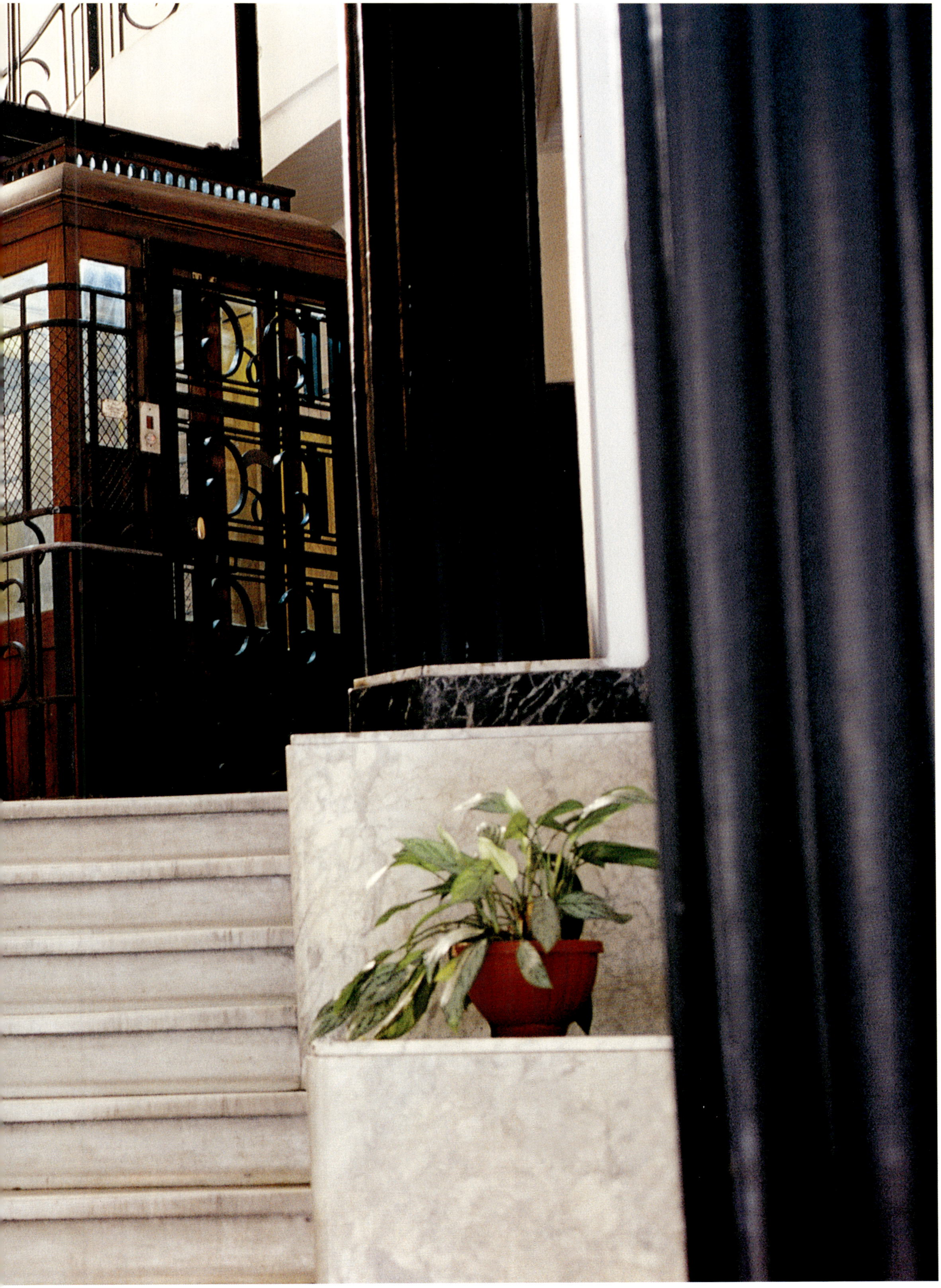

*An elevator in Zamalek, Cairo*

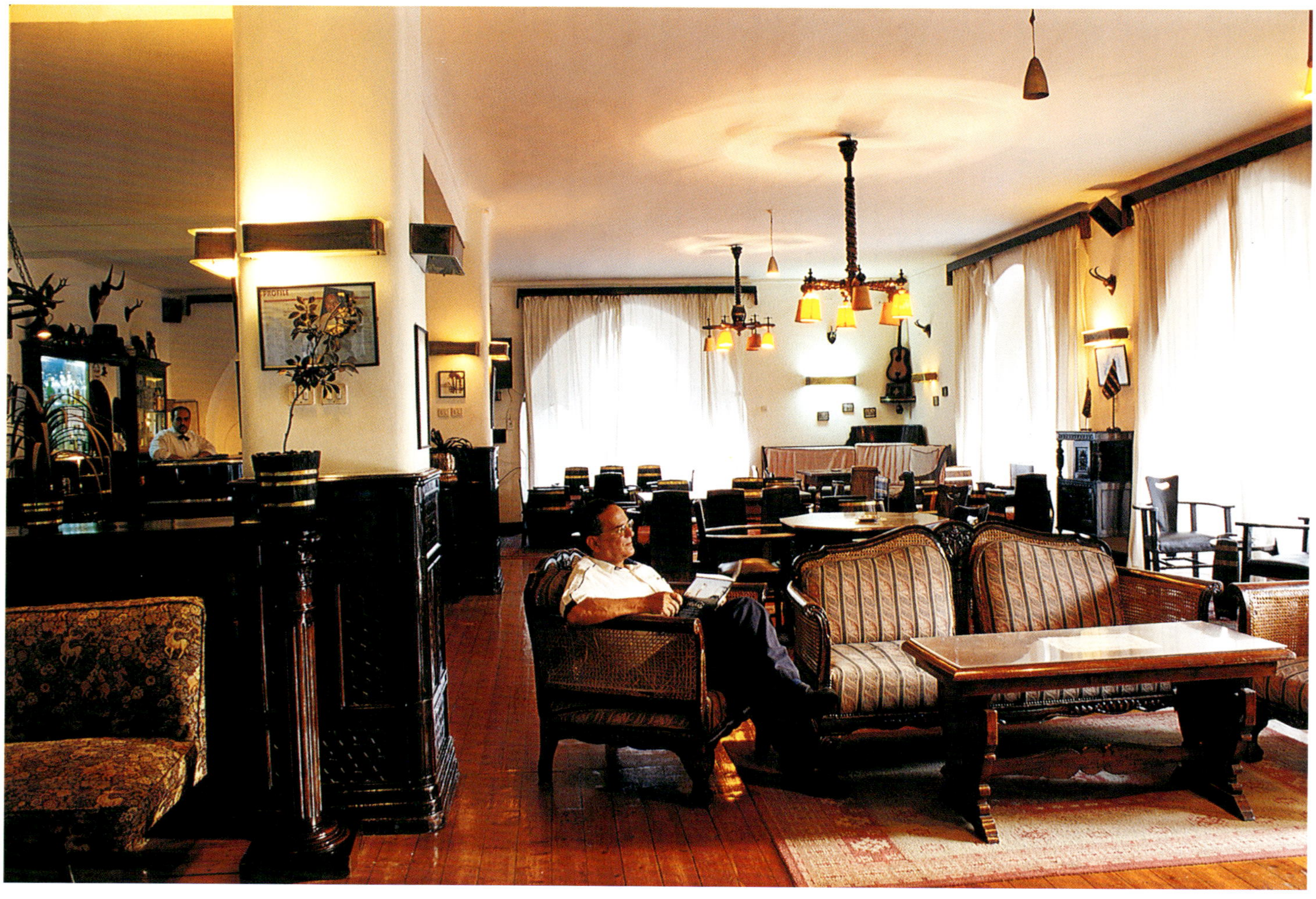

*The bar of the Windsor Hotel, Cairo*

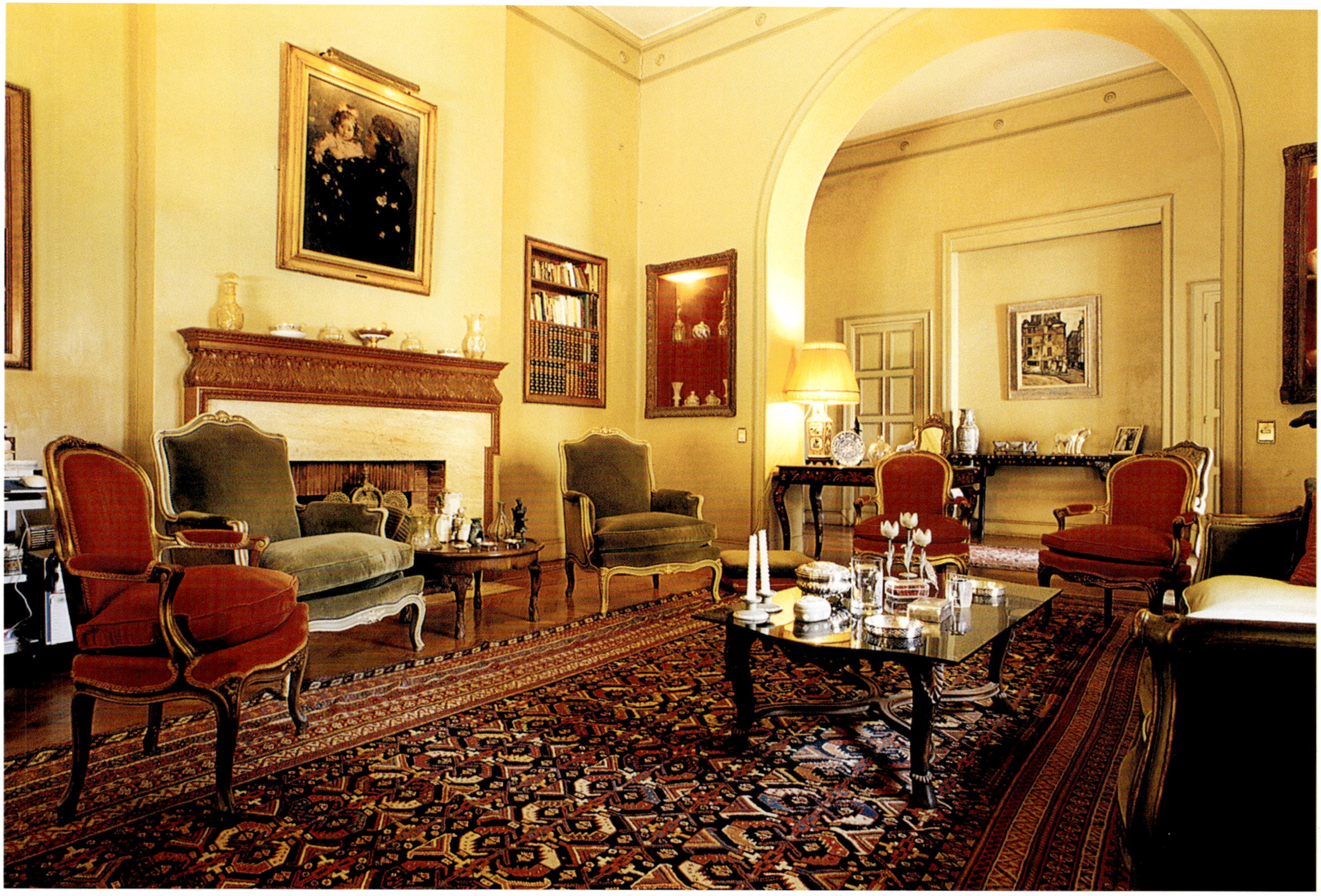

*Sherif Sabry Pasha Palace, Alexandria*

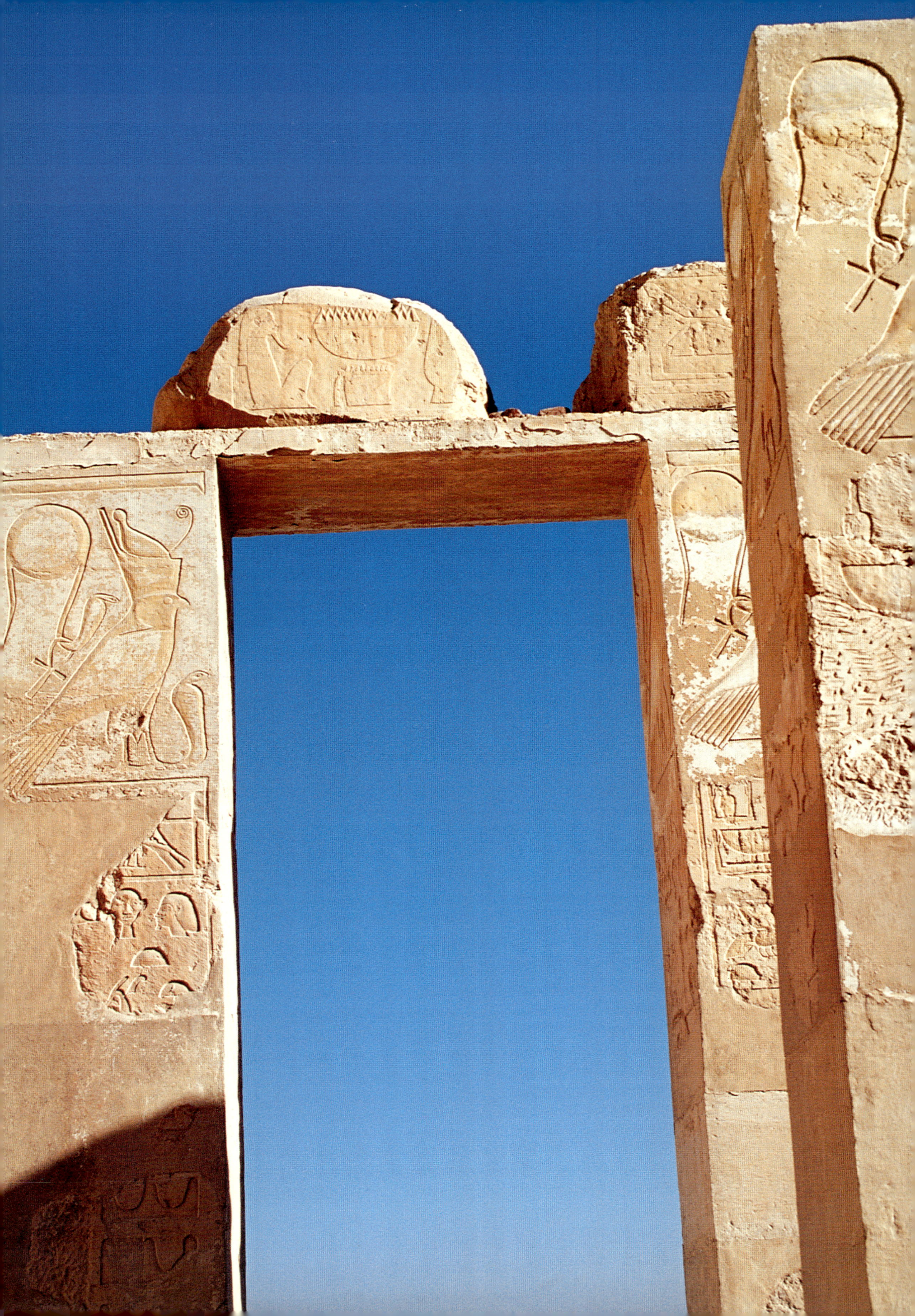

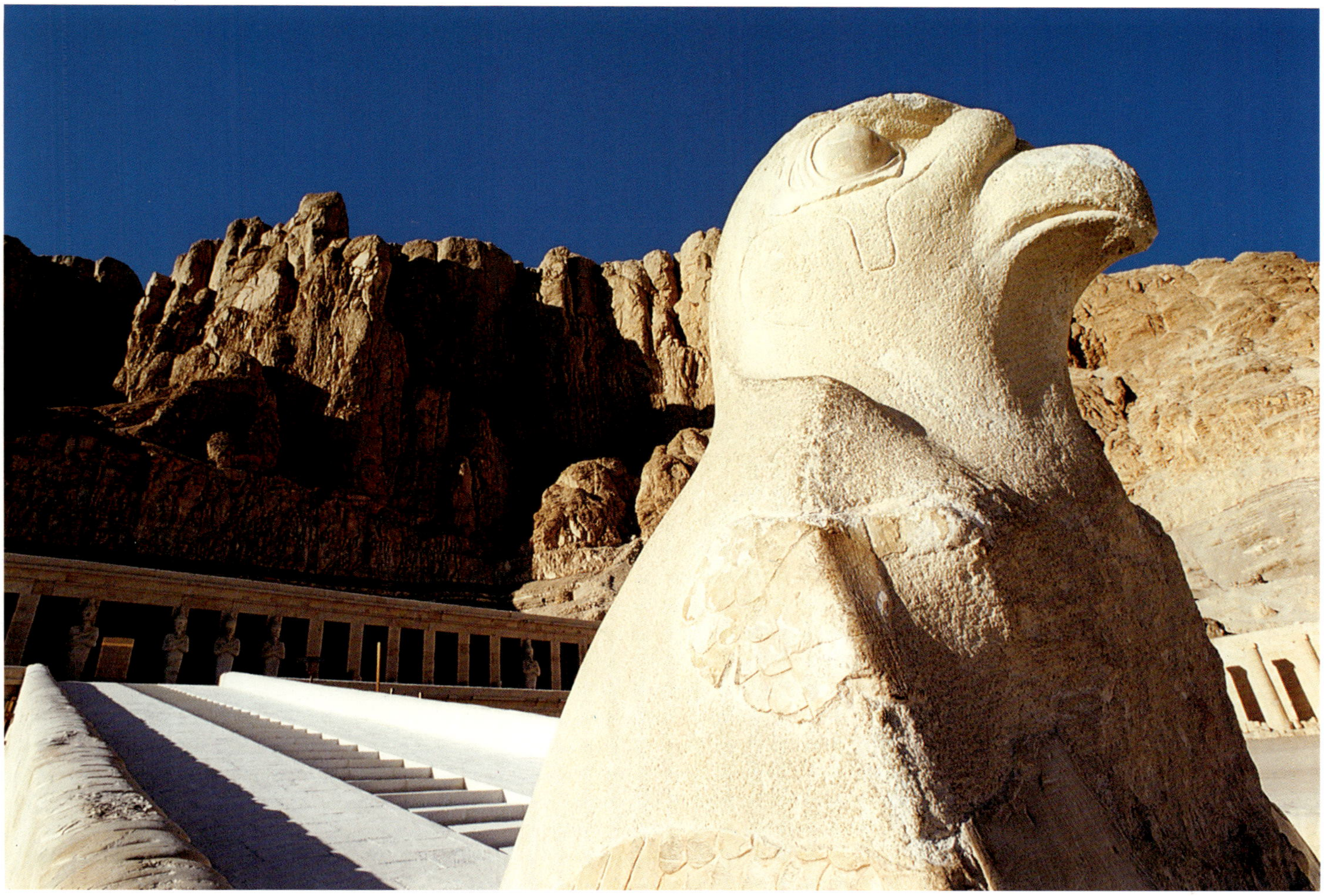

*The Temple of Hatshepsut, Luxor*

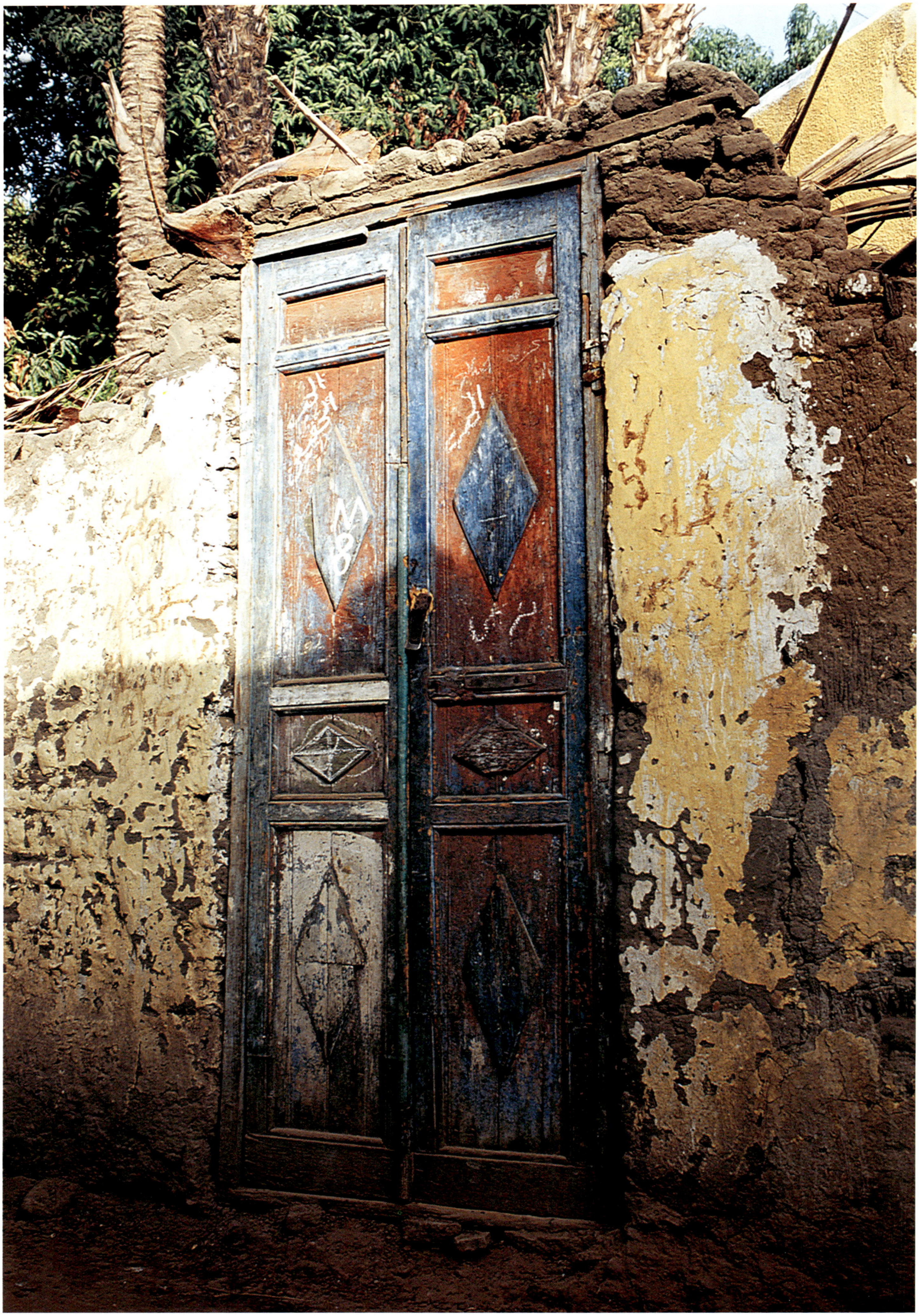

*In a Nubian village, Aswan*

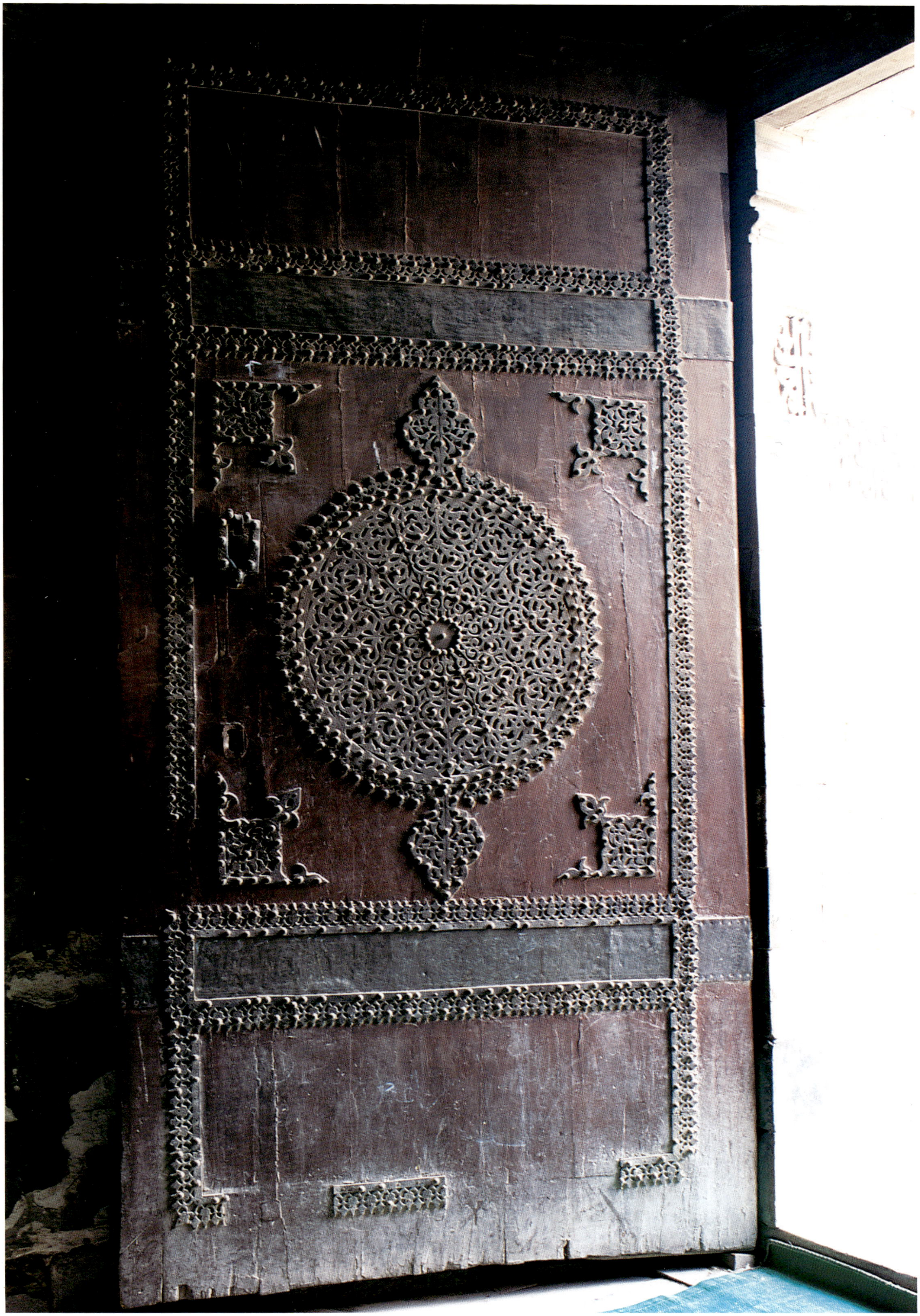

*The door of the Mausoleum of Qaitbay, City of the Dead, Cairo*

*Next page: One of the coffins of Tutankhamun, Egyptian Museum, Cairo*

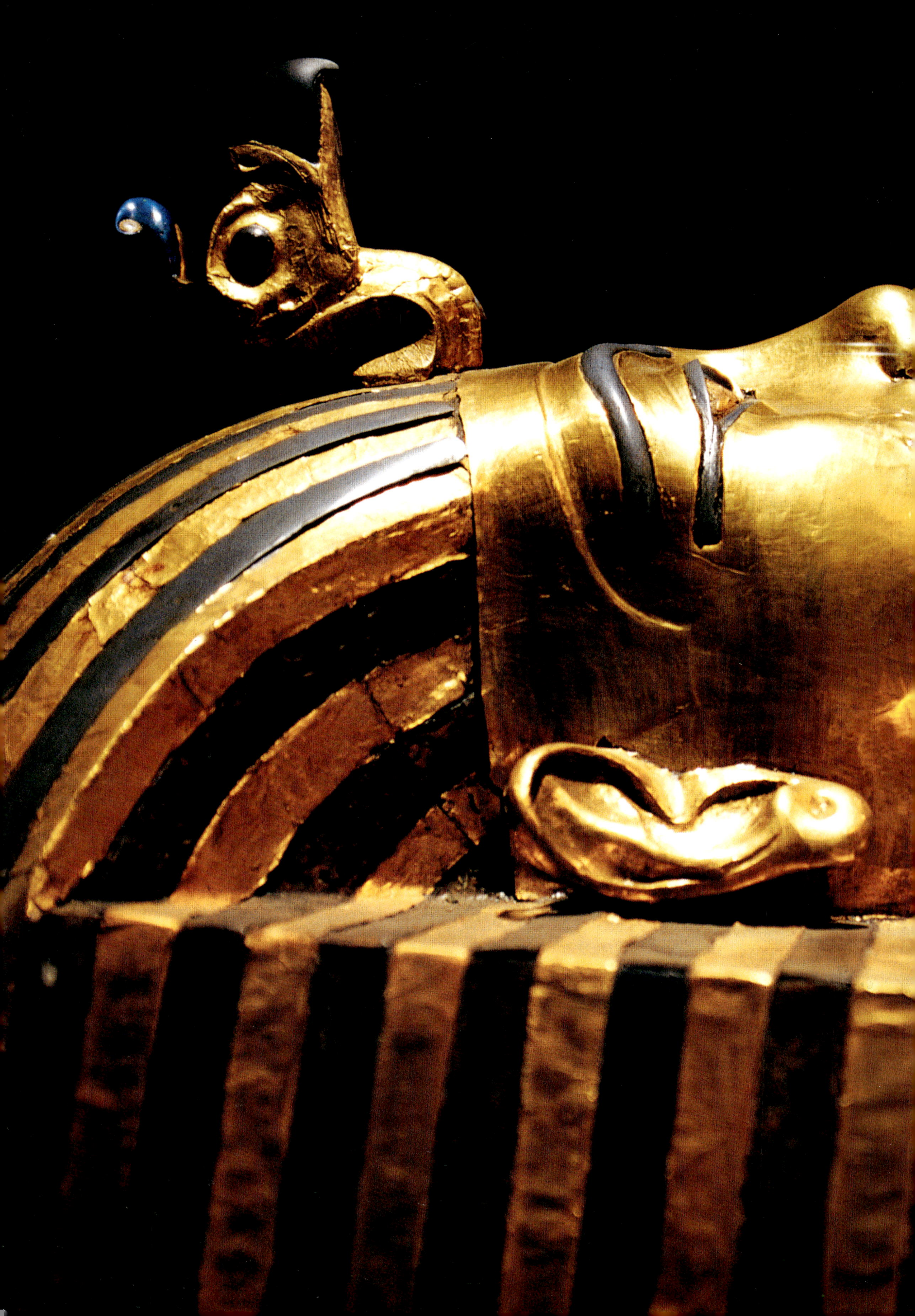

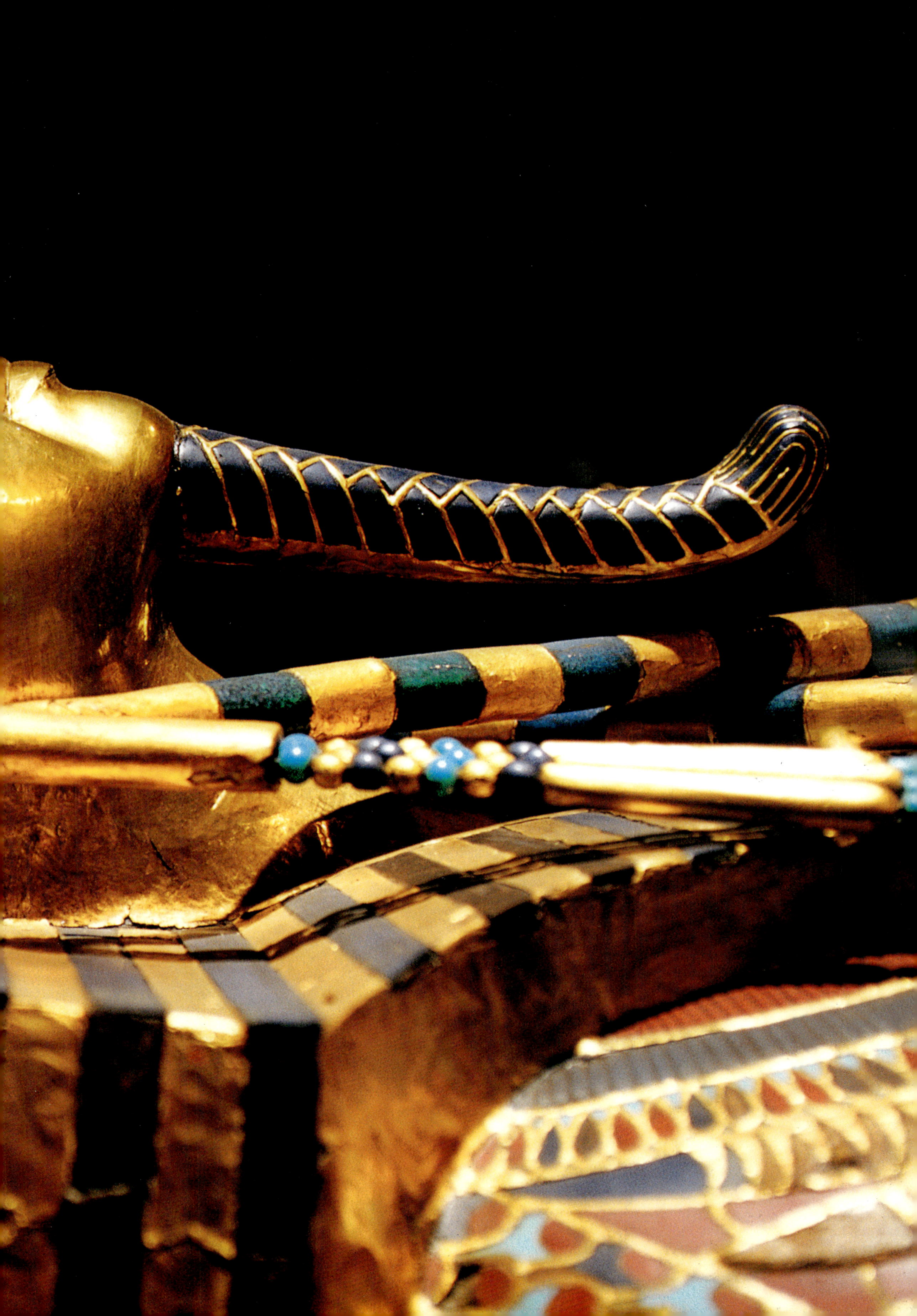

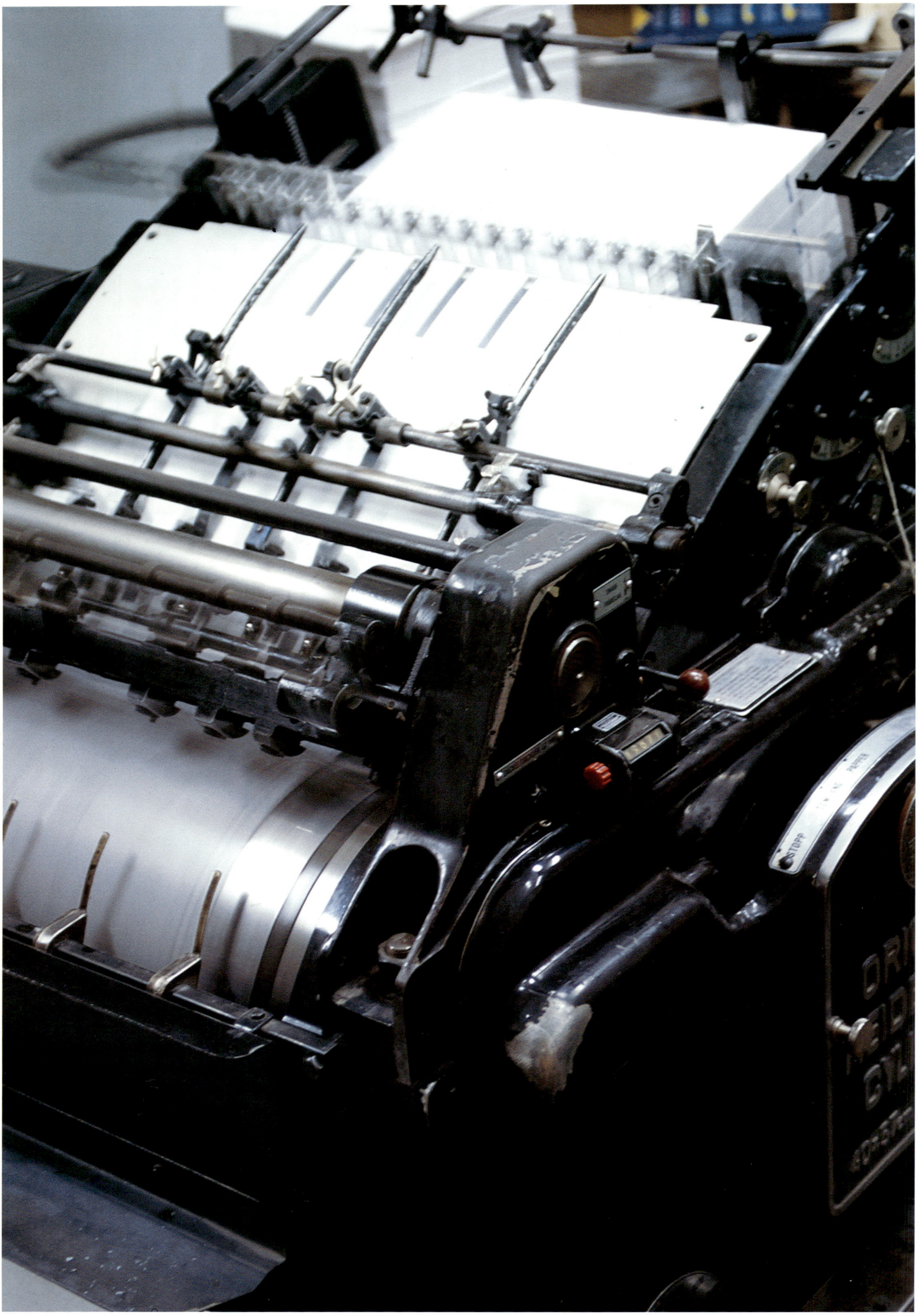

*Printing machine, Cairo*

*The wreck of a German Stuka combat plane from the Second World War, Western Desert*

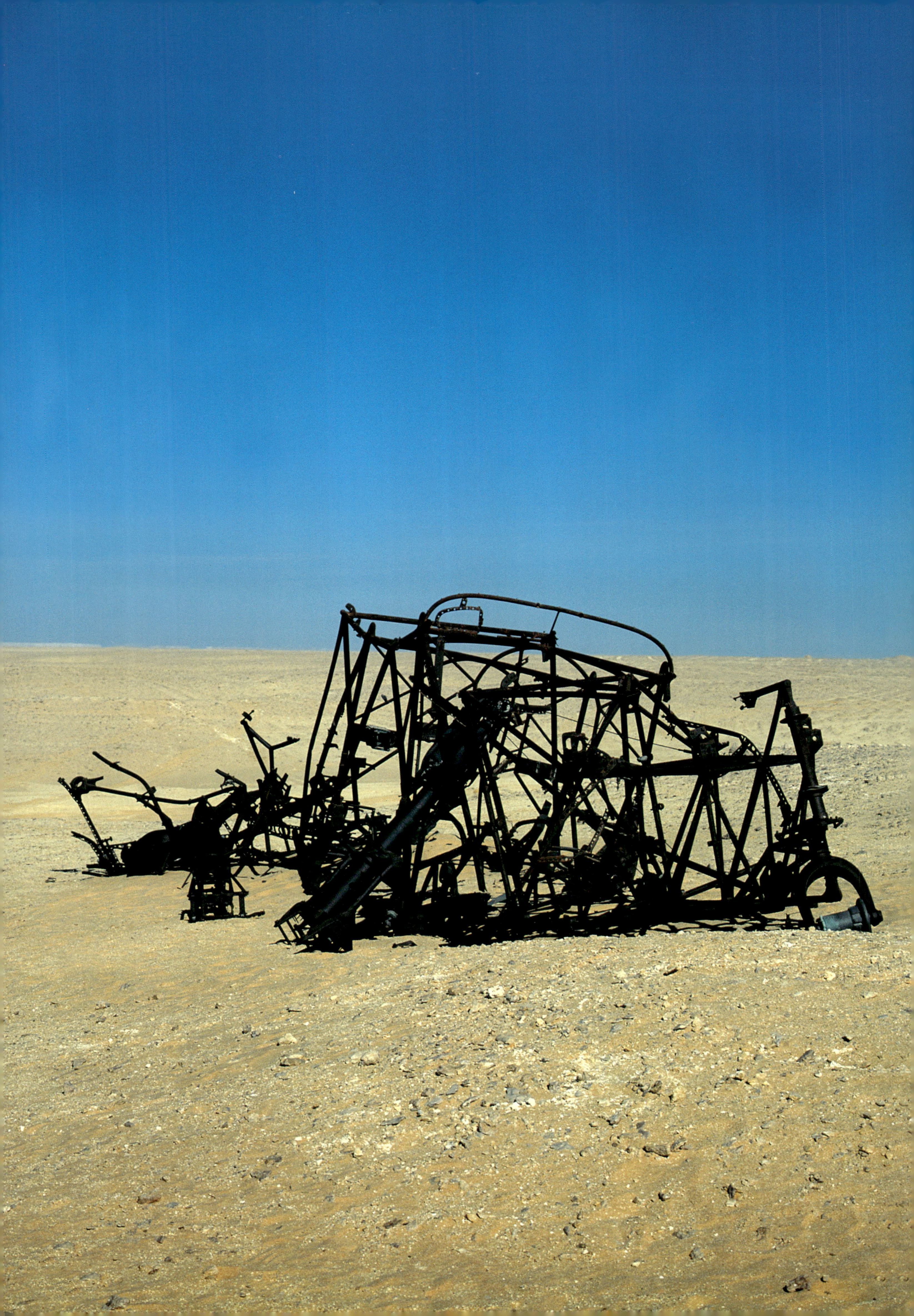

## Ahmed El-Barkooky

*Geologist*

When Ahmed El-Barkooky looks at the Egyptian desert, he does not see just an endless, undulating expanse of sand. He sees the past.

"Layers is the magic word, because they are history," says El-Barkooky, a geologist who grew up and studied in Cairo, and did part of his doctoral work in Germany. "Each layer provides one page of the history book, which includes lots of hints and ciphers of old life, environments, climate, ecosystems, and so forth."

The main information comes from fossils, which are animal and plant remains. These tell about the kinds of organisms that existed in the past, as well as their habits. "The work of geology is to try to sort out the puzzle of what you see from the record of the rocks, and inside those rocks you have old life, vegetation, everything."

During one trip to the Fayoum desert west of Cairo, El-Barkooky pointed out circular fossils known as angels' coins. These give an indication that at one time, about forty million years ago, the desert was an ocean—the waters of the Mediterranean extended even to the southern section of Egypt. "Then about thirty-five million years ago," says Barkooky, "or something around there, it was forest and savannah and such things."

El-Barkooky's frame of reference is hard to grasp—in conversation he brings up "millions of years" the way the rest of us talk about last week, and he can create a mental picture of what the landscape looked like during that ancient time. Nonetheless, the record that was left millions of years ago is far from straightforward. Not everything leaves a trace, after all. As El-Barkooky explains it, each layer is related to a certain period of time, but the thickness of the layer does not always correspond to the expanse of time. "You can have a very thin layer containing a condensed period," he says, "and you can have a very thick layer that was deposited in only a few hours."

El-Barkooky cannot say for sure where he discovered his interest in the rocks that hold the keys to Egypt's past. "I only remember visiting the Geological Museum in secondary school," he says. "I kept going there, but I didn't know that I'd be working in that field." Upon finishing secondary school, however, he became certain that geology was his calling—"from day one of being admitted to the Faculty of Science at Cairo University," he notes.

Even after years of study, he remains deeply drawn to the Egyptian landscape. "I love the desert," he exclaims. "I feel peaceful there. Especially if you are there at the right moment, at the right time, it looks very beautiful. I never feel lonely in the desert. There's some sort of harmony with the landscape."

As well as an intimate glimpse of history.

*T. E.*

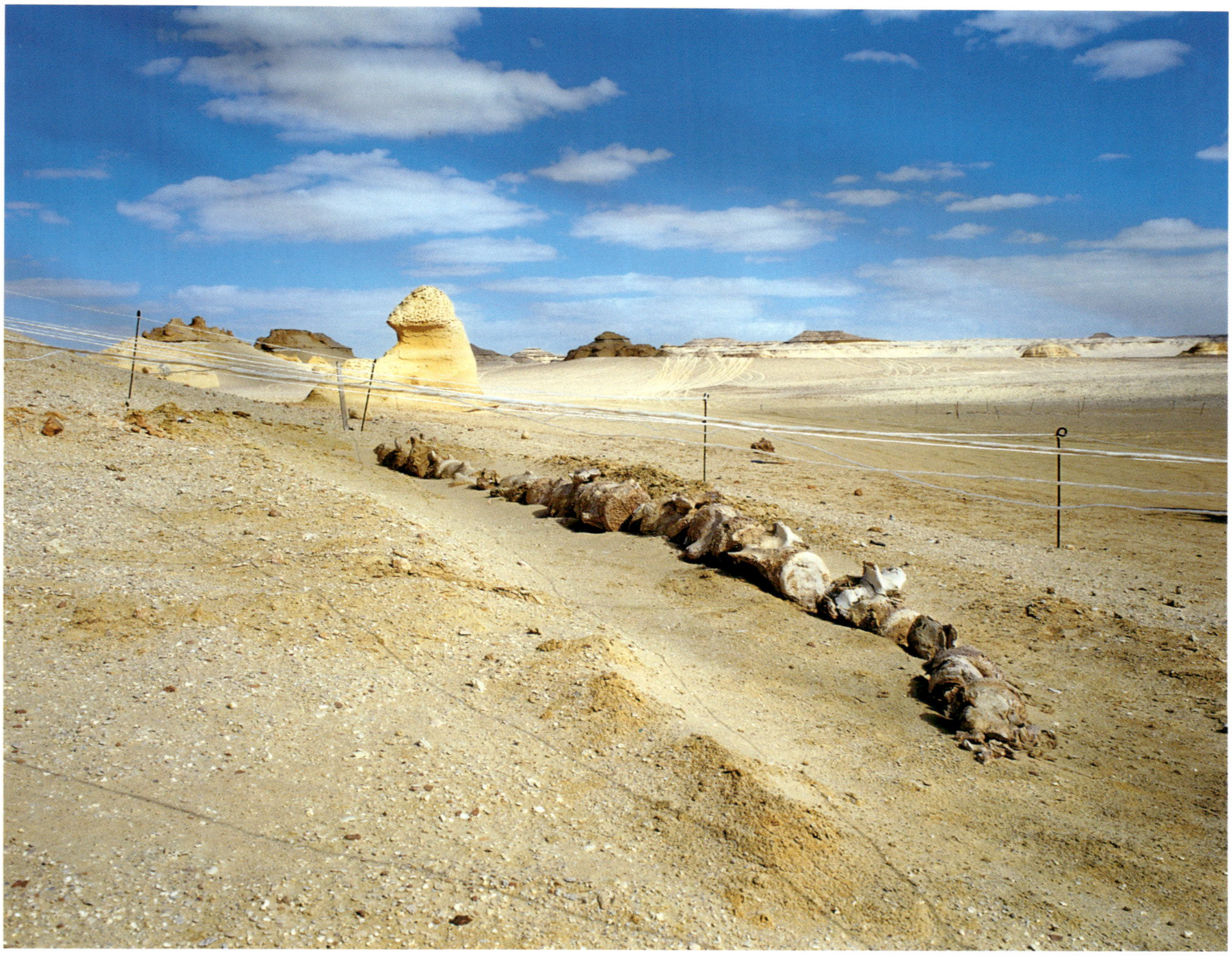

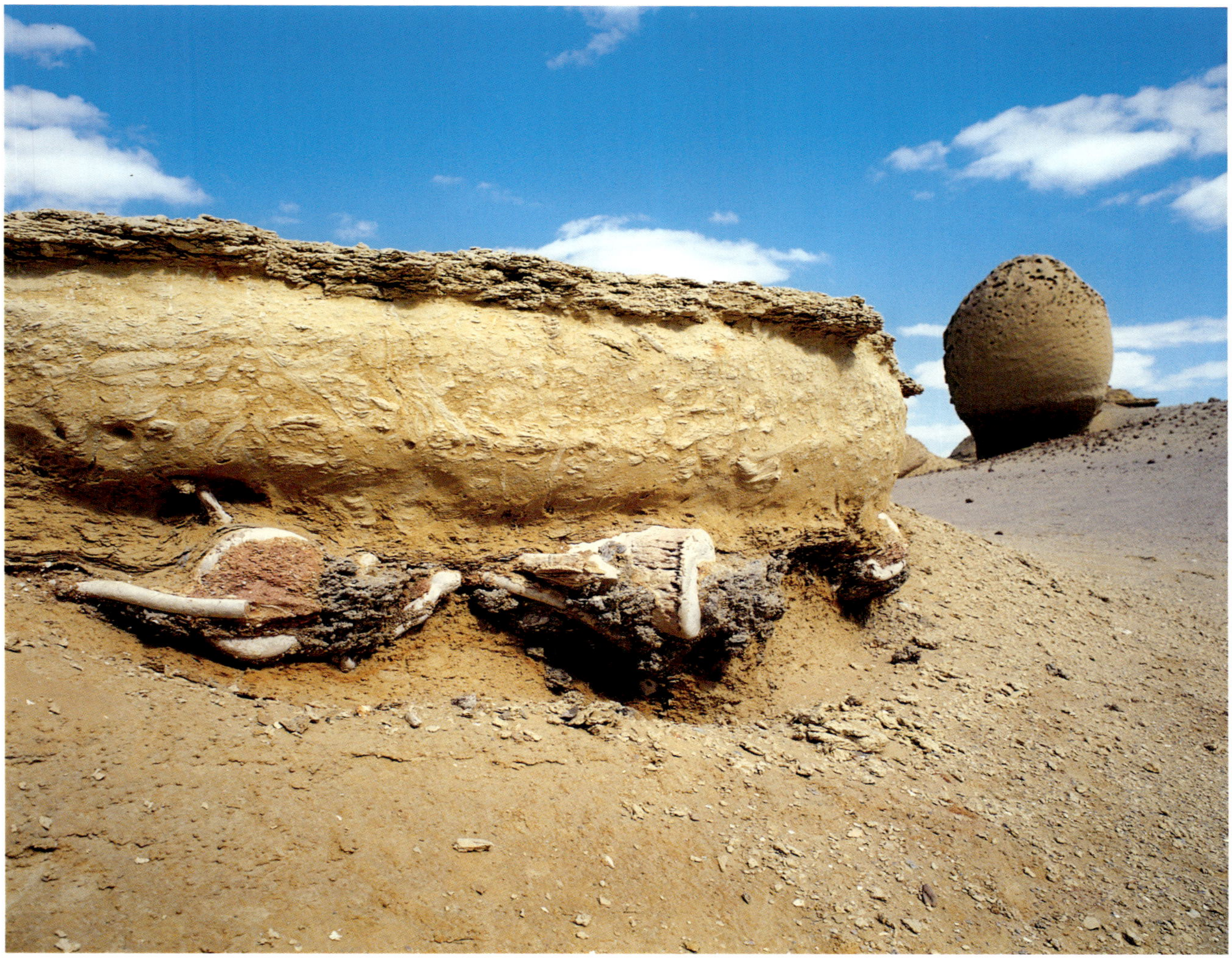

*Skeletons of ancient whales, Valley of the Whales, Western Desert*

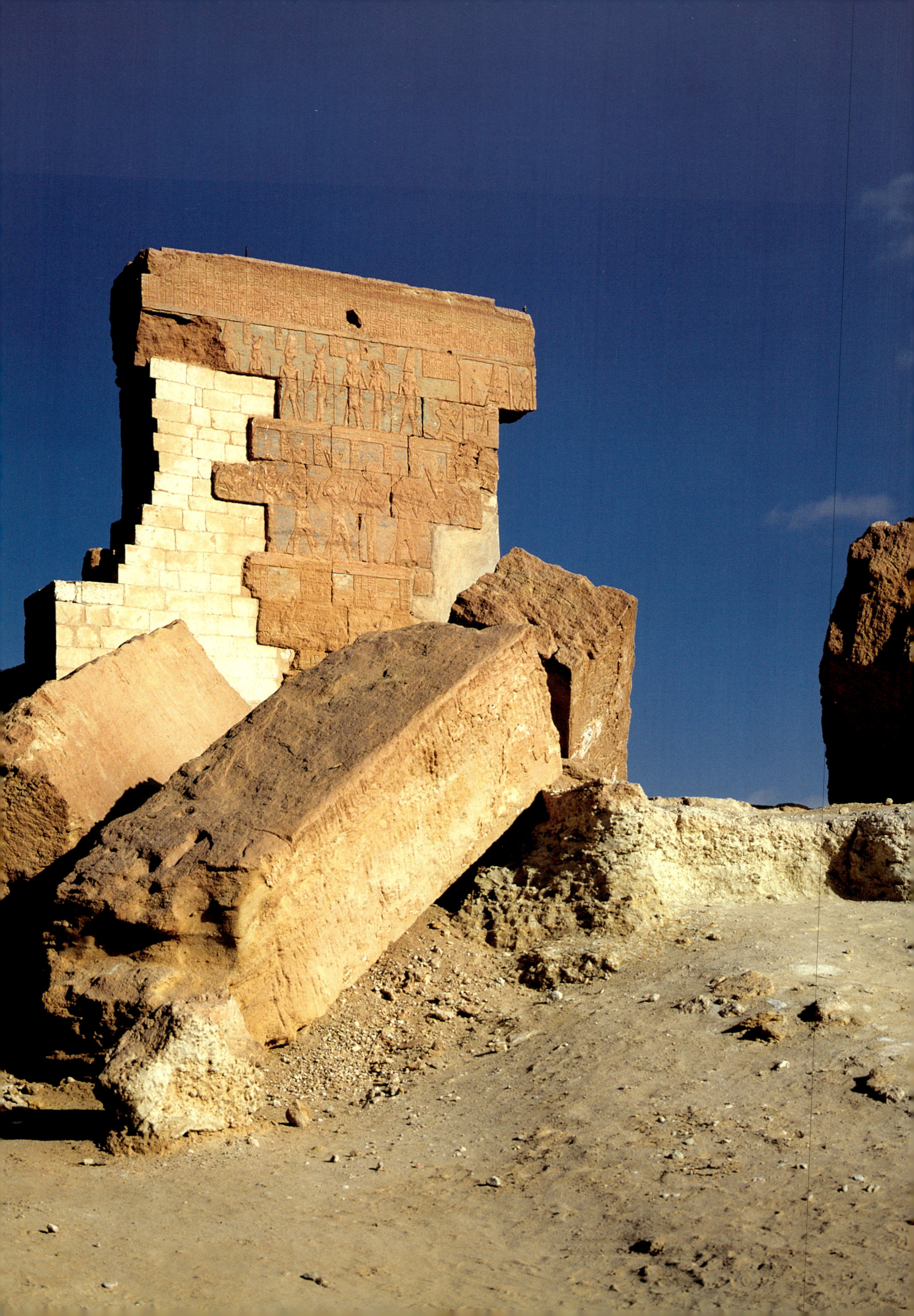

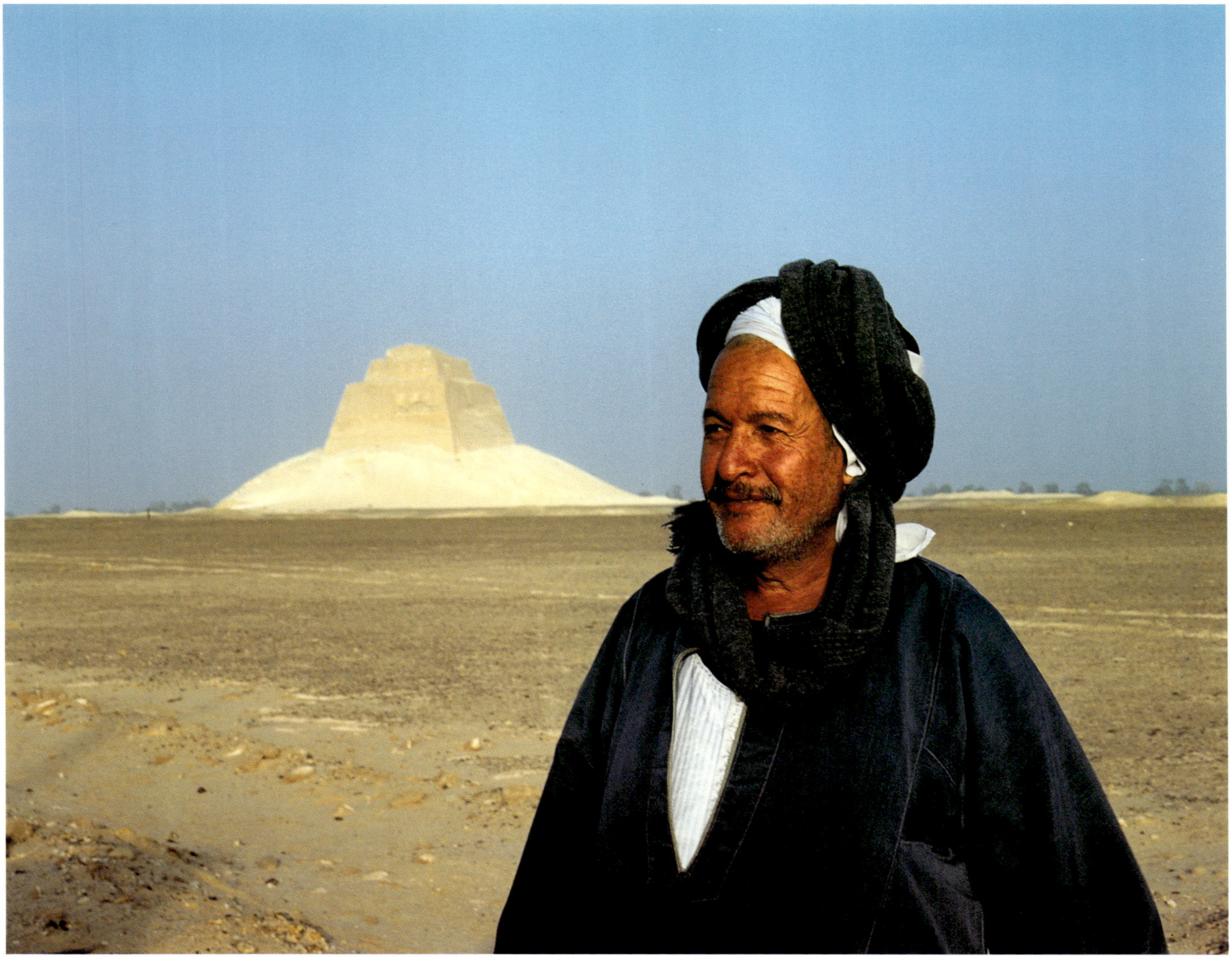

*The ruins of the Temple of Umm 'Ubayd, Siwa Oasis*

*In front of Maydum Pyramid, Beni Suef*

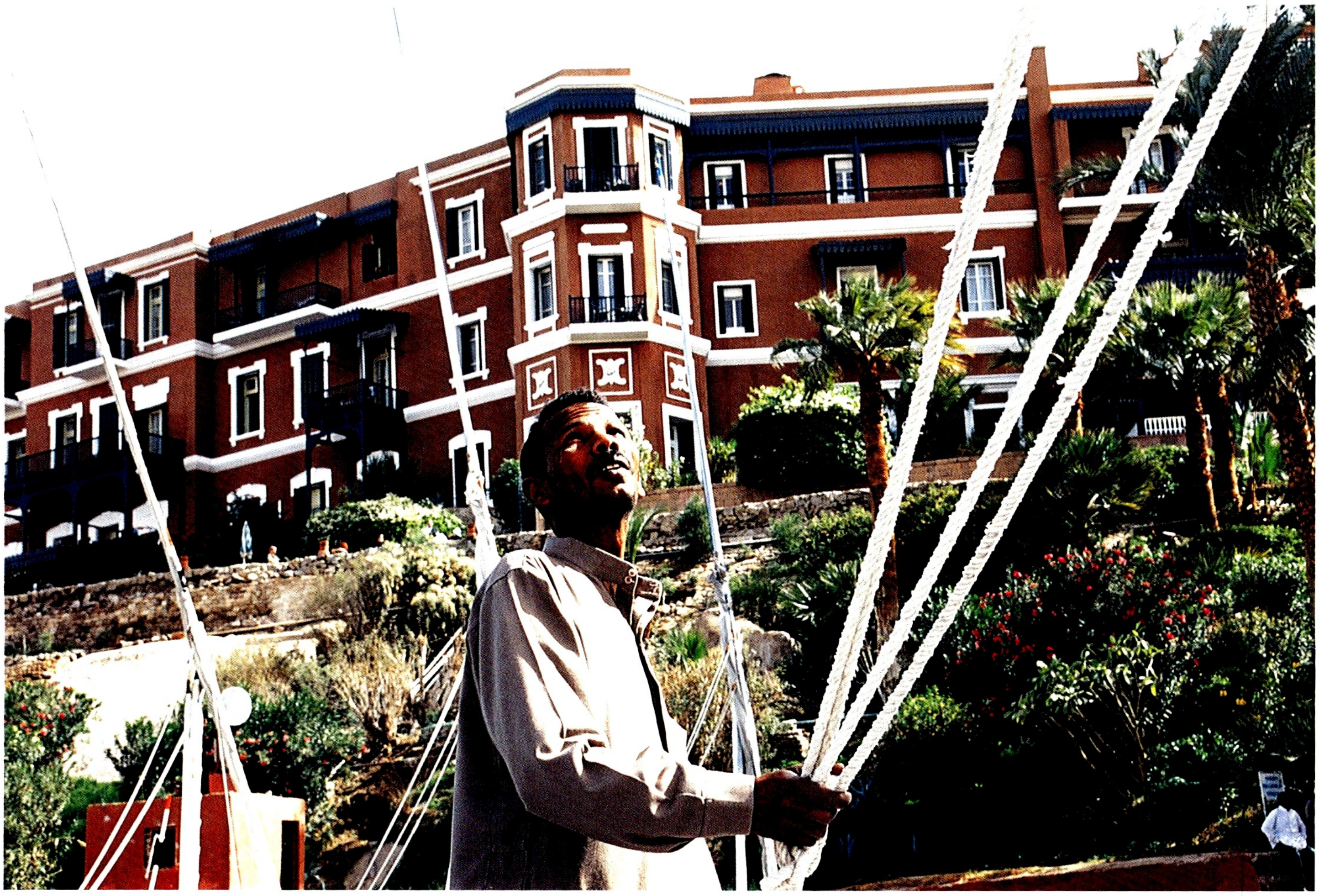

*The Old Cataract Hotel, Aswan*

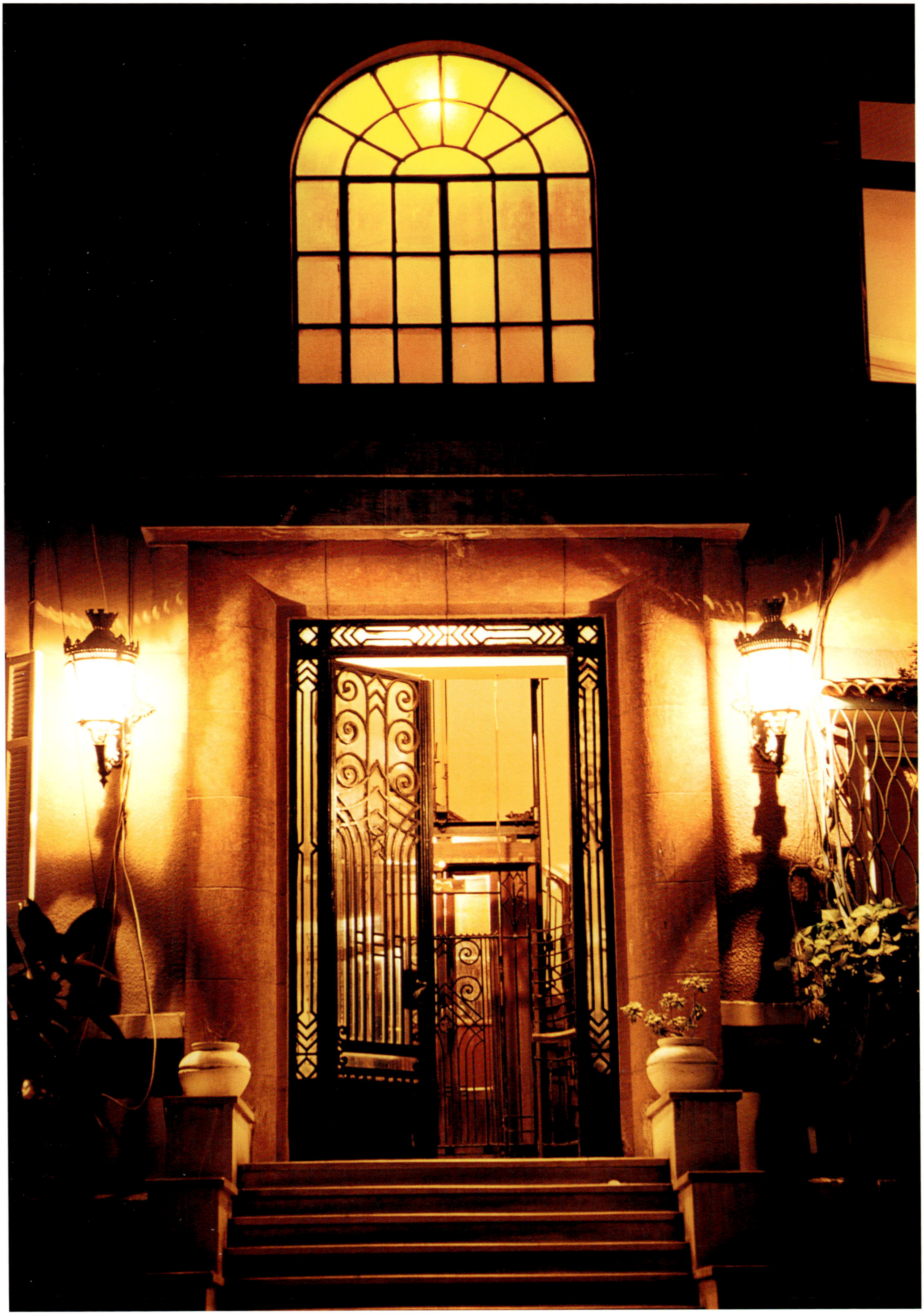

*A residential building in Zamalek, Cairo*

# Future

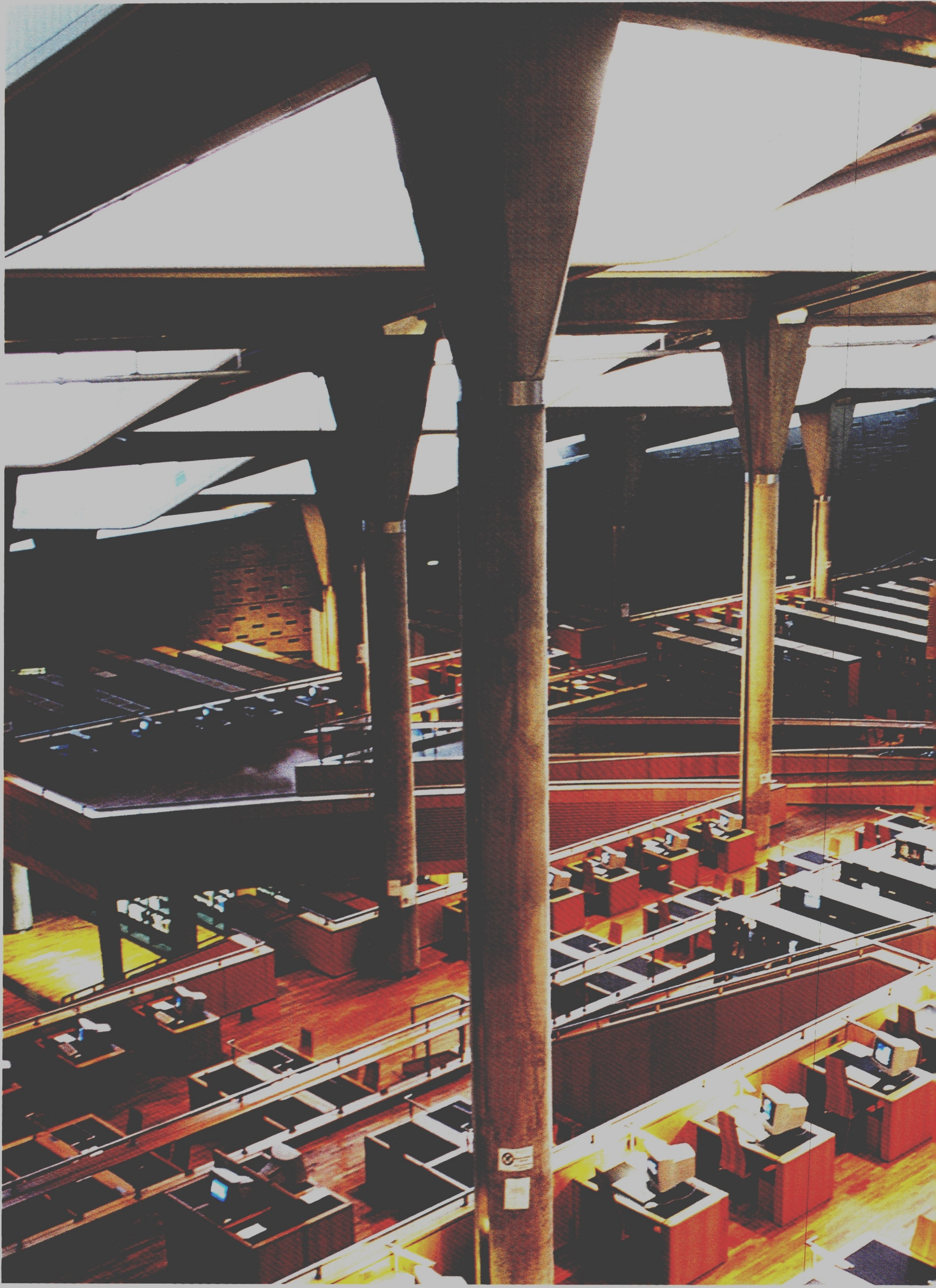

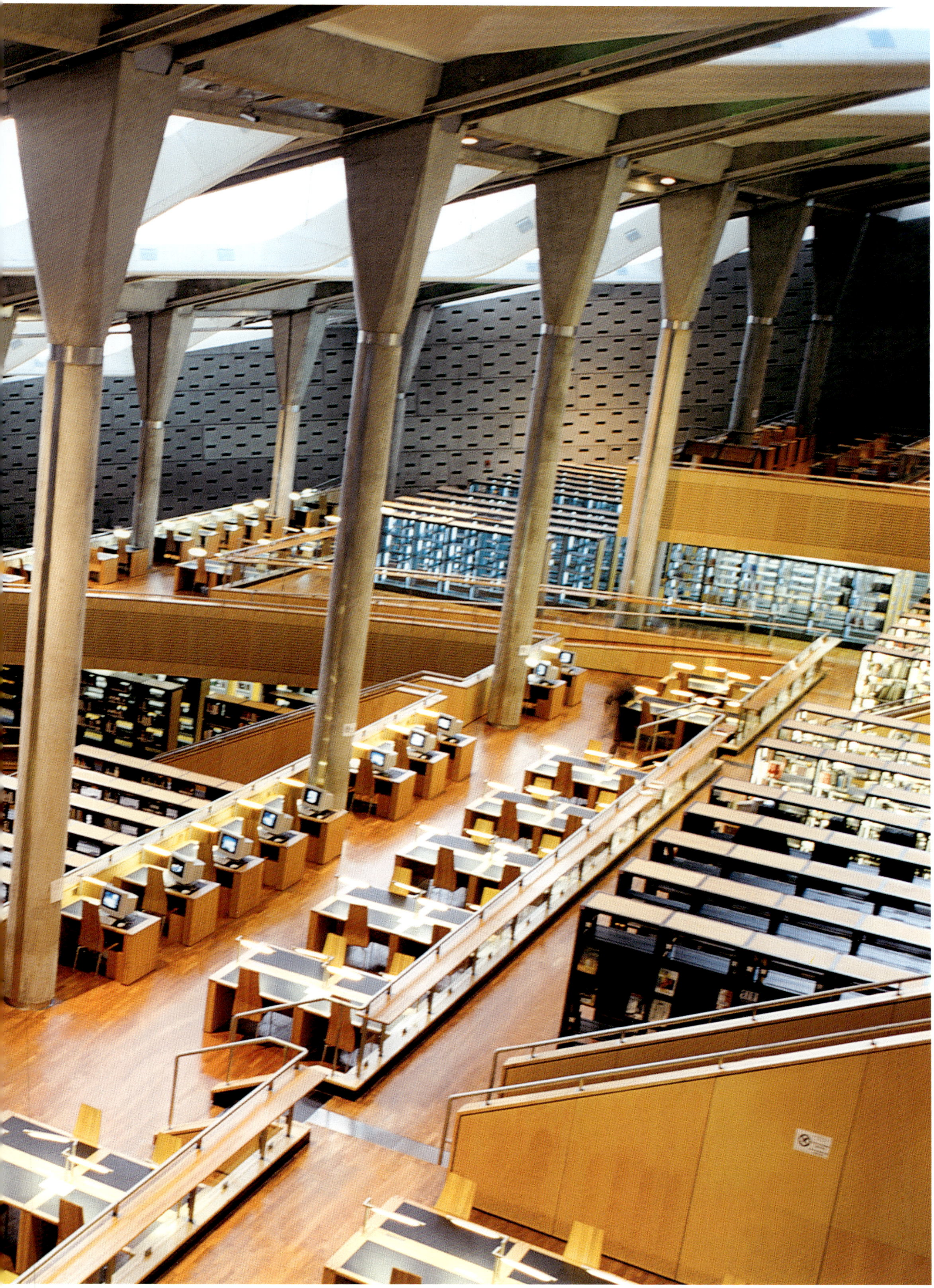

*Inside the Bibliotheca Alexandrina, Alexandria*

Egypt is famous as an ancient land, but it is a country heading decidedly into the future. Perhaps the best example of the way the country's forward-looking goals are grounded in its heritage is the new Alexandria library, the Bibliotheca Alexandrina, a modern construction built on the edge of the Mediterranean Sea, facing out toward the world.

The legendary ancient library of Alexandria was a massive repository for knowledge: it planned to gather books from all the world's people, and it also housed a remarkable effort to translate other cultures' works into Greek. The library was first mentioned around 150 b.c. by a Jewish scholar chronicling the translation of the Old Testament into Greek by seventy-two rabbis. The new library is a continuation of the past but, more importantly, a bridge to the future, with an aim to use technology to expand the country's access to information. And the library is just one part of a revitalized waterfront that is the pride of the present-day city of Alexandria. A broad new Corniche skirts the sea from Montazah in the east all the way west to the library, from where it curves through the old downtown with its lovely European-era hotels, to the old Fort Qaitbay, which has recently undergone a facelift.

A two-hour train ride from Alexandria brings us back to Cairo, where the future can be seen most clearly in the modern buildings and hotels that have changed the cityscape over the past few years. These gleaming structures cannot be ignored among the more disheveled gray and brown buildings that make up most of downtown. Here, the past and the future often seem to be at odds with each other, rather than examples of the modern learning from and building upon the past. Nonetheless, the skyscrapers and sleek international hotels remind the city's residents that this traditional society, with its honored history, cannot settle for old glories.

This is something that many visitors to Egypt already realize. After having their fill of the ancient monuments of Luxor and Aswan, foreign visitors often head to Egypt's Red Sea coast. In recent decades, resort cities like Sharm al-Sheikh and Hurghada have sprung up literally out of nothing. These places now offer the most modern of amenities: hotels such as the Four Seasons, classy restaurants, even golf courses.

The course of Egypt's future naturally depends on its people. One of the brightest flickers of promise comes from Tahani El-Gebali, who was appointed at the beginning of 2003 to be Egypt's first sitting female judge. Gebali's grace in the face of her groundbreaking role should serve as an inspiration to all young Egyptian girls—as well as to the rest of the country's people, and indeed the world.

*T. E.*

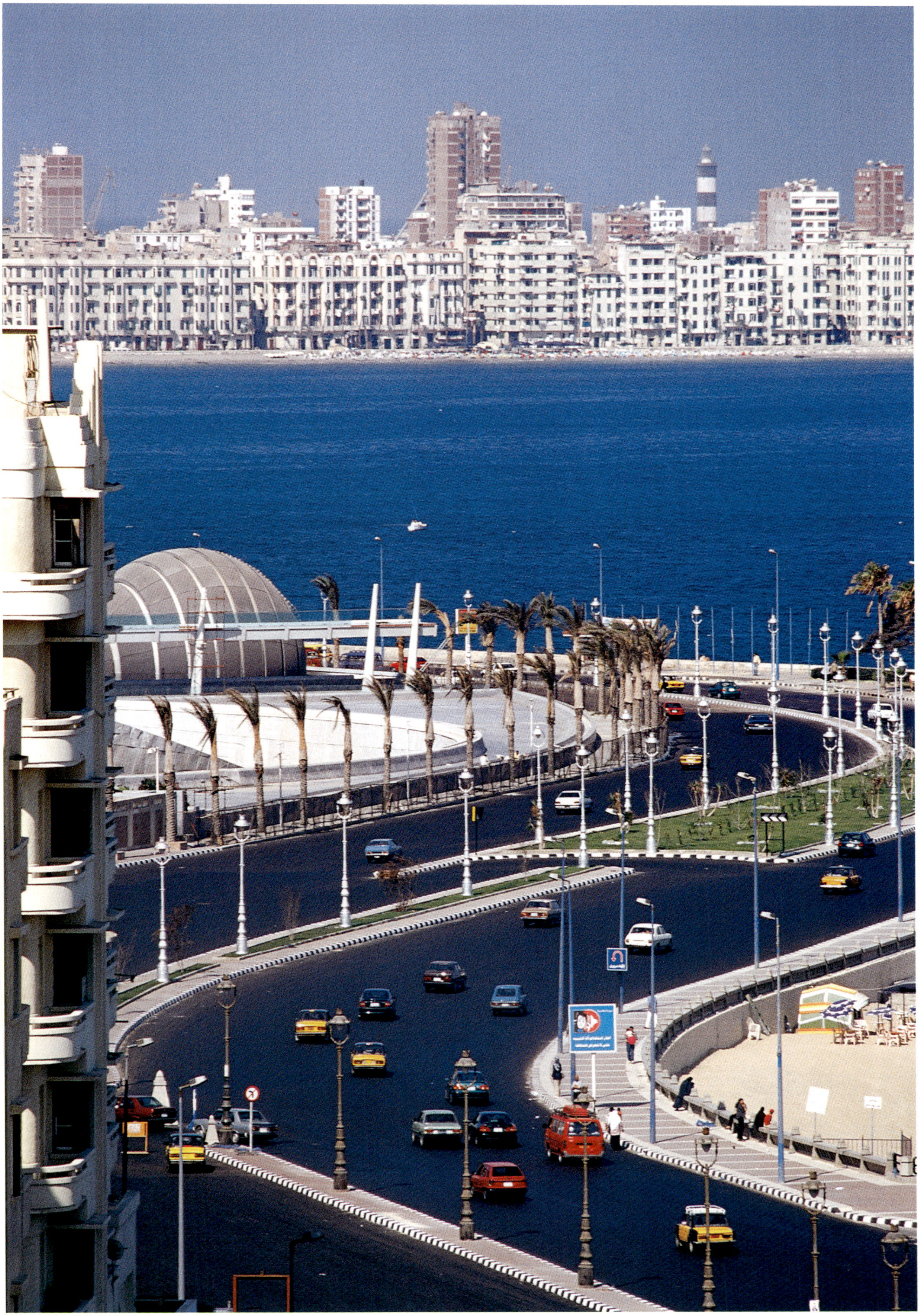

*The Corniche, Alexandria*

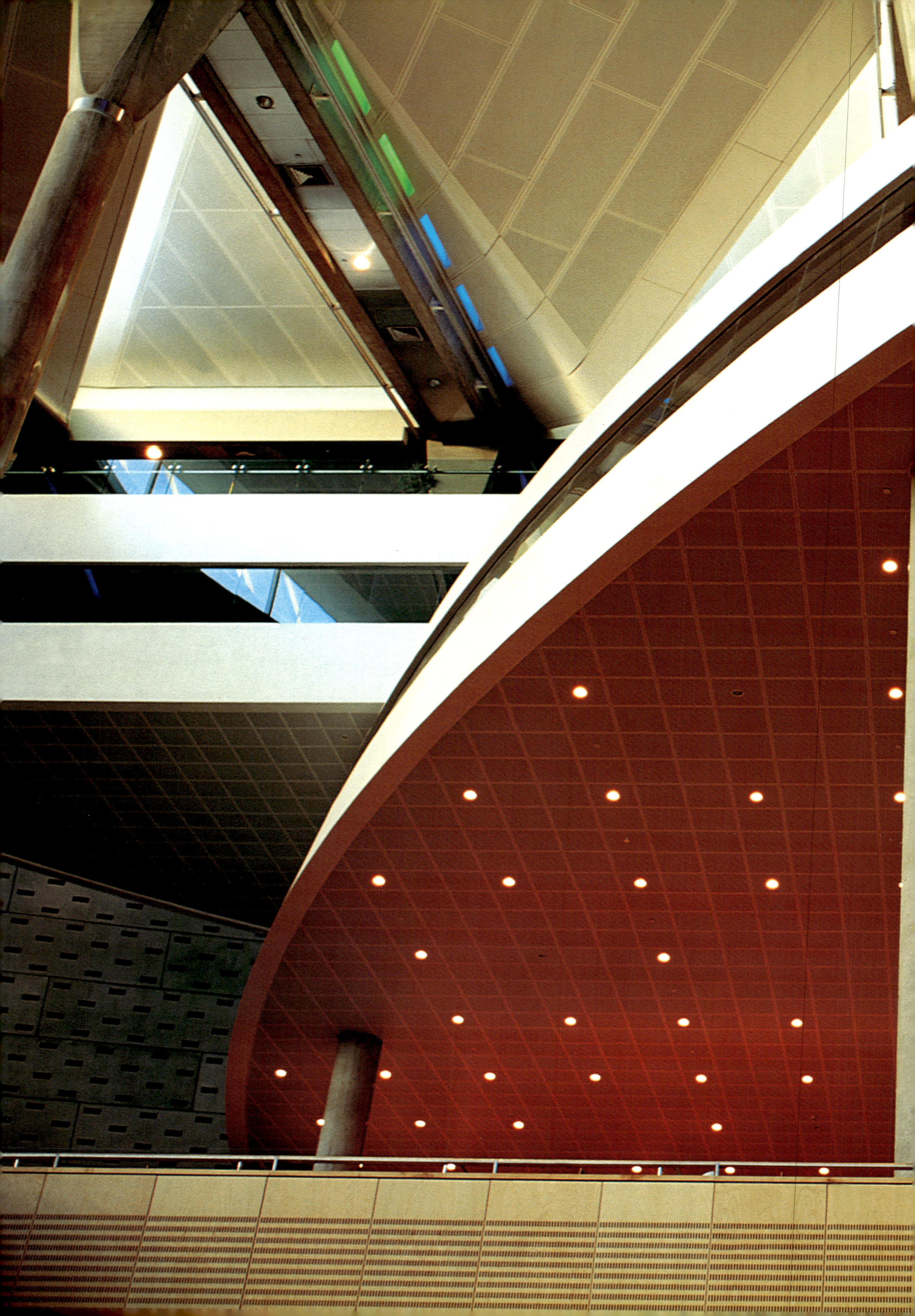

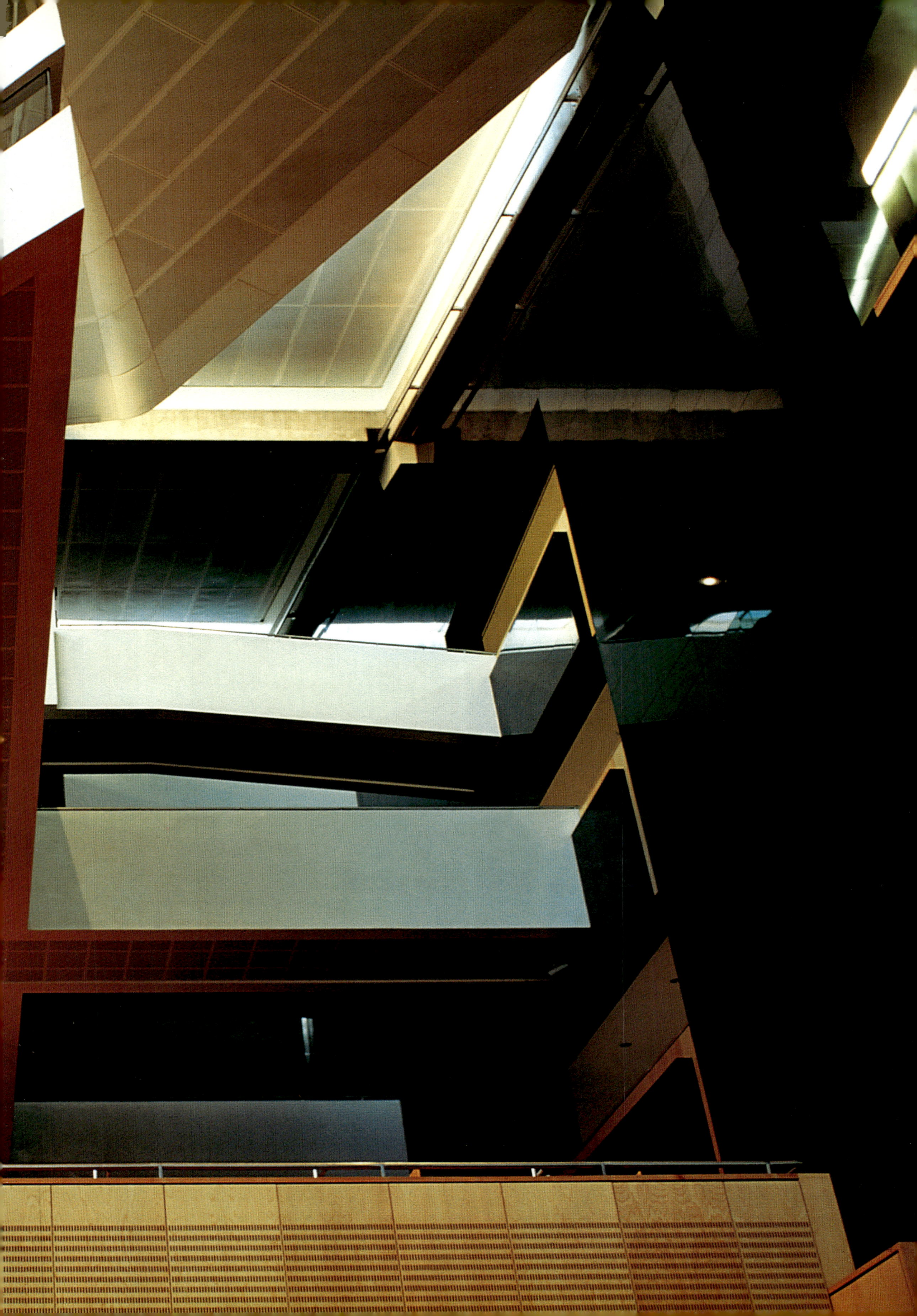

**Ismail Serageldin**

*Director of the Bibliotheca Alexandrina*

"The Library of Alexandria is really a rebirth not just of an intellectual tradition, but of a great cultural tradition," says Dr. Ismail Serageldin, the director of the Bibliotheca Alexandrina since May 2001.

The ancient library of Alexandria, founded in the third century b.c., was the western world's most important center of learning, housing books and manuscripts from all cultures. For Serageldin, the resurrected library has a similarly global mission. "We are aiming to be Egypt's window on the world and the world's window on Egypt, as well as a leading institution of the digital age, able to rise to the challenges of new technologies. It has to be the space of freedom, a forum for dialogue and understanding between people, cultures, and nations."

The director explains that the Alexandria library is not just one building but a vast complex of interconnected institutions: three museums, two permanent exhibitions, six art galleries, seven research institutes (one of which is in Cairo), a children's exploratorium, a planetarium, a conference center, six specialized libraries, an internet archive, and the central library.

What role can a library play in a country's life? "We are moving very rapidly to the digital age, which is going to raise new definitions above and beyond the book," says Serageldin. As a result, the management of information and copyright will have to change. Libraries will have to play a role in the mediation between society's needs, the protection of the author's rights and the needs of the younger generation, who are growing up with computers and the internet.

"Libraries will serve a triple purposes," says the director. "First, they will continue to be the container of the collective memory of humanity." Much of this will now take the form of internet archives and new technologies. "Second, they will increase people's access to information," he continues, stressing the importance of reference facilities that provide factual information, something necessary in this age of information overload. "Third, the library will be more proactive in making information available online." Serageldin would like to avoid the arcane way of physically going to a library's card catalog, copying a code, asking for the book, waiting for it to come, consulting it for a limited time, and returning it. "Our younger generation needs new ways to approach what we consider the most valuable of the human heritage, the product of the human mind," he explains. "Our collective judgment should be exercised and translated in a forward-looking vision, and not be tightly bound to the past."

Without a doubt, the role of books and reading can be improved in Egypt. "Contrary to what people imagine," says Serageldin, "computers will not displace the book, but will simply complement and add to it." To better explain this point Serageldin mentions a three-year study in the United States that showed that people continue to buy books even if they are online. "It is like music," says Serageldin. "Why would people buy records if they can listen to them for free on the radio? But they do!"

Along with technology, Serageldin thinks that the main priority in Egypt should be to provide inexpensive reading material. Making all the great classics available in cheap editions would be a good first step.

Egyptians seem to appreciate the new library. "There is a lot of pride in Egypt about this library," explains the director. Numbers certainly confirm it. "We have between one thousand and two thousand daily visitors. At the beginning we had seven to eight thousand people a day—it was not manageable!" On an average day, three-quarters of the visitors are Egyptians and one-quarter foreigners, mainly visitors.

Serageldin sums up by noting: "As we say here, the Bibliotheca Alexandrina was the past's gift to the present, Mubarak's gift to Egypt, and Egypt's gift to the world. The library is a contribution to improve the future of our country. It is the space for Egyptian talent to flourish."

*S. D.*

*Previous page: Inside the Bibliotheca Alexandrina, Alexandria*

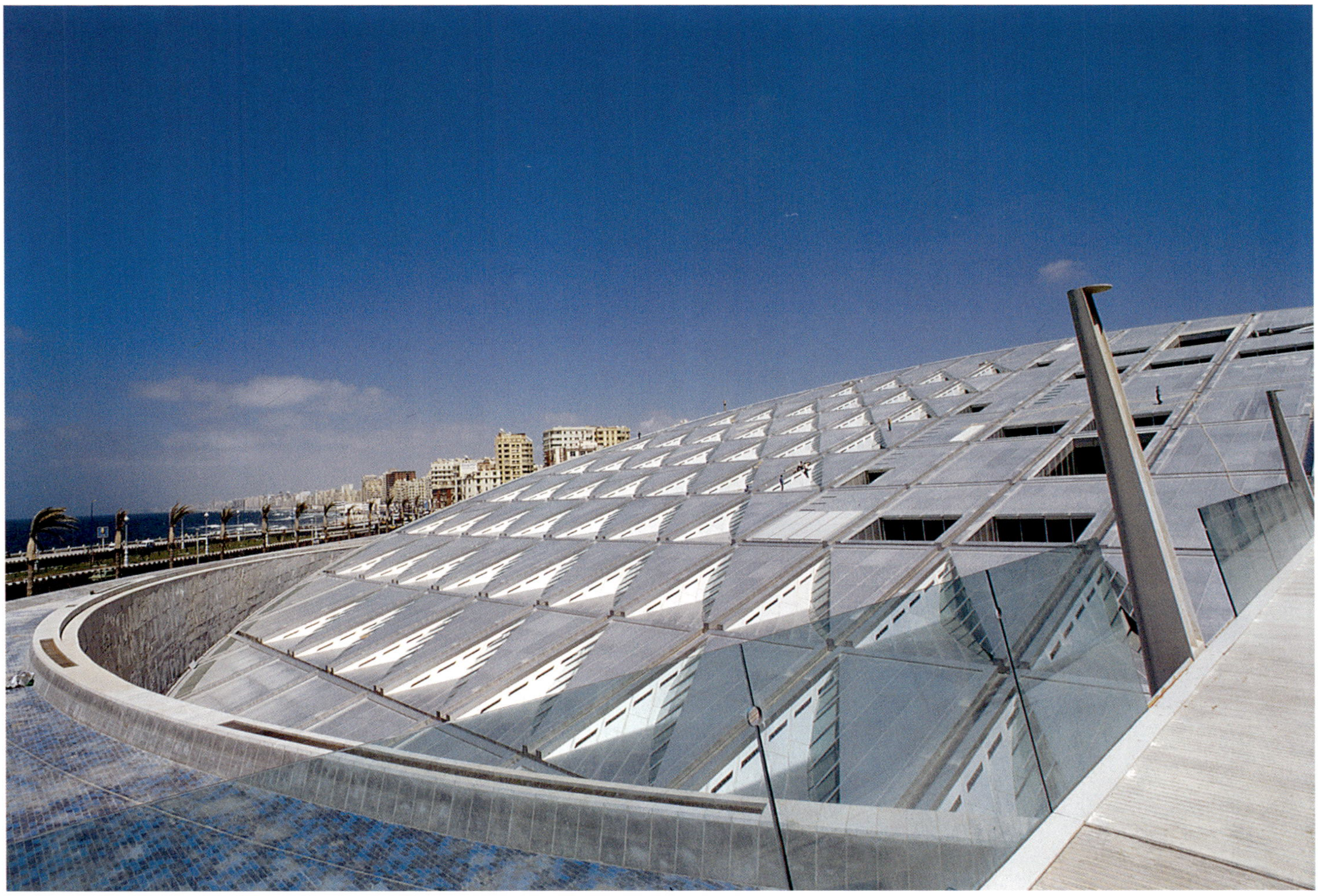

*The Bibliotheca Alexandrina, a modern construction built on the coast of the Mediterranean Sea, facing out toward the world*

*Next page: The new Hyatt Hotel, Cairo*

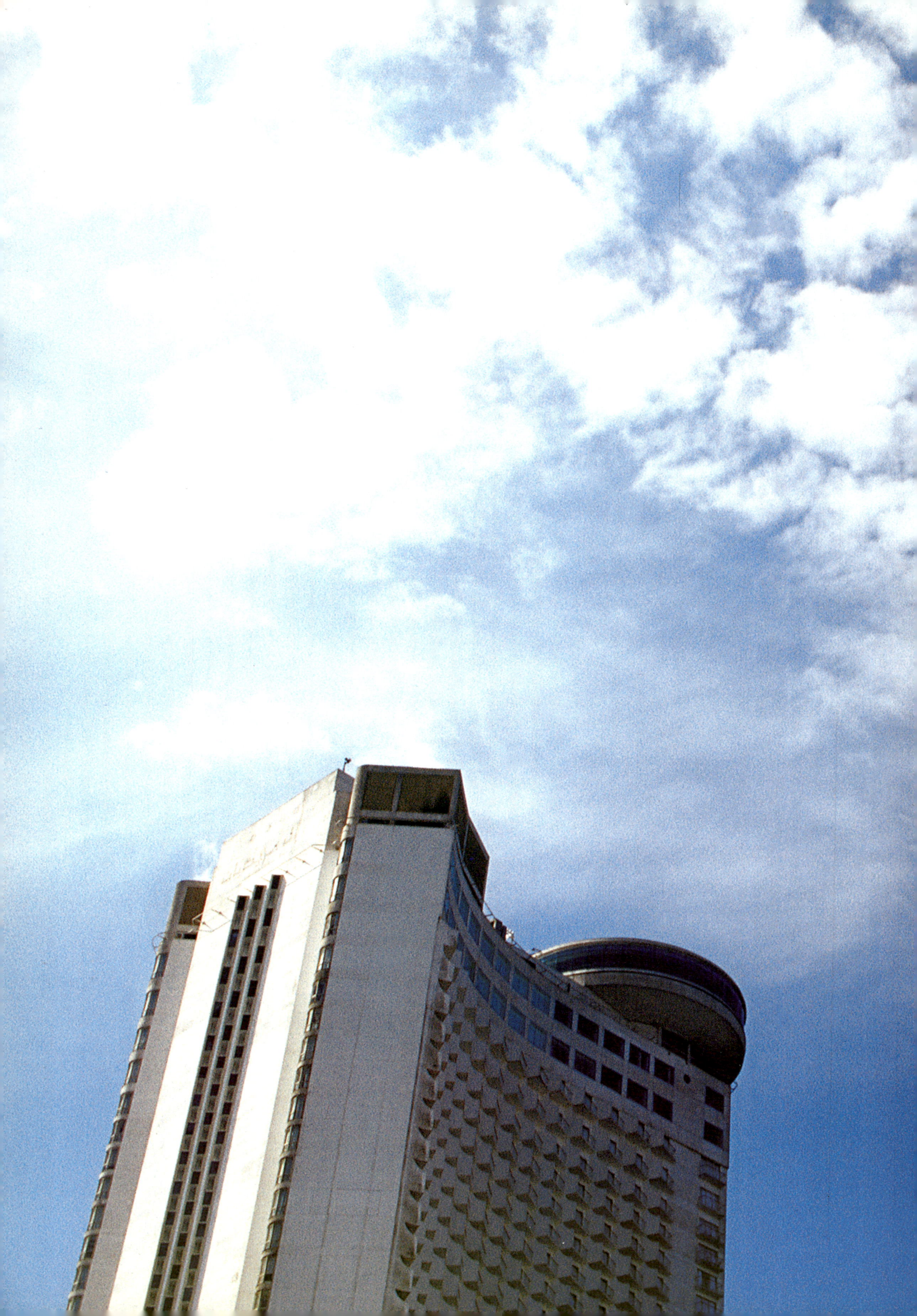

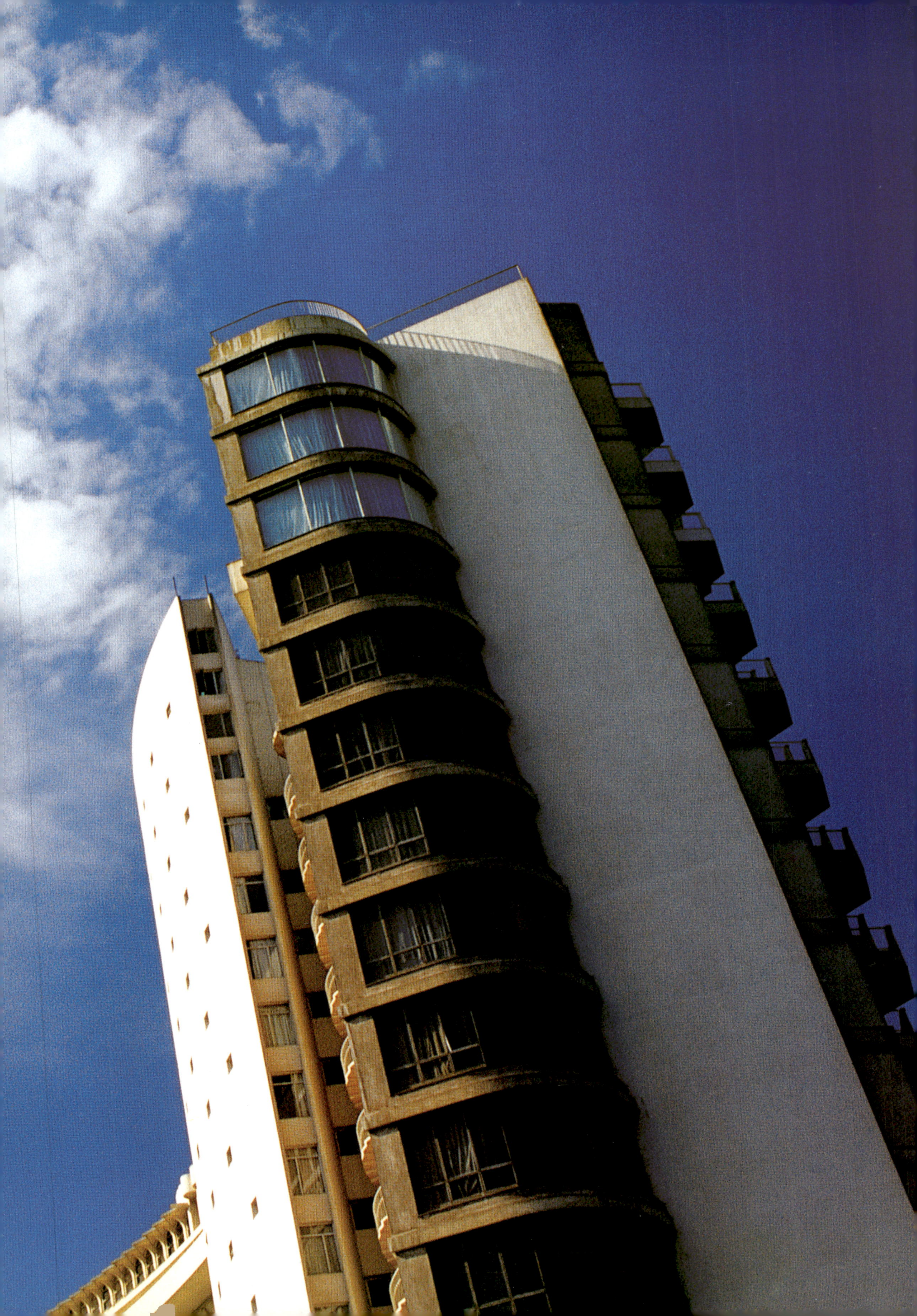

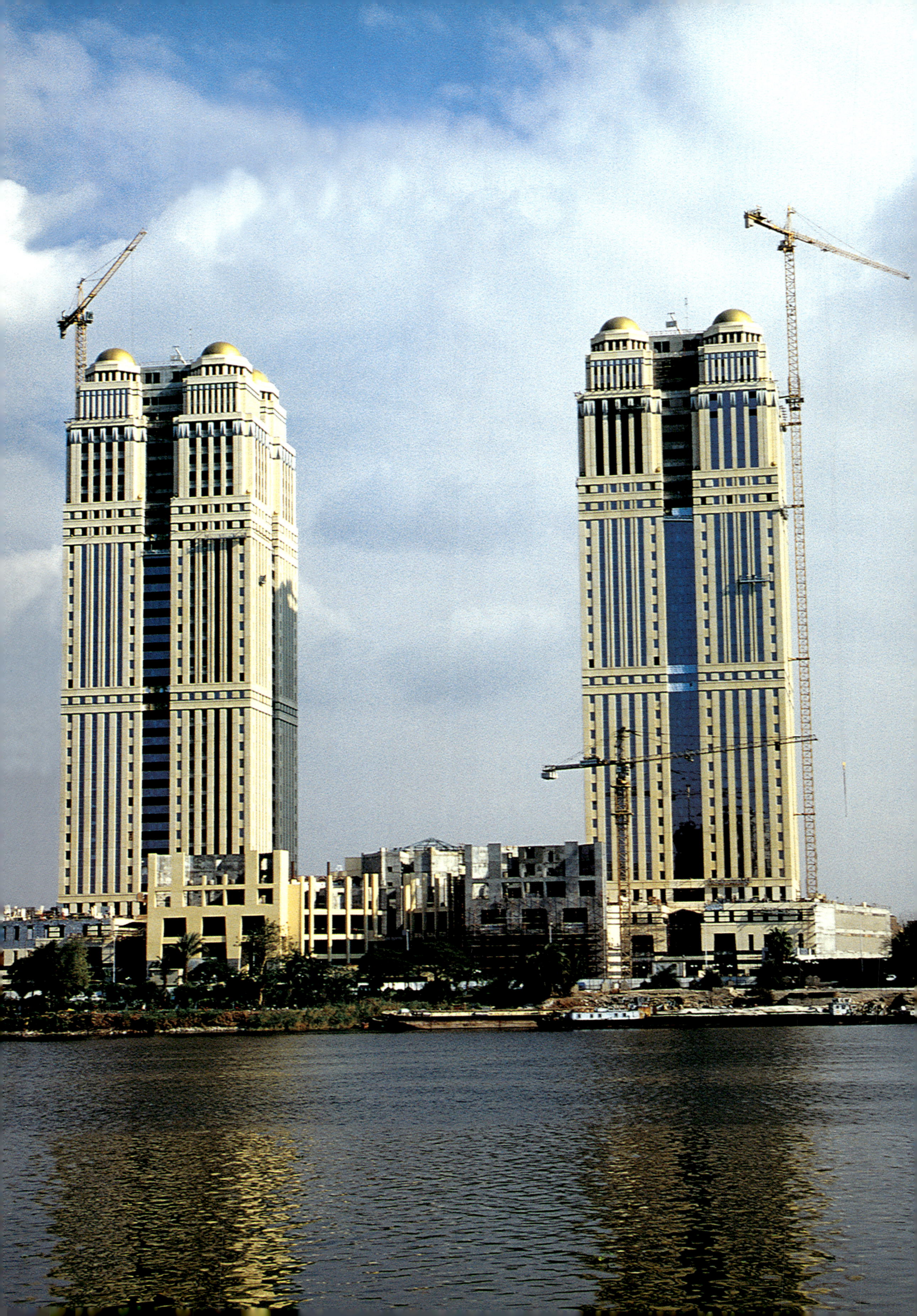

**Samih Sawiris**

*Businessman*

"Popular? No, I don't think we are very popular. Education, timing, and my father's background are the three points that have contributed to our success as a business family," says Samih Sawiris, one of the three well-known Sawiris brothers, leaders in Egypt's business world.

His father Onsi ran a construction company in the 1950s, but it was nationalized during Nasser's rule. Onsi went to Libya, but then when the post-socialist era arrived in Egypt, he decided to return. At the time, his three sons were studying abroad: Nassef in Chicago, Naguib in Zurich, and Samih in Berlin. When the brothers graduated and went back to Egypt, they found that their father was ready to teach his children how to be successful in life. "That gave us an enormous advantage over many other families, whose parents were too old to start a business again," says Sawiris.

The three sons went in different business directions. Naguib chose telecommunications and mobile networks, Nassef went into construction, and Samih pursued real estate and hotels.

The timing was very good. "Egypt was opening up and there was lots of potential for business expansion," remembers Sawiris. "Quick buck, hit and run is the typical business of a post-socialist economy," he explains. But the Sawirises chose a different strategy. "The long-term investment philosophy that we all followed was something unknown to Egypt," says Sawiris. "Even now, Egyptians are not used to it."

The Sawiris brothers were willing to wait fifteen years for a return on their investments. "We were completely alone, with zero competition! We could pick and choose!" While Sawiris maintains a short-term business to pay for immediate needs, his success comes from having faith in long-term matters. And the strategy has paid off: the Orascom Group, the family empire, has interests ranging from construction and building materials through restaurants, hotels, resorts, telecommunications, and satellite technology.

Nonetheless, Sawiris is very realistic about the options in Egypt. Certain popular places have been overbuilt. "In Sharm al-Sheikh or in Hurghada there are too many players," he says. "Many people are now suffering because they put too many rooms in the same place and at the same time." He looks for something different. "I like to go completely outside, take huge pieces of land that are worth nothing and keep investing in that area for ten or more years," says Sawiris. He encourages people to live and work in the places where he builds hotels. "The development becomes a town, not just one or two hotels. This is the way of making money on everything!" confesses the businessman. El Gouna, a resort just north of Hurghada, is one of Sawiris's investments. "It took ten years to build this town, and only now it is starting to become rewarding."

Considering the economic crisis that Egypt faces, Sawiris thinks that the "brick" is the safest investment. "We have a country that is growing fast but it still needs tons of houses for everybody. The construction material produced will always be a top priority for underdeveloped countries, where cement and bricks are exactly like bread," he says.

But it is not always so easy to conduct proper marketing research in a country like Egypt, where the government's decisions are often erratic. New malls, supermarkets, and shops are developed and then suddenly pulled down. "One day we have decisions that sponsor investments, growth and success, and then the next day the government is going backward. But it is too late, as you already started," he notes with a sigh.

Egypt's past is mainly to blame for the current economic situation. "Being a colony did not help, as the best way to control colonies is to impose a bureaucracy. The twenty years of socialism did not help either," says Sawiris. "If we want to change this, we need to get the system to adapt itself so that it is no longer fully controlled, and this takes time."

Although Sawiris considers a contractor to be only an executor, not someone responsible for what is good or bad for the country, his and his family's projects have contributed to the future of Egypt: twelve hospitals, a fertilizer factory, many new railway lines, bridges over the Nile and the Suez Canal, and many five-star hotels.

"I personally think we will improve because the younger generation will take over by the law of nature. They are better educated than the current generation that is now in power. They are not brainwashed by the socialist era and they all travel and watch television. The younger generation will have enough ambitions to do a better job."

Looking at the future of Egypt, Sawiris is convinced that an explosion of prosperity will come soon. "When I sit and just think of how many things can be done yet, I run out of time."

*S. D.*

*The two Sawiris Towers under construction, Cairo*

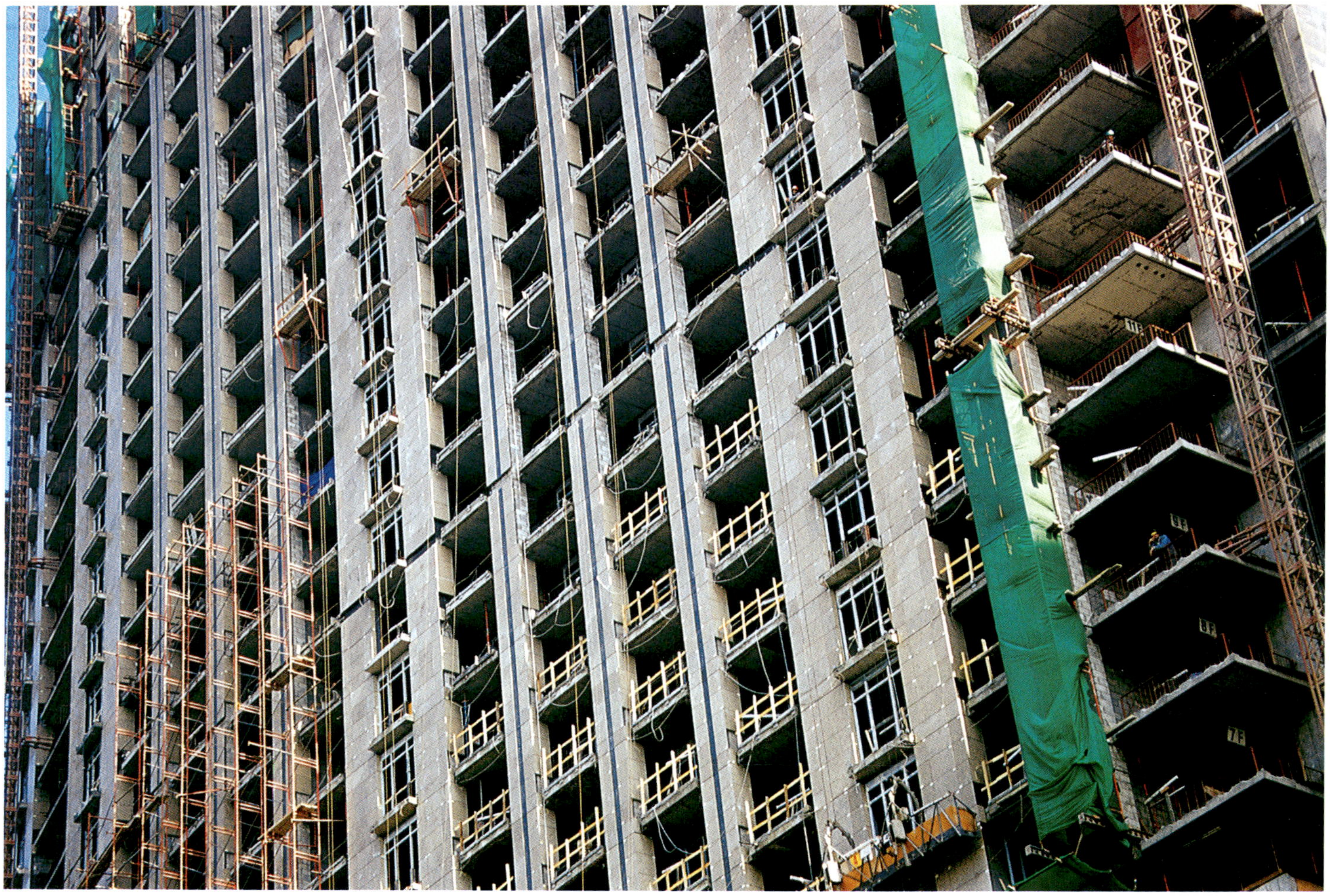

*A hotel under construction, Cairo*

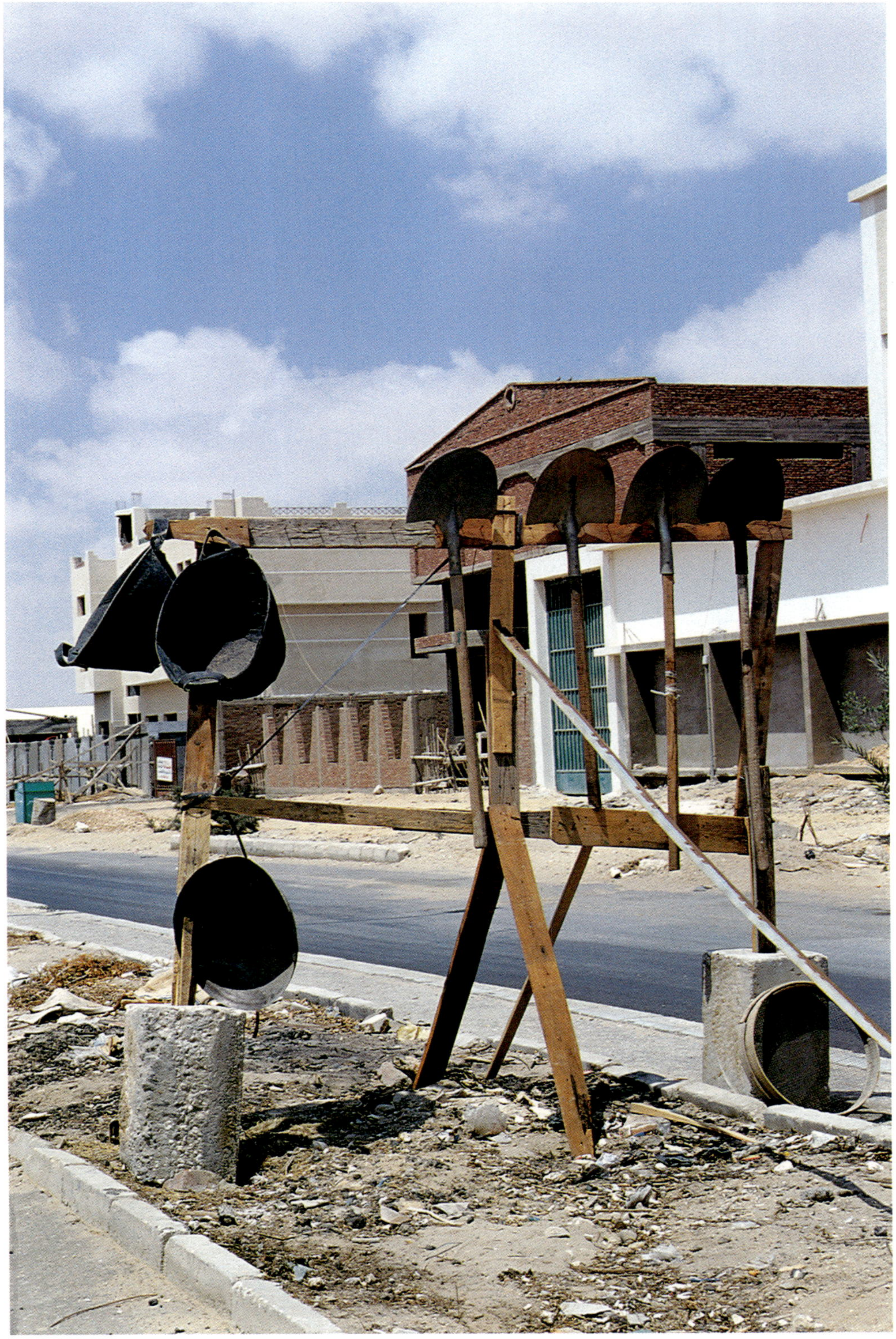

*Sixth of October City, the recently constructed Cairo suburb*

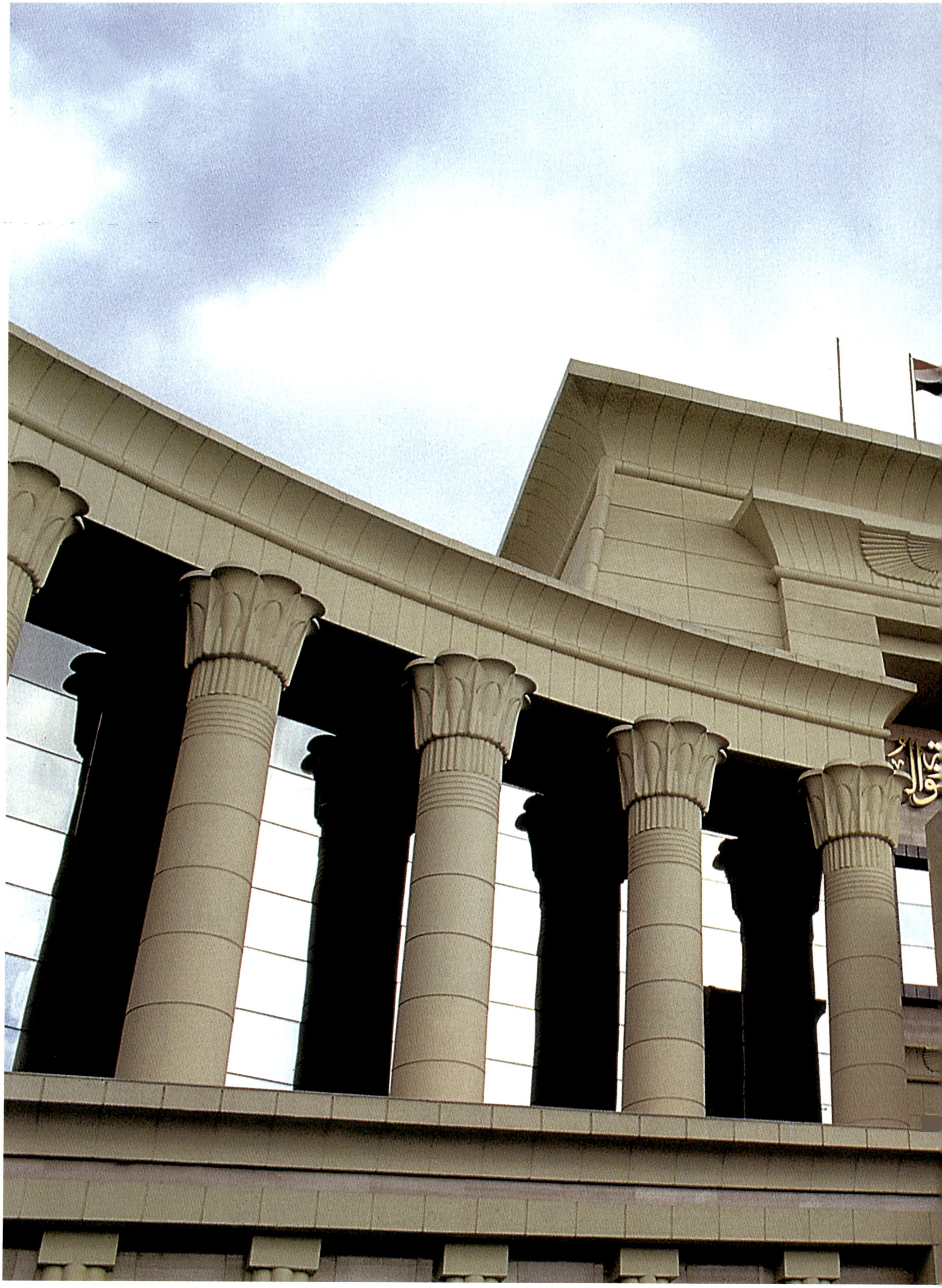

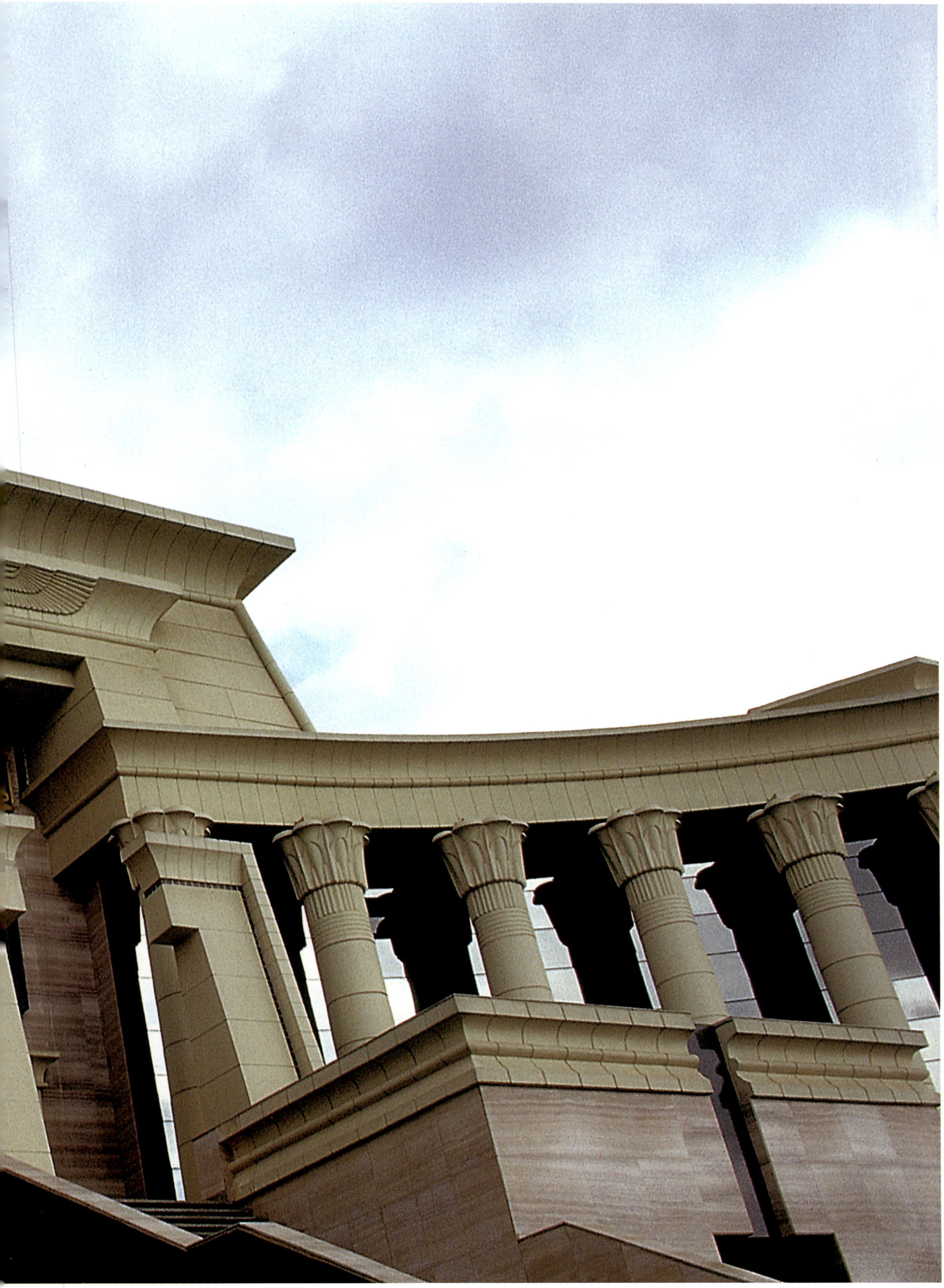

*The Constitutional Court, Ma'adi, Cairo*

## Tahani El-Gebali

*First female judge in Egypt*

Tahani El-Gebali has played an important role in Egypt's history—and she will certainly influence the country's future. Her appointment at the beginning of 2003 to the Supreme Constitutional Court made her Egypt's first sitting female judge.

"I worked as a lawyer after I graduated from the Faculty of Law at Cairo University in 1973," explains El-Gebali. "During that period, I lived the dream of the Egyptian woman to be part of the judicial system, since it is the third branch of authority in society. The Egyptian woman has participated successfully in the executive branch of government through the various ministries, and in the legislative branch in the People's Assembly. She has surrounded the judge's bench from all sides—she worked as a lawyer, she taught law, and worked with the Judicial Administrative Authority." Nonetheless, Egyptian women had never possessed judicial authority. "This," declares El-Gebali, "was an unacceptable situation."

Many women had fought to become judges, offering their applications and even filing lawsuits. When this appointment finally came, it was welcome—and unexpected. "It was a surprise for me as well," El-Gebali says. And the surprise was not only because she is a woman, but because she has taken up many causes unpopular with the government. "I have always been in the political opposition," she explains. "I was always very active and very loud." She has worked for human rights, the respect of the constitution and of individual freedoms, and other political and social causes.

Considering El-Gebali's confidence and grace, Egypt could not wish for a better person in such a historic role. "I have never felt the pressure of being a woman in a field that was mostly dominated by men," she notes. "So that is why I see things very differently than other activists working in the field of women's rights, because I always put more of a burden on women when it comes to justice. We must be stronger and confident in ourselves."

Women have definitely made gains in Egypt in recent years, although there is still a long way to go. El-Gebali is very straightforward when assessing the situation. "The problem is not the man—he's not the obstacle to the woman," she says. "The man is as much a victim in the society because of old cultural norms, old ways of thinking and living with the problems we are faced with. And this is pressuring him, so it manifests itself in the form of mistreatment of women."

El-Gebali's view of women's role in society is especially insightful. "We often only gather statistics about the women who work in the official sectors," she points out, "and that is wrong, because I believe that you must also assess those working outside the official sectors, starting from the farmer. She produces and is part of the economy. Besides, the unofficial sectors have a great effect on our economy, even if it's not written down. But the problem is that women have not yet participated sufficiently in the political areas of society and not yet very effectively as decision-makers."

She would also like to see more attention given to young women who are just about the graduate and enter the workforce. "I believe this group needs more concentrated effort in order to make them more active in the political, social, and economic life. We need to get them to be more active and more positive in the way they think because I believe that they are depressed over the lack of employment possibilities and the high unemployment rate they face," El-Gebali explains. "They need more effort and support because they are the future. They are also distracted by the idea of raising families and establishing their lives—they are faced with great difficulty. At the same time, they are faced with the shift to consumerism rather than production."

Despite the long time it took to appoint a woman as a judge, El-Gebali is warmly optimistic about her country's future. "I have complete faith in the ability of the Egyptian woman and in the mind and conscience of the Egyptian people, because they value the contribution of women. And when there is a qualified woman, the society surrounds her with support and respect and accepts her in a position of leadership."

When asked to name her role models, El-Gebali mentions her mother. "She was one of the Egyptians who were educated in 1920s and worked in the 1930s when women didn't work. She fell in love with my father and married him. She was an Arabic and religious studies schoolteacher, and she was very good at her job and very elegant. I always saw her as the great example of the woman who takes care of herself." She also mentions the singer Umm Kulthum, who rose from being a peasant to become a famous artist who wielded great social, political, and economic power. Then El-Gebali declares, "I don't believe in the single role model. I see a role model in any individual I meet, no matter how humble they are. So I might find my maid a role model because she works very hard, she takes care of her family and her ill husband. She deserves my respect and of course for me to try to follow her example."

As she continues, it is clear that El-Gebali does not take this subject lightly. "I think that women should always think carefully when they are selecting a role model, even a religious role model, because there are a lot of misleading role models when it comes to religion, which encourage you to follow blindly and not question what you are told. I think this is dangerous, because women have to think and read and understand and decide for themselves, and not simply take the ideas that others give to them as fact or truth."

And will young Egyptian women try to emulate El-Gebali? "I don't know if I will or will not be a role model," she says modestly. "But what I can say is that I will be happy to tell the youth how I lived my life, and it is up to them to decide if they want to follow it or not."

*T. E.*

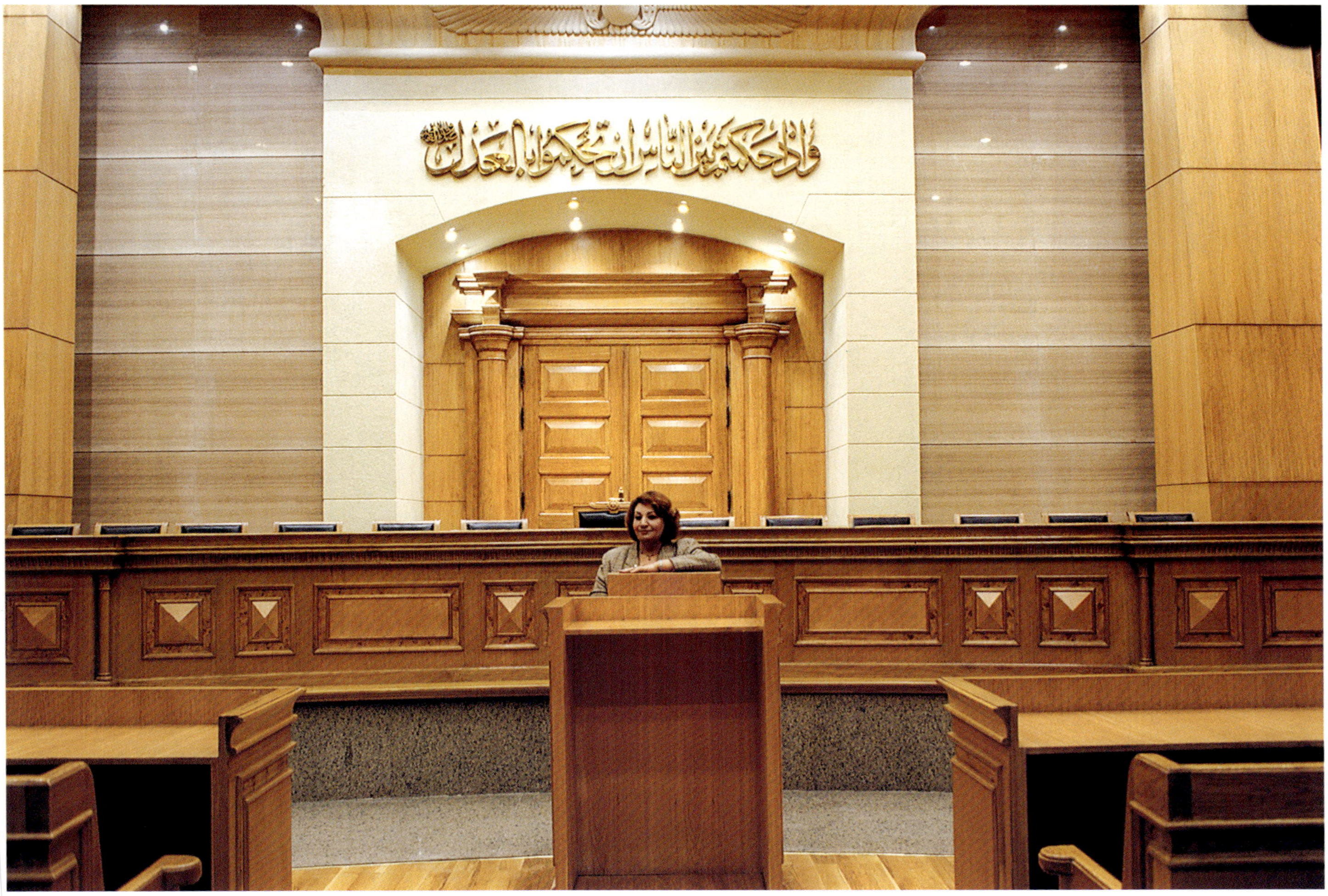


*Tahani El-Gebali, Egypt's first sitting female judge, appointed in early 2003*

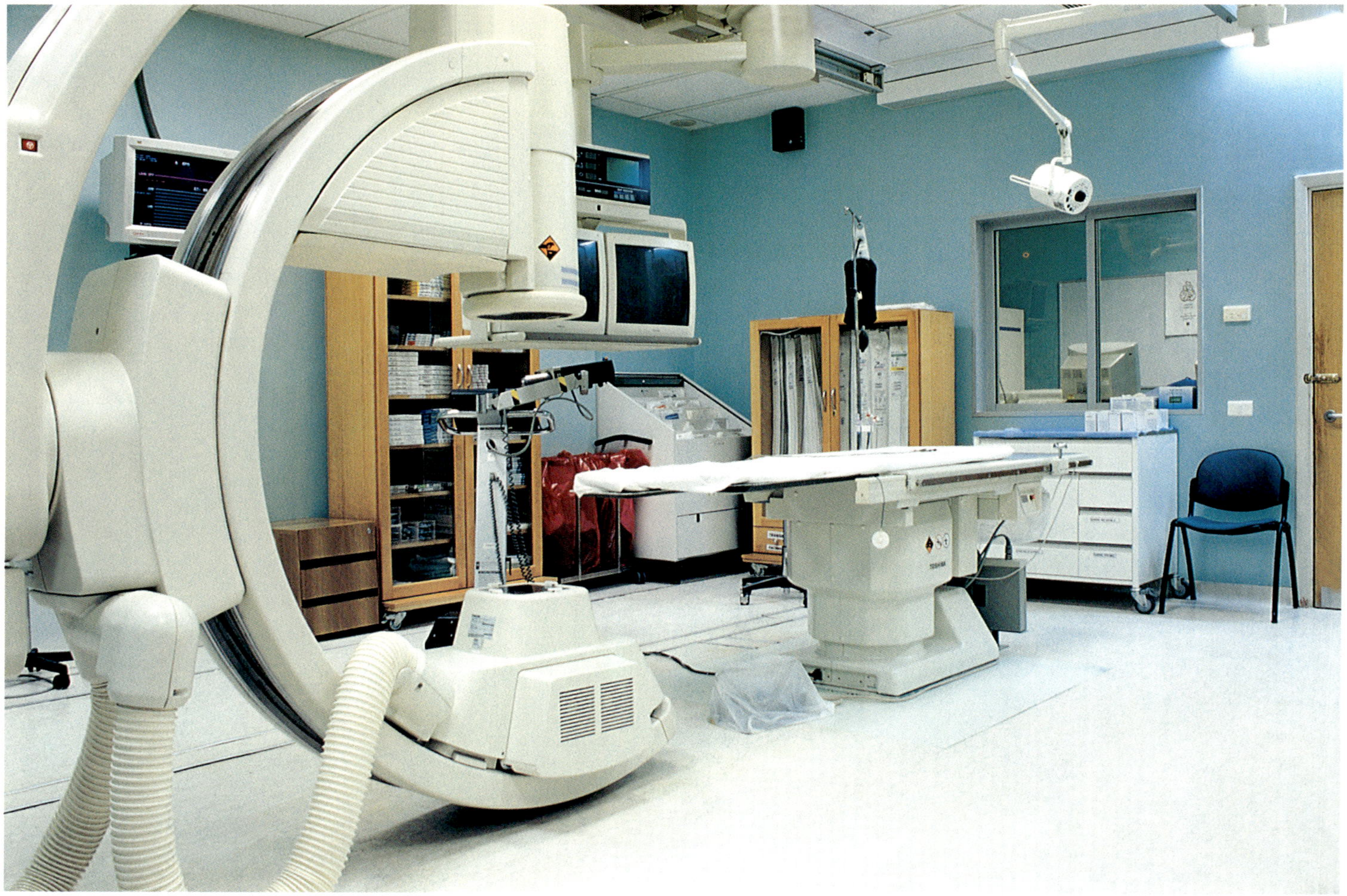

*Dar al-Fu'ad Hospital, Sixth of October City, Cairo*

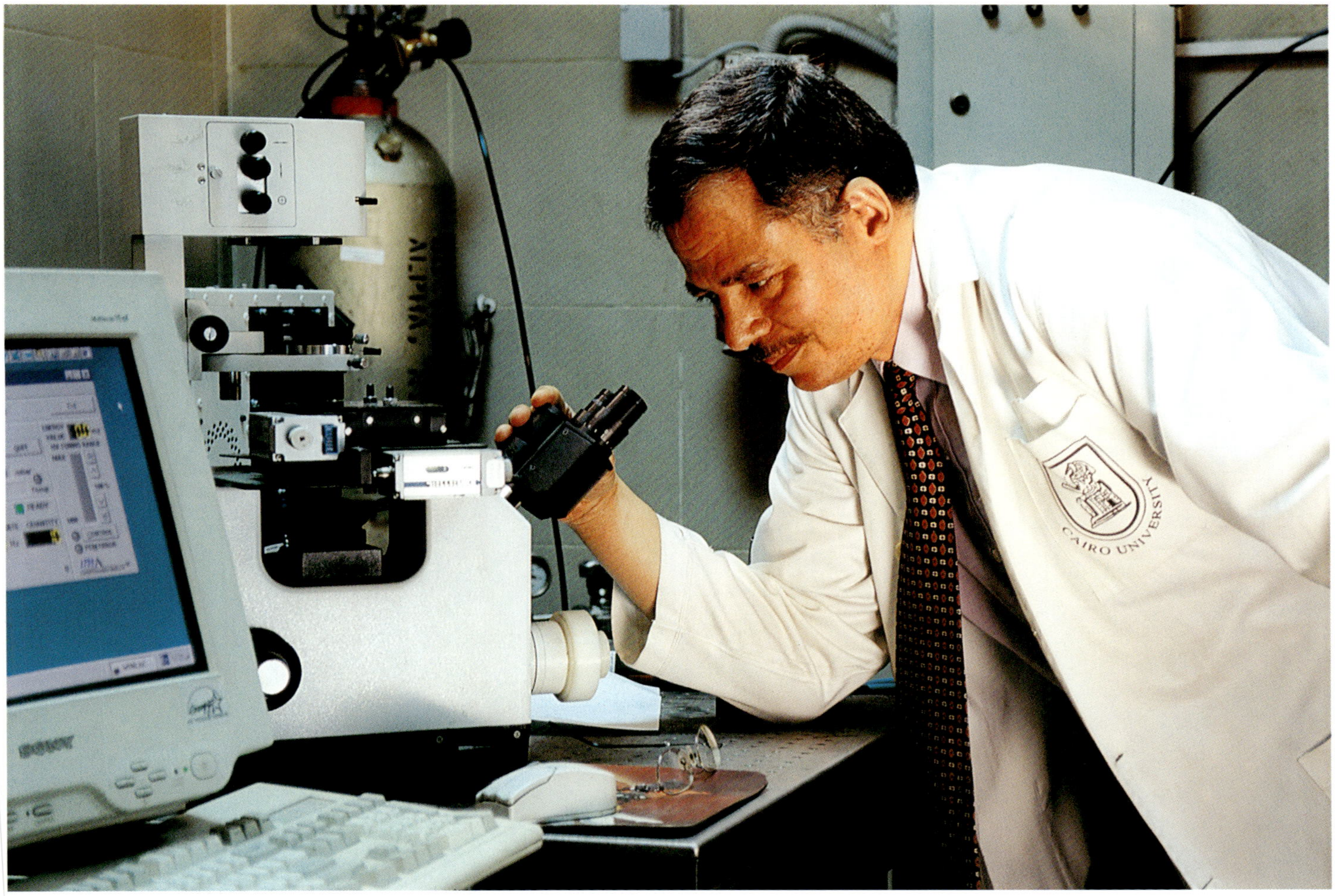


*Dr. Yehia Badr at the National Institute of Laser Enhanced Sciences, Cairo*

## Sabina Pilgram

*Foreign resident*

"Becoming a mother here in Egypt has certainly been the most important experience of my life," says Sabina Pilgram, an Italian woman who delivered her twin girls in Cairo. "It is also the strongest emotion that this country could ever give me."

Pilgram arrived in Egypt in August 2000 with her German husband, who teaches at the Deutsche Schule der Borromäerinnen in Cairo. At first she was excited by the eastern style of life. After three years as a foreign resident she learned to be more realistic, recognizing the good and the not-so-good sides of the place. For her, the hospitals and doctors who bring the future of Egypt into the world are on the good side.

"When I realized that I was pregnant I really didn't know whether I should have the babies here or in Europe," she admits. "As always happens with twins, my due date was uncertain. I knew that my husband couldn't leave his job for more than a few days, and I didn't want to be far from him. Through the Italian and the German embassies, as well as some foreign friends' advice, I found a good gynecologist," she says. "Following his suggestions I decided to personally check all the best local hospitals. Although Egyptian women think that visiting the intensive care department brings bad luck, I was aware of the importance of it, as twins are often born premature."

When she was six months pregnant, she went on a business trip to Germany, where she used to live with her family. The trip was tiring, and in order to avoid problems with her pregnancy, her German doctor ordered her to spend two weeks in a clinic. "To be honest, while in the clinic I felt like I was a foreigner in Europe! It was then when I decided to have my babies in Egypt."

Back in Cairo she chose her hospital and waited for the uncertain day. On October 1, 2001 Lisa and Lara were brought into the world.

"Although Lisa had to spend twenty-six days in the incubator, my delivery experience was extremely positive," says Pilgram. "I am sure that in Germany I wouldn't have had such a close relationship with my gynecologist and my midwife, who gave me private preparatory classes and helped me before and after the delivery. There, you can't have a personal midwife, and until the very last minute you don't even know the name of the doctor who will be in the delivery room with you! What western doctor would ever give out his personal mobile number?"

Pilgram describes her Egyptian private maternity hospital as a five-star hotel, where you can book the room of your choice: standard, deluxe, or superior. Nonetheless, she admits that local hospitals are not as well equipped as American or European ones. "I have been told that Egyptian hospitals are not able to save babies under one kilogram. In developed countries they can often exceed this limit," she says. "Lisa was only one kilo and three-hundred grams when she was born."

Pilgram noticed another shortcoming. "Most of the nurses are not specialized, and sometimes unprofessional," she says. "I was disappointed when some of them asked my husband for tips just a few minutes after the delivery"

But Pilgram has continued to feel safe. "The twins' pediatrician is one of the best doctors in Cairo. The girls suffer from asthma, and he was able to save Lisa during one of her worst and most dramatic attacks."

Egypt offers a lot to children. "It is a safe country, where you are relieved of the fears of the kinds of tragedies that happen in the west, particularly with children. But you also fear the simple things like diseases carried by unboiled water or by something not properly washed."

Then she continues, "The warm weather allows children to play outside. The desert and the sea are something unique in this country, and kids love it. The international schools and atmosphere help children to open their mind to different languages, people, and cultures. The vision of the world is wider: they know what life is in Egypt, and in Europe as well."

Would she have another baby in Egypt if she had the chance to chose? "Of course yes!" Pilgram answers. "If a friend ever asked me for my advice, I would certainly urge her to have her baby here in Egypt!" she says with a smile.

*S. D.*

*Vittoria Valeria Gertrud Avogadro, the author's Cairo-born daughter, Western Desert*

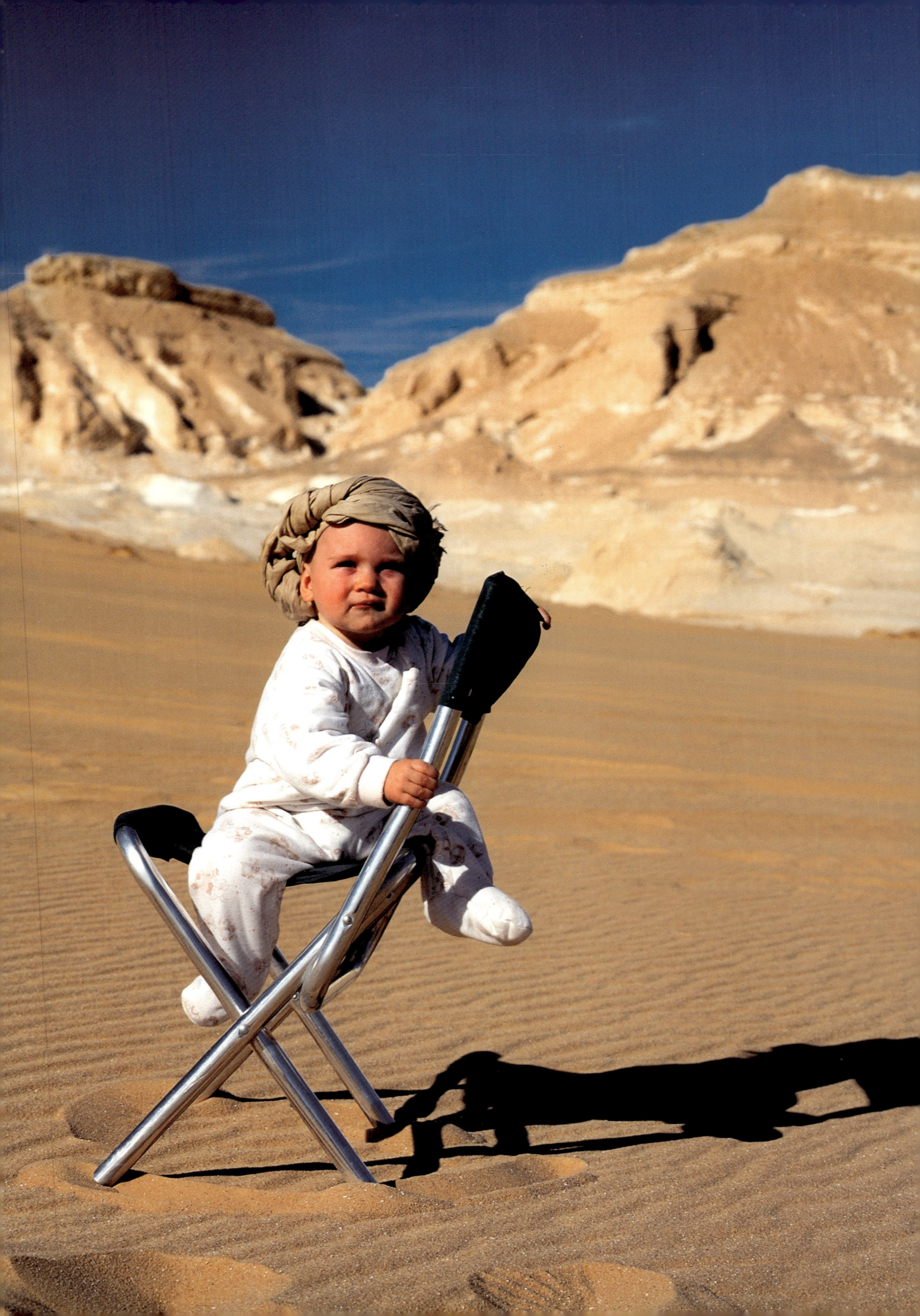

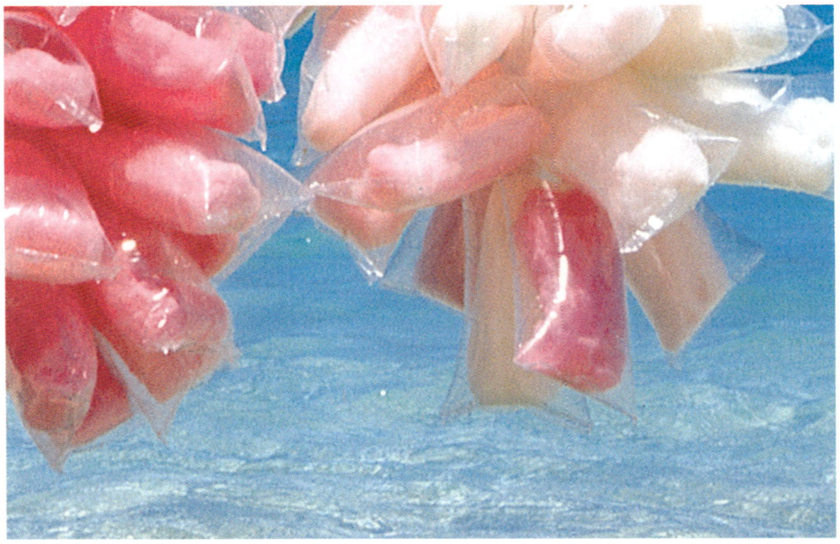